VRIJE UNIVERSITEIT TE AMSTERDAM

ARAB CONTRACT OF EMPLOYMENT

Conflict and Concord

PROEFSCHRIFT

TER VERKRIJGING VAN DE GRAAD
VAN DOCTOR IN DE RECHTSGELEERDHEID
AAN DE VRIJE UNIVERSITEIT TE AMSTERDAM,
OP GEZAG VAN DE RECTOR MAGNIFICUS DR. F. DE ROOS,
HOOGLERAAR IN DE FACULTEIT DER ECONOMISCHE WETENSCHAPPEN,
IN HET OPENBAAR TE VERDEDIGEN OP VRIJDAG 3 JULI 1964
DES NAMIDDAGS TE 3.30 UUR IN HET WOESTDUINCENTRUM,
WOESTDUINSTRAAT 16, TE AMSTERDAM

DOOR

HISHAM RIF'AT HASHEM
geboren te Nablus (Palestina)

MARTINUS NIJHOFF / 'S-GRAVENHAGE
1964

Promotor: PROFESSOR MR. W. F. DE GAAY FORTMAN

STELLINGEN

I.

Codification is more useful to developing countries than the evasive form of an unwritten law.

II.

The lack of a strict doctrine of judicial precedence in the Code countries prejudices the certainty which codification aims at.

III.

No system of law can be complete without the doctrine of equity, the legitimate child of natural justice and reason.

IV.

International law is gaining more sanctions in recent years, and yet it is in a more precarious position than ever, both on account of the prevailing 'balance of terror' in the world.

V.

An administrative decision is law from without and official policy from within.

VI.

The Moslem law is characterised by realism, practicability and progressive outlook.

VII.

The first draft of a constitution should not be written by lawyers.

VIII.

Collective agreements and collective contracts are an excellent compass for the labour legislator.

VRIJE UNIVERSITEIT TE AMSTERDAM

ARAB CONTRACT OF EMPLOYMENT

Conflict and Concord

PROEFSCHRIFT

TER VERKRIJGING VAN DE GRAAD
VAN DOCTOR IN DE RECHTSGELEERDHEID
AAN DE VRIJE UNIVERSITEIT TE AMSTERDAM,
OP GEZAG VAN DE RECTOR MAGNIFICUS DR. F. DE ROOS,
HOOGLERAAR IN DE FACULTEIT DER ECONOMISCHE WETENSCHAPPEN,
IN HET OPENBAAR TE VERDEDIGEN OP VRIJDAG 3 JULI 1964
DES NAMIDDAGS TE 3.30 UUR IN HET WOESTDUINCENTRUM,
WOESTDUINSTRAAT 16, TE AMSTERDAM

DOOR

HISHAM RIF'AT HASHEM
geboren te Nablvs (Palestina)

MARTINUS NIJHOFF / 'S-GRAVENHAGE
1964

Promotor: PROFESSOR MR. W. F. DE GAAY FORTMAN

FREE UNIVERSITY AT AMSTERDAM

ARAB CONTRACT OF EMPLOYMENT

Conflict and Concord

THESIS

FOR OBTAINING THE DOCTOR'S DEGREE IN LAW AT THE FREE UNIVERSITY, AMSTERDAM ON THE AUTHORITY OF THE RECTOR MAGNIFICUS DR. F. DE ROOS, PROFESSOR IN THE FACULTY OF ECONOMICS, WHICH THESIS WILL BE UPHELD ON FRIDAY JULY 3, 1964 AT 3.30 P.M. IN THE "WOESTDUINCENTRUM", 16 WOESTDUINSTRAAT, AMSTERDAM

by

HISHAM RIF'AT HASHEM

born at Nablus (Palestine)

MARTINUS NIJHOFF / THE HAGUE

1964

ISBN 978-94-011-8188-4 ISBN 978-94-011-8836-4 (eBook)
DOI 10.1007/978-94-011-8836-4

TO MY MOTHER

AND THE MEMORY OF

MY LATE FATHER

PREFACE

The contract of employment is the legal instrument which regulates the conditions of employment of the vast majority of the working people of the world.[1] More than any other civil contract based on mutual rights and obligations, this contract is characterised by the importance of its human elements. Sir William Blackstone once underlined the human and legal significance of the relationship, by classifying it immediately after the two great human relationships of husband and wife and of parent and child.[2] The contract is thus nationally and internationally important. In 1927 the International Labour Conference adopted a resolution "requesting the governing body of the Office to consider the possibility of placing the question of the general principles of contracts of employment on the agenda of a future session of the Conference."[3] This question was regrettably not followed up. The reason though not the justification, lies in the difficult task of limiting the bounds of the contract and of reconciling the different legal systems in the various countries. The effort spent by the I.L.O. during the last few years towards the adoption of an international recommendation on the termination of the contract, which is yet to bear fruit, illustrates the difficulties involved.

In the Arab countries the importance of the contract of employment was more felt since the introduction of industry thirty years ago. A great deal of interest in the contract has since developed in these countries in the labour, judicial, professional and academic circles, especially in the U.A.R. This shows the increasing awareness of the importance of the contract of employment in the every-day life of the Arab countries. The modest industrial development in these countries

[1] *Vide* E. Herz in an article entitled *The Contract of Employment*, in the *International Labour Review* (published monthly since 1921 by the International Labour Office, Geneva, hereinafter called I.L.R.), Vol. 31, 1935, p. 838.

[2] *Vide The Law of Master and Servant*, by Batt, F. R., 4th ed., 1950, London, p. 1 (hereinafter called Batt); *vide* also Report VII (1), 1961, of the *International Labour Office* (hereinafter called I.L.O.), p. 7.

[3] I.L.R., Vol. 31, 1935, p. 837; *vide* also the introduction to *Al-Mawsu'ah Al-Kadai'-yyah Fi Munaza'at El-'Amal*, by El-Hawwari, I, 1960, in Arabic, Cairo (hereinafter called El-Hawwari).

has so far resulted in the creation of a nucleus of a working class, both in industry and agriculture. But the further envisaged development is expected to increase the ranks of that class and thus propagate more interest in the contract. The relationship between the members of that class was and in the main still is individual in character, and is exemplified by the contract of employment. This, in the first instance, accounts for the selection of the contract of employment as the subject of this study.

The fact that the contract of employment was the subject of legislation in the Arab countries, is a second reason for the selection. In all these countries it came to be recognised that there was need for the special protection of the worker as the weaker party of the contract. This protection was provided by the statutory regulation of the contract with penal sanctions which bestowed upon it a public character.

A third reason for the selection is the general tendency noticed in the area of legislative cross-reference, so much so that almost identical provisions are sometimes found in the relevant enactments of these countries. The fact that the legal systems in these countries are not all identical, gives rise to the conflict of law difficulties.[4] A comparative study will assist in this respect, but the writer is not aware of a relevant comparative study.

A fourth reason for the selection is the rapid development of legislation regulating the contract in the Arab countries.[5] This has one main goal. The goal is that of providing more protection for the worker by means of filling in the gaps in legislation. So it is hoped that the present study will assist in this filling-in process, mainly by pointing out the legal difficulties involved. It is further hoped that it will assist in the comprehensiveness of the collective contracts and agreements, which have started to be made in some of the Arab countries. These in due course are supposed to assist in the said filling-in legislative process.

Finally the Arab League manifested its interest in the contract of employment by issuing recommendations in 1954, concerning the statutory regulation of the contract, to be used as a legislative source by the member states for the further development of their enact-

[4] Though there are many scholars in the Arab countries who are experts in one or the other of these legal systems, which are mainly the English Common Law and the French Law in addition to the Moslem *Shari'a* law, it can be safely assumed that those who have good knowledge of both the English Common Law and French Law are not many.

[5] To take but one example, Libya legislated on the subject in 1952, 1957 and 1962. The last one seems to be still under amendment at present. This of course is attributable to the rapid development of oil exploration and drilling.

ments.[6] The goal was and still is that of unification within the framework of the general unification movement in the area. It is hoped that the present study will assist in this unification process.

As the law inspiration in the Arab countries, at least as concerns the legislative provisions which regulate the contract of employment, is either a Latin and in the main a French inspiration, or that of the English Common Law,[7] these countries were divided into two groups. The first group comprises the U.A.R., Iraq, Kuwait, Qatar, Saudi Arabia, Lebanon, Jordan, Libya, Tunisia, Algeria and Morocco. The second group comprises the Sudan, Bahrain and Aden. As no comparative study can be properly carried out between more than two countries, the U.A.R. and Sudan were selected as representative countries of these two groups. The selection is further discussed in the *Introduction*.

The legislative provisions which regulate the contract of employment in the U.A.R., are mainly contained in Chapter II of Book II of the U.A.R. Labour Code and in sections 674–698 of the U.A.R. Civil Code. The relevant provisions in Sudan are mainly contained in the Employers and Employed Persons Ordinance of 12 February 1949.[8] Of these two the former were selected as the basis of this study, because:

(a) they were developed seperately in the U.A.R., as was done in all the Arab countries in the abovementioned first group, and contrary to what has been done in Sudan. Even the U.A.R. Labour Code which was the first attempt at comprehensive enactment dealing with labour matters, has preserved a seperate chapter for the contract of employment. In due course it was realised that "the contract of employment is the basis of all labour legislation";[9] and this warranted the special

[6] These recommendations were a legislative source for the U.A.R. Law No. 91 of 5 April 1959—*Al-Jaridat-ul-Rasmiyyatu* No. 71 (bis) B, dated 17 April 1959, legislated in Arabic for Egypt and Syria of which the United Arab Republic was then comprised—*vide* the Explanatory Note thereto. This law will hereinafter be called the U.A.R. Labour Code. The translation of the Code into English was undertaken by the writer, because the I.L.O. translation which was issued in its Legislative Series (hereinafter called L.S.)-1959-U.A.R. 1, was rendered indirectly through a French translation and is not all correct. The writer's translation is his responsibility.

[7] The Moslem *Shari'a* Law, whose principles were codified in the *Majallah* in the days of the Turkish Empire, does not any more regulate the contract of employment in the Arab countries, as is clear from their enactments, though it is a judicial authority in the U.A.R. by virtue of section 1(2) of Law No. 131 of 1948 (hereinafter called the U.A.R. Civil Code), and in the rest of the Arab countries.

[8] *The Laws of the Sudan*, Vol. 8, Title XXII, Sub-Title 8, the Government Printing Press, Khartoum, hereinafter called the Sudan Ordinance. The Ordinance was legislated in English.

[9] *Sharh Tashree' El-'Amal Fi Misr*, by El-Areef, A., 2nd ed., 1955, in Arabic (hereinafter called E.-Areef), Vol. I, p. 7, *vide* also pp. 5 and 25; and *vide* a book of the same title by Badawi, Z., 1953, in Arabic, Cairo (hereinafter called Badawi, Z.), Vol. I, p. 5. *Vide* also footnote 12, infra.

juridical attention which has for more than twenty years been paid to the contract in the U.A.R.;

(b) they are more comprehensive than those of Sudan. So they afford a wider scope of study.

As the provisions in the two countries do not deal with certain matters which properly fall within the law of agency, torts or the criminal law, these were excluded from the scope of this study.[10] The conditions of employment of special categories of workers like women, young persons, miners and disabled persons were also excluded, because their regulatory legislative provisions are usually seperate from the provisions which regulate the contract of employment.[11] Their special provisions indeed merit separate studies. Hours of work were also excluded, mainly because they are dealt with independently of the contract of employment in the U.A.R. Labour Code. This independent treatment is understandable because the hours of work do not usually engage the attention of the individual worker when he enters into a contract of employment. He presumes that the hours of work will be more or less the same not only in his establishment, but also in the country as a whole. On the other hand, his attention, besides wages, is expected to be directed to leaves and holidays, which may differ in their upper limitations from one establishment to the other. This may explain and indeed justify the inclusion of leaves and holidays in the contract of employment provisions in the U.A.R. Labour Code, and the resultant inclusion thereof in this study. Finally the settlement of disputes arising from the contract of employment was excluded from this study, because it deserves a seperate study embracing all the relevant procedural matters.

This study is a lawyer's study. So the social and economic aspects of the contract of employment are not discussed except briefly, and

[10] So the study does not claim to be a full study of the law of 'master and servant' in the traditional English sense. It does not embrace the rights of the parties against and their liability to third parties, nor the employer's liability to compensate the worker for an industrial injury or a professional disease, nor the criminal liability of either party.

[11] Witness the particular attention devoted to women and young persons in the *Versailles Treaty* (Clause 427, Chapter XIII, Part II), and the I.L.O.'s relevant Conventions and Recommendations. *Vide* I.L.R., Vol. 7, 1923, p. 182: "The beginning of labour legislation was marked by the prohibition of employment of young children. This was followed by the limitation of the hours of work of women and young persons." *Vide* El-Areef, p. 28: "The French Act of 22 March 1841 regulating the employment of young persons, is the first piece of labour legislation." And *vide* I.L.R., Vol. 28, 1933, p. 681, and Vol. 34, 1936, pp. 84 and 85, for the evidence of the early and independent legislative treatment of women and young persons in Lebanon and the U.A.R., respectively.

only when this is necessary for the better appreciation of the legal problems of the contract.[12]

The treatment of the contract of employment in this study is a comparative treatment. The main goal is to clarify the *conflict and concord* in the provisions which regulate the *Arab contract of employment,* such conflict and concord as are expected from the influence of two or more legal systems in one country or area. The contract is given the description 'Arab' because the study generally embraces one area which accomodates all the Arab countries. However, it is hoped that the study will also be useful especially to some of the young African countries which face similar conflict of law difficulties.

The study was designed in a setting which would enable the reader who is only conversant with either the English Common Law or the French Law, to appreciate it. It is also written in a form which, it is hoped, will be of use and interest not only to the academic expert, but also to those who have to deal with labour, whether they are employers, trade unionists, workers or labour officials.

Part I of the study is allotted to the selection of the U.A.R. and Sudan and to the emergence of their legislation on the contract of employment. The enactments of the other Arab countries are briefly mentioned. Part II is allotted to the treatment of the contract of employment in seven chapters. These deal with definitions, formation of the contract, rights and obligations of the parties, wages, leaves and holidays, suspension frustration and termination of the contract, and the termination gratuity, respectively. Every chapter is followed by a summary which recapitulates the conclusions.

ACKNOWLEDGEMENTS

Finally I wish to record my appreciation and thanks to all those who helped to make this study a reality, whether by financial assistance or by providing the necessary academic contacts or by their useful remarks. In particular I wish to thank H.E. the Minister of Education, Arts and Sciences in the Netherlands and Miss E. Talsma, senior

[12] *Vide* O. Kahn-Freund in *The System of Industrial Relations in Great Britain, its History, Law and Institutions*, ed. by A. Flanders and H. Clegg, 1954, London (hereinafter called Flanders and Clegg), p. 54, where he says: "The relationship between the employer and the individual employee is normally irrelevant to the social scientist, at any rate in so far as he is interested in the social and economic factors which contribute to the development of wages and other conditions of employment. For the lawyer, however, this individual relationship between employer and employee is the cornerstone of the edifice. Everything hinges upon what is called the 'contract of employment' or 'contract of service'."

official of the Department of International Cultural Relations in that Ministery, and her Staff, for the scholarship award and the financial grant, which helped me in completing this study and in defraying some of the printing costs. Professor E. de Vries, the Rector of the Institute of Social Studies of the Hague, thankfully helped me in the necessary academic contacts before I came to the Netherlands, and by putting the good facilities of the Institute at my disposal. In this respect I wish also to thank Professor H. Chabot, the Dean of Studies at the said Institute, and Dr. C. W. Van Santen, the Deputy Legal Adviser at the Ministry of Foreign Affairs in the Netherlands, both of whom contributed in providing the said academic contacts. I owe a word of thanks to Mr. J. N. van der Vlugt, the Librarian of the Institute and his staff, for their cheerful assistance; and to Dr. B. Landheer, Director of the Peace Palace Library in the Hague and his staff; and all those in the Ministry of Social Affairs in the Netherlands who did not grudge any assistance. The staff of the Social Affairs Department of the Arab League in Cairo, and the library staff of the League's Centre for Higher Studies in Cairo, have both been of some assistance in some way or another.

His Honour A. S. Diamond, Master of the Supreme Court in England, Professor O. Kahn-Freund of London University, Professor M. H. Murad of Heliopolis University in Cairo, *Sayed* S. A. Habeeb of the Law Department of the Arab League, Dr. A. Barakat of the I.L.O., Geneva, and Dr. A. El-Maraghi the I.L.O. representative in Cairo, have all thankfully assisted with useful remarks in the preliminary stages of this study.

Mr. J. L. Roberts, Senior Lecturer in the Victoria University of Wellington, New Zeeland, was kind enough to read the manuscript and to make some valuable remarks. And a word of thanks goes to *Sayed* M. Th. Taher who kindly assisted in the proof reading.

I wish to express my appreciation of the provoking encouragement I received from *Sayed* A. M. Atabani, the ex-Attourney General of the Republic of Sudan, with whom I worked in the Ministry of Justice in Khartoum.

Last but not least my wife stood it all with lots of forbearance and cheerfulness, and to her goes my final word of thanks. With her I also thank Haneen and Usama who will in due course appreciate my great obligation to them.

TABLE OF CONTENTS

Preface IX
Table Of Cases XXI
Abbreviations XXIX

PART I. INTRODUCTION 1

Section I. Selection Of The U.A.R. (Egypt) And The Sudan And The Legal Systems Of Both Countries 3

Section II. Emergence And Evaluation Of The Legislation Which Regulates The Contract Of Employment In The U.A.R. And Sudan 7

Section III. Legislation Regulating The Contract Of Employment In The Other Arab Countries 17

PART II. THE CONTRACT OF EMPLOYMENT

CHAPTER I. DEFINITIONS

Section I. The Contract Of Employment 23
The Elements Of The Contract:
(1) Work 25
(2) Remuneration 27
(3) Control 30
The Consensual Nature Of The Contract 37
Distinction Of The Contract Of Employment From Related Contracts:
(a) The Contract of Independent Work Or Of Services . . . 41
(b) The Contract Of Agency 45
(c) Partnership 48

Section II. The Employer 51

Section III. The Worker 53

Controversial Contracts Of Certain Persons:
(i) Persons Performing Work Of A Religious Character . . 56
(ii) Teachers 57
(iii) Advocates 57
(iv) Journalists 59
(v) Doctors 59
(vi) Company Directors 60
(vii) Commercial Travellers, Representatives, Local Salesmen And Other Intermediaries 61
(viii) Artists 62
(ix) Kerosine Distributors 63
(x) Drivers 63
(xi) Shoe-Makers 65
Certain Persons Expressly Excepted From The Definition Of The Worker:
(a) Casual Workers 66
(b) Dependent Members Of The Employer's Family 68
(c) Domestic Servants 70
(d) Government Officials And Workers 73
(e) Apprentices 76
(f) Agricultural Workers 79
(g) Maritime Workers 80
(h) Other Workers 81

Summary 81

CHAPTER II. FORMATION OF THE CONTRACT OF EMPLOYMENT

Section I. Capacity And Consent Of The Parties 83

Section II. Form Of The Contract 84

Section III. Duration And Renewal Of The Contract 88
Duration Of The Contract:
(a) The Limited Contract:
(i) Contract For A Definite Period Of Time 90
(ii) Contract For Seasonal Work 92
(iii) Contract For Specific Work 93
(iv) Long-Term Contracts And Contracts For Life 93
(b) The Unlimited Contract 95
Renewal Of The Contract 96

Section IV. Novation And Vicarious Performance Of The Contract 98
Section V. Terms Of The Contract 101
Summary 106

CHAPTER III. RIGHTS AND OBLIGATIONS OF THE PARTIES

Section I. Rights And Obligations Of The Parties Arising At The Commencement Of And During Employment 109
(a) Transportation. 109
(b) Provision Of Work By The Employer And Personal And Exclusive Service By The Worker:
(i) Provision Of Work By The Employer. 111
(ii) Personal Service Of The Worker 113
(iii) Exclusive Service By The Worker 114
(c) Faithful Service Of The Worker And The Bona Fides Of Both Parties:
(i) The Care Of A Reasonable Man In The Performance Of The Work. 115
(ii) The Employer's Orders 116
(iii) Care For The Work Materials And Equipment 120
(iv) Preservation Of Professional Secrets 121
(v) The Bona Fides Of The Parties 122
(d) Work Rules 124
(e) Disciplinary Rules And Measures. 127
(f) Medical Treatment And Protection From Dangers At Work 134
(g) Housing And Food 137
(h) The Worker's Inventions 140

Section II. Rights And Obligations Of The Parties Arising On And After The Termination Of Employment 144
(a) Transportation 144
(b) Certificate Of Service And Return Of The Worker's Papers 147
(c) The Worker's Competition With The Employer After The Termination Of The Contract 151

Summary 158

CHAPTER IV. WAGES

Section I. Defintion And Kinds of Wages 160

Section II. Agreement On Wages 172

Section III. Protection Of Wages 175
(a) Payment Of Wages In Legal Tender 176
(b) The Worker's Freedom Of Purchase 178
(c) Time, Place And Periodicity Of Payment Of Wages During Employment 179
(d) Payment Of Wages At The Termination Of The Contract . 181
(e) Deductions From Wages:
(i) Disciplinary Deductions. 184
(ii) Compensatory Deductions. 184
(iii) Deductions In Satisfaction Of Loans 185
(iv) Other Deductions 186
(f) Attachment And Assignment Of Wages 187
(g) Priority Of Wages 189
Summary 190

CHAPTER V. LEAVES AND HOLIDAYS

Section I. Annual Leave 193

Section II. Sick Leave. 203

Section III. Public Holidays 207

Section IV. Other Leaves 210

Summary 211

CHAPTER VI. SUSPENSION, FRUSTRATION AND TERMINATION OF THE CONTRACT OF EMPLOYMENT

Section I. Suspension And Frustration Of The Contract 213
Particular Causes:
(a) Sickness 214
(b) Disability 218
(c) Criminal Offences And Imprisonment 219
(d) Military Service 222
(e) Strikes, Lock-Outs And Other Work Stoppage 224
(f) Death 226

(g) Bankruptcy, Winding Up And Closing Down Of The Establishment 227
Section II. Termination Of The Contract 229
(a) Legal Termination 229
(1) Termination Of Limited Contracts 230
(2) Termination Of Unlimited Contracts By Either Party With Notice 231
(3) Termination By Either Party Of Unlimited Contracts Without Notice Or Limited Contracts Before Expiry:
(i) Failure to Carry Out Contractual Obligations . . . 236
(ii) Misrepresentation 239
(iii) Assault 241
(iv) Breach Of Safety Regulations 243
(v) Criminal Offences, Dishonesty And Immorality . . 245
(4) Termination By The Employer Of Unlimited Contracts Without Notice Or Limited Contracts Before Expiry:
(i) The Worker's Absence from Work. 246
(ii) Serious Material Damage To The Employer's Property 249
(iii) Disclosure Of Professional Secrets 250
(iv) Intoxication 252
(v) During Probation 253
(b) Unjustifiable And Wrongful Termination 254

Summary 261

CHAPTER VII. THE TERMINATION GRATUITY

Section I. Conditions Of Entitlement And Calculation Of The Gratuity 265

Section II. Substitution Of The Gratuity By Other Benefits . . 274

Section III. Distribution Of The Gratuity Or The Substituted Benefits Among Beneficiaries 277

Summary 281

Selected Bibliography 284

Index 290

TABLE OF CASES

(Refer to the Alphabetical List of Abbreviations for the full titles of the Law Reports)

English: Arranged in alphabetical order.
French: Arranged in alphabetical order.
Indian: Arranged in alphabetical order.
Sudanese: Arranged in alphabetical order.
U.A.R.: Arranged according to Courts, year and case number.

ENGLISH CASES

Page

Addis *v.* Gramophone Co. (1909), A.C. 488 . . . 260
Allen *v.* Rawson (1845), 1 C.B. 551 143
Armour *v.* British International Pictures (1930), 23 B. 367 62
Athersmith *v.* Drury (1857), 7 W. R. 14 178
Attwood *v.* Lamont (1920), 3 K.B. 571 155
Baillie *v.* Kell (1838), 6 Scott, 739 238
Bartonshill Coal Co. *v.* Reid (1858), 3 Macq. 266. 245
Bason *v.* Sandford (1689), 2 Salk., 440 31
Baster *v.* London and County Printing Works (1899), 1 Q.B. 901 . . . . 123, 250
Bell *v.* Lever (1932), A.C. 161 123
Bettini *v.* Gye (1876), 1 Q.B. 217
Bloxam *v.* Elsee (1825), 1 C. & P. 558 143
Boston Fishing Co. *v.* Ansell (1888), 39 C.D. 399 123, 238
Bound *v.* Lawrence (1892), 1 Q.B. 226 55
Bouzourou *v.* Ottoman Bank (1930), A.C. 271 . . 120
Brace *v.* Calder (1895), 2 Q.B. 253 236
British Celanese Ltd. *v.* Moncrieff (1948), Ch. 564. 143
British Reinforced Concrete Engineering Co. *v.* Lind (1917), 86 L.J. (Ch.) 486. 143
Bromley *v.* Smith (1909), 2 K.B. 235. 156
Browning & Ors. *v.* Crumlin Valley Collieries Ltd. (1926), 1 K.B. 522. 226
Bunning *v.* Lyric Theatre Ltd., 71 L.T. 396. . . 113
Burton *v.* Pinkerton (1867), L.R. 2 Ex. 340. . . 245
Carrol *v.* Bird (1800), 3 Esp. 201 150
Cassidy's Case (1951), K.B. 343 60
Castigan Gray *v.* Bovier (1925), 41 T.L.R., 372 . 98
Castilia, the (1822), I Hag. Adm. 59 238
Clayton *v.* Oliver (1930), A.C. 209 260
Clayton *v.* Waller (1830), A.C. 209. 113
Clouston & Co. Ltd. *v.* Corry (1906), A.C. 122 . . 238
Collier *v.* Sunday Referee Publishing Co. (1940), 2 K.B. 647 101
Collins *v.* Herfordshire County and Anr. (1947), 1 A.E.R, 633 44
Cooper *v.* Phillips (1831), 4 C. & P. 581 136
Cuckson *v.* Stones (1858) L.J.Q.R. 25 . . . 206, 216
Cunningham *v.* Fonblanque (1883), 6 C & P 44 N.P. 122
Davidson *v.* Reeves (1892), 8 T.L.R. 391 227
Davies *v.* Ebbow Vale Urban District Council (1911), 27 T.L.R. 543 205
Davies Contractors Ltd. *v.* Fareham U.D.C. (1956), A.C. 696 214
Deane *v.* Wilson (1906), 2 T.R. 405 165
Dennis & Sons *v.* Tunnard Bros & Moore (1911), 56 Sol. 162 260
Devonald *v.* Rosser (1906), 2. K.B. 728. 165
Deyong *v.* Shenburn (1946), 1 A.E.R. 226 . . . 124
Dunston *v.* Imperial Gas Light Co. (1881), 3 B & Ad. 60
East Anglican Railways Co. *v.* Lythgoe (1851), 20 L.J.C. P. 841 122
Edwards Ltd. *v.* Comber, 42 T.L.R. 247 89
Elliott *v.* Liggens (1902), 2 K.B. 84 206
Farron *v.* Wilson, L.R. 4 C.P. 744 227
Federal Supply & Coal Storage of South Africa *v.* Angehrn, 103 L.T. 150 254
Fillieul *v.* Armstrong (1837), 7 A. & E., 557. . . 249
Foxall *v.* International Land Credit Co. (1867), 16 L.T. 673. 165
French *v.* Brooks (1830), 6 Bing. 354. 147
General Billposting Co. Ltd. *v.* Atkinson (1909), A.C. 118 155
Gold *v.* Essex County Council (1942), 2 K.B. 293 60
Gordon *v.* Potter (1859), 1 F. & F. 644 147
Gould *v.* Webb, 4 E. & B. 236 . . . . 239, 250

Page
Grand Trunk Railway Co. of Canada v. Robinson (1915), A.C. 740 45
Gravely v. Barnard (1874), 18 L.R. Eq. 518. . . 155
Gutsell v. Reeves (1936), 1 K.B. 372 40
Hall v. Wright (1859), E B. & E. 746 227
Hands v. Simpson (1928), 44 T.L.R. 295 252
Hardaker v. Idle District Council (1896), 1 Q.B. 335 42
Harmer v. Cornelius, 5 C.B.N.S. 236 . . . . 219, 240
Harrington v. Churchward, 29 L.J. Ch. 521 . . . 164
Harvey v. Crampain Fishing Co. Ltd. (1934), L.J.N.C.C.R. 405 238
Helmore v. Smith (1886), 35 Ch. D. 449 122
Hepworth Manufacturing Co. v. Ryott (1920), 1 Ch. 1, p. 33 154
Higgins v. Hopkins (1848), 18 L.J. Ex. 133 . . . 28
Hill v. Beckett (1951), 1 K.B., 578. 50
Hillyer's Case (1909), 2 K.B. 820 60
Hivac Ltd. v. Park Royal Scientific Instruments Ltd. (1946), Ch. 169 . . . . 115, 122
Horton v. McMurtry, 5 H. & N. 667 250
Hughes v. The Overseers of the Parish of Chatham (1843), 5 Man & G. 54 163
Inglis v. East India Co. (1851), 18 L.T.O.S. . . . 206
Jacoby v. Whitmore (1883), 49 L.T. 335 156
Johnson v. Shrewsbury & Birmingham Railway Co. (1853), 3 De G.M. 914 261
Jones v. Scullard (1898), 2 Q.B. 565 115
Keen v. Henry (1894), 1 Q.B. 292 64
Kennedy v. Broun (1863), 13 C. B.N.S.. 57
King v. Michael Faraday and Partners Ltd. (1939), K.B. 753 189
Konski v. Piet (1951), 1 Ch. 530. . . . 155, 171. 236
Lacy v. Osbaldiston (1837), 8 C. & P. 80 123
Lake v. Campbell, 5 L.T. (N.S.) 582 170
Langeton v. Carleton (1873), 9 Ex. 57 . . . 98, 231
Latchford Premier Cinema v. Ennion (1931), 2 Ch. 409 235
Law v. Redditch Local Board (1892), 1 Q.B. 127 . 156
Liste v. Romford Ice and Cold Storage Co. Ltd. (1957), A.C. 555 115
Lloyd v. Midland Railway Co. (1914), 30 T.L.R. 247 115
L.M.S. Railway v. National Union of Railwaymen (Award No. 1602 of 13 November 1934)–I.S.D.L., Vol. 10, 1936, p. 30 119
Lomax v. Arding (1855), 10 Ex. 734 238
Manubesn v. Leon (1919), 1 K.B. 208 168
Marbe v. G. Edwardes (Daily's Theatre), (1928), 1 K.B., 269. 112
Marina, the, (1881), 50 L.J.P. 33 238
Marshall v. Glanville (1917), 2 K.B. 97 224
Marshall's Case (1937), A.C. 97 60
Matsoukis v. Priestman & Co. (1915), 1 K.B. 681 . 214
Measures Bros. Ltd. v. Measures (1910), 2 Ch. 248. 155
Morison v. Thompson (1874), 9. Q.B. 48 123
Morris v. Saxelby (1916), 1 A.C. 688 . . . . 155, 157
Nathan v. Gulkoff & Levy Ltd. (1933), Ch. 809 . 112
Neyger v. London Passenger Transport Board (1935), L.J.N.C.C.R. 46 238
Nicoll v. Greaves (1864), 17 C.B.N.S. 27 73

Page
Nokes v. Doncaster Amalgamated Collieries Ltd. (1940), A.C. 1014 . . . . 99, 101
Nordenfelt v. Maxim – Nordenfelt (1894), A.C. 535 154
Nordman v. Rayner and Sturges (1916), 33 T.L.R. 87. . . . . 214, 221
Nugent v. Smith (1876), 1 C.P.D. 423 214
O'Neil v. Armstrong, Mitchell & Co. (1895), 2 Q.B. 418 245
Orman v. Saville Sportswear Ltd. (1960), 3 A.E.R., p. 105 217
Ottoman Bank v. Chakarian (1930), A.C. 277 . . 120
Paradine v. Jane (1647), Aleyn, 26. 214
Pearce v. Foster (1886), 17 Q.B. 536 . . . . 122, 246
Penman v. Fife Coal Co. (1936), A.C. 45 189
Penny v. Wimbledon Urban District Council (1898), 2 Q. B. 212. . . . . 35, 42
Philipps v. Foxall (1872), L.R., 7 Q.B. 666 . . . 254
Price v. Webb (1931), 2 K.B. 367 151
Quarman v. Burnett (1840), 6 M. & W. 499 . . . 31
Re African Association, Ltd., and Allen (1910), 1 K.B. 396 229
Re Mirams (1891), 1 Q.B. 594. 189
Re Young ex. p. Jones (1896), 2 Q.B. 484 . . . 50
Reeve v. Reeve (1858), 1 F. & F. 28
Reid. v. Explosives Co., 19 Q.B. 264 236
R. v. Bailey (1871), 12 Cox 56 46
R. v. Macdonald (1861), Le & Ca 85 50
R. v. National Arbitration Tribunal, ex. p. Crowther (1948), 1 K.B. 424 261
R. v. Negus (1837), 2 C.C.R. 36, 46, 62
R. v. Walker, 27 L.J.M.C. 207 46
Rigby v. Connol (1880), 14 Ch. D. 482 261
Rishton v. Grissell, 5 Eq. 326 164
Robinson v. Davidson (1871), L.R. 6 Exch. 269 . 217
Rogers v. Booth (1937), 2 A.E.R. 751 C.A., 30 B. W.C.C. 189 56
Russel v. Austin Fryers (1909), 25 T.L.R. 414. . 189
Ryan v. Jenkinson (1835), 25 L.J.Q.B. II. . . . 229
Ryan v. Mutual Tontine Westminister Chambers Association (1893), 1 Ch. 116 261
Sadler v. Henlock, 4 E. & B. 57 44
Saxby v. Gloucester Wagon Co. (1883), Griffin's Patent cases, 1888, pp. 54 and 56 143
Scarman v. Castell (1795), 1 Esp. 270 136
Sellers v London Counties Newspapers (1951), 1 A.E.R. 544 183
Siddall v. Wallsey Corporation (1932), I.S.D.L., Vol. 8, 1934, p. 28. 260
Smith v. Allen (1862). 3 F. & F. 157 N.P. . . . 243
Smith v. General Motor Cab Co. Ltd. (1911), A.C. 188 64
Spain v. Arnott, 2 Stark 256, N.P.. . . 230, 238, 240
Speak v. Phillips (1839), 5 M. & M., 279 252
Spotswood v. Burrow (1850), 5 Ex. 110 238
Squire v. Bayer & Co. (1901), 2K.B. 299 128
Stewart v. Casey (1892), 1 Ch. 104. 28
Stocker v. Brocklebank (1851), 3 Mac. & G. 250 . 50
Storey v. Fulham Steelworks Co. (1907), 24 T.L.R. 89. 217

Page

Swain *v.* West (Butchers) Ltd. (1936), 3 A.E.R. 261 123
Taylor *v.* Caldwell (1863), 38 & S. 826 214
Taylor *v.* Rowan (1835), 7 C. & P. 70 151
Tolhurst *v.* Associated Portland Cement Manufacturers (1900) Ltd., (1902), 2 K.B. 660 . . . 98
Triplex Safety Class Co. *v.* Scorah (1938), Ch. 211 . . . . 122, 143
Turner *v.* Bayley, 4 De G.J. & Sm. 332 164
Turner *v.* Goldsmith (1891), 1 Q.B. 544 113
Turner *v.* Mason (1845), 14 M. & W. 112 116
Turner *v.* Sawdon & Co. (1901), 2 K.B. 653 . 112, 113
Unger *v.* Preston Corporation (1942), 1 A.E.R. 200 222
University of London Press Ltd. *v.* University Tutorial Press Ltd. (1916), 2 Ch. 601. 57
Venables *v.* Smith (1895), 2 Q.B. 279 64
Walker *v.* Hirsch, 27 Ch. D. 641 50
Wallis *v.* Day (1837), 2 M. & W. 273. 94
Warburton *v.* Cooperative Wholesale Society (1917), 1 K.B. 663. 219
Wennall *v.* Adney, B. & P. 247 136
Wennhak *v.* Morgan (1888), 20 Q.B. 635 151
Wilson *v.* Cookson (1863), C.B. (N.S.) 496 . . . 178
Wise *v.* Wilson, 1 C. & K. 662 252
Woodley *v.* Metropolitan Railways (1877), 2 Ex. 384 241
Yardley *v.* Laws (1957), Law Yearbook No. 1260 235

FRENCH CASES

Ballot *v.* Auzémery (1931), Dalloz Hebdom., 1932, 90. 255
Bellet *v.* Planque èsqualiés (1933), Dalloz Hebdom., 1933, 2, 77 61
Bonfiglio *v.* Carmona (1936), Dalloz Hebdom., 1936, 298. 46
Bon Marché *v.* Rongeat (1932), Gaz. du Palais, 1932, 2, 140 255
Bonnières et Colombes *v.* Viguier (1937), Gaz. du Palais, 1937, I, 387 232
Cauzier *v.* Dame Malude (1929), Gaz. du Palais, 1930, I, 143 255
Comptoir d'excompte et autres *v.* Duboisset(1937), D.H., 1937, 30 228
Desmarais Frères et Compagnie d'Assurance "l'Urbaine et la Seine" *v.* Debrand (1932), Dalloz Hebdom., 1932, 210 35
Duclos *v.* Sèbe (1933), Dalloz Hebdom., 1933, 275. 60
Dumont *v.* l'Ami du Peuple (1932), Dalloz Hebdom., 1933, 79 232
Jomard *v.* Omnium Automobile (1934), Gaz. du Palais, 1934, 2, 633 104
Journal de Valence *v.* Veuve Giraud-Mangin (1936), Sirey, 1937, I, 16 89
Journal des débats *v.* Masqulier (1934), Gaz. du Palsis, 1934, 2, 724 42
Keller-Dorian *v.* Chrétien (1937), Gaz. du Palais, 1937, 1, 408 171
Lamiot *v.* Poiret (1927), Gaz. du Palais, 1927, 1, 457 120
Manufacture Lyonnaise de Chaussures du Sud-Est *v.* Mrs. Brunet (1927), Gaz. du Palais, 1927, 2, 395 232
Martin *v.* Limonsis (1931), Sirey, 1931, 1, 175 . . 162
Mercier *v.* Chemins de fer de l'Est (1935), Gaz. du Palais, 1935, 1, 933 166
Mouclin *v.* Consorno (1934), Dalloz Hebdom., 1934, 326. 149
Noury *v.* Banque Populaire Morbihannaise (1932), Dalloz Hebdom., 1932, 410 89
Pautrat *v.* Gallo (1934), Gaz. du Palais, 1934, 1, 998 70
Petit *v.* Chemins de fer Paris – Orléans (1931), Dalloz Hebdom., 1931, 533 97
Picot et Prunier *v.* Steam Pacific (1933), Dalloz Hebdom., 1933, 2, 29 91
Romestant *v.* Pical (1936), Gaz. du Palais, 1937, 1, 142 233
Sabatier *v.* Cheysson Administrator of the Concarcio Alamgrera (1932), Gaz. du Palais, 1933, 1, 567 90
Société Au Bon Marché *v.* Staudenmeyer (1936), Dalloz Hebdom., 12, 265 255
Société Carbel *v.* Société Cranion fils et Compagnie et Ragon (1936), Dalloz Hebdom., 1936, 380 . 153
Société Chaleur et Froide (1931, Gaz. du Palais, 1931, 2, 659 122
Société d'apprêts et teintureries roannaises *v.* Vernisse (1933), Dalloz Hebdom., 1933, 553. . 124
Société d'Electricité Ouest-Lumière *v.* Moulin (1931), Gaz. du Palais, 1931, 1, 134 124
Société des Tournées Baret *v.* Castella et Rivier (1930), Dalloz Hebdom., 1930, 312. 42
Société Faux et Lafon *v.* Padovani (1935), Sirey, 1935, 1, 45 125
Société Frères *v.* Lapointe (1934), Dalloz Hebdom., 1934, 484. . . . . 91, 153
Société lyonnaise des Cafés Torredo *v.* Ramus (1936), Gaz. du Palais, 29–30 March, 1936 . . 153
Société Pharmacie Centre du Nord *v.* Dame Eysseric (1937), Dalloz Hebdom., 1937, 512 . . . 102
Société Secrestat *v.* Crozatier (1926), Receuil de la Gazette des Tribunaux, 1926, 1, 164 60
Vauvrecy *v.* Marsil (1925), Gaz. du Palais, 1925, 2, 279 237
Vernet *v.* Compagnie d'assurances la Préservatrice (1935), Gaz. du Palais, 1935, 20, 12 166
Veuve *v.* Picard (1929), Sirey, 1929, 1, 230 . . . 29
Weick *v.* Société générale et banque française du Syrie (1932), Gaz. du Palais, 1932, 140 120

INDIAN CASES

Amar *v.* Karam Singh, A.I.R., 1914, Lah. 82 . . 209
Beg Mohammed *v.* Kavasji (1900), 2 Bomb. L.R. 514 181
Chatra Serampore Co-operative Credit Society *v.* Becharam Sarkar & Ors., A.I.R., 1938, Calc. 1829 249
East Indian Railway Co. & anr. *v.* Shewbex Roy Chanshyamdas (1925), 32 C.W.N. 805 225
Goolbai *v.* Pestonji, A.I.R., 1935, BoHbay, 333 . 44

Page

K.R.V. Alagappa Chettiar *v.* Sundaram Annuvi & Ors., 49 M.L.J. 516 238
Middleton *v.* Playfair (1925), A.I.R. Calc. 87 . 123, 124
Nagpur Electric Light & Power Co. Ltd. *v.* Anand, I.L.R., 1944, Nag. 66 229
Ramaswamy Aiyar *v.* Madras Times Printing & Publishing Co. Ltd., A.I.R., 1918, Mad., 1257 . 240
Sardar Gulab Singh *v.* Punjab Zemindari Bank Ltd. (1940), A.I.R., Lahore, 243 61
Seshagiri Row *v.* Nawab Askur Jung (1907), 30 Mad. 438 181
Sunderesan *v.* C.O. & Berar, A.I.R., 1946 Nag. 273 229
The Indo Union Assurance Co. Ltd. *v.* T. Srinivasan (1947), I.L.R., Madras, 170 47
Wechsler *v.* Johnston & Hoffman (1928), Calc. suit 455 254

SUDANESE CASES

Page

Ali El-Hag Mansour *v.* El-Hag Ahmed Abu Zeid and Mohamed Tewfik Hussein (1959), HC-CS-214 137
Bakheita Ibrahim Khalil *v.* Hamad Mahayoub (1957), AC/REV/8 6
El-Sayed El-Hag El-Dosh *v.* President, Ahlia Intermediate School (1958), AC/REC/164-58 . . . . 236, 260
Fatma Sharif *v.* Mansour El-Sheveli and Others (1920), A.C. 1 App. 3 5
Hamad El-Nur *v.* Modern Aluminium Works (1958), HC-CS-603 137
Heirs of Ibrahim Kalil *v.* Ahmad Hassan Abdel Moneim & Brothers (1926) A.C./App. 2. . . . 6
Shawgi Khalil Akasha *v.* Heirs of Khalil Akasha (1958), AC-App-34. 69
Vassili Bamboulis *v.* Osman Abdulla (1960), KHC-Revision-167-1960 239
Yousef Abdel Raziq *v.* Heirs of John Pothitos (1960), AC-Revision-394 170

U.A.R. CASES

High Court of Appeal

Case No.	*Date*	*Page*
Unnumbered	18 May, 1950	124
„	19 April, 1952	59
„	9 April, 1953	249
„	11 February, 1954	124
367	1954	103
131	1956	131
Unnumbered	22 November, 1956	132
202	1957	131
283	„	126
289	„	33, 65
362	„	125, 126
Unnumbered	28 November, 1957	164
74	1958	216
202	„	255
210	„	256
1774	„	53
11	1959	196, 199
27	„	138
99	„	53
248	„	91
269	„	135
Unnumbered	11 February, 1960	164
228	1960	256
332	„	91
441	„	103

The Council Of State

667	1950	63
13919/11/1951	30 December, 1951	127, 130
Unnumbered	December, „	31
„	23 March, 1953	135
2/5/2/2	1953	204
Unnumbered	18 May, 1954	135

Case No.	*Date*	*Page*
„	20 September, 1954	139
„	10 September, 1955	209
903	26 January, 1957	74
Unnumbered	24 July, 1957	71
„	5 July, 1958	138, 139

The Court Of Appeal

Alexandria

210	1950	162
Unnumbered	6 January, 1953	164
97	1954	102
140	„	242
143	„	165, 221
18	1955	200
52	„	195
74	„	242
85	„	204
88	„	62
296/101	„	200
305	„	99, 227
369	„	170
116	1956	247, 248
148	„	242
321	„	118
400	„	267
167	1957	232, 256
176	„	268
288	„	122
326	„	259
360	1957	49
227	1958	247
1319	„	89
271	1959	64

Case No.	*Date*	*Page*
322	1959	169
362	„	103
428	„	254
524	„	269
Almansourah		
17	1954	169
Cairo		
Unnumbered	21 July, 1930	153
132	1948	163
Unnumbered	18 January, 1948	166
764	1951	102
876	„	89
Unnumbered	27 April, 1952	114
25	1953	103
54	„	105
113	„	165
444	1954	117
509	„	248
580	„	148
671	„	87
804	„	57
836	„	34
35	1955	118, 120
61	„	169, 171
116	„	103
222	„	100
300	„	114
563	„	100
625	„	232
801	„	240
1021	„	205, 216
1102	„	62
1103/1031	„	199
1104	„	165
1142	„	195
1244	„	118, 170, 199
1295	„	59
5	1956	104
67	„	64
253	„	195
361	„	248
410	„	244
597	„	247
1332	„	265
1334	„	247
30	1957	138
53	„	202
99	„	165, 169
215	„	253
340	„	57
474	„	213, 267
1196	„	268
22	1958	173
63	„	101
100	„	125
182	„	99
192	„	35

Case No.	*Date*	*Page*
374	1958	162
768	„	125
923	„	58
1159	„	259
1	1959	103
23	„	169
25	„	118
40	„	103
41	„	242
50	„	167
64	„	169
67	„	180
69	„	58
73	„	74
81	„	164
98	„	104
99	„	58
110	„	221
807	„	100
857	„	89
1021	„	257
1145	„	91
1206	„	238
1279	„	249
14	1960	169
223	„	169
283	„	169
329	„	168
486	„	122
655	„	114, 122
676	„	84
987	„	97, 104, 149
1000	„	97, 104, 149
1185	„	123
1254	„	249
1388	„	256
1429	„	58
	The Court Of Cassation	
Alexandria		
471	1949	201, 254
1802	„	254
159	1950	165, 270
331	„	220
999	„	219
1302	„	201
534	1953	199
568	„	199
1098	„	110, 144
1765	„	56
2254	1954	200
952	1955	253
2031	„	259
870	1957	247
871	„	248
1753	„	250
1978	„	258
1504	1958	241, 242
126	1959	122

Case No.	*Date*	*Page*
171	1959	148
757	„	91
1326	„	59
Cairo		
3426	1949	63
1582 (Commercial)	1951	241
723	1952	256
1225 (Commercial)	„	256
Unnumbered	13 November, 1952	72
„	17 December, 1953	91
229	1953	72
415	„	200, 254
780	„	227
1697	„	200
1770	„	234
1911	„	196
2275	„	66
2353 (Commercial)	„	161
2490	„	165
2504	„	195
2548	„	251
2551	„	62
2735	„	66
3031	„	200
3097	„	218
3415	„	200
3447	„	200, 242
3553	„	93
37	1954	64
103	„	195
114	„	200
271	„	242
287	„	240
473	„	254
490	„	200
1284	„	148
1287	„	162
1323	„	97
1454	„	35
1481	„	71
1518/35 (Commercial)	„	62
1657	„	242
1851	„	135
1869	„	196
2032	„	200
3844	„	97
Unnumbered	10 October, 1954	249
55	1955	256
70	„	253
214	„	71
392	„	267
415	„	237
605	„	89
631	„	169
792	„	200
832	„	135
923	„	268
1083	„	165

Case No.	*Date*	*Page*
1205	1955	216
1240	„	148
1312	„	71
1326	„	214
1445	„	194
1492	„	204
1716	„	242
1954	„	245
142	1956	58
265	„	103, 194
324	„	240
479	„	169
991	„	200, 221
1072	„	70
1317	„	253
1467	„	148
140	1957	221
1041	„	268
1116	„	149
1162	„	216
1462	„	220
1591	„	164
1709	„	242
1713	„	251, 253
1844	„	148
35	1958	91, 253
216	„	116
641	„	36, 41
672	„	123
734	„	169
1029	„	74
1878	„	169
2158	„	122
17	1959	220
157	„	99, 103
199	„	35
931	„	172, 270
1079	„	96
1151	„	242
1165	„	242
1201	„	103
1253	„	242
1326	„	34
1339	„	123
1486	„	216
1529	„	41
1733	„	269
1976	„	117
2271	„	269
4304	„	96
299	1960	99
430	„	163
El-Geeza		
130	1956	258
322	„	196
229	1958	254
Shbeen El-Koum		
194	1951	57

Case No.	*Date*	*Page*
Suez		
119	1954	89
Tanta		
280/66	1952	103
	The District Court	
Abdeen		
1397	1949	149
2288	„	220
3718	1950	119
90	1952	60
Bandar El-Geeza		
949	1949	63
Bandar El-Zakazeek		
Unnumbered	3 October, 1952	66
Beni Sweif		
Unnumbered	11 May, 1951	97
37	1954	97
Cairo		
16	1945	114
21 (Commercial)	1949	254
Unnumbered „	19 February, 1949	201
„ „ „	3 April, 1950	201
1017 „	1950	242
	The Labour Court	
Alexandria		
553	1952	200
57	1953	56
354	„	200
2014	„	150
Cairo		
2585	1952	194
215	1953	200
328	„	200
1339	„	165
1697	„	200
1790	„	270
1857	„	60
1933	„	200
1962	„	200
2480	„	256
2768	„	71
2966	„	232
3447	„	200
4052	„	200
5517	„	77
501	1954	200
1903	„	256
2020	„	87
3598	„	87
3833	„	71
5574	„	244

Case No.	*Date*	*Page*
5597	1954	170, 198, 209
5683	„	71
7120	„	86
7352	„	64
1619	1955	59
2320	„	71
2459	„	64
3437	„	200
3611	„	71
3655	„	71
4433	„	77
5979	„	253
6565	„	253
7010	„	100
530	1956	87
1103	„	232, 270
1418	„	64
4029	„	108
4655	„	247
4716	1957	62
1034	1958	71
1711	„	42
1912	„	221
2150	„	149
3280	„	247
364	1959	257
1541	„	238, 247
1687	„	220
2626	„	58
2717	„	71
3620	„	216
4534	„	120
4921	„	100
4958	„	162
5131	„	242
5282	„	231
5285	„	93
5322	„	122
5483	„	195
5654	„	103
5722	„	201
5755	„	170
5767	„	199
6169	„	63
6242	„	169
6261	„	101
6252	„	194
77	1960	91
140	„	213
193	„	256
195	„	256
196	„	256
198	„	256
472	„	172
568	„	163
744	„	91
989	„	119
1106	„	256
1378	„	256

Case No.	*Date*	*Page*
1572	1955	167
2087	„	108
2863	„	71
	The Court Of Arbitration	
Alexandria		
9	1953	118
10	„	118
57	„	169
25	1954	165
14	1955	162
12	1956	169
57	„	165
Asyout		
8	1954	173
12	„	138
14	„	139
Cairo		
133	1952	202
12	1953	65
54	„	169
57	„	167
63	„	169
72	„	111
78	„	165

Case No.	*Date*	*Page*
118	1953	165
231	„	180
245	„	63
265	„	130
277	„	103
4	1954	71
111	„	162
128	„	225
143	„	194
176	„	208
181	„	172
189	„	165
206	„	167
221	„	164
244	„	100
286	„	173
291	„	167, 168
6	1955	52
13	„	208
34	„	208
Unnumbered	9 January, 1955	111
57	1956	63
	The Mixed Courts	
Unnumbered	May, 1936	59
„	18 May, 1936	233

ALPHABETICAL LIST OF ABBREVIATIONS

A

A. & E.	Adolphus & Ellis (King's Bench Series).
A.E.R.	All England Law Reports.
Aleyn	Aleyn's Law Reports (King's Bench Series).

B

B.	Beavan's Law Reports.
B. & Ad.	Barnewall & Alderson (King's Bench Series).
Badawi, K. M.	Reference Book For The Law of The Individual Contract of Employment And The Legal Principles Relating to Industrial Injuries And Professional Diseases (*vide* the Bibliography).
Badawi, Z.	Commentary On The Labour Legislation In Egypt (*vide* the Bibliography)
Barwell and Kar	Law of Service In India, Vol. I., Master And Servant (*vide* the Bibliography).
Batt	Law of Master And Servant (*vide* the Bibliography).
Bing	Bingham's Law Reports.
British Legal Papers	Edited by A.K.R. Kiralfy (*vide* the Bibliography).
B. & P.	Bosanguet & Puller Law Reports.
Butros and Rajab	Commentary On The Legislation Regulating The Contract of Employment (*vide* the Bibliography).
B.W.C.C.	Butterworth's Workmen's Compensation Cases.

C

C.B.	Common Bench Law Reports.
C.B.N.S.	Common Bench New Series.
C. & K.	Carrington and Kirwan Law Reports.
C. & P.	Carrington and Payne Law Reports.
Cheshire and Fifoot	The Law of Contract (*vide* the Bibliography).
Cooper	Outlines of Industrial Law (*vide* the Bibliography).
Cox	Cox's Equity Reports.
C.P.D.	Common Pleas Division Law Reports.

D

Dalloz Hebdom.	Dalloz Hebdomadaire.
De G.M. & G.	De Gex, Macnaghten & Gordon Law Reports.
D.G.J. & Sm.	De Gex, Jones & Smith Law Reports.
Diamond	The Law of Master and Servant (*vide* the Bibliography).

E

E.B. & E.	Ellis, Blackburn & Ellis Law Reports.
E. & B.	Ellis & Blackburn.
El-Areef	Commentary On The Labour Legislation In Egypt (*vide* the Bibliography).
El-Fakahani	The Labour Handbook (*vide* the Bibliography).
El-Hawwari	The Judicial Encyclopaedia of Labour Disputes (*vide* the Bibliography).
El-Sa'eed	Some Rights And Obligations Of The Workers And The Employers In The Iraqi Labour Code (*vide* the Bibliography).
Eq.	Equity (The Official Law Reports).
Esp.	Espinasse Law Reports.
Ex. or Exch.	Exchequer Reports.

F

F. & F.	Foster and Finlason Law Reports.
Faheem	The Law Of The Individual Contract Of Employment And Court Judgements (*vide* the Bibliography).
Fawzi	The Labour Movement In The Sudan (*vide* the Bibliography).
Flanders and Clegg	The System Of Industrial Relations In Great Britain (*vide* the Bibliography).

G

Gaz. du Palais	Gazette du Palais.

H

H. & N.	Hurlstone and Norman Law Reports.
Habeeb	Commentary On The Contract Of Employment In The Unified Labour Code (*vide* the Bibliography).
Hag Adm.	Haggard Admiralty Law Reports.
Halsbury	Halsbury's Laws of England, Vol. 25 (*vide* the Biblio-ography).
Husseini and Hawwari	The Labour Encyclopaedia (*vide* the Bibliography).

I

I. & L.	Industry and Labour (*vide* the Bibliography).
I.L.O.	International Labour Office.
I.L.R.	International Labour Review (*vide* the Bibliography).
I.S.D.L.	International Survey of Decisions On Labour Law (*vide* the Bibliography).

L

Le & Ca	Leigh and Cave Law Reports.
L.J.(Ch.)	Law Journal Reports New Series (Chancery).
L.J.C.P.	Law Journal Reports New Series Common Pleas.
L.J.Exch.	Law Journal (Reports) Exchequer.
L.J.M.C.	Law Journal Magisterial Cases.
L.J.N.C.C.R.	Law Journal Newspaper County Court Reports.

L.J.P.	Law Journal Probate Division Reports.
L.J.Q.B.	Law Journal Queen's Bench Division Reports.
L.R.Eq.	Law Reports Equity.
L.R.Ex.	Law Reports Exchequer.
L.T.	Law Times Reports.
L.T. (N.S.)	Law Times (New Series).
L.T.O.S.	Law Times Old Series.

M

M. & M.	Moody and Malkin Law Reports.
M. & W.	Meeson and Welsby Law Reports.
Mac. & G.	Macnaghten and Gordon Law Reports.
Macdonell	The Law of Master and Servant (*vide* the Bibliography).
Macq.	Macqueen (Sc.) Reports.
Majalla	The Moslem Law Codified (*vide* the Bibliography).
Man. & G.	Manning and Granger Law Reports.
Murad	The Labour And Social Insurance Laws (*vide* the Bibliography).

N

Naguib and Bakr	The Unified Labour Code – Theory And Practice (*vide* the Bibliography).

R

Rashed and Hashem	The Basic Legislation On The Contract Of Employment – The Individual Contract Of Employment Law – A Comparative Study Of The Successive Enactments (*vide* the Bibliography).

S

Sabbour	A Handbook On The Individual Contract of Employment (*vide* the Bibliography).
Salk.	Salkeld's King's Bench Law Reports.
Samuels	Industrial Law (*vide* the Bibliography).
Scott	Scott's Law Reports.
S.L.J.R.	The Sudan Law Journal And Reports.
Smith	A Treatise On The Law of Master And Servant (*vide* the Bibliography).
Sol.	The Solicitor's Reports.
Stark.	Starkie's Law Reports.

T

T.L.R.	Times Law Reports.
T.R.	Term Reports (by Durnford & East).

W

W.R.	Weekly Reporter.

Z

Zaki	Resumé Of Labour Legislation (*vide* the Bibliography).

PART I

INTRODUCTION

SECTION I: SELECTION OF THE U.A.R. (EGYPT) AND THE SUDAN AND THE LEGAL SYSTEMS OF BOTH COUNTRIES

(a) The U.A.R.

The labour law in the U.A.R. is Latin inspired. The inspiration in the main is French. This can be deduced from the comparison of the legislative provisions in the two countries,[1] and the frequent reference in the U.A.R. to the French jurisprudence.[2] The preparatory work

[1] To mention but some examples, cf. section 51 of the U.A.R. Labour Code, with section 51 of Book I of the French Labour Code – *Vide* the *International Survey of Legal Decisions on Labour Law* (issued yearly by the I.L.O., since 1926, but regrettably stopped in 1939, hereinafter, called I.S.D.L.), Vol. 1, 1926, p. 114; cf. section 74 with section 23 of these two Codes, respectively – *Vide* I.S.D.L., Vol. 2, 1927, p. 103; section 85 with 23 of the two Codes, respectively – *Vide* I.S.D.L., Vol. 7, 1933, p. 101; cf. section 86 with section 24 of the two Codes, respectively – *Vide* I.L.R., Vol. 79, 1959, p. 633; cf. sections 91 and 92 with section 31 c of the two Codes, respectively – *Vide* I.S.D.L., Vol. 1, p, 105. Section 75 (6)of the U.A.R. Labour Code was copied from a French Act dated 19 July 1928 – *Vide* I.S.D.L., Vol. 4, 1929, p. 56. Section 86 of the U.A.R. Labour Code, was copied from the French Law, as reported in *Sharh El-Kawaneen Al-Munadhema Li 'Akd El-'Amal*, by Butros, R., and Rajab, A. E., 1957, in Arabic, Cairo (hereinafter called Butros and Rajab), p. 327. Section 676 of the Civil Code was copied from section 29 K of Book I of the French Labour Code – *Vide Al-Wageez Fi Kanun El-'Amal*, by Zaki, M. J. E., 1962, in Arabic, Cairo (hereinafter called Zaki), p. 143; and *vide* I. L. R., Vol. 32, 1935, pp. 374, 384 and 492, for the comparison of section 676 with the French, Italian and Swiss legislation, respectively. Sections 686 and 687 compare well with the French and Swiss legislation – *Vide* I.L.R., Vol. 32, 1935, pp. 380 and 498, respectively. Section 688 compares well with the Swiss and Italian legislation – *Vide* I.L.R., Vol. 83, 1961, pp. 38 and 49 and 43, respectively.

[2] For some examples, *vide Al-Marje' Fi Kanun 'Akd El-'Amal El-Fardi Wa Al-Mabade' El-Kanuniya Likanunai Isabat El-'Amal Wa Amradh El-Mihna*, by Badawi, K. M., 1955, in Arabic, Cairo (hereinafter, called Badawi, K. M.), p. 285, for the reference to a French decision, reported in Dalloz Hebdomadaire, 1927, p. 378, for the purposes of section 72 of the U.A.R. Labour Code; refer to the same author, p. 301, for the judicial history of the doctrine of justification of the termination of the contract in France, for the purposes of section 74 of the Labour Code; refer to the same author, p. 388, for the reference to a French decision, reported in Dalloz Hebdom., 1937, p. 519, for the purposes of section 76(7) of the Labour Code; refer to the same author, p. 273, for the comparison of sections 71 and 679 of the Labour and Civil Codes, respectively, with the French decision reported in Dalloz Hebdom., 1949, p. 598; refer to Butros and Rajab, pp. 96–7, for the comparison of section 683 of the Civil Code, with the French decision of Cass. Civ. on 22 December 1925; cf. section 684(3) of the Civil Code, with the French decision in *Bel V. Servonnet* (1925), Rev. Prud., 1925, p. 174 (I.S.D.L., Vol. 1, 1926, p. 117) – and cf. in this respect, the decision of Cass. Civ., on 7 May 1913 (mentioned in Butros and Rajab, p. 95); *vide* also the last mentioned author, pp. 346–7, for a comparison of section 686(1) of the Civil Code, with the French jurisprudence. *Vide* the reference to the French legal term *lien de subordination*, by the Cairo Labour Court, in case No. 3258 of 1954

for the Civil Code of 1948, contains abundant evidence of the Latin inspiration.[3]

In this capacity, the U.A.R. can, as a subject of study, represent those Arab countries which are either well known to administer legal systems of law very akin to the French Legal system, and have labour legislation similar to that of France, like Tunisia, Algeria and Morocco,[4] or those whose civil laws are similar to that of the U.A.R., like Iraq, Syria, and Lebanon, or those whose labour laws bear various degrees of resemblance to that of the U.A.R., like Iraq, Kuwait, Qatar, Saudi Arabia, Lebanon, Jordan and Libya. The 1958 Labour Codes of Iraq and Kuwait have a lot in common with the U.A.R. Decree Law No. 317 of 1952, which was superseded by the U.A.R. Labour Code. The 1962 Labour Code of Qatar bears a great resemblance to the Kuwaiti Labour Code. The 1963 Labour Code of Libya drew closer in its provisions to the U.A.R. Labour Code.[5]

(b) The Sudan

The law in Sudan is inspired by the English Common Law. This has in the main resulted from the early recruitment of British judges, whose pronouncements bear witness to the inspiration.

Section 4 of the Civil Justice Ordinance of 1900, re-enacted in section 5 of the Civil Justice Ordinance of 1 May 1929,[6] provides for the administration of 'justice, equity and good conscience,' in personal law matters, where there is no Sudanese enactment. Section 9 of the same Ordinance provides that, "in cases not provided for by this or any other enactment for the time being in force, the court shall act according to justice, equity and good conscience."

Acting in accordance with 'justice, equity and good conscience,' was and still is a good sanction for the judicial resort to the principles of foreign law without limitation. However, resort to the U.A.R. or French law, was thereunder rejected, as early as 1920, by judicial pronouncement. "I have considerable hesitation," said *Dun*, C.J. of

(in Badawi, K. M., p. 32); *vide* the reference to the French writer *Durand*, by the Cairo Court of Cassation, in case No. 415 of 1953 (in Badawi, K. M., p. 201); *vide* the reference, in the last-mentioned author, p. 182, to the French writers *Planiol et Ripert* and others; and *vide* the use of the French term *règlement de travail* (the counterpart for the English term *work rules*), by the same author, p. 247, and by Butros and Rajab, p. 321.

[3] *Vide El-Areef*, p. 5; and Zaki, pp. 98 and 100.

[4] *Vide* the *Labour Survey of North Africa*, published by the I.L.O. in 1960, Geneva, (hereinafter, called the Labour Survey of North Africa), pp. 209, 253 and 254.

[5] *Vide* Sections II and III of the present Part I, *infra*

[6] *The Laws of the Sudan*, Vol. 10, Title XXVI, sub-Title 1.

the Sudan,[7] "in applying the principles of French or Egyptian law, partly because it is much more difficult for an English lawyer to discover how to apply the French law to any particular set of facts than it is to discover how to apply the English law, and therefore, I should not as a rule apply the principles of the French Law, Egyptian or any other law except English law, in cases in which I am directed by Section 4 of the Civil Justice Ordinance 'to act according to justice, equity and good conscience,' unless the result of applying English law was repugnant to my ideas of justice, equity and good conscience." *Fleming*, J, in the same case added, "I quite agree with what the learned Chief Justice has said as to the difficulty which the members of a bench, recruited in the manner set out in Section 6 of the Courts Ordinance, must always have in applying consistently the principles of Egyptian law.... I therefore think that in the absence of Sudan legislation or a previous decision of this Court, we should, especially in purely commercial matters, be guided mainly by the legal principles with which we are familiar, and make use of other systems of law merely to assist us in exceptional cases in arriving at the principles of justice, equity and good conscience." That these pronouncements were carried further so as to establish a consistent practice for the Sudan based on the English Common Law, is clear from the words of the same Judge: "It is difficult to see how a consistent practice can be arrived at unless, in cases not governed by Sudan legislation or the previous decisions and practice of the Court, we apply, with such modifications as justice may require, the legal principles in which we have been educated." *Williamson*, J, in the same case put a stamp, as it were, on the whole matter by saying: "I do not say that there may not be cases in which it may be equitable to apply the principles of Egyptian law or even any other law if the principles of English Law are not in accordance with the principles of justice, equity and good conscience when applied to a particular case in this country, but as a general rule I am of opinion that the application of English Law is more likely to confer justice than the application of any other law." So the resort was mainly left to the English Common Law, as administered in England and India. That explains the frequent legislative and judicial reference to these two countries in the Sudan. Comparison of the Sudan Labour legislation with the British and Indian legislation, affords good examples of this reference.[8] In this process, the Sudan seems to have followed in the footsteps of India, where the

[7] *Fatma Sharif V. Mansour El-Sheveli and others* (1920), A.C./App. 3.
[8] *Vide* Chapter VII of *The Labour Movement in the Sudan*, by Fawzi, S. E., 1957, Oxford University Press, London, hereinafter called Fawzi.

term 'justice, equity and good conscience' was coined,[9] and the reception of the English Common Law seems to have gone through the same process.[10] The reception of the English Common Law in Sudan was further widened in scope by the adoption of the principles of the English Statute Law, whenever they were in consonance with 'justice, equity and good conscience.' Evidence of the justification thereof was afforded by *Bell*, C.J. of the Sudan, who said: "English Common Law has been modified by Statute Law from time to time because it has been found to be unsuited to changed conditons. The law to be administered in this country is laid in Chapter II (i.e. section 9) of the Civil Justice Ordinance, and in my opinion the Sudan courts are fully entitled to consider English Statute Law and to adopt or reject it according to whether or not it is in consonance with the provisions of Chapter II, having due regard to conditions in the Sudan."[11] A cautionary remark applicable both to Sudan and India, was afforded in the same case, by *Owen*, J, when he said: "We are guided but not governed by English Common Law and Statute Law." This case is an early case in which the Sudan rejected the English Law, for not being in consonance with 'justice, equity and good conscience.'[12]

In line with these judicial pronouncements, the laws were enacted in English; and this continued even after independence in 1956, though side by side with enactment in Arabic.[13]

In this capacity, the Sudan can, as a subject of study, represent the Arab countries which are well known to administer similar legal systems, and are possessed of labour laws resembling that of the Sudan, like Bahrain and Aden.

[9] *Vide The Reception of the Common Law in Sudan*, by E. Guttmann, in the *International and Comparative Law Quarterly*, Vol. 6, 1957, p. 401. For further enlightenment, refer to *Justice, Equity and Good Conscience*, by D. M. Derrett, in p. 114, of the *Changing Law In Developing Countries*, edited by J. N. D. Anderson, 1963, George Allen and Unwin Ltd., London.

[10] *Vide The Law Relating to Service in India, Vol. I, The Law of Master and Servant*, by Barwell, N., and Kar, S. S., 1st ed., 1952, Orient Longmans Ltd., Bombay, (hereinafter, called Barwell and Kar), p. 253.

[11] *The Heirs of Ibrahim Khalil V. Ahmad Hassan Abdel Moneim and Brothers* (1926), A.C./App. 2.

[12] *Bakheita Ibrahim V. Hamad Mahayoub* (1957), AC/REV/8 (reported in *The Sudan Law Journal and Reports*, 1957, The Sudan Bookshop, Khartoum, p. 25, hereinafter, called the S.L.J.R.), is a modern case, in which the English Common Law was rejected, for the same reason.

[13] The Arabic text has precedence over the English text. The writer, while serving in Sudan, first as a judge, and later as a Legal Counsel to the Sudan Government, from 1956 to 1962, was the Secretary, for two and a half years, of the Law Arabisation Committee, which was charged with the rendering into Arabic, of the eleven volumes of the pre-independence laws, which were enacted in English. The task is yet to be accomplished.
The legal education in the University of Khartoum, is still rendered in English.

SECTION II: EMERGENCE AND EVALUATION OF THE LEGISLATION WHICH REGULATES THE CONTRACT OF EMPLOYMENT IN THE U.A.R. AND SUDAN

(a) The U.A.R.

The contract of employment under the Moslem and Roman laws, used to be considered as a lease contract.[14] Leases used thereunder, to be divided into leases of things and leases of persons.[15]

The new ideas of the French Revolution failed to change this classification of the contract of employment. So Code Napoleon preserved the lease characteristic of the contract.

The first Civil Code in the U.A.R. dated 1883[16], which was inspired mainly by the French law,[17] contained only five sections (401–405), regulating the contract of employment.[18] These sections, which were the first piece of legislation on the contract, bore a great similarity to the provisions of Code Napoleon. They thus preserved the lease characteristic of the contract.

To be sure, not much notice was taken of these provisions, because the employment market was then still limited to handicrafts, some of which were very ancient, dating back to the days of the *Pharaohs*. The employment relationship was still controlled either by the rules of the guilds, which were still prevailing, not only in the U.A.R. but in the area as a whole,[19] or by the family ties which prevailed and still,

[14] *Vide* Book II of the *Majallah*; El-Areef, p. 148; and *Sharh 'Akd El-'Amal Fi El-Kanun El-Muwahhad*, by Habeeb, S. A., 1959, in Arabic, Cairo (hereinafter, called Habeeb), p. 24.

[15] *Vide* Zaki, p. 77.

[16] Law No. 131 of 28 October 1883; i.e. one year after the British occupation. It is indeed surprising that the direct British influence in the country, which continued for many years thereafter, did not effectually change the course of the U.A.R. legal system, which was already set upon the French inspiration, ever since the days of Napoleon in the country.

[17] *Vide* Badawi, Z., Vol. I, p. 20.

[18] The equivalent sections of the Civil Code, which used to be applied by the Mixed Courts, were sections 489–493 (vide Badawi, Z., Vol. I., p. 20). The Mixed Courts were established in 1875, while the country was still governed by the Turks, to try civil and commercial cases, in which the parties were of different nationalities. The capitulations, which permitted the establishment of these courts, resulted in the development of privileges for the foreign nationals, over the native population. The British Government inherited these capitulations by occupation; and it preserved the Mixed Courts. These Courts were finally abolished on 15 October 1949. For further enlightenment on the Mixed Courts, *vide The Mixed Courts of Egypt*, by Brinton, J. Y., 1930, New Haven Yale University Press.

[19] *Vide Sharh Wa Tahleel Kanun El-'Amal El-Kuwaiti Fi El-Kita' El-Ahli*, by Madkour, M. T., 1960, in Arabic, Kuwait, p. 16, for an interesting example of the guild system, which was prevailing in the pearl fishing industry. All this, of course, is reminiscent of the pre-industrial revolution days in Europe.

in some cases, do prevail over any legal employment relationship between the members of the same family. These guilds continued to operate, until the whole system was abolished by a Decree dated 9 January 1890.[20] The cancellation of the guild system left the contract of employment to the said five sections of the 1883 Civil Code, and to the general law.

That the provisions of the Civil Code were, from the start, insufficient, is clear from the fact that, like the Roman and Moslem law provisions, they did not distinguish between the concept of the contract of employment or 'service' and that of 'services.' The industrial development, which took place in the U.A.R., mainly as a result of the inflow of foreign capital after the British occupation, soon exposed the futility of these provisions. Repugnance to the lease characteristic of the contract of employment, showed its effect; and the concept of distinguishing the contract of employment from the other similar contracts, by the element of control which the employer exercises over his worker, started to develop. The Courts, both national and mixed,[21] were thus obliged to fill in the legislative gaps which were exposed.

The First World War and the resultant import difficulties prompted industrial development in the U.A.R.[22] This created the industrial working class, and contributed to its organisation in trade unions. The 1919 revolt did not fail to have some effect on the working class, which began to show better consciousness of the need to improve the working conditions.[23] The successive governments soon began to feel the power of the working class, and most of them did not fail to use this class as a power-weapon. Thenceforward, the working class began to have some political influence and some say in the legislation of the future governments.

The futility of the 1883 Civil Code provisions on the contract of employment, however, persisted. No legislative measures were taken, for a considerable number of years to come, to repeal or amend these provisions. The reason lay in the relative weakness of the working class, as against the employers who were backed by the Government.

In 1927, after the working conditions developed into a miserable

[20] *Vide* El-Areef, p. 24; Zaki, p. 24; and Badawi, Z., Vol. I., p. 12.

[21] The first I.L.O. expert, invited in 1932 by the U.A.R., in order to assist in the writing up of its labour laws, recommended among other things, the reference to the jurisprudence of the Mixed Courts, as a legislative source – *vide* Badawi, Z., Vol. I., p. 21.

[22] *Ibidem*, p. 12.

[23] The political consciousness of the working class against the British rulers, was partly translated into a social consciousness and struggle, against the British and other foreign investor – employers.

state,[24] the Government had to set up a special committee, to study and recommend measures for the regulation of industrial relations, including the individual contract of employment.[25] The committee made 102 recommendations.[26] But all of these were practically neglected, except for the setting up of a Labour Department, mainly because of the said relative weakness of the working class. The I.L.O. expert who was invited in 1932, advised the gradual enactment of labour legislation, instead of the comprehensive draft recommended by the 1927 committee.[27]

Further industrial development followed in the inter-war period,[28] and reached unprecedented levels during the second World War. This further strengthened the workers and spurred their unitary efforts, particularly from 1930 onwards. For the first time, they participated in an international labour conference in Madrid in 1931.

These developments were the direct reason of the enactment of the first labour law in the U.A.R., to regulate the individual contract of employment. That law was Law No. 41 of 15 August 1944.[29] This marked the second legislative stage.

In Law No. 41, the contract provisions began to gain a public character and to have an instant effect on current contracts,[30] by means of imperative provisions with penal sanctions, which are the main characteristic of labour legislation.[31] Thenceforward, the contract, instead of being exclusively civil, entered the precincts of the criminal and

[24] In 1909, the Government was obliged to provide some protection for employed children, by enacting Law No. 14, which was the first piece of modern labour legislation in the U.A.R. – *Vide* El-Areef, pp. 24–5; and Zaki, p. 30.

[25] *Vide* El-Areef, p. 25; and Badawi, Z., Vol. I., p. 13.

[26] These recommendations included the first draft of a labour law, to regulate the contract of employment – *Vide Ibid.*, p. 20.

[27] *Vide Ibid.*, p. 14; and Zaki, p. 31. The acceptance of the expert's advice explains the deplorable consistent Government policy of piece-meal enactment, until the policy was reversed, for the first time, in 1959, when the U. A.R. Labour Code was enacted.

[28] Customs protective barriers, which were imposed in 1930, encouraged the development of the national industry – *Vide* Badawi, Z., Vol. I., p. 13.

[29] *Al-Jaridat-ul-Rasmiyyatu*, No. 69 of 8 June 1944, in Arabic. This law was issued by the I.L.O., in its L.S., in English. It is interesting to note that the first draft of this law was introduced in the Parliament in 1935 – *Vide* Badawi, Z., Vol. I., p. 21.

[30] *Vide* Badawi, K. M., p. 284. This instant effect was conditioned by a saving clause for the contract terms, which are more beneficial to the worker – *vide Kanun El-'Amal El-Muwahhad 'Ilman Wa 'Amalan*, by Naguib, F., and Bakr, A. E. R., 1959, in Arabic, Cairo (hereinafter, called Naguib and Bakr), p. 28; *vide* also Habeeb, pp. 214–7. The instant effect on the current contracts, does not amount to a retrospective effect of the law – *vide* Badawi, Z., Vol. I., pp. 20, 24, and 27; and Naguib and Bakr, p. 22 – *Vide* a different opinion, in Butros and Rajab, pp. 49, 68 and 318; and in Habeeb, pp. 213–4.

[31] The newly acquired public character of the contract (*l'ordre public*), was mainly due to the legislator's new projected intention of providing protection, for a larger section of the community – *Vide* Badawi, Z., Vol. I., p. 8; *vide* also I.L.R., Vol. 31, 1935, pp. 839 and 841–3; and Vol. 84, 1961, p. 175. This is understandable for social reasons, and re-

administrative laws.[32] What is more important is that in this law, the U.A.R. legislator, for the first time, recognized the element of control, as the distinguishing element of the contract from the other similar contracts. Thus the contract of 'service' and that of 'services' were finally distinguished. The lease characteristic of the contract, under the provisions of the 1883 Civil Code, began to vanish, and thereby, the human element of the contract gained gerater influence in the development of legislation.

The scope of the 1944 Law was limited to those employed in commerce and industry,[33] thus leaving those employed in agriculture, to the futile provisions of the 1883 Civil Code and to the general law. This was due to the lack of organisation of the working class in the agriculture sector, and their resultant weakness in the face of the big and powerful land-owners who dominated agriculture, as they have always done from time immemorial. So the old provisions of the Civil Code survived, and in their survival, created an embarassing situation which continued for the next four years. On the other hand, section 22(3) of Law No. 41 introduced for the first time, the doctrine of justification of the termination of the contract of employment.[34] The 1883 Civil Code (sec tion 404) limited compensation to the worker's dismissal without notice.[35]

On 16 July 1948, the new Civil Code was enacted.[36] It contains new, though general provisions,[37] which regulate the individual contract of employment. These are contained in sections 674 to 698, comprising Chapter II of Part III of the Code.[38]

asons related to the public order. The protective character of this legislation is characterised, mainly by the provision of minimum standards, below which no contract can provide – *Vide* El-Areef, p. 420; Naguib and Bakr, p. 33; and I.L.R., Vol. 7, 1923, pp. 183 and 185–6. These standards are minimum standards, in as far as the interests of the worker and not the employer, are concerned: cf., for instance, sections 44 and 58 of the U.A.R. Labour Code, re the maximum period of probation, and the minimum length of the annual leave, respectively.

[32] *Vide* the introduction to *Al-Tashree' El-Asasi Li 'Akd El-'Amal Kanun 'Akd El-'Amal El-Fardi Dirasat Mukarana 'Ala Al-Nusus*, by Rashed, J. E., and Hashem, M. K., 1954, in Arabic, Cairo, (hereinafter, called Rashed and Hashem).

[33] *Vide* I.L.R., Vol. 34, 1936, p. 87.

[34] It is interesting to note that this marked the introduction of the new concept of the justification of the termination of the contract, in some of the Near East Arab countries, excepting those inspired by the English Common Law.

[35] That is still mainly the case, in England, India and Sudan.

[36] This is Law No. 131 of 1948 (the U.A.R. Civil Code), which repealed the Civil Code of 1883.

[37] *Vide* section 675 of the U.A.R. Civil Code, quoted in footnote 42, *infra*.

[38] *Vide* El-Areef, p. 5, where he says: "The general trends that began to show in the *International Survey of Legal Decisions on Labour Law*, had a great effect on the drafting of these provisions of the Code... However, the Code was inspired in some of these provisions, by modern legislation, especially that of Poland, the Swiss *Code des Obligations* and the French and Italian legislation."

The lease characteristic of the contract vanished in these new provisions. The element of control was made therein, the most essential element of the contract.[39] This in part, completed the legislative process of Law 41 of 1944. In the other part, the doctrine of justification of the termination of the contract, which was introduced in Law No. 41, found its place in section 695(2) of the Civil Code. As the provisions of this section are general in their nature,[40] difficulties of interpretation and procedure resulted.

The enactment of these new provisions in the Civil Code, marked the third stage of legislative development in the U.A.R.[41] This third stage is characterised by two main landmarks. The first is the recognition by the U.A.R. legislator of the special nature of the contract of employment, justifying the enactment of independent provisions more comprehensive than those in the 1883 Civil Code. And the second is the recognition of the importance of the labour legislation, to the extent that the provisions of the U.A.R. Civil Code were relegated to a place second to that of the special labour laws.[42] Thus the provisions of Law 41 of 1944 were in effect given precedence over the provisions of the Civil Code.

The 1944 Law and the Civil Code spurred the juridical interest in the contract of employment.

The industrial and social development in the U.A.R., in the following years, coupled with the revolution of 23 July 1952, marked the fourth stage of legislative development of the contract of employment.

The year 1952 witnessed the enactment of Decree Law No. 317.[43] This law, which superseded Law No. 41 of 1944, revealed, together with other legislation of the same year, a Government interest in the development of social legislation, not witnessed before. The new revolutionary regime professed to champion the cause of the working class, not

[39] *Vide* the definition of the contract, in section 674, in Part II, Chapter I, *infra*.

[40] *Vide* Section 675 of the U.A.R. Civil Code, quoted in footnote 42, *infra*.

[41] This was the last stage, as far as the Civil Code is concerned, because sections 674–698 were never amended.

[42] Section 675 provides:

"The provisions of this Chapter shall only apply in so far as special labour laws do not expressly or impliedly derogate therefrom.

"The said laws shall specify the categories of workers to which the provisions of this Chapter shall not apply."

[43] *Al-Jaridat-ul-Rasmiyyatu* No. 157 (bis), 8 December 1952, in Arabic, (issued by the I.L.O. in its L.S., in 1952). The Explanatory Note to this law says: "Industry has developed in the country, to the extent that the effective laws were lagging behind. This prompted the introduction of new legislation, to cope with the new situation, and to do away with unrest, by further regulating the relationship between the workers and the employers, and their respective rights and obligations."

only in commerce and industry, but also in agriculture. Its championship in the latter was exemplified, not only by its land distribution programme and the resultant breaking up of the power of land-owners, but also by widening the scope of the new Law of 1952, so as to cover agricultural workers,[44] for the first time. Its beneficial provisions were also extended to a bigger number of persons, particularly with regards to the leaves and the termination gratuity.

This fourth stage of legislative development heralded in the U.A.R., the greatest volume of litigation on the principles of the contract of employment.[45]

The industrial development which followed, mainly prompted by Government planning and participation, necessitated the amendment of the 1952 Law, in order to meet the new needs which arose. Law No. 165 1953,[46] which added section 39(b) to the 1952 Law, was the most important amendment. By enacting new elaborate provisions, it met to a great extent the difficulties occasioned by the general provisions of section 695(2) of the Civil Code, in as far as the worker's unjustifiable dismissal is concerned.

The fifth and last stage of legislative development of the contract of employment commenced in 1959. That year witnessed the enactment of Law No. 91 of 5 April 1959.[47] This law came to be known as the unified Labour Code, because the Code unified most of the labour legislation of Egypt and Syria, by way of comprehensive enactment or re-enactment.[48] This new trend of comprehensive enactment necessitated the inclusion of the legal provisions, regulating the contract of employment, in the Code. However, they were kept separate, mainly in Chapter II of Book II of the Code.

Though the U.A.R. Labour Code was widened in its protective scope, it does not contain many new substantial provisions, regulating the contract of employment, as compared with the Law of 1952.

Such were the stages of development in the U.A.R., over a period of three quarters of a century.

[44] It is worth noting that the agricultural workers form the largest section of the working class, in the U.A.R.

[45] It also produced the bulk of the academic work, on the contract of employment.

[46] *Al-Jararidat-ul-Rasmiyyatu* No. 30 (*bis*), Extraordinary, 9 April 1953.

[47] The U.A.R. Labour Code.

[48] *Vide* the Explanatory Note to the Code.

(b) The Sudan

Before the Anglo-Egyptian conquest of Sudan towards the end of the last century, the legal system in Sudan was Moslem. The Moslem *Shari'a* Law was the only reference.[49] All the legislation which was passed by the various kingdoms in the different parts of Sudan, was inspired by the Moslem *Shari'a*.

So whatever notion there was of labour contracts emanated from the Moslem Law concept of the lease contract.[50] This persisted during the administration of the Sudan by the *Mahdia*,[51] who abrogated the Turkish Law, because the *Mahdia* adhered to the strict *Shari'a* law.[52] This we may call the spring board or the first stage, from which the contract of employment started to develop in Sudan.

Although *Lord Cromer* assured the inhabitants of the Sudan in 1899, that the Moslem Law would be applicable in Sudan under the Condominium[52], the law administered in the Sudan quickly took the shape which it has preserved upto the present times. That this Law was, and still is mainly inspired by the English Common Law, was fully expounded above.[53]

This meant an early encroachment by the English Common Law upon the 'lease' characteristic of the contract, in the Moslem notion of labour contracts. It also meant the introduction, for the first time in the history of Sudan, of the concept of the contract of employment or 'service,' distinguished from that of 'services' and other similar contracts, mainly by the element of control. This marks the second stage of development of the contract of employment in Sudan.

Throughout this second stage, which continued for nearly half a century, the contract of employment essentially remained within the bounds of the civil law, like any other civil contract, much the same as it was, and basically still is in England, and to a lesser extent in India. However, the conditions of employment of domestic servants[54] and apprentices[55] were regulated by The Domestic Servants Ordinance,

[49] Both as codified in the *Majallah*, and otherwise.

[50] *Vide* Section I of the present Part, *supra*.

[51] 1884–1898.

[52] E. Guttmann, in the *International and Comparative Law Quarterly*, Vol. 6, 1957, p. 402.

[53] *Vide* Section I of the present Part, *supra*.

[54] Domestic servants are excepted from the U.A.R. Labour Code and the Sudan Ordinance – *Vide* Part II, Chapter I, *infra*.

[55] Apprentices are expressly excepted from the Sudan Ordinance. Provisions, separate from Chapter I of Book II of the U.A.R. Labour Code, regulate the conditions of employment of apprentices.

1921,[56] and The Apprentices Ordinance, 1908,[57] respectively. Both of these Ordinances basically affected the contracts of domestic servants and apprentices, by bestowing upon them a public character with penal sanctions.

The third stage of development of the contract of employment began in 1948, when the bulk of labour legislation was enacted. This was mainly the result of organised labour agitation which culminated in that year. "The events of 1947–8," says *S. E. Fawzi*, "had clearly shown the need for promulgating legislation on welfare and industrial relations as soon as possible.... For this purpose, an expert from the British Ministry of Labour[58] and National Service was seconded to the Sudan, and by the time he left the country in April 1948, a corpus of labour legislation had been drafted, most of which became law later in that year."[59]

The relevant enactment is The Employers And The Employed Persons Ordinance, of 12 February 1949.[60] That enactment contained for the first time in Sudan as a whole, provisions of a public character and an instant effect on current contracts, by means of penal sanctions, regulating the contract of employment. Henceforward, the contract which was only civil in its nature, entered the fields of criminal and administrative laws.[61]

Although this Ordinance contains many provisions equivalent to those in the U.A.R. legislation, one can easily see from the comparison of the two, that there are matters which were not dealt with in the Ordinance, but were left to the English Common Law, the traditional source of reference. It is worthy of mention, however, that workers in agriculture were not all excepted from the provisions of the Sudan Ordinance (S. 3), whereas in the U.A.R. all agricultural workers were excepted from the labour law provisions up to 1952, when they were totally covered by Law No. 317.

[56] *The Laws of the Sudan*, Vol. 8., Title XXII, Sub-Title 3.

[57] *Ibidem*, Sub-Title 2.

[58] The British Labour Party was in power, at the time.

[59] Fawzi's book (*vide* footnote 8, *supra*), is the main reference on the subject, under discussion. Chapter VII thereof is illuminating. Two articles by O. M. Osman, which appeared in the I.L.R., Vol. 78, 1958, p. 329, and Vol. 86, 1962, p. 235, are also illuminating. However, Sayed Osman attributes the late enactment of the labour legislation in Sudan, to "the fact that practically all urban wage labour had for a long time been employed by one employer who had sufficient moral obligations to maintain a high standard of working conditions and terms of employment-namely the Sudan Government" (Vol. 78, p. 340). That this is not totally correct, is clear from the labour agitation, which preceded the enactment of the said legislation, and was clamouring for benefits, much wider than those envisaged by the Government.

[60] The Sudan Ordinance.

[61] Much the same as what happened to the contract of employment in the U.A.R., by the enactment of 41 Law of 1944 – *Vide* Section I of the present Part, *supra*.

The third stage of development, which is mainly marked by the enactment of the said Ordinance, has continued up to the present days, because the Ordinance was never superseded by any other enactment.

The effect of the I.L.O. Conventions[62] and that of the English Common Law and Statute[63] and of the Indian legislation, on the Sudan labour legislation, is apparent.

Such was the development of legislation in Sudan, on the contract of employment, during the equivalent period of development in the U.A.R.

From the above sketch of legislative developments in the U.A.R. and Sudan, we can compare the two in two main respects, one historical and the other actual:

(a) Labour agitation in both countries was one of the main reasons of labour law enactment. The agitation in both cases was of course against the employers. But while the Government in Sudan was and still is the biggest employer in the country,[64] as we have seen above, the U.A.R. Government was otherwise up to the late sixties of this century, when the bulk of labour laws in U.A.R. was already enacted. This difference between the two Governments, *vis a vis* employment, coupled with the fact that industrial development started much earlier in the U.A.R. than in Sudan, should have led the Government in the former, to develop labour laws, including provisions on the contract of employment, much earlier than it did. It was indeed surprising that the distinction of the contract of employment from similar contracts by the element of control, did not find its way into the U.A.R. law until 1944, by the enactment of Law No. 41 in that year. The Civil Code did not so distinguish the contract until 1948; in other words, about the same time the Sudanese labour legislation was enacted. The contrast between the history of the two contracts in the U.A.R. and Sudan, becomes more apparent, when we remember that long before 1948, the contract in Sudan was under the English Common Law, already dis-

[62] Cf., for instance, Articles 3 and 6 of Convention 64 (*The Contracts of Employment (Indigenous Workers) Convention*, 1939), with sections 4 and 6 of the Sudan Ordinance, respectively, (*vide* Part II, Chapter II, *infra*).

[63] That a British expert was the draftsman of the Sudan Legislation, coupled with the English Common Law inspiration already accepted in Sudan, explains that effect. Cf., for instance, section 4 of the Sudan Ordinance, with the (now repealed) section 4 of the English Statute of Frauds, 1677 (*Vide* Party II, Chapter II, *infra*); and cf. section 10(2) of the Sudan Ordinance, with the English Common Law (*Vide* Part II, Chapter VI, *infra*).

[64] The Sudan Railways and the other Government departmants employ the highest percentage of workers in Sudan.

tinguished as mentioned above. This earlier juridical appreciation of the contract of employment in Sudan is worthy of notice, as the practical need for such appreciation arose in the U.A.R. much earlier than it did in Sudan. The 'lease' characteristic of the contract of employment under the Roman and Moslem Laws, has long vanished in Sudan, whilst in the U.A.R. it did not vanish until 1948.

This earlier commendable development in the two countries was, however, rather unconscious, as it mainly resulted from the two different courses the legal systems in the U.A.R. and Sudan took. The early English Common Law acceptance in Sudan, with the contract of employment distinguished by that Law as aforementioned, when compared with the French inspiration in the U.A.R., with the 'lease' characteristic attached to the contract by French Law, exposes the said unconscious development. But under the French Law the contract was rid of its lease characteristic, long before it was in the U.A.R. This somehow reduces the apology of unconscious development.

(b) The repugnance of the English Common Law to the interference by Statute in the freedom of contract,[65] and the legislative tradition of codification in France, showed themselves in the labour enactments of Sudan and the U.A.R., respectively. The former accordingly, came out more sketchy than the latter, which contains more comprehensive provisions on the contract of employment. As a result, the matters that are left for decision in accordance with 'justice, equity and good conscience' in Sudan,[66] are more than those left for decision in accordance with 'equity' in the U.A.R.,[67] bearing in mind that in both countries the said decisions can only be with civil sanctions.[68] The apparent conclusions are that the worker and the employer in the U.A.R. are in a better position to know their respective rights and obligations, than they are in Sudan, on the one hand, and the worker in the former has wider protection by means of penal sanctions than the worker in Sudan, on the other hand. The developing nature of the economies of the two countries, and the general lack of collective agreements in Sudan,[69] renders the U.A.R. legislative tradition in a more favourable position.

[65] This repugnance explains the general lack of legislation, on the contract of employment, in England.

[66] *Vide* Section I of the present Part, *supra*.

[67] *Vide* section 1(2) of the U.A.R. Civil Code.

[68] It is only by virtue of the labour legislation, that penal sanctions were applied to the contract of employment.

[69] Collective agreements usually contain details of the rights and obligations of the employers and the workers, and are good vehicles for filling in the gaps in the labour legislation.

SECTION III: LEGISLATION REGULATING THE CONTRACT OF EMPLOYMENT IN THE OTHER ARAB COUNTRIES

It is not within the scope of this study, to detail the legislative developments in the rest of the Arab countries. So what follows is a sketch of these developments, just sufficient to render the reference to the laws of these countries more understandable.

Iraq's Civil Code, Law No. 40 of 1951, depended for its provisions, on the draft of the U.A.R. Civil Code.[70] The Iraqi Labour Code, Law No. 1 of 1958,[71] drew a lot on the Decree Law No. 317 of 1952 of the U.A.R., as is clear from the comparison of the two. This code superseded Law No. 72 of 1936, and was one of the achievements of the new regime, which started with the revolution of 14 July 1958. It is thus reminiscent of the enactment of the said Decree Law in the U.A.R., after the revolution of 23 July 1952.

The Kuwaiti Labour Code in the Private Sector, of 15 March 1959,[72] was drafted with the assistance of experts from the U.A.R. This accounts for the similarity between the Code and the U.A.R. Decree Law No. 317 of 1952. The development of the oil industry after the second World War in Kuwait, accounts for the enactment of the Code.

The Qatari Labour Code, Law No. 3 of 1962,[73] was drafted with the assistance of experts from the U.A.R. The direct inspiration was from the Kuwaiti Labour Code. The striking and exploitation of oil in the late fifties accounts for the enactment of the Code.

The Saudi Arabian Labour and Workman's Regulations, of 10 Octo-

To the knowledge of the writer, only two collective agreements have so far been made in Sudan. The first is in the Misr Printing Works in Khartoum, and the second is in the Soap Factory in Khartoum North. Both agreements were signed on 5 September 1963, as reported in *Al-Thawra* Newspaper, No. 1043, dated 6 September 1963.

[70] *Vide Min-Hukuk Wa wagebat El-'Ummal Wa Ashab El-A'amal Fi Kanun El-'Amal El-'Iraqi*, by El-Sa'eed, S. M., 1962, in Arabic, Baghdad, (hereinafter, called El-Sa'eed), p.11. The Code will, hereinafter, be called the Iraqi Civil Code.

[71] *Al-Jaridat-ul-Rasmiyyatu* No. 4115 of 16 March 1958, in Arabic. The Code will, hereinafter, be called the Iraqi Labour Code. An English translation of the Code was issued by the I.L.O., in its L.S., 1961 – Iraq 1. But the writer referred to the Arabic text, as he did with the other Arab Labour Codes, legislated in Arabic, and did his own translation when necessary.

[72] *Al-Jaridat-ul-Rasmiyyatu*, No. 216 of 15 March 1959, in Arabic. The Code will, hereinafter, be called the Kuwaiti Labour Code. It is interesting to note that the British protection in Kuwait, from 1899 to 1961, when Kuwait became independent, did not result in the adoption of the English Common Law principles, whether in the labour law or generally in the Civil and criminal laws.

[73] *Al-Jaridat-ul-Rasmiyyatu*, No. 2 of 2 April 1962. The Code will, hereinafter, be called the Qatari Labour Code. It is interesting to note that reference to the U.A.R. law, directly and *via* Kuwait, was not precluded by the fact that Qatar was, and still is under British protection.

ber 1947,[74] were drafted and first administered, with the help of U.A.R. experts.[75] This accounts for the inspiration from the U.A.R., which by 1947 had only three years of development of the modern concept of the contract of employment, after it had been rid of the lease characteristic by Law No. 41 of 1944. The enactment of the regulations came as a result of the development, after the Second World War, of the big oil industry.[76]

The Jordanian Labour Code, Law No. 21 of 14 May 1960,[77] was partly inspired by the U.A.R. legislation, as is clear from the comparison of the two, and from the participation of an expert from the U.A.R., though in the capacity of an I.L.O. expert, in the drafting of the Code, jointly with another I.L.O. expert from Pakistan.

The Libyan Labour Code, of 22 November 1962,[78] or more precisely its predecessor, Law No. 100 of 1957, seems to have gone through legislative processes, similar to those through which the Jordan Labour Code had gone. The 1957 Law was indeed one of the legislative sources of the Jordanian Labour Code, for the same I.L.O. expert from Pakistan had already worked in Libya, before he came to Jordan.

The Lebanese *Code des Obligations* of 1934, was inspired by the French Law, and even more so than the U.A.R. Civil Code.[79] The Lebanese Labour Code, of 23 September 1946,[80] was also French inspired; and there is some similarity between it and Law No. 41 of 1944 of the U.A.R.

The Syrian Civil Code, Legislative Decree No. 84 of 18 May 1949,[81] is the best example of orthodox U.A.R. inspiration, as the similarity

[74] They were published by the Government Printing Press, in 1947. These will, hereinafter, be called the Saudi Regulations.

[75] *Vide Pan-Arabism and Labour*, by Beling, W. A., 1960, Harvard, p. 69.

[76] The Arabian American Oil Company (Aramco) has brought about this development. The Company employs the biggest percentage of workers, in the country.

It is interesting to note the enactment of these regulations, within the context of the Moslem Law, otherwise applicable in the country. The writer watched the application of these regulations closely, whilst in the employment of Aramco, as a Labour Law Analyst, from 1952 to 1955.

[77] *Al-Jaridat-ul-Rasmiyyatu*, No. 1491 of 21 May 1960, p. 511, in Arabic. This will, hereinafter, be called the Jordanian Labour Code. A translation of the Code in English, was issued by the I.L.O., in its L.S.- Jord.1, 1960.

[78] *Al-Jaridat-ul-Rasmiyyatu*, No. 17 of 24 November 1962, p. 3, in Arabic. This will, hereinafter, be called the Libyan Labour Code.

[79] The Lebanon and Syria were under the French Mandate, from 1920 to 1946. This explains the direct influence of the French legal system. The Code will, hereinafter, be called the Lebanese Civil Code.

[80] This was legislated in Arabic. The I.L.O. issued an English translation of the Code, in its L.S., 1946–Leb. 1, but indirectly through a French translation. The Code will, hereinafter, be called the Lebanese Labour Code.

[81] *Al-Jaridat-ul-Rasmiyyatu*, No. 27 of 21 May 1949, in Arabic. The I.L.O. issued an English translation of sections 640–664 thereof, which regulated the contract of employment, in its L.S., 1949–Syr. 1.

between it and the U.A.R. Civil Code, is very clear.[82] The U.A.R. Labour Code of 1959 was, as was previously mentioned, legislated for both Egypt and Syria.

The Tunisian Labour Code, No. 60–18 of 1960,[83] is basically a consolidation of the previous legislation. The Code was French inspired.[84]

The labour law provisions in Algeria and Morocco will be referred to, as can be found in the I.L.O.'s *Labour Survey of North Africa*, 1960. The law inspiration in both countries is French.[85]

The Bahraini Labour Code, of 28 December 1957,[86] bears a great similarity to the Sudan Ordinance; and the main source of reference in the island is the English Common Law.[87] It is surprising that the Labour Code was enacted as late as 1960, whereas the oil was discovered as early as 1932.

The Adenese Contracts of Employment (Indigenous Workers) Ordinance of 1945,[88] also bears a great similarity to the Sudan Ordinance; and the source of reference in Aden is the English Common Law.[89]

[82] Reference to this Code will not be necessary, because its provisions are almost identical with the relevant provisions of the U.A.R. Civil Code.

[83] *Al-Jaridat-ul-Rasmiyyatu*, No. 36, of 29 July 1960, in Arabic. This Code will, hereinafter, be called the Tunisian Labour Code.

[84] The fact that Tunisia was under the French protection, from 1881 to 1956, accounts for the direct influence of the French Law.

[85] France legislated for Algeria, from 1830 to 1962, when Algeria became independent. Morocco was under French protection, from 1912 to 1956; and this explains the direct influence of the French Law.

[86] An English translation of the Code was published, by the British Political Resident in the Persian Gulf; and appears in L.S., 1957–Bah.1. This is the only text of the Code, which the writer could obtain. The Code will, hereinafter, be called the Bahraini Labour Code.

[87] The fact that Bahrain came under the British protection since 1880, explains the reference to the English Common Law.

[88] This was legislated in English, as was the Sudan Ordinance. This will, hereinafter, be called the Adenese Ordinance.

[89] The fact that Aden was a British colony from 1839, until it was annexed in 1963, to the still British protected South Arabian Federation, accounts for the reference to the English Common Law.

PART II

THE CONTRACT OF EMPLOYMENT

CHAPTER I

DEFINITIONS

SECTION I: THE CONTRACT OF EMPLOYMENT[1]

There is no definition of the contract of employment in the U.A.R. Labour Code. A definition of the contract may, however, be inferred from section 42 thereof,[2] re application of the Code. So the express definition of the contract in section 674 of the Civil Code, is left as the only refernece. This section defines the contract as "a contract whereby one of the parties undertakes to work in the service of the other and under his direction and control, in return for remuneration which the other party undertakes to pay."[3]

From this definition, three basic elements of the contract can be discerned: (a) an undertaking by the worker to work for the employer, (b) under the employer's control, and (c) in return for the employer's undertaking to pay remuneration to the worker. As we shall see later, control is the only one of the said three elements, which distinguishes the contract of employment from similar contracts.

In Sudan the contract of employment[4] was expressly defined in

[1] The term 'contract of employment' will on the whole be used in this study, and that of 'contract of service' will be avoided, because the term 'worker' and not 'servant' will be used therein (*vide* Section III of this Chapter, infra). Furthermore, the term 'contract of employment,' will be used to indicate the 'individual contract of employment.'

[2] Section 42 provides: "This Chapter shall apply to any contract, by virtue of which a worker undertakes in return for remuneration to work under the direction or supervision of an employer." Another definition can be deduced from the definition of 'worker,' in section 2 of the Code (*vide* Section III of this Chapter, *infra*). It is believed that the contract should have been defined in the Labour Code. This seems to be advisable for easy reference, and because of the apparent development towards the enactment of a special Labour Code in contra-distinction to the Civil Code, much the same as what happened in France.

[3] Section 900(1) of the Iraqi Civil Code defines the contract in similar terms. The Iraqi Labour Code does not define the contract, but a definition can be drawn from that of the 'worker' in section 1 thereof, as can be done from section 2 of the U.A.R. Labour Code. The same can be said of the Kuwaiti Labour Code, which does not expressly define the contract. Section 1 of the Saudi Regulations connotes a similar definition. Section 15 of the Jordanian Labour Code contains an express definition, similar to the U.A.R. Civil Code definition, and so does section 10(1) of the Libyan Labour Code. In Lebanon the Labour Code does not define the contract, nor can a definition be deduced from the definition of the 'employer' in section 1 thereof. But the Lebanese *Code des Obligations* of 1934, contains a definition similar to the U.A.R. definition. The Tunisian Labour Code defines the contract in section 6, much the same as it was defined in the U.A.R.

[4] The term 'contract of service,' is used in the Sudan Ordinance, because of the English Common Law inspiration and terminology.

section 2 of the Sudan Ordinance,[5] as "any contract whether written or oral, express or implied, whereunder any person is employed,[6] either for any period of time or for the execution of any work for remuneration in money or money's worth."[7] The elements of the contract in this definition are only two: (a) employment, and (b) remuneration. The first element is ambiguous, and is not an exact counterpart of the elements of 'work' and 'control' in the U.A.R. definition. More important is that these two elements in Sudan do not distinguish the contract of employment from similar contracts. The decisive factor of distinction, which is the element of 'control,' is not clear in the definition; and this deprives the definition of its importance. Under the English Common Law, which was the only reference before the enactment of the Sudan Ordinance, 'control' was and still is the decisive element of the contract.[8] So the filling-in of the gap in the Sudan definition, by reference to the English Common Law is mandatory, for otherwise, the Sudan Ordinance would be, contrary to expectations and the legislator's intention, an incomplete statement of the previous Common Law position in Sudan. Furthermore, the Sudan definition contains matters related to the formation and form of the contract, which should properly have been kept in separate provisions in the Ordinance.

On comparison of the definitions of the contract in the two countries, it is easy to see that the U.A.R. definition is legall ymore comprehensive than the Sudan definition. The former is self-sufficient, whereas the latter is valueless without reference to the English Common Law.

We shall now discuss the contract elements of work, remuneration and control, respectively.

[5] Originally legislated in English; *vide* Part I, *supra*.

[6] The definition of 'employed person' in the same section, unlike the definition of worker in section 2 of the U.A.R. Labour Code, mentions the contract only by name.

[7] Cf. the same wording of the definition of the contract, in section 3(e) of the Bahraini Labour Code. The Adenese Labour Law does not expressly define the contract. But section 3 of the Adenese Ordinance, re application of the Ordinance, contains a definition similar to the Sudan definition, though it is limited to manual workers. The English Common Law definition of the Contract presumably applies to other workers.

[8] The relationship of 'master' and 'servant' is that "between two persons where by agreement between them, express or implied, the one called the 'servant' is under the control of the other called the 'master'": *The Law of Master and Servant*, by Diamond, A. S., 1946, London, (hereinafter called Diamond), p.l.

The elements of the contract

(1) Work

Both in the U.A.R. and Sudan it is the undertaking to work[9] and not the work itself, which forms the first element of the contract of employment. Once this is underlined, an inference may be drawn therefrom that the worker's availability and readiness for work, and not the actual performance of the work by him, is sufficient for the fulfilment of his undertaking to work,[10] with the exception of the case in which the contract is for the performance of specific work.[11]

The form of work is immaterial.[12] It may be mental or physical[13] or a mixture of both. However, it must be possible of performance

[9] Section 674 of the U.A.R. Civil Code, expressly mentions the undertaking to work. In Sudan the definition of the contract connotes, but does not expressly mention the undertaking to work. However, the English Common Law, as stated by Batt, p. 5, emphasises the importance of this undertaking: "The servant must be under the duty of rendering personal services to the master or to others on behalf of the master, otherwise the contract is a contract of sale of goods or the like."

[10] Section 692 of the U.A.R. Civil Code provides: "Whenever a wage-earning or salaried worker attends for the day's work in pursuance of the contract, or announces that he is ready to perform it in the course of the said day and is only prevented from so doing by a circumstance for which the employer is responsible, he shall be entitled to the wages for that day"; *vide* Habeeb, pp. 45–7; and Butros and Rajab, p. 129; and *vide* the somewhat similar provisions in section 10, but cf. with section 131(2) of the Iraqi Labour Code; *vide* also I.L.R., Vol. 32, 1936, pp. 68–9. In Sudan the words "whereunder any person is employed either for any period of time" in the definition of the contract, connote the same meaning, though not in such a definite manner. "Where the contract of hiring provides for the payment of certain wages (not in proportion to the work done), although it may be optional on the part of the master to find work, and he may if he pleases, discontinue his business, yet he must nevertheless pay wages agreed upon whether he find work for the servant or not": *A Treatise on the Law of Master and Servant*, by Smith, C. M., 7th ed., 1931, London (hereinafter called Smith), p. 49. From these words, it is discernible how the availability for work was made the basis of the undertaking to work. This follows from the general rule that the employer is not obliged to find work for the worker (*vide* Chapter III, *infra*). It is interesting to note in this respect, that section 425 of the *Majallah* provides that "the worker is entitled to his remuneration, if during the currency of his employment, he is present for work. His actual performance of the work is not necessary but he cannot refuse to work, and if he so refuses, he shall not be entitled to any remuneration."

[11] Section 678(1) of the U.A.R. Civil Code provides that "the contract of employment may be made for a particular service..." Section 2 of the Sudan Ordinance provides that the contract may be "for the execution of any work"; vide also Diamond, p. 93. This rule follows from the exceptions to the general rule, that the employer is not obliged to find work for the worker (*vide* Chapter III, *infra*).

[12] "The Law has not defined work, so it covers all human activity": Naguib and Bakr, p. 68.

[13] *Vide* El-Areef, p. 146: "Work is the physical or mental effort, which the worker undertakes in return for the remuneration"; *vide* also *Kanun-ul-'Amal Wa Al-Ta'meenatu Al-Ijtima'iyyatu*, by Murad, M. H., 1961, 4th edn., Cairo, in Arabic (hereinafter called Murad), p. 252. For Sudan, *vide* Diamond, p. 18. Refer to Section III of this Chapter, *infra*.

and must be legally permissible.[14] It may be positive or negative.[15]

There are, however, some types of work which are excepted both in the U.A.R. and Sudan, from the provisions on the contract of employment in the U.A.R. Labour Code and the Sudan Ordinance, respectively. Section 88(a) of the U.A.R. Labour Code, as we shall see later, excepts temporary work which does not last for more than six months, and is outside the scope of the employer's business. Section 3(a) of the Sudan Ordinance excepts casual work which is out of the scope of the employer's trade or business.

The specification of the details of the work in the contract is immaterial[16]. Though details of the work are usually specified in the contract, it happens more often than not, that such details are left without specification to be implied from the custom of the trade or locality.[17] Section 682 of the U.A.R. Civil Code provides for the determination of the "nature and extent of the duties which the worker is required to perform," by the custom "in the trade or occupation" or in the place of work, "where the individual or collective contract or the rules of employment do not" determine the nature or details of the work. In default of custom, the said section provides that the Court shall determine the nature of the work in "an equitable manner."[18]

In the Sudan Ordinance there is no relevant provision. However, reference to the custom of the trade or locality is sanctioned in the English Common Law, by means of an implied term in the contract. "By not expressly laying down the terms of their contract, the parties have agreed implicitly to incorporate into their contract those terms, which are customary in the trade and district, possibly in the undertaking."[19]

[14] *Vide* Sections 132 and 134 of the Civil Code; *vide* also Murad, p. 253; El-Areef, p. 147; and Naguib and Bakr, p. 69. For Sudan, *vide Outlines of Industrial Law*, by Cooper, W. M., 7th edn. by J. C. Wood, 1962, London, (hereinafter called Cooper), p. 16. Refer to Chapter II, *infra*.

[15] A classical example is the posing by models, for painters or sculptors: *vide* Murad, p. 252; and Habeeb, p. 191. However, this does not cover an undertaking to abstain from doing a certain or any work, like an undertaking not to compete: El-Areef, pp. 145 and 147.

[16] *Vide* Murad, p. 252; Zaki, p. 137; and El-Areef, p. 147, who quotes section 133 of the U.A.R. Civil Code, as an authority for the necessity of specifying the worker's profession (though not the details of the work), as such specification ascertains the legal contractual obligation of the worker.

[17] *Vide* I.L.R., Vol. 32, 1936, p. 60: "The nature of the work to be done is to be determined in the first place by the contract of employment, and where its terms are not specific, by the custom of the occupation or of the locality." This is true both in the U.A.R. and Sudan.

[18] Zaki, p. 137, criticizes the provisions of section 682, re determination of the nature of the work, as ambiguous. He adds that the contract should be void, if the Court cannot determine the nature of the work.

[19] O. Kahn-Freund in Flanders and Clegg, p. 48.

The amount of remuneration is not material, nor is it material whether remuneration is fixed or variable,[20] or in money or in kind.[21]

Finally, work for one employer, or exclusive service as it is called, is not necessary for the fulfilment of the undertaking to work under the contract.[22]

Such is the significance of the element of 'work' in the contract of employment.[23] The undertaking to work constitutes the *causa contractus* of the worker, or the 'consideration' which he offers to the employer, in return for the employer's undertaking to pay remuneration.

(2) Remuneration[24]

The definitions of the contract of employment in section 674 of the U.A.R. Civil Code, and as inferred from sections 2 and 42 of the Labour Code, make 'remuneration' the counterpart of the worker's obligation to work. The definition of the contract in section 2 of the Sudan Ordinance likewise makes remuneration the said counterpart. So from the definitions in the two countries, we can easily appreciate that remuneration is an element in the contract.

That remuneration is an element in the contract of employment is all the more emphasized in the U.A.R., by section 681 of the Civil Code, which provides that "every service performed shall be deemed to be in return for remuneration, where it is not the custom that the work to which the service relates is carried out without return, or where the work belongs to the trade or occupation of the person performing it."[25]

[20] *Vide* Habeeb, p. 190.

[21] Section 684 of the U.A.R. Civil Code provides that "tips and meals may in some industries, be the only remuneration the worker receives." The definition of the contract of employment in section 2 of the Sudan Ordinance, provides that remuneration may be in money's worth. Refer to Chapter IV, *infra*.

[22] Section 676 (1) of the U.A.R. Civil Code applies the contract provisions to commercial travellers, insurance agents and other intermediaries, who work for more than one employer, provided they are under the control of the employer (the section is quoted in section III of this Chapter, *infra*); *vide* also Habeeb, p. 190. The Sudan Ordinance is silent in this respect. In the English Common Law, there is no absolute rule like the U.A.R. rule. The position there is governed by the terms of the contract: *vide* Batt, pp. 195–196. Refer to Chapter III, *infra*.

[23] "The emphasis on the human and social aspects of the element of 'work' in the contract of employment, has led to the interference by the legislator, in the various countries, in order to regulate work much earlier than he did interfere to regulate wages": Zaki, p. 146.

[24] Remuneration or wages will be discussed in detail, in Chapter IV, *infra*. What concerns us here, is the appreciation of remuneration as the second essential element in the contract of employment.

[25] *Vide* Murad, p. 253. This legislative provision seems to have been necessitated by the prevalent habit in the U.A.R. and in the area as a whole, of volunteering assistance but not without the hope of getting some return; *vide* similar provisions in section 903 of the Iraqi Civil Code.

This section, by encouraging the implication of a contract from conduct where there is no written agreement between the parties, stresses the importance of remuneration as an element in the contract of employment.

The Sudan Ordinance has no similar provisions. Reference to the English Common Law seems to be of some, though not of full and direct assistance in this respect. In such cases the Common Law is not as prepared as the said section in the U.A.R., to imply a contract, though it tries to save some return for the person who performs the work, through the doctrine of *quantum meruit.*[26] "It is by no means a matter of law," said *Martin B.*, in *Roberts v. Smith,*[27] "that a person shall be paid for his services, it is a matter of contract."[28]

The definitions of remuneration or wages in section 3 of the U.A.R. Labour Code and section 2 of the Sudan Ordinance,[29] again consider the worker's remuneration as the return and consideration for the work, respectively. This is a further evidence of remuneration forming an essential element in the contract of employment.

Once it is appreciated that remuneration is an element of the contract, it is immaterial whether the amount of remuneration is fixed in the contract or not. If it is not so fixed, section 682 of the U.A.R. Civil Code provides for its determination by custom in the trade or locality, by employment rules or collective agreements or by equity.[30] The Sudan

[26] *Vide* Cheshire and Fifoot, pp. 13 and 549–51, for a vivid exposition of the *quantum meruit*; *vide* also Batt, pp. 207 and 41: "A right to claim remuneration for service rendered does not arise in law, unless in fact there is an agreement, express or implied, to pay for them." In the U.A.R. there is an equivalent to the English doctrine of *quantum meruit*, in the doctrine of 'unjust enrichment' (*Vide* footnote 8 to Chapter IV, *infra*); *vide* also and cf. sections 437 and 563–5 of the *Majallah.*

[27] (1859), 4 H & N 315. The same Judge in *Reeve v. Reeve* (1858) I. F. & F. p. 280, said: "An action cannot be maintained for remuneration, merely because it may appear to be reasonable." Barwell and Kar, p. 217, submit that "a person who undertakes to labour and to provide materials, is not to be presumed to work for nothing." They cite *Higgins v. Hopkins* (1848) 18 L.J. Ex. 113, in their support. *Stewart v. Casey* (1892) 1 Ch. 104 seems to be in their support too. So the judicial authority seems to be in favour of the presumption of a 'contract of service' in such cases, and of the resultant payment of remuneration.

[28] Smith, in pp. 125–6, summarises the English Common Law position, by saying: "In cases where services have been rendered without any express contract to pay for them, the servant cannot maintain an action for wages, unless the circumstances are such as to afford evidence sufficient to justify a jury in finding that there was an implied contract to pay for such services." If the payment or non-payment of remuneration appears to have been left to the discretion of the employer, there is no contract of service (*Ibid.*, p. 129); *vide* also Diamond, p. 81; Halsbury, Vol. 25, p. 473; Cooper, p. 97; and Batt, p. 165.

[29] Refer to these definitions in Chapter IV, *infra*.

[30] *Vide* section 682 quoted in Section II of Chapter IV, *infra*; *vide* also Zaki, pp. 86–7, where he criticises the ambiguity of these determinants of remuneration.

Ordinance is silent on this question; but the English Common Law assists in this respect with rules similar to the U.A.R. rules.[31] The form of remuneration is not material. It may be in money or in kind.[32] Whether remuneration is a sum certain or variable is also immaterial.[33] Nor is it material whether remuneration is adequate or not.[34] Finally it is immaterial whether remuneration is payable by the employer or some one on his behalf.[35]

Remuneration then, irrespective of its form, determination, variability or payment, is an essential element of the contract of employment. Its legal significance is that the employer's undertaking to pay remuneration to the worker constitutes the former's contractual *causa contractus* to the latter, or the 'consideration' which he offers to the worker, in return for the worker's undertaking to work.[36]

The logical conclusion from this legal significance of remuneration, is that remuneration is not due without work in return. The rigidity of such conclusion has been mitigated by the legal insistence upon the worker's availability and readiness for work, rather than the actual performance of the work, as we have seen above.[37] On the other hand, this conclusion was the reason which led the legislator both in the U.A.R. and Sudan, to interfere in order to prescribe for workers annual holidays

[31] *Vide* O. Kahn-Freund in Flanders and Clegg, p. 48; *vide* also Barwell and Kar, pp. 116–7.

[32] *Vide* footnote 24 to this Chapter, *supra*; *vide* also Habeeb, p. 51; and Zaki, p. 87: "Remuneration may consist of a certain right or benefit as when an agricultural worker's remuneration consists of a part of the crop, though remuneration in kind has dwindled in modern times". For Sudan, *vide* Batt, p. 42.

[33] *Vide* Habeeb, pp. 190 and 198. Section 676 of the U.A.R. Civil Code, re commercial travellers, insurance agents and other intermediaries, makes the contract of employment provisions applicable to them, even where they are paid on a commission basis, which is usually variable with the volume of the work done. In the Sudan, there is no similar provision. But the English Common Law recognises the variable form of remuneration for the purposes of a 'contract of service': *Vide* Batt, pp. 42–3 and 170; *The Law of Master and Servant*, by Macdonell, J., London, Stevens and Son, 1883, (herinafter called Macdonell), p. 412: "A man may be the servant of another, though his remuneration may not be called wages, but profit or commission"; and Cooper, p. 13: "A servant may be paid a varying commission."

[34] For the U.A.R., *vide* Habeeb, p. 190. For Sudan, *vide* Batt, p. 42. The legal irrelevance of the adequacy of remuneration to the contract, has led to the legislator's interference by laying down the minimum wage provisions, both in the U.A.R. and Sudan.

[35] Section 3 of the U.A.R. Labour Code considers as wages, the tips payable by customers (*vide* Section I of Chapter IV, *infra*); *vide* also Zaki, pp. 86 and 88; and El-Areef, pp. 150 and 279–80; and *vide* the French decision in *Veuve V. Picard* (1929), Sirey, 1929, 1,230 (in I.S.D.L., Vol. 5, 1930, p. 970). This is also warranted in Sudan, by the English Common Law rules on agency.

[36] *Vide* for Sudan, Diamond, p. 3; and Batt, p. 42. For the U.A.R., *vide* El-Areef, p. 147; and Habeeb, p. 139. For the human and social aspects of remuneration, *vide* Zaki, pp. 106–7 and 123–4.

[37] Refer to the first part of the present Section in this Chapter, *supra*. *Vide* Habeeb, p. 45, for the U.A.R. legal decisions in support of this contention.

with pay, paid sick-leave, public holidays with pay, and pay during some periods of military service.[38]

So far we have discussed the two elements of work and remuneration. But as we shall presently see, these two elements are not sufficient to distinguish the contract of employment from similar contracts. The real factor of distinction is control by the employer of the worker's performance of his contractual duties.

(3) *Control*[39]

As we have seen above, the definition of the contract of employment in the U.A.R. expressly makes control one of the elements of the contract. The definition in Sudan, however, does not; but the English Common Law does. What then is meant by 'control'? And how did it become an element of the contract?

In the U.A.R. control has been defined as "that dependent relationship which arises from the performance of work for an employer, and the subjection of the worker during his performance of the said work, to the orders of the employer, to his supervision and to the disciplinary measures imposed by the employer on the worker, if the latter neglects or fails to carry out the prescribed work, or to abide by the terms of the contract or the work rules or the provisions of the law."[40] So there are two essentials of control in the U.A.R.: (a) the worker's obligation to carry out the orders of the employer concerning the performance of the work,[41] and (b) the worker's subjection to the employer's disciplinary measures in the warranted circumstances.[42]

The origin of the element of control in the contract of employment has in the U.A.R. been attributed to "the employer's right to benefit from the worker's efforts to the utmost."[43] The right to manage the work cannot be properly exercised, without the right to say how the work should be done.[44] And it is this last mentioned right which ne-

[38] This legislative interference in the rule that remuneration is the return for work, has led to a big controversy in the U.A.R., concerning the nature of pay in these cases, as to whether it is remuneration or not (*vide* Section I of Chapter IV, *infra*).

[39] *Lien de subordination* or *Lien de dépendance*, as it is called in France.

[40] Cairo Court of Cassation in case No. 1529 of 1959 (in El-Hawwari, p. 37); see also Cairo Court of Appeal in appeal No. 98 of 1959 (Ibidem, p. 61). *Vide* Badawi, K. M., p. 29; Naguib and Bakr, p. 69; Rashed and Hashem, p. 6, believe that control is characterised by the non-participation of the worker, in the management or in responsibility. But this seems to be too wide, as there are many workers of high standing, who do take part in management and share in the responsibility.

[41] *Vide* also section 685 (b) of the U.A.R. Civil Code, in Section I, C, of Chapter III, *infra*.

[42] Refer to Section I, E, of Chapter III, *infra*.

[43] Badawi, K. M., pp. 33.

[44] *Vide* Zaki, p. 256.

cessitated control, whence arose the element of control in the contract of employment.[45]

In the English Common Law, "a person is under the control of another, if he is bound to obey the orders of that other, not only as to the work which he shall execute, but also as to the details of the work and the manner of its execution."[46] This mentions the first essential of control in the U.A.R. But there is no mention of the second essential of discipline.

The origin of the element of control in the 'contract of service' in England, dates according to *A.S. Diamond*, to *Quarman v. Burnett* (1840), 6 M. & W., 499. But we may go further back to *Bason v. Sandford* (1689) 2 Salk, 440, which decided that the "master is responsible for the acts of his servant." This responsibility could not be fully fixed upon the 'master,' without the master's power of 'control' over the 'servant.'

The difference between the U.A.R. law, on the one hand, and the English Common Law and consequently the law in Sudan, on the other hand, in their outlook on discipline, will be discussed in more detail further on.[42] But it suffices here to say that, while the employer's right in the U.A.R. to take disciplinary measures against his worker in the warranted circumstances, flows automatically from the making of the contract, that right in England and Sudan is purely contractual, or in other words, it is exercisable only if the contract authorises the employer to exercise such right.[47] The U.A.R. law in this respect has generally followed in the footsteps of the French Law.[48]

On comparison of the two laws of the U.A.R. and Sudan, it is easy to appreciate the dangers that arise from the law in the former, however practical and logcal it may seem. But it is these dangers (which lie in the automatic and undefined disciplinary powers of the employer), that led the legislator in the U.A.R. to interfere, so as to curb these powers in the interests of the worker. On the other hand, the contractual

[45] Previous to 1950, there was a big controversy in the U.A.R., as to whether control included the employer's disciplinary powers or not. But the Council of State, in an opinion rendered in December 1951, has set the course in favour of implying these disciplinary powers from control (*vide* Rashed and Hashem, p. 142). Thenceforward, Court judgements began to lean in favour of the said implication, until it came to be taken for granted a few years later, as appears from the cases quoted in footnote (40), *supra*.

[46] Diamond, p.l; *vide* also Batt, p. 5; and Barwell and Kar, p. 34.

[47] *Vide* Cooper, p. 117; Samuels, p. 45; O. Khan-Freund in Flanders and Clegg, p. 49.

[48] *Vide* El-Areef, p. 198. The German law, however, refuses to consider the employer's disciplinary powers as an element of control (*Ibid.*, p. 199).

sanction of these powers in Sudan is neither logical nor practical.[49] So legislative interference in Sudan for the definition and limitation of these powers, seems to be mandatory. Such legislative interference had indeed taken place, as early as 1927, when the Officials Discipline Ordinance of 15 July 1927, was enacted.[50] But this Ordinance is not of general application in the Sudan, as its effect is limited to Government 'employees.' And because it was intended for them it contains provisions peculiar of application to Government departments. So non-governmental workers are left in this respect to the unsecure contracts which they make with their employers, who have no statutory limitations on their disciplinary powers, if they assume them in these contracts.[51]

The element of control, which we have noted as an essential in the contract of employment both in the U.A.R. and in Sudan, needs further limitation, as early in this century an attempt to graft 'economic control' of the worker by the employer, upon the element of 'legal control,' had been made, especially by some of the Continental jurists.[52] Hitherto, control was limited to what came to be called 'legal control,' in contra-distinction to 'economic control.'

The almost total dependence of the worker for his sustenance and that of his family, or his 'economic dependence' on the employer[53] as it came to be called, and as it became noticeable with the development of industry in Europe, gave rise to the said 'grafting' upon the element of 'legal control' in the contract. On the other hand, the influence of the protectionists of the last and present centuries, fortified by the new socialist revolutionary ideas,[54] as opposed to the *laissez faire* protagonists, accounts, it is believed, for the appearance of the theory of economic dependence on the scene. This influence, especially on some of the French jurists,[55] was particularly noticeable, when home workers,[56] though totally dependent for their living on the employers, could not benefit from all the new protective social legislation, because they were not legally controlled in the performance of their work by their em-

[49] *Vide* O. Kahn Freund in Flanders and Clegg, p. 49, quoted in Section I of Chapter III, *infra*.

[50] *Laws of the Sudan*, Vol. 1, Title II, Sub-title 3.

[51] The necessity of legislative interference has started to arise and will gain force, because of the industrial development in the private sector, that has already started in Sudan.

[52] Zaki, p. 126; Habeeb, p. 157.

[53] *Subordination économique ou sociale*, or *dépendance économique*, as it is called in France.

[54] *Vide* Habeeb, p. 157.

[55] So jurists in the U.A.R., could not avoid the discussion of the theory of economic dependence.

[56] *Travailleurs à domicile*, as they are called in France.

ployers.[57] Indeed the said influence was all the more exercised, because the emergence of the said legislation was due mainly to the total economic dependence of the worker on the employer. But this theory did not find many advocates among the French jurists,[58] and was expressly rejected by the highest judicial tribunal in France.[59] The U.A.R. Courts were for some time also influenced by this theory, mainly because of the abundance of home workers. But the theory was finally rejected by them in 1957.[60] This rejection came late in the trail of the Civil Code of 1948, as the definition of the contract of employment therein (section 674), read jointly with section 676 (which did away with the notion of exclusiveness in employment[61]), left no legal significance for economic dependence.

In England the theory of 'economic dependence' did not find any serious advocates. This, it is believed, is due mainly to the emphasis on 'legal control' as an essential of the 'contract of service,' much earlier than the time when industrial development led to the common phenomenon of the worker's total economic dependence on the employer. So the limitation of control by the English Common Law, to the "servant's undertaking to serve another and to obey his reasonable orders within the scope of the duty undertaken,"[62] came completely free of any notion of 'economic dependence.'

Thus both in the U.A.R. and Sudan economic dependence does not, from a legal view, have anything to do with the element of control in the contract of employment,[63] and what counts is what came to be called 'legal control.'

This 'legal control' must further be distinguished from 'statutory control,' or in other words, control in the public field, which is derived "not from agreement between controller and controlled, but from obedience by the latter to the provisions of a statute, or obedience owed and rendered by the one as the occupier of an inferior office to the other

[57] *Vide* Zaki, p. 127.

[58] *Vide* El-Areef, p. 146.

[59] Dalloz Hebdom., 1931, 1, 121 (in El-Areef, p. 146); and so did the German and Italian laws (*vide* Habeeb, p. 171, footnote 1).

[60] *Vide* the High Court of Appeal in Appeal No. 289 of 1957 (pp. 160, 167 and 171); *vide* also the review of the judicial decisions in *Al-Mudawwant-ul-'Ummaliyyatu*, by El-Fakahani, H., 2nd edn., 1959, Cairo, in Arabic (hereinafter called El-Fakahani), Book I, Vol. I, p. 32 *et seq.*

[61] Refer to section 676, in footnote 22, *supra*.

[62] *Halsbury's Laws of England*, 3rd ed., Vol. 25, 1958, London (hereinafter called Halsbury, Vol. 25), p. 448.

[63] *Vide* I.L.R., vol. 31, 1935, pp. 846 and 948, for a study of the importance of economic control as differentiated from legal control, with reference to the contract of employment and labour legislation as a whole.

as occupier of a superior office."[64] As the 'statutory control' does not derive from an agreement, it cannot have anything to do with 'legal control' in the contract of employment.

Both in the U.A.R. and Sudan, 'legal control'[65] can be of different forms. It can be technical,[66] professional,[67] or administrative,[68] depending on the nature of the work and the employer's ability to exercise his right of supervision and direction of the work. It can be in one or more of the said forms, according to the circumstances of the case. But in whatever form of the three it is, the crucial test in the U.A.R. is whether or not it amounts to a power for the employer to issue orders regarding the details and manner of performance of the work, and to take disciplinary measures against him if he disobeys these orders. In Sudan the test is whether it amounts to the employer's power to issue such orders to the worker.

The determinants of the said test are the terms of the contract and all the surrounding circumstances.[69] These circumstances, whose importance mainly arises when the contract is not in writing, must be examined together, as every one taken alone may not be sufficient to indicate 'legal control' and may indeed be immaterial to the issue.

[64] Diamond, p. 2. This is also true in the U.A.R.: *vide* Cairo Court of Cassation in case No. 1029 of 1958, (in El-Hawwari, p. 38).

[65] *Dépendance Juridique*, as it is called in France.

[66] *Dépendance Technique*, as it is called in France. It presupposes the continuous and direct exercise by the employer, of the work in which he should be an expert. This happens only in small workshops (Habeeb, p. 154); *vide* also Zaki, p. 125; and *vide* I.L.R. Vol. 31, 1935: "It implies a close personal relationship, between the person employed and the employer" (p. 847). In England this form of control is the original form of legal control, as is clear from the emphasis on the control of the details and manner of performance of the work: *vide* Halsbury, vol. 25, p. 1, and Diamond, p. 2.

[67] *Dépendance Professionelle*, as it is called in France. This is typical in large scale establishments, where personal exercise of the power of control by the employer is impossible, and the exercise thereof is usually effected by delegation (Habeeb, p. 155). This dependence is practically exclusive of technical dependence: El-Fakahani, Book I, Vol. 1, 1959, p. 32 et seq.; *vide* also Zaki, p. 126. In England, "control by the master, which may be a large corporation, is often physically impossible, contemporary economic organisation rests upon an organised hierarchy of delegation": Cooper, p. 6; *vide* also Batt, p. 5.

[68] *Dépendance Réglementaire*, as it is called in France. This is limited to the control of the conditions of work, e.g. hours of work, leaves etc. (Habeeb, p. 155). Zaki, p. 126, says that this type of control had not been accepted as sufficient to constitute the contract element of 'legal control,' without some "objections by jurists and hesitation in Courts, mainly on behalf of employers in the free professions"; *vide* also Badawi, K.M., p. 31; and Cairo Court of Cassation in case No. 1326 of 1959 (in El-Hawwari, p. 67). In England this form of control may be sufficient: *vide* Batt, p. 5.

[69] "In marginal cases, therefore, the existence of a subordinate relation must be determined by other considerations": I.L.R., Vol. 31, 1935, p. 848. This is true both in England and hence in Sudan, and in the U.A.R. *Vide* Diamond, pp. 5 and 6; Cooper, p. 4; and Batt, p. 5. For the U.A.R., the Explanatory Note to the Civil Code says: "The circumstances of the individual case are the determinants of control. The more effective the power of control is, the more probable the contract of employment relationship is"; and Cairo Court of Appeal in case No. 836 of 1954 (in Habeeb, p. 156).

But what is clear is that, on account of coding in the U.A.R. and case-law in England and hence in Sudan, the reference to these circumstances is more necessary in the latter than it is in the former. The said circumstances are mainly the form and extent of control, the form ot the work,[70] the kind, amount and manner of payment of remuneration,[71] the exclusiveness of service for and control by the employer,[72] the contract duration[73] and the provision by the worker of his own tools and equipment.[74]

It is not necessary that control be direct[75] nor continuous.[76] But what is necessary is the existence of the right or power of control for the employer.[77]

[70] As we have seen in the first part of the present Section of this Chapter, *supra*. *Vide* I.L.R., Vol. 31, 1935, p. 847; and Diamond, p. 6: "The fact that an employee is employed to exercise skill and an independent judgement," is one of the considerations.

[71] Refer to the second part of the present Section in this Chapter, *supra*. *Vide* also El-Areef, p. 145; and Cooper, p. 5.

[72] *Vide* footnote 22, *supra*; Cairo Court of Appeal in appeal No. 192 of 1958 (in El-Hawwari, p. 68); and I.L.R. Vol. 31. 1935, p. 847, 848, and vol. 32, 1936, pp. 385 & 497. For England and Sudan, *vide* Diamond, p. 5. *Vide* also Section I, B, iii, of Chapter III, *infra*.

[73] Though the definition of the contract of service in Sudan, mentions duration of the contract, it does not mention control which is left out for inference from the English Common Law. So no more bearing of duration on control can be inferred there than in England. The first U.A.R. definition of the contract of employment in section 1 of Law no. 41 of 1944, like Sudan, mentions duration; but the definition of the contract in section 674 of the Civil Code omits it. Some writers in the U.A.R. (e.g. Habeeb, p. 35; and Zaki, p. 190), consider duration as the fourth essential of the contract of employment. However, section 678(1) provides independently for the duration of the contract (*vide* Section III of Chapter II, *infra*), thus indicating clearly that duration is not an essential, said as the writers allege.The wording of the Sudan definition of the Contract does not make duration an essential in the contract.

[74] *Vide* the High Court of Appeal in case No. 289 on 4 April 1957 (*vide* footnote 59, *supra*); and Cairo Court of Cassation in case No. 199 of 1959 (in El-Hawwari, p. 62). In England, *vide Penny v. Wimbledon Urban District Council* (1898) 2 Q. B. 212, where the plaintiff was employed to construct a sewer and was held, on account of the power of control over the work having been reserved for the defendants, to be their servant, even though he used his own equipment. *Vide* I.L.R., Vol. 31, 1935, p. 847: "As a rule the work must be carried out with materials and equipment belonging to the employer; this is the normal practice in the modern industrial undertakings. At the same time, it must not be forgotten that a subordinate relation may exist when this condition is not fulfilled."

[75] Refer to footnote 66, *supra*, where control by delegation was shown to be the most prevalent form of legal control.

[76] *Vide* Section 676 (*vide* footnote 22 of this Chapter, *supra*), re commercial representatives etc...; and El-Areef, p. 145. For England and Sudan, *vide* Diamond, p. 12: "Power of control need not be continuous."

[77] *Vide* Cairo Court of Cassation in case No. 1454 of 1954 (in Habeeb, p. 156): "Proof of the employer's ability (*faculté*) to exercise the right of supervision and control guaranteed to him by the law, is sufficient. Actual exercise by him of the said right is not of essential importance"; *vide* also the French case of *Desmerais Frères et Compagnie d'Assurance "l'Urbaine et la Seine" v. Debrand*, Dalloz Hebdom., 1932, p. 210, (I.S.D.L., Vol. 8, 1934. p. 97–8). For England and Sudan, refer to Cooper, p. 6, where he says: "The question therefore, is not whether the control is exercised, it is where is the right to control?"

After we have defined and noted control or 'legal control' as an element in the contract of employment, and we have discussed the forms and determinants thereof, the next question that arises is its evaluation in the contract.

Work and remuneration, as we have seen above, form the *causa contractus* or 'consideration,' for one or the other of the two contracting parties. In this capacity they cannot distinguish the contract of employment from other contracts under which work is carried out, like contracts of agency, independent work and partnership. The distinction between the contract of employment and these contracts, will be discussed in detail later on. It suffices here to say that what distinguishes the contract of employment from these contracts, is the employer's right of control, as defined above. This distinctive value of control makes it the most important element of the contract of employment.[78] In the U.A.R. this importance had been further emphasized, by making it attract some persons into the category of workers, where otherwise on account of the nature of their work, they would not be accepted as workers for the purpose of the contract of employment.[79] In England the importance of control as an element in the contract has been emphasized, to the extent of sometimes defining the contract relationship exclusively by this element.[80]

Finally, control is the basis of the rules of the law, both in the U.A.R. and Sudan, which govern the assignment of contracts of employment,[81] though this is more apparent in the latter than in the former. On the whole, a worker cannot without the consent of the employer, assign his contractual duties to another, because of the lack by the employer of the legal control of the assignee.

So control is the main element of the contract of employment which distinguishes it from related contracts, and is of particular importance

[78] *Vide* Zaki, p. 128; Habeeb, p. 160; El-Areef, pp. 144–5, 197; Rashed and Hashem, p. 5; *vide* also Cairo Court of Cassation in case No. 641 of 1958: "If no control is present in the contract the provisions of the law will not be applicable thereto" (in El-Hawwari, p. 64); and *vide* I.L.R., Vol. 31, 1935, p. 845. For Sudan, *vide* Diamond, p. 10, where he says: "The essence of the relationship is not the appointment, payment of wages or power to dismiss, but control." *R. v. Negus* (1837), 2 C. C.R., is the classical English case for the proposition, that control is the most important element of the contract.

[79] Commercial representatives, insurance agents and other intermediaries, were covered by the Civil Code (section 676), only because of control. The English Common Law also considered such persons as 'servants,' because of the element of control.

[80] *Vide* footnote 8, *supra*. Such definition by the element of control only, is due mainly to the doctrine of consideration in the English Law, without which as a general rule, no contract whether of 'service' or otherwise is valid. So work and remuneration, which constitute the consideration for both parties, are more or less taken for granted.

[81] Refer to Section IV of Chapter II, *infra*.

in the assignment of the contract. That in a nutshell is the significance of control in the contract of employment.

After we have defined the contract and its constituent elements, and before we distinguish it from related contracts, we shall now discuss the consensual nature of the contract.

The consensual nature of the contract

We are not here concerned with the well-known juridical controversy (which raged in the nineteenth century, between the *laissez faire* protagonists and the protectionists, before and after the emergence of labour legislation), concerning the contracting freedom, and consequently the consensual nature of the contract of employment.[82] This controversy took place outside the U.A.R. and Sudan and all the Arab countries, much earlier than the time when the contract of employment as defined above, began to form a part of the respective laws of these countries. But what concerns us here is the evaluation of the consensual nature of the contract of employment, in the laws of the U.A.R. and Sudan, taking into consideration the relevant labour legislation in these two countries.[83]

The contract of employment both in the U.A.R. and Sudan is still a civil contract. Like other civil contracts, the formation of the contract is subject to offer and acceptance.[84] So the consent of the parties, without which offer and acceptance cannot operate, is the basis of the contract.[85] But mandatory provisions mainly in the U.A.R. Labour Code and the Sudan Ordinance, which purport to regulate the contract of

[82] Reference may be made to *The Theory of Legislation* by Jermey Bentham, 1950, 1950 ed; *The Province and function of the Law*, by Julius Stone, 1950, Sydney; Cheshire and Fifoot; and Habeeb.

[83] "The individual problems of labour law have their roots in the fundamental problem of the conflicting principles of the freedom of contract and industry, on the one hand, and state and collective regulation of the relation between employers and workers on the other." (from the Preface to Vol. 13 of the I.S.D.L., 1939).

[84] Section 433 of the *Majallah* provides: "The contract of hiring persons is formed by offer and acceptance, like the contract of sale."

[85] *Vide* section 89 of the U.A.R. Civil Code; Rashed and Hashem, p. 4: "The contract of employment is originally a consensual contract which cannot be completed without the meeting of the two intentions." Consent is the basis of acceptance in the English Common Law. It may here be interesting to note the essential difference, between the French (and the U.A.R.) conception of the contract and the English (and the Sudan) conception. In the former, it is the meeting of the two intentions of the parties, whereas in the latter it is the 'bargain' between the parties. "The English Common Law has long stressed the commercial flavour of its contract. An Englishman is liable, not because he has made a promise, but because he has made a bargain": Cheshire and Fifoot, p. 21. However, "behind all forms of contracts, no doubt, lies the basic idea of assent" (*Idem*). This is true of the French and the English contracts.

employment, have affected the consent of the two parties to the contract, as follows:

Firstly, section 6 of the U.A.R. Labour Code, which gives an instant effect to the Code on the effective contracts, so as to render void any term of the contract conflicting with the provisions of the Code except terms more favourable to the worker,[86] marks the most important effect of the Code on the consent of the parties, especially that of the employer.[87] "The regulation of work by the legislator, amounts in Civil Law, to a restriction on the will of the parties in entering contracts... to the extent that any term of the contract conflicting with the said regulation... is void, and the employer cannot request the worker to abide by it.... If the latter refuses any such request and is as a result dismissed, his dismissal will be unjustifiable."[88] This regulation, together with the legal sanction of collective contracts and the development of work-rules, had partly acquired for the contract of employment the description of adhesion (*contrat d'adhésion*),[89] which connotes limitation on consent.

In Sudan there is no exact equivalent to the said section 6 of the U.A.R. Labour Code. However, section 35 of the Sudan Ordinance[90] provides by implication to the same effect, as it permits "benefits to any employed person which are more favourable" than the provisions of the Ordinance.[91] Due to the serious nature of the effect of such legislative provision on the contract, it is believed that the said section should not have left the deduction of such effect to implication.

[86] The section is quoted in Section V of Chapter II, *infra*. Refer to Part I, *supra*, especially footnote 16.

[87] The Explanatory Note to Decree Law 317 of 1952 (which was superseded by the Labour Code), says that "the legislator's interference by providing norms and rules concerning workers, means that the legislator intended to interfere with the freedom of contract between an employer and a worker. The intention is the furtherance of public interest. Thus the contract terms which conflict with the provisions of this Law, will be void, especially if they amount to an injustice to the worker whom the legislator intended to protect." Again, "the main reason behind this protection, is the appreciation by the legislator of the economic inequality of the employer and the worker, especially after the guilds were abolished, and the resultant inability of the latter to exercise his free will, so as to give a proper consent": Habeeb, p. 15. Before the legislator interfered in 1944 (Law No. 41 of that year, whose section 38 is the first ancestor of the said section 6 of the Labour Code), the contract of employment was socially characterized by the obligation (arising from economic need) to submit to the terms the employer offers (*Ibid.*, p. 17).

[88] Zaki, p. 189.

[89] *Vide* Habeeb, p. 21. *Vide* also Cheshire and Fifoot, p. 24. This description of adhesion has been further emphasised by the development of the collective contracts and the collective agreements in France and England, respectively, on the one hand, and the development of work-rules in the undertaking, on the other hand.

[90] The section is quoted in Section V of Chapter II, *infra*.

[91] The Sudanese legislator, without saying it in express and forceful terms as the U.A.R. legislator did, has in section 35 demonstrated his intention of bestowing protection upon the worker.

The description of adhesion, which was acquired for the contract in the U.A.R., does not equally stick to the contract in Sudan. This should be due to the less detailed mandatory provisions in the Sudan, regulating the contract of employment, as will be gathered from the following chapters. On the other hand, work-rules are more developed in the U.A.R. than in Sudan. Finally, collective agreements are little known in Sudan, whereas in the U.A.R. collective contracts have legal sanction.

Secondly, Section 677 of the U.A.R. Civil Code provides that the contract of employment can be in any form. Section 43 of the Labour Code, though it requires a written form for the contract, it does so in a directive and not in a mandatory provision, thus basically preserving the effect of section 677.[92] So the contract is left to the consent of the parties as the main basis.[93]

Section 4 of the Sudan Ordinance, on the other hand, prescribes writing for certain contracts. And section 6 prescribes attestation of the contract in certain circumstances.[92] So consent of the parties in Sudan is burdened with formalities, more than it is in the U.A.R.

Thirdly, the English Common Law resistance to too much legislative interference in the freedom of contract,[94] on the one hand, and the non-recognition thereby of collective contracts, on the other hand, had some effect in Sudan.[95] The effect of the English Common Law was further felt through its doctrine of implying statutory provisions as terms in the contract. "The freedom of contract between master and servant has, in many respects, been affected by statute;"[96] but the Common Law has tried to preserve the freedom of contract by the said doctrine of implication. "The term in the contract of employment by virtue of which holidays can be claimed, can either be express or implied from a usage established by the employer himself in his undertaking, or it can be implied by virtue of a collective agreement, or it can be compulsorily implied by virtue of a wage regulation order made on the basis of the Wage Councils Acts, the Catering Wages Act or the Agricultural Wages Acts."[97] But "it is by reason of the contract of employment,

[92] The U.A.R. and Sudanese sections are quoted in Chapter II, *infra*.

[93] *Vide* Habeeb, p. 32.

[94] A very interesting example is the non-acceptance of the *Lord Amulree Committee* (1938) recommendation, that "legislation should be introduced ...making provision for holidays with pay in industry generally": *Industrial Relations*, Ministry of Labour, 1961, London, p. 199.

[95] This effect partly accounts for the delay in enacting the Sudan Ordinance and the bulk of the Labour legislation in Sudan (*vide* footnote 59 to Part I, *supra*).

[96] Halsbury, Vol. 25, p. 457.

[97] *The Law of Paid Vacation*, by O. Kahn-Freund, in the *British Legal papers*, pre-

that the employer is liable to pay remuneration for holidays."[98] In the U.A.R., though the doctrine of implication exists, it is submitted that it is not as effective and as apparent as it is in England. The Labour Code gives legal sanction to collective contracts. The individual contract of employment is automatically affected by the collective contract, sometimes without the consent or even the simultaneous knowledge of the two parties.[99] Section 68 of the Labour Code makes it obligatory on the employer who employs 15 or more workers, to make work-rules for his undertaking.[100] When these work-rules are binding on the worker and the employer, they are so binding in the U.A.R., by implication of terms in the contract. But the effect of the collective contracts on the individual contracts as mentioned above, is more direct than implied.

Fourthly, sections 686 and 687 of the U.A.R. Civil Code,[101] which restrict the operation of covenants in restraint of trade, have practically the same effect on the contracting freedom and consent of the parties, as the rules of the English Law.[102] However, section 686(b) in the U.A.R. prescribes for the validity of restrictive covenants, that the worker should not be a minor, at the time of making the contract. But in England apprentices may continue to be bound by the restrictive covenants, which they entered into when they were minors. So in this respect we may say that there is more limitation on the consent of the parties in the U.A.R. than in Sudan.

The conclusion that may be drawn from the above considerations, is that, although consent has the same importance in the legal systems of both countries, the contracting freedom in the Sudan is more apparent than in the U.A.R.

Distinction of the contract of employment from related contracts

We now turn to distinguish between the contract of employment and the related contracts. These are mainly contracts for independent

sented to the Fifth International Congress of Comparative Law, in Brussels, in 1958, London (hereinafter referred to as the British Legal Papers), p. 267. "This compulsory normative effect, or compulsory implication of minimum norms in the relevant contracts of employment, was for England, defined by the Court of Appeal in the case of *Gutsell v. Reeves* (1936), 1 K.B. 372" (*Ibid.*, p. 269).

[98] *Ibid.*, p. 267.

[99] Section 94 of the U.A.R. Labour Code permits adherence to collective contracts, by registration with the competent authorities.

[100] The section is quoted and discussed in Section I, D, of Chapter III, *infra*.

[101] The two sections are quoted and discussed in Section II, C, of Chapter III, *infra*.

[102] There are no legal provisions in Sudan, re covenants in restraint of trade; vide Section II, C, of Chapter III, *infra*.

work, contracts of agency and partnerships.[103] The distinction is the measure of application of the labour legislation, both in the U.A.R. and Sudan.[104]

Neither the U.A.R. Labour Code nor the Sudan Ordinance contains any provision, to distinguish the contract of employment from the said related contracts.[105] So the distinction should be sought in the definitions of the relevant contracts, in the relevant legislation or law.

(a) *The contract of independent work of or services*[106]

Section 646 of the U.A.R. Civil Code defines the contract for independent work or 'services,' as "a contract by virtue of which one of

[103] Contracts of 'tenancy' and contracts of 'bailment' are usually distinguished, from the contract of 'service' in the English text-books. But such relationships do not belong to our topic of distinction here, as they properly belong to the general law, both in the U.A.R. and in England and Sudan. Whether an occupier of a certain premises does so as tenant or worker, properly belongs to the law of tenancy, and has nothing to do with the application of the labour law to him. Likewise, whether a taxi-driver or a milk-distributor for instance, holds the taxi or the milk-carriage, as the case may be, as bailee or not, is immaterial to our distinction. What would be material in such instances, is to decide whether the taxi-driver or milk-distributor is a worker, bound by a contract of employment or an independent contractor or a partner, as we shall see later on.

[104] "If control is not an element of the contract, the provisions of the Labour Code shall not be applicable thereto": Cairo Court of Cassation in case No. 641 of 1958 (in El-Hawwari, p. 64); "An agent remunerated by commission, is not a worker, so he cannot benefit from the provisions of the Labour Code, but is subject to the Commercial Code": Cairo Court of Cassation in case No. 1529 of 1959 (*Ibid.*, p. 37) – However, this case should be read subject to the provisions of section 676(1) of the Civil Code, which are quoted in Section III of this Chapter, *infra*; *vide* Murad, p. 226; El-Areef, pp. 374, 154, and 165–6: where he discusses 'mixed' contracts of employment which contain agency provisions, and distinguishes them from 'several' contracts or contracts of employment coupled though independently, with contracts of agency.

Barwell and Kar say what is applicable to Sudan, taking into consideration the rights and duties of the parties to the contract of 'service,' as affected by the Sudan Ordinance: "The importance of distinguishing between the several relationships... is further enhanced by the fact that, by each of (these) relationships, are created quite different rights and liabilities from those, which arise from contracts of service" (p. 155); moreover, "a contract of service may, in particular circumstances, involve the servant in one or more of the other relations alluded to" (p. 154); *vide* also I.L.R., Vol. 31, 1935, p. 846.

[105] The only Arab Country, whose civil law expressly distinguishes between a contract of employment and a related contract, viz. a contract of 'services,' is Iraq. Section 900 of the Iraqi Civil Code provides for this distinction, after it defines the contract of employment. It is believed, however, that such express provision is not necessary, as long as the various contracts are defined and thus can be compared. Section 933 of the Draft Civil Code of 1948 in Egypt, provided like the said section 900 in Iraq. But it was not adopted in the Code.

[106] *Contrat de louage d'ouvrage ou contrat d'entreprise*, as it is called in France. It is of particular importance to distinguish this from the contract of employment, as "it is considered as the most related contract to the contract of employment, and the circumstances of both contracts are very similar and inter-related": El-Areef, p. 155. As we have already seen, these two contracts were always treated as one contract under the Roman and Moslem Laws, and under Code Napoléon and the first U.A.R. Civil Code of 1883. The distinction between the two contracts "depends on the real relationship and its operation, and not merely on the words used by the parties": Cairo Labour Court in

the parties binds himself to manufacture something or perform some work, in return for remuneration which the other party undertakes to pay." This definition, when compared with the definition of the contract of employment, at once reveals that the former has the two elements of work and remuneration, whereas the latter has in addition to these two elements, the third element of control. The work in the former is performed independently of the supervision by the other party, but in the latter it is performed under his supervision and control. Such then is the real and basic distinction between the two contracts.[107]

However, three more distinctions, which are not as basic as the said distinction, should be mentioned. The first two emanate from the fact that in the contract of employment the person of the worker and the personal performance of the work by him are characteristic of the contract, whereas they are not generally speaking, so characteristic of the contract for independent work or 'services.' The first of these can be deduced from the provisions of section 692 of the U.A.R. Civil Code.[108] Whilst by virtue of this section, the worker will, except in certain circumstances, be entitled to his remuneration if he is available and ready for work, a contractor will not be entitled to any pay for the work, unless he actually performs it.[109] Furthermore, the worker will

case No. 1711 of 1958 (in El-Hawwari, p. 54). In England, "the distinction between a servant and an independent contractor, is one which is continually occupying the attention of the Courts": Batt, p. 8. How difficult in any individual case it may be to say, whether a person is a servant or an independent contractor, is illustrated by the cases of *Hardaker v. Idle District Council* (1896) 1 Q.B. 335; and *Penny v. Wimbledon Urban District Council* (1898) 1 A.B. 212 (*Ibid.*, pp. 10–11).

[107] Section 933 of the Draft Civil Code expressly provided for this distinction. *Vide* El-Areef, p. 155: "The only difference is that the right of control exists in the contract of employment, but does not exist in the other contract"; *vide* also Murad, pp. 227–8. The French Law and most of the jurists in France hold that control is the only difference between the two contracts (Murad, p. 228; Zaki, p. 130; and Habeeb, p. 162); and *vide* the French decision in *Journal des débats v. Masquelier* (1934) Gaz. du Palais, 1934, 2,724 (in I.S.D.L., Vol. 10, 1936, p. 85): "A cyclist carrying newspapers of a Company everyday, is not the Company's.... worker as the Company has no means of controlling or supervising him, and the cyclist provides the service at his own risk"; and in *Société des Tourneés Baret v. Castella et Rivier* (1930), Dalloz Hebdom., p. 312 (in I.S.D.L., Vol. 6, 1931, p. 71): "An artist (operatic) is a worker if she is in a subordinate position, i.e. cannot interpret her part but performs under the supervision of the employer"; the German judgement of R.G. of 26 January 1937, III/41/36 (J.W., 1937, p. 1234) in I.S.D.L., Vol. 13, 1939, p. 177, ran as follows: "The concept of a 'job contract' implies some pieces of work, which the contractor undertakes to complete on his own responsibility (section 631 of the Civil Code). In the case of a contract of service, on the other hand, the working effort as such forms the substance of the contract." The same opinion was expressed by the Supreme Court of the Netherlands on 1 December 1961: *vide* Nederlandse Jurisprudentie, 1962, Nr. 79.

[108] The section is quoted in footnote 10, *supra*.

[109] It is interesting to note that the Moslem law, which does not make a distinction between the two contracts, does however, similarly distinguish between them in the entitlement to remuneration (*vide* sections 424 and 425 of the *Majallah*).

be entitled to his remuneration if the object of his work while in his charge is damaged, because the duty of care for the said object imposed upon him by section 685(c) of the Civil Code,[110] does not fix him with absolute liability. But a contractor will not be entitled to any pay for his work, if the object thereof is damaged or lost while in his hands (section 665 of the Civil Code). The second distinction can be deduced from the provisions of section 685(a) of the Civil Code.[110] This section provides that the worker should "perform the work himself." But unless the contract otherwise provides, there is no such obligation on the independent contractor in the Code. From this distinction follows the further distinction of the non-assignability of the contract of employment by one party without the consent of the other, whereas assignment is generally permitted in the other contract.[111] The third distinction is the most prominent among the distinctions which result from the applicability of the labour legislation, especially the Labour Code, to workers,[112] and their inapplicability to independent contractors. This lies in the manner of termination of the contract. While the contract of employment of indefinite duration is terminable by notice,[113] the contract for independent work is terminable without any notice prescribed by law (section 663 of the Civil Code). Moreover, the doctrine of unjustifiable dismissal is applicable to the former, but not to the latter.[113]

As the said three distinctions serve as indicators rather than form the bases of the distinction between the two contracts, control as defined above, remains the measure of distinction. The manifestation of the value of this measure will further be demonstrated, when we later discuss and distinguish the contracts of certain persons.[114]

In Sudan control is not clear in the contract of 'service,' as we have seen it defined in section 2 of the Sudan Ordinance. So the definition of the contract does not except for the name, provide any criterion of distinction between the two contracts. The two elements of employment and remuneration that form the contract in the definition, are

[110] The section is quoted and discussed in Section I, C, iii, ofChapter III, *infra*.

[111] Section 661 of the U.A.R. Civil Code permits such assignment; *vide* El-Areef, p. 156. Section 87 of the Labour Code, however, provides exceptions to this rule of assignability: *vide* Section IV of Chapter II, *infra*.

[112] Some U.A.R. writers try to devise numerous distinctions, in addition to control, from the exclusive applicability of labour legislation to workers, and from the rules of the general law, re vicarious liability (which was excepted from the scope of this study, *vide* Preface, *supra*): *Vide* Zaki, p. 129; and Habeeb, pp. 161–62.

[113] *Vide* section 72 of the Labour Code, in Section II, A of Chapter VI, *infra*, and the doctrine of justification in Section II, B, thereof.

[114] Refer to Section III of this Chapter, *infra*.

indeed the same elements of a contract for independent work. But reference to the English Common Law, which we have seen is mandatory in these circumstances in Sudan, provides the necessary criterion of distinction, viz. that of control. An independent contractor has been defined as "one who undertakes to produce a firm result, but so that in the actual execution of the work, he is not under the control of the person for whom he does it, and may use his own discretion in the things not specified beforehand."[115] Again "a contractor is a person who has entered into a contract to execute a certain specific work... unlike the servant, he is not under the control of the employer."[116] This definition distinguishes the independent contract from that of 'service,' by the emphasis on the existence of control in the latter, and its absence in the former.[117] So like the U.A.R., control is the basic and real distinction between the two contracts.

The first of the other three distinctions between the two contracts in the U.A.R., re entitlement to remuneration, is equally applicable in Sudan.[118] The second of those distinctions, re assignability of the contract, is also applicable in Sudan. "In contemplation of the relative law, there is consequently, apart from specific agreement, no room for substitution on the part of a servant of someone else to perform the services which he has agreed to render."[119] However, the non-assignability of a contract of 'service' seems to be more strict in Sudan than

[115] Samuels, p. 7; *vide* also Batt, p. 8.

[116] Diamond, p. 16; *vide* also Cooper, who defines in p. 12, the independent contractor in an interesting way: "An independent contractor," he says, "is a person doing that which a principal wishes to delegate, but doing it unfettered by any control except as to the end to be achieved." Section 10 of the Employers and Workmen Act, 1875, in England, which is applicable to both contracts, does not clearly distinguish between them: "whether the contract", it says, "be a contract of service, or personally to execute any work or labour"; *vide* Macdonell, p. 60, where it is mentioned how Lord Justice *Brett* properly distinguished between the two contracts in 1877, before the Select Committee on Employers' Liability.

[117] "The power of control which the master enjoys over the work of his servant, is the decisive factor distinguishing the servant from an independent contractor": Batt, p. 1; *vide* also *Sadler v. Henlock* (4 E & B 570), in which *Compton J.*, said: "The greater the amount of direct control exercised.... the stronger the grounds for holding it to be a contract of service, and similarly the greater the degree of independence of such control the greater the probablility that the services rendered are of the nature of professional services, and that the contract is not one of personal service"; and *vide* the Indian case of *Goolbai v. Pestonji*, A.I.R., 1935, Bombay 333, which was quoted by Barwell and Kar, p. 34, as the authority in India, for the distinction; they also quoted the modern English case of *Collins v. Hertfordshire County and Anr.* (1947) 1 A.E.R., 633, as a case "in which the connotations of the phrases Contract of Service and Contract of Services are expressly mentioned"; *vide* Halsbury, Vol. 25, pp. 452, 498.

[118] *Vide* footnote 10, *supra*.

[119] Barwell and Kar, p. 59. However, if the contract of services is personal, i.e. the personal skill of the contractor is material, the contract is not assignable (*Ibid.* 59-footnote 1).

the assignment of a contract of employment in the U.A.R.[120] As for the third distinction, re termination of the contract of 'service' by notice, section 10(1) of the Sudan Ordinance [121] forms the basis of distinction. The English Common Law doctrine of 'reasonable notice,' which is applicable when the contract does not provide for notice, is limited to the contract of 'service.'

The conclusion is that, like the U.A.R., the measure of distinction between the two contracts in Sudan remains to be control, but of course as defined and distinguished from control in the U.A.R., as we have seen above.

(b) The contract of agency

"The relationship of principal and agent," says *W. M. Cooper*,[122] "is one which often overlaps that of master and servant... the difficulty usually arises where there is an informal relationship." *F. R. Batt*[123] emphasises the nature of the difficulty, by saying that "all servants are in some matters the agents of their masters, but all agents are not servants." The difficulty is further complicated by the interesting fact that "it is possible for a master to be his own servant's agent in a transaction created by a contract of service,"[124] while it is impossible for a 'master,' during the currency of a 'contract of service' with his 'sevant,' to be the 'servant' of the said 'servant.' This difficulty of distinction in England and hence in Sudan, is even more acute in the U.A.R., as we shall see later on.[125]

Section 699 of the U.A.R. Civil Code defines a contract of agency as "a contract by virtue of which an agent binds himself to carry out some work of a legal nature on behalf of the principal."[126] The explanatory

[120] *Vide* reference to statutory exceptions to this rule, in footnote 111, *supra*.

[121] Refer to Section II, A, of Chapter VI, *infra*. Unless the contract of 'service' expressly provides for notice, the English Common Law recognises the necessity of service of a 'reasonable notice.'

[122] Pp. 12 and 13.

[123] P. 6; *vide* also Diamond, p. 166, for the five cases in which the "master is bound by the acts done or entered into by the servant with third persons on his master's behalf." However, he properly adds that "the 'authority' of a servant is properly part of the law, not of master and servant, but of principal and agent"; refer in this respect to Samuels, pp. 24–6; and Macdonell, pp. 14–5.

[124] Barwell and Kar, pp. 186–7, who quote the "curious modern case" of *Grand Trunk Railway Co. of Canada v. Robinson* (1915) A.C. 740, as an instance of such difficulty. It was held therein, that a master who, on sending his servant on a business journey, and had contracted with the Railway Co. (whose services were used for the journey), so as to fix the liability for any accident to the servant, with the said Co., without the servant's objection, did so contract with it as an agent for his servant and not as his master.

[125] *Vide* Habeeb, p. 195; El-Areef, p. 159, where he underlines the difficulty of distinction, when the worker is also an agent.

[126] *Vide* section III of this Chapter, *infra*, re advocates.

Note to the Civil Code says that "the agent carries out some legal work, and that is what distinguishes a contract of agency from a contract of employment." This criterion of distinction, which the Explanatory Note ventured to state, has given rise to a great juridical controversy.[127] It is submitted that the Explanatory Note is unwarranted in stating the said criterion, and that the real distinction between the two contracts in the U.A.R. ultimately lies in the element of control. An agent is independent of his principal's control, as we defined it, but a worker is not.

In England and hence in Sudan, "an agency agreement is one by which the agent is authorised to establish privity of contract between his employer, called the principal, and a third party."[128] If the question of distinction between the contract of 'service' and that of agency, rested with the said definitions of the agent and his contract, the same difficulties which arose in the U.A.R., would have arisen in England. But as far back as 1858, it was decided in *R. v. Walker*,[129] that "a principal has the right to direct what the agent has to do, a master has not only that right but also the right to say how it is to be done."[130]

[127] Some of the U.A.R. writers go to the extent of saying that control is not the measure of distinction, but the distinction lies in the nature of the work and whether it is 'legal' or 'material' (Habeeb, p. 196, who therein quotes other U.A.R. and French authors and some old cases decided under the old Civil Code of 1883, in his support). Other writers take the view that control is the real measure of distinction (Murad, pp. 231–2; El-Areef, p. 159; Badawi, K. M., p. 39, and other U.A.R. and French authors who were listed in Habeeb, p. 195). The fallacy of the first group is exposed, by the proviso which section 676(1) of the Civil Code itself prescribes for the admission of insurance agents etc... as workers, viz. that of control (*vide* footnote 25, *supra*). The above quotation from the Explanatory Note to the Civil Code, should not as was done by these authors, be taken on its face value, nor is it any authority when section 699 of the Code is confronted with section 676(1), both of which should be read together with section 674, when a distinction is sought between the two contracts. The question has not been forcefully mooted, it seems, but the Council of State, on 15 April 1953, delivered an opinion that "the essential difference between a worker and an agent, is that the former is subject to the supervision and control of his employer, whereas the agent's will is independent of his principal's will" (in Habeeb, p. 195, footnote 4; this author, whose support for the first view has been noted, contradicts himself in p.197, when he says that "the contract of a commercial representative is a contract of employment, if he does not preserve his total independence in the performance of his work"). The said first group of writers claim that the law in France supports their view. However, *Trib. de Rouen*, 23 July 1929, Recueil de Rouen et Caen, 1930, 1, 30 (in I.S.D.L., Vol. 6, 1931, p. 69), decided that "a commercial representative is not an agent.... where he is in a dependent and subordinate relation to the firm employing him"; *vide* also *Bonfiglio v. Carmona* (1936) Dalloz. Hebdom. (in I.S.D.L., Vol. 12, 1938, p. 144) to the same effect. It is worthy of mention here, that 'control' is the measure of distinction also in Belgium (I.L.R. Vol. 32, p. 225), in Switzerland (*Ibid.*, p. 498), in Germany (*Ibid.*, p. 211), and in the Netherlands (*vide* footnote 107, *supra*).

[128] Cheshire and Fifoot, p. 386.

[129] 27 L.J.M.C. 207.

[130] *Vide* Diamond, p. 13; Samuels, p. 7; Macdonell, p. 52; and Smith, p. 36; *vide* also *R. v. Bailey* (1871), 12 Cox 56; and *R. v. Negus* (1873), L.R. 2 C.C.R. 34, both decided after *Walker's* case, and when compared together, underline the same distinction (*vide*

This criterion of control, as the basic distinction between the two contracts, continued in its validity upto the present time, without the challenge we saw posed in the U.A.R.

The said definitions of agents, both in the U.A.R. and Sudan, do not make remuneration an essential element in their contracts. Therein lies the second distinction between a contract of agency and a contract of employment. In the U.A.R. section 709(1) of the Civil Code considers an agent's contract to be gratitous unless provided otherwise.[131] In England and hence in Sudan, the law presumes an agency, in "the case of cohabitation,"[132] for instance; and that is a good demonstration of the gratitous nature of a contract of agency. This gratitous nature of the contract has in the U.A.R., occasioned the further provision in the said section 709, that, notwithstanding any agreement as to the remuneration of an agent in his contract, the Court may at the request of either party in the warranted circumstances, decrease or increase the remuneration, as the case may be. In this the contract of agency differs from that of employment, where remuneration cannot be altered without the consent of both parties. In England, however, an agent's contractual remuneration cannot be interfered with by the Court, and its decrease or increase lies only with the principal and the agent themselves. So the contract of agency, if remunerative to the agent, does not differ in this respect from the contract of 'service.' The difference between the two positions in U.A.R. and Sudan is clear.

The third distinction between the two contracts lies in their manner of termination. In the first place, a contract of employment for a limited period is not ordinairly terminable in the U.A.R., before the expiry of its period (section 694(1) of the Civil Code), and a contract for an unlimited period is not ordinarily terminable without notice (section 694(2), and section 72 of the Labour Code).[133] But a contract of agency is terminable by either party at will, unless the contract is remunerative (sections 715 and 716 of the Civil Code). In England and hence in Sudan,

Cooper, p. 12). Section 188 of the Indian Contract Act of 1875, recognizes the discretion which the agent exercises in his work and which is not open for a servant: – *The Indo-Union Assurance Co. Ltd., v. T. Srinivasan* (1947), Indian Law Reports, Madras, 170, is an authority for the said distinction between a 'servant' and an agent. *Vide* also I.L.R., Vol. 32, 1936, p. 382.

[131] *Vide* the history of the gratitous nature of the contract of agency, commencing with the Roman Law, in Zaki, pp. 138–40 *et seq.*, and Habeeb, pp. 193 *et seq.*, though of course this contract has everywhere developed to be remunerative (*vide* Murad, p. 232); El-Areef, p. 159, points to the lawful guardian's agency on behalf of the minor, as an instance of agency without remuneration.

[132] Cheshire and Fifoot, p. 387. Section 185 of the Indian Contract Act of 1875, provides that no considereation is necessary to create an agency.

[133] Cf. section 85 of the Labour Code – Refer to Section I, G, of Chapter VI, *infra*.

"the relation of agency may be terminated at any time in the absence of agreement to the contrary, whereas the relation of master and servant requires some period of notice for its termination."[134] So in this respect, the U.A.R. and Sudan are similar. In the second place, a contract of agency in the U.A.R. automatically comes to an end on the death of the principal (section 714 of the Civil Code). But the death of the employer does not so terminate the contract of employment, "unless the employer's personal qualities were taken into consideration when the contract was made" (section 697(1) of the Civil Code). In England and hence in Sudan, the death of the principal determines the agency.[135] Section 12 of the Sudan Ordinance provides that, "unless otherwise expressly provided in the contract, every contract of service shall terminate on the death of the employer." Thus the effect of the employer's death on the contract of employment in Sudan and in England,[136] is the same as the effect of the principal's death on the agency contract, whereas in the U.A.R. such effect is different.

The fourth and last distinction between the two contracts both in the U.A.R. and Sudan, is that an agent can be a legal person, whereas a worker should be a natural person.

Such then are the grounds of distinction between the contract of employment and that of agency. But the first ground of control stands out as the basic measure of distinction, though more clearly in Sudan than in the U.A.R., whereas the other three grounds really follow rather than play a decisive role in the distinction between the two contracts.

(c) Partnership

The difficulty of distinguishing between a contract of empolyment and a partnership agreement is, both in the U.A.R. and Sudan, particularly important, where the worker shares in the profits of his employer, in total or partial fulfilment of his entitlement to remuneration. Section 691(1) of the Civil Code permits such kind of remuneration.[137] The definition of the contract of 'service,' in section 2 of the Sudan Ordinance, also implies such remuneration.[138]

[134] Batt, p. 7, adds: "unless it is coupled with an interest held by the agent"; *vide* also Cheshire and Fifoot, pp. 411 and 412. Refer to Section II, A, 2, of Chapter VI, *infra*, for the statutory notice-requirements in Sudan.

[135] *Vide* Cheshire and Fifoot, p. 415.

[136] Refer to footnotes 111 and 121, *supra*.

[137] The section is quoted and discussed in Section I of Chapter IV, *infra*. *Vide* also Zaki, pp. 97–8, and 131–2; Habeeb, p. 181; and El-Areef, p. 160.

[138] "Arrangements are frequently made in trade between masters and... servants employed by them, under which (the latter) are remunerated... by a sum calculated with reference to the gross or net profits of their masters": Smith, p. 31; "A man may be

Section 505 of the U.A.R. Civil Code defines a partnership, as "a contract whereby two or more persons bind themselves to contribute in a financial business by some capital or some work, and to share whatever profits or losses result therefrom." This contribution and sharing between partners presupposes the equality, though not the absolute equality[139] in the management of their business. In other words, it excludes any notion of control by one partner over the other.[140]

The definition of the partnership mentions the sharing of losses by the partners. In this some U.A.R. writers have tried to find a second distinction between a partnership agreement and a contract of employment, depending apparently on section 515 of the Civil Code, which renders a partnership void if a partner is, by the terms of the partnership agreement, exempted from losses.[141] It is submitted that, although the sharing of losses may be a good 'marker' for distinction, yet the final test for the distinction is control and not the sharing of losses.[142]

A second distinction is clear from the comparison of section 507 of the Civil Code, which holds the partnership agreement null and void if it is not in writing, with section 43 of the Labour Code which does not do so with the contract of employment. In other words, the partnership agreement is a formal contract, but the contract of employment is not. A third but subsidiary distinction lies in the effect of the death

the servant of another, though his remuneration may not be called wages but profit or commission": Macdonell, pp. 41–2; "A contract for the remuneration of a servant, employed by a person engaged in a business, does not of itself make the servant a partner in the business": Halsbury, Vol. 25, p. 452; and *vide* cases quoted therein to the same effect. *Vide* section 2(3, b) of the English Partnership Act of 1890, which provides to the same effect. The difficulty is further complicated because "every partner may take part in management of the partnership business, but no partner is entitled to remuneration for so doing": Encyclopaedia Britannica, Vol. 17, p. 344.

[139] *Vide* sections 519 and 520 of the Civil Code; *vide* also Zaki, p. 132; Habeeb, pp. 182–3 (who quotes the French expression *collaboration sur un pied d'egalite*, and the Moslem Law, to the same effect).

[140] *Vide* Murad, p. 235; and El-Areef, p. 160, where he mentions the familiar but interesting example of an agreement, between a land-owner and a farmer, under which the latter farms the land of the former and both share the crop. If the former controls the work of the latter, the agreement is a contract of employment. If he does not, it is a tenancy agreement of husbandry, governed by section 619 of the Civil Code. The element of control which decides the nature of the contract, in the case where workers are remunerated by a share in the profits of the employer's business (section 691(1) of the Civil Code), is not affected by the provisions of the same section, which make it obligatory on the employer in these cases, to permit the worker to consult his (the employer's) accounting books, in order to verify the profits (*vide* Habeeb, p. 183).

[141] *Vide* Murad, p. 237; and Habeeb, p. 181 – footnote 5; Badawi, K. M., p. 96; El-Areef, p. 265; and *Kanun 'Akd El-'Amal El-Fardi Wa Ahkam El-Kadha'*, by Faheem, M., 1955, Cairo, in Arabic (hereinafter, called Faheem), p. 38.

[142] *Vide*, however, Alexandria Court of Appeal in appeal No. 360 of 1957 (in Habeeb, p. 183), in which it was held that the contract was that of employment and not of partnership, as long as one of the parties was under the control of another, even though the party controlled was liable to carry the losses of the business.

of one of the parties on the agreement. We have seen that the death of the employer does not automatically terminate the contract of employment. But the death of one partner automatically dissolves the partnership (section 528 of the Civil Code).

In Sudan section 3 of the Partnership Registration Ordinance of 15 November 1933[143] defines a partnership, as "the association of two or more persons for the purpose of carrying on business together, and dividing its profits between them." The same deduction concerning the lack of control, which was made out from the U.A.R. definition, follows from the Sudan definition.[144]

Although sometimes the distinction in England and hence in Sudan, between a contract of 'service' and a partnership, is based on the sharing of losses,[145] the sharing of losses is taken as one of the important considerations but not the final measure of distinction. "The sure guide," says *W. M. Cooper*, "is the intention of the parties."[146] This sure guide, it is submitted, ultimately rests on the power of control of one party by the other.[147] There does not seem to be a division of opinion in England as we saw in the U.A.R., concerning the distinctive value of the sharing of losses.[148]

The second distinction pointed out in the U.A.R., is also clear in Sudan, from the comparison of section 5 of the Partnership Registration Ordinance with the definition of the 'contract of service' in section 2 of the Sudan Ordinance.

[143] *Laws of the Sudan*, Vol. 4., Title XIII, Sub-Title 6; *vide* the similar wording of the definition of a partnership, in section 1 of the Partnership Act of 1890 in England.

[144] In *Stocker v. Brooklebank* (1851)3 Mac. & G. 250, it was decided that, a manager of a firm who had "no controllable discretion" in the management of the firm, was a mere servant, although the firm exploited a process discovered by the manager, and the manager was remunerated by a percentage of the profits ,and had the option of buying the business on certain conditions. In *Hill v. Beckett* (1951) 1 K.B., 578, it was decided that the simple test for the distinction was, "whether one of the parties is under the control and bound to obey the orders of the other; if so there is the employment relationship"; *vide* Samuels, p. 8.

[145] *Vide R. v. Macdonald* (1861) Le. & Ca. 85, where the accused, who was employed as a cashier at a certain annual salary and a commission on profits, was held to be a servant, because he was not liable to share in the losses.

[146] p. 14.

[147] The weight of judicial authority is to the same effect. In *Walker v. Hirsch*, 27 Ch. D. 641, it was decided that a servant who was remunerated by a fixed salary and a share in the profits, but was also liable to share in the losses, was not a partner, because of the power of control his master had over him; *Re Young ex. p. Jones* (1896) 2 Q.B. 484, is an authority to the same effect, and is all the more interesting, because its facts are similar to the facts of the U.A.R. case, quoted in footnote 142, *supra*.

[148] When Diamond, p. 24, says that, "if the person in question is a partner, he is liable to contribute to the losses of the business, if he is merely a servant he is not so liable," he is, it is believed, aiming at emphasising the importance of the distinction, rather than defining the measure of that distinction.

The third subsidiary distinction pointed out in the U.A.R., is not applicable to Sudan, because as the death of a partner in England dissolves the partnership,[149] the death of the employer likewise terminates the contract of 'service', as we have seen before. So in this respect, the position in Sudan is different from that in the U.A.R.

SECTION II: THE EMPLOYER

Section 1 of the U.A.R. Labour Code defines an employer, as "any person or body corporate employing one or more workers, for a wage of any kind." Section 2 of the Sudan Ordinance defines an employer, as "any person or body of persons whether incorporated or not, who has entered into a contract of service, and includes the Government and any Local Government Authority."

On the comparison of these two definitions, it is clear that the employer, both in the U.A.R. and in Sudan, does not have to be a natural person, as he can be a legal person such as a company.

However, the Sudan definition is wider, in that it permits any body of persons not incorporated to be an employer. Thus a partnership, which both in Sudan and in the U.A.R. is an unincorporated group of persons,[150] can in Sudan be an employer, while it cannot be so in the U.A.R.[151]

On the other hand, neither definition is complete for our purpose, without reference to the relative definition of the contract of employment. In the U.A.R. definition, the word 'employing' does not necessarily connote the power of control, as we have previously seen. Either a complete definition should have been enacted, expressly referring to the power of control, or the words "any person or body corporate" would have sufficed as a definition, provided there is an express reference to the definition of the contract in the Code. Such express reference to the contract of 'service' in the Sudan definition, renders that definition more clear and so more useful than the definition in the U.A.R.

Finally, the definition of the employer, both in the Sudan Ordinance and as can be deduced from the definition of the contract of 'service'

[149] Encyclopaedia Britannica, Vol. 17, p. 344.

[150] "Under English Law the firm is not a corporation, nor is it recognised as distinct from the members composing it" (*Ibid.*)

[151] The difficulties which may arise from such provision in Sudan, are not far-fetched. "Servants of such bodies," says Batt, "may find themselves in serious difficulties in discovering who in law is their master, and whom to sue should there be a breach of the contract" (p. 37).

in England, does not make it a condition for a person, in order to be an employer of another person, necessarily to employ that other person in his own profession. A person can be a 'servant' of another, even though he serves him in a capacity not related to the 'master's' profession.[152] Though in the U.A.R. the position is the same,[153] some juridical doubts provoked a controversy in this respect, which led to the appearance of some advocates of the 'profession' restriction on the employer. Such contention of course, if it is legally warranted, would lead to the limitation of the scope of application of the Labour Code. It is believed that these juridical doubts originally emanated from two sources: (a) the Explanatory Note to Decree Law 317 of 1952, which defines the employer, as "any natural or legal person, who carries out his work as his profession or craft, either for profit like advocates and doctors and factories or commercial companies, or for the fulfilment of social or educational purposes, like philanthropic societies, first-aid societies or educational institutions." After it so defines the employer, the Explanatory Note concludes that, "as a result, persons who without taking their work as their own profession or craft, and have others perform it for them, like a house owner hiring a builder to build the house for him, or a carpenter to make the house furniture, cannot be employers";[154] and (b) the belief that control in the contract of employment should necessarily be technical control.[155] It is clear that this belief is also shared by the authors of the Explanatory Note. However, it is submitted that the Explanatory Note to Decree Law 317 of 1952 is not legally warranted in providing the said definition of the employer,[156] and thus limiting the scope of application of the Labour Code. The said Law did not provide any definition for the employer. So reference

[152] The definition of 'employer' in section 3(h) of the Bahraini Labour Code, is similar to the Sudan definition; and so is the definition in section 2 read with section 3 of the Aden Ordinance.

[153] The definition of the employer in section 1 of the Kuwaiti Labour Code, expressly imposes the 'profession' restriction on the employer; and so does section 1(2) of the Iraqi Labour Code – (this was only added by amendment of the Code by Law 82 of 1958). But the definition in section 2(11) of the Jordan Labour Code, section 1 of the Lebanese Labour code, section 2 of the Saudi Regulations, and as can be deduced from section 10(1) of the Libyan Labour Code, do not impose such restriction on the employer.

[154] Contrary to the English and hence the Sudan law, Explanatory Notes in the U.A.R. are interpretative references of first instance.

[155] *Vide* Butros and Rajab, p. 15; *vide* also Badawi, K. M., p. 27; Badawi, Z., Vol. I, p. 23; El-Fakahani, Book I, Vol. I, p. 32, who impliedly contradicts himself in p. 92 *et seq.*

[156] The Explanatory Note definition does not seem to have been put to serious testing in Courts. The Cairo Court of Arbitration decision in dispute No. 6 of 1955 (mentioned in Habeeb, p. 245), which adopted the 'profession' restriction on the employer, is not an authority to depend on, as it is a decision of a minor Court, and does not seem to have been followed by the same or any other Court.

should then have been limited to the definition, which could have been deducted from the definition of the contract of employment in section 674 of the Civil Code and the provisions of section 1 of the said Decree Law,[157] re its applicability. Such deduction certainly rejects any 'profession' restriction on the employer. The sole measure of applicability of that Law was the element of control in the contract of employment. That measure, which is the same measure of applicability of the Labour Code, can, as we have seen above, be technical, professional or administrative. So in the example of the house owner quoted by the Explanatory Note, if the builder's or the carpenter's contract is not a contract of employment, and indeed is in most cases a contract for independent work,[158] the reason lies in the lack of any notion of control by the house owner over the builder and the carpenter, and not in his lack of technical control. If the house owner is not able to exercise technical or professional control, even through an expert worker (also bound to him by a contract of employment), he can still exercise administrative control which is enough for the prupose.[159] The examination of the contract terms, in order to ascertain the existence or absence of control, is the test, and not a super-imposed and unwarranted 'profession' restriction on the employer.[160]

SECTION III: THE WORKER[161]

Section 2 of the U.A.R. Labour Code defines a worker as "any male

[157] Section 1 of Decree Law 317 of 1952 was exactly worded as section 42 of the Labour Code (which was quoted in footnote 2, *supra*).

[158] *Vide* Habeeb, p. 252.

[159] Administrative control is, as we have previously seen, enough to constitute control. *Vide* also Cairo Court of Appeal decision in appeal No. 1774 of 1958 (in Habeeb, p. 175); and the same Court in appeal No. 99 of 1959 (in El-Fakahani, Book I, Vol. I, p. 61); and *vide* Murad, pp. 241–2.

[160] The advocates of the 'profession' restriction on the employer, have also tried to find some support in (a) the use of the term 'the other party,' in the definition of the contract of employment in section 674 of the Civil Code, while the term 'employer' was used in the said Decree Law (and the Labour Code), which two terms according to their view, cannot mean the same thing, (b) the exclusion by the Labour Code, of domestic servants and persons performing work "not within the scope of the employer's business" (*vide* Section III of this Chapter, infra). However, the use of the different terms without the definition of the term 'the other party' in the Civil Code, on the one hand, and the use of a term other than "the other party" in the Civil Code itself (sections 676, 684, 686, 687, 690), on the other hand, means that these terms are no more than synonyms. The express exclusion of domestic servants from the Labour would not be necessary, if the profession restriction on the employer were valid. Finally, the exclusion of persons performing work which falls outside the scope of the employer's business, is not absolute, as it is limited by the Code itself to the work not lasting for more than six months.

[161] The traditional legal term 'servant' was and is still being used in England, to denote the person who works for another, under the latter's direction and control. The contract

or female, working for a wage of any kind in the service[162] of an employer, under the latter's authority or supervision." Section 2 of the Sudan Ordinance defines an 'employed person,' as "any person not under the age of fifteen years and not specifically excluded from the provisions of this Ordinance, who has entered into a contract of service with an employer."

Contrary to what we saw in the definition of the employer, the U.A.R. definition of the worker is clearer and legally more concise[163] than the definition of 'employed person' in Sudan.[164] The Sudan definition would have been more concise, if the words 'to serve an employer' had been used instead of "with an employer."[165] Both definitions, on the other hand, contain either provisions unnecessary or irrelevant to the definition of the worker. The words 'male or female' in the U.A.R. definition are not necessary, because the word 'person' would have sufficed. The words "not specifically excluded from the provisions of this Ordinance" in the Sudan definition are not necessary, because the effect of the exclusion provisions in the Ordinance are clear. The words "not under the age of fifteen years" in Sudan are irrelevant to

which regulates the relationship, was as a result called the 'contract of service.' These terms, on account of their acquisition of certain legal connotations, continue to be used in spite of the fact that "the terms servant and master have become unpopular in legislation, the popular ear finding presumably too great a similarity between servile and service": Batt, pp. 4–5. In Sudan, though the term 'employed person' and not 'servant' is used in the Ordinance, the term 'contract of service' was illogically used instead of the term 'contract of employment.' In the U.A.R. the term *ajeer* (in Arabic), which means a 'hired person' and denotes the term 'servant' rather than any other, was used in the first Civil Code of 1883. This was understandable, because, as was pointed out in Part I, *supra*, the contract under which the *ajeer* used to work was a lease contract. But the term *ajeer* was finally discarded, since the enactment of Law 41 of 1944. The term 'worker' was used instead, to denote any one bound by a contract of employment, irrespective of the nature of his work, whether it is predominantly mental or manual, i.e. whether he is, to use the English terms, an 'employee' or a 'workman.' Since the Sudan Ordinance uses the term 'employed person' to denote the U.A.R. term 'worker,' the use of the latter term in this study was decided on as a convenient term. The term 'worker' connotes no 'servility' or 'lease,' both of which are not in consonance with the modern spirit of democracy and that of labour legislation.

[162] The word 'service' in this definition, which is a relic of the past, is not necessary for the definition. The words 'for an employer' would have been better than the words 'in the service of the employer.'

[163] Section 1(a) of the Iraqi Labour Code, and section 1 of the Kuwaiti Labour Code contain definitions similar to that of the U.A.R. But section 2(10) of the Jordanian Labour Code, section 2 of the Lebanese Labour Code, and section 1(3) of the Saudi Regulations, are useless, without reference to the definition of the contract of employment.

[164] Section 3(g) of the Bahraini Labour Code contains a definition, like the Sudan definition. The definition of a 'worker' as can be deduced from the contract of service definition in section 3 of the Adenese Ordinance, is also similar.

[165] The typical English definition of a 'servant' is "one who for consideration, agrees to work subject to the orders of another": Macdonell, p. 34; *vide* also Cooper, p. 3; and Batt, p. 1.

the definition, because they relate to the capacity of the 'employed person,' and they should have been kept separate.

It is clear from the said two definitions of the worker that he should be a natural person.[166] This was presumed by the legislators in the two countries, at least on account of the legislative provisions concerning leaves and some powers of dismissal and the general tenor of labour legislation, all of which are only applicable to natural persons.

Finally, neither definition makes a distinction between 'workman' and 'employee,' or workers whose work is predominantly 'manual' or 'mental,' respectively.[167] Such distinction cannot be conclusively implied from the different treatment accorded to monthly-paid workers and workers paid otherwise, in some of the provisions of both the U.A.R. Labour Code and the Sudan Ordinance,[168] because the pay-category of the worker does not necessarily follow his category of work.

The definition of the worker in Sudan does not basically differ from the definition of 'servant' in the English Common Law. The definition of the worker in the U.A.R. depends in fact on the definition of the contract of employment in section 674 of the Civil Code. So both in the U.A.R. and Sudan, the distinctive feature of a worker is that he performs his work while under the control of another. The measure of deciding whether a certain person is a worker or not, for the purposes

[166] *Vide* Murad, p. 224; Habeeb, p. 189, who depended on section 685(a) of the Civil Code, which provides that the worker should perform the work himself; El-Areef, p. 139; and Faheem, p. 6; El-Sa'eed, pp. 4 and 7, did the same in Iraq. *Vide* also the I.L.R., Vol. 31, 1935, p. 847.

[167] *Vide* Murad, p. 225. The only Arab Countries, which make an express distinction between a 'workman' and an 'employee,' are Iraq (section 1 a & b of the Labour Code), and Lebanon (section 3 of the Labour Code). Such distinction is familiar in some of the European countries, especially France and Germany. The distinction is material in England, e.g. in the application of the Employers and Workmen Act 1875, which was limited in its application to 'manual' work. *Bound v. Lawrence* (1892) 1 Q.B. 226, decided the distinction, according to whether manual labour was "the real and substantial part of the employment.... or merely accessory and incidental to the real employment" (*vide* Samuels, p. 40). The I.L.O. tries to treat workmen and employees separately, in some of its reports, recommendations and conventions.

[168] Both treat the two categories of wrokers differently, in respect of termination of the contract (Chapter VI, *infra*). Sudan treats them differently in the termination gratuity entitlements, but the U.A.R. does not (Chapter VII, *infra*). Section 66 of the U.A.R. Labour Code (vide Chapter III, *infra*), makes a distinction between the two categories of workers, in the length of the period during which a disciplinary penalty may be inflicted. The trend in the U.A.R., which used to differentiate as aforementioned, much more than Sudan ever did, is to equate the two categories of workers. This is clear, when the Labour Code is compared with its predecessor Decree Law 317 of 1952, which used to accord different treatment in the termination gratuity and sick-leave. The said Decree Law itself equated the two categories of workers, in the length of the probation period, which was not the same under Law 41 of 1944.

of the applicability of the labour legislation to him, is that distinctive feature of control.

We now proceed to the testing of the said measure in certain categories of persons, who were and still are the subject of much litigation and juridical discussion.

Controversial contracts of certain persons

(i) Persons performing work of a religious character

In the U.A.R. such a person whether Moslem or Christian, is bound by and benefits from the provisions of the Labour Code, if "his religious office is for remuneration paid to him... by the principality to whose control and dismissal powers he is subject, irrespective of the spiritual nature of his duties, because spiritual work is so well connected with and cannot be independent of mental work."[169] So the criterion of control was held to be applicable to religious work.

In England the "relationship is governed not by the law of contract but by the law of the Church. The priest is conceived under that law, as serving the Godhead only."[170] Again, "the relation between incumbent and curate, or bishop and curate in the Church of England, is not that of employer and employed, for a curate is the holder of an ecclesiastical office."[171] In *Rogers v. Booth*,[172] it was held that a Salvation Army Officer was not a workman (for the purpose of the Workmen's Compensation Act); his relationship is spiritual and not that of 'service.' Thus the English notion of control in the contract of 'service' is not applicable to persons performing work of a religious nature. As the notion of control in the contract of 'service' in Sudan is that of the English Common Law, the English Law as stated above, will, it is submitted, be held applicable in Sudan in the Christian Community. However, as long as the reception of the English Law in Sudan is in accordance with 'justice equity and good conscience,'[173] it is submitted that such reception will not be warranted in respect of the Moslem Community. According to this submission, the position will be the same both in the U.A.R. and

[169] Alexandria Court of Cassation in case No. 1765 of 1953 (in Badawi, K. M., p. 34; and Butros and Rajab, p. 14, both of whom report the case without much comment). *Vide* also Barwell and Kar, p. 43, where they affirm that the remunerated *muezzin* (the Moslem crier for prayers), is a 'servant' in the full sense, when he is under the control of the religious committee concerned.

[170] Barwell and Kar, p. 42.

[171] Halsbury, Vol. 25, p. 451.

[172] (1937), 2 A.E.R. 751 C.A., 30 B.W.C.C. 188

[173] Refer to Part I, *supra*.

Sudan, in as far as Moslems are concerned, but it would still be different as far as Christians are concerned.[174]

(ii) Teachers

Teachers are workers and they benefit from the Labour Code in the U.A.R., as long as they are subject to the control of the institution they work for, whether this control be technical or simply administrative.[175]

In England and hence in Sudan, the position seems to be the same, as the question is also determined by control. "There is no doubt," says *W. M. Cooper*,[176] "a teacher is the servant of the local authority by whom he is employed."[177]

So both in the U.A.R. and Sudan, the test of the worker here is also control. If there is no control, the teacher would be held an independent contractor.[178]

(iii) Advocates

Before the modern practice of employing advocates in big commercial or industrial establishments, the relationship of advocates with their customers was exclusively that of counsel and client. The latter relationship, which is completely free of any notion of control by the client over his counsel, no doubt was and still is that of agency.[179] This is true both in the U.A.R.[180] and Sudan.[181]

[174] It is believed that, due to the lack of any protection for Moslems engaged in religious work, apart from remuneration and charitable treatment, the application of the Labour Law to the said persons in the U.A.R. and Sudan, is sound, though in neither country do such persons seem to avail themselves much of the opportunity. The application of the U.A.R. Labour Legislation to Christians engaged in religious work, is purely academic, as their establishments usually take care of them in their own way.

[175] *Vide* Shbeen El-Koum Court of Cassation in case No. 194 of 1951 (in Habeeb, p. 177); Cairo Court of Appeal in appeal No. 804 of 1954 (in Badawi, K. M., p. 35); and the same Court in appeal No. 340 of 1957 (in El-Fakahani, Book I, Vol. I, p. 35). Section 935 of the Draft Civil Code of 1948 contained an express provision to the same effect; but the section was not adopted.

[176] P. 6; *vide* also Barwell and Kar, pp. 49–50, who in footnote 2 p. 34, quote the interesting case of the *University of London Press Ltd., v. University Tutorial Press Ltd.* (1916), 2 Ch. 601, as an authority for holding an outside-examiner of an educational institute, an independent contractor and not a servant. The temporary nature of the examiner's work contributed, it is believed, to the making of this decision.

[177] The word 'employed' here, which, it is believed, is used as a synonym for the word 'controlled,' is reminiscent of the use of the word 'employed' in the Sudan definition of the 'contract of service.' The term 'employed' is, however, an unhappy term, as it may just mean 'given work,' and does not necessarily indicate 'control.'

[178] *Vide* the distinction between a contract of employment and a contract for independent work, in section I of this Chapter, *supra*.

[179] *Vide* the distinction between a contract of employment and a contract of agency, in Section I of this Chapter, *supra*.

[180] *Vide* El-Areef, p. 163; Habeeb, p. 194; and Badawi, K. M., p. 39, who adds that, if an advocate works in the office of another and under the latter's control, he would be a worker.

[181] This is deducible from *Kennedy v. Broun* (1863) 13 C.B.N.S., 677: "We consider

The difficulty of deciding the nature of the relationship arose with the said modern practice of employing advocates in establishments. The difficulty was further complicated by the part-time retainer of advocates, who usually carry out their duties in their own offices. This difficulty, which emanates from the nature of the advocate's work and the untraditional or unfamiliar notion of control of an advocate by another person, occasioned in the U.A.R. a juridical and judicial division of opinion, concerning the nature of the advocate's relationship with that other person. The majority opinion, both judicial and juridical, is in favour of holding that the relationship is a contract of employment relationship, if there is control by the employer over the advocate, as when the latter is employed permanently as a legal adviser of an establishment at a fixed salary.[182] The minority opinion seems to depend mainly on section 19 of the Advocates Law 98 of 1944, which does not permit the practice of the profession in Court by the advocate, while holding an office with a company or an individual employer.[183] The latter opinion, by reference to the said Law, puts a limit on but could not altogether reverse the majority opinion. It is submitted that, although it is generally difficult to ascertain control in the case of advocates, it is not impossible to do so. So, subject to such ascertainment, it is conceivable that an advocate can be a worker, provided that the provisions of the Advocates Law are not violated.[184]

... that the relation of counsel and client renders the parties mutually incapable of making any contract of hiring and service, concerning advocacy in litigation"; *vide* also Macdonell, p. 84; and Barwell and Kar, p. 33, who consider that a solicitor would be an independent contractor.

[182] *Vide* Cairo Court of Appeal in appeal No. 99 of 1959 (in El-Hawwari, p. 61): "The relationship between an advocate and another person is subject to the Labour Code, if legal and not necessarily technical control is present"; the same Court in appeal No. 923 of 1958 (in El-Fakahani, Book I, Vol. 1, p. 103), held that the Labour Code did not apply to the advocate when there was no notion of control – as also when the advocate carried out his duties in his own office; Cairo Labour Court in case No. 2626 of 1959 (Ibid. p. 51); *vide* also Murad, pp. 232–3, 176; El-Areef, pp. 163–4; Rashed and Hashem, p. 8, where they quote section 935 of the Draft Civil Code of 1948, as an authority to the same effect; El-Fakahani, Book I, Vol. 1, pp. 108–9; I.L.R., Vol. 31, 1935, p. 846: "...a doctor or lawyer can enter into such a contract of employment, if their work is to be performed in a subordinate relation."

[183] Cairo Court of Cassation in case No. 142 of 1956; and Cairo Court of Appeal in appeal No. 69 of 1959 (both in El-Fakahani, Book I, Vol. 1, p. 103 and 99, respectively), confirmed the said limitation by the Advocates Law, but ruled that this did not prevent an advocate from doing legal work as a legal adviser to a Company or any other employer, and from being bound to the employer by a contract of employment. However, the minority opinion persisted in spite of a later decision by the Cairo Court of Appeal in appeal No. 1429 of 1960, to the same effect as its 1959 decision.

[184] If control can thus be ascertained, one cannot see why an advocate should still be deprived of the protection, provided by the Labour Code and the other labour legislation.

In Sudan the Advocates Ordinance of September 1935,[185] does not place a restriction on advocates similar to that in the U.A.R. On the other hand, the determination of the nature of the relationship between a legal adviser and a company, has never been mooted; nor has it been very much mooted in England.[186] However, it is submitted that there is nothing in the Sudan Ordinance to prevent its application to an advocate, who is 'employed' as full-time legal adviser by a company or other employer.[187] But difficulties may arise in the case of regular part-time advisers, though the more probable view is that these would also be covered, if control forms an element in their contracts.

(iv) Journalists

It is clear that the criterion of control in the U.A.R. is the test of whether a journalist is a worker or an independent contractor.[188] The similar position in England and Sudan, is likewise clear.[189]

(v) Doctors

Both in the U.A.R. and in England and hence in Sudan, a doctor's relationship with his patient is that of independent work.[190] The difficulty arises, however, when a doctor is bound by a contract to work for an establishment. In the U.A.R. the weight of judicial authority leans strongly in favour of the application of the Labour Code to doctors, if they work for and are controlled by the said establishments.[191] There

[185] *The Laws of the Sudan*, Vol. 10, Title XXVI, Sub-Title 2.

[186] The decision quoted in footnote 181, *supra*, is on the traditional agency relationship between a client and a counsel, of which we have previously spoken.

[187] It is conceivable that an advocate can be a 'servant' in England, "even though the nominal control resting in the master, is made almost illusory by his lack of the particular skill involved": Cooper, pp. 6–7.

[188] The old decision of the Mixed Courts in May 1936 (reported in El-Areef, p. 164), to the effect that a journalist is an independent contractor, if he is "independent in his editing duties," need not bother us, because then control had not yet developed to embrace administrative control.

[189] *Vide* cases in Diamond, pp. 183, 282 and 283.

[190] For U.A.R., *vide* El-Areef, p. 162, who quotes French authorities to the same effect. For England, *vide* Cooper, p. 6: "a patient's contract with his doctor will rarely be a contract of service, for effective control cannot be asserted"; *vide* also Barwell and Kar, p. 33.

[191] *Vide* the High Court of Appeal on 19 April 1952 (in Badawi, K. M., p. 34); Alexandria Court of Appeal in appeal No. 97 of 1956 (in El-Fakahani, Book I, Vol. I, p. 111); Alexandria Court of Cassation in case No. 1326 of 1959 (in El-Hawwari, p. 68), both of which decided that the administrative control of the doctor is sufficient, and that his control need not be technical; in the Cairo Court of Appeal decision in appeal No. 1295 of 1955, it was held that there was no control in the contract of a doctor with his establishment, where only a certain general fee per patient was agreed upon. The Cairo Labour Court decision in case No. 1619 of 1955, which was contrary to all the above-quoted decisions, is of no serious concern, as it is of a minor Court, and does not seem to

does not seem to be a real division of opinion concerning doctors, as we saw concerning advocates.

In Sudan it is submitted that there is nothing in the Ordinance to prevent its application to doctors, if they are controlled by the persons who 'employ' them. This will not be very much affected by the difficulties, which arose in England in this respect, because those difficulties were vicarious liability difficulties.[192]

So both in the U.A.R. and Sudan, doctors can be workers, if they are controlled by their employers, though this seems to be more settled in the former than in the latter.

In both countries, however, nurses are always workers, if they are controlled by their employers.[193]

(vi) Company Directors

The law in the U.A.R. is clearly settled in favour of considering a company managing director as a worker, provided he is remunerated for his work, and is in the performance of his duties controlled by his company.[194] This is on the same lines of the law in France.[195]

In England "a director of a limited company is not its servant... His payment, unless made under some special provision, is in the nature of a gratuity."[196] However, a "director may at the same time also be employed as a servant."[197] So no contract of 'service' will be implied in the case of a company director. It is submitted that the Sudan definition of the 'employed person' would include a remunerated

have been followed. The position in the U.A.R., is similar to the position in France: *vide Duclos v. Sèbe* (1933), Dalloz Hebdom. – (in I.S.D.L., Vol. 9, 1935, p. 75). *Vide* also I.L.R. Vol. 31, 1935, p. 846.

[192] "And this difficulty of controlling professional service, is responsible for the problems which have been before the Courts in relation to doctors employed by or working in hospitals": Cooper, p. 6. The difficulties encountered in deciding the said vicarious liability arose in cases like *Hillyer's* case (1909) 2 K.B. 820, which was followed by more logical decisions in *Marshall's* case (1937) A.C., and *Cassidy's* case (1951) K.B. 343. *Vide* Diamond, p. 9; Batt, p. 10; and Barwell and Kar, p. 49, who state that resident doctors would if controlled, be 'servants,' but not the visiting doctors.

[193] Cairo Labour Court in case No. 1857 of 1953; and Abdeen District Court in case No. 90 of 1952 (both in El-Fakahani, Book I, Vol. 1, pp. 121 and 124, respectively). For England and Sudan, *Gold v. Essex County Council* (1942) 2 K.B. 293, finally settled the law; *vide* also Diamond, p. 3.

[194] *Vide* Murad, p. 233; and Habeeb, p. 195, who adds that the agency powers of a general manager of a Company, should not be mixed with his 'service' duties, even though both these powers and duties are provided for in his contract of employment; and he quotes other U.A.R. writers and some French decisions in support.

[195] *Vide Sociéte Secrestat v. Crozatier* (1926) – Receuil de la Gazette des Tribunaux, 1926, 1, 164 (in I.S.D.L., Vol. 2, 1926, p. 102).

[196] Smith, p. 126. The question seems to have been first mooted and decided in England, in *Dunston v. Imperial Gas Light Co.* (1881) 3 B & Ad.

[197] Diamond, p. 274.

managing director of a company, and that the doubt which arose in England would not arise in Sudan.[198]

On the other hand, both in the U.A.R. and Sudan, the position of a company director, who only attends the Board meetings a few times each year, and is remunerated either yearly or per attendance, would, it is submitted, be that of an independent contractor, contrary to what we have seen in the case of a managing director.

(vii) Commercial travellers,[199] *representatives,*[200] *local salesmen,*[201] *and other intermediaries*

Section 676(1) of the U.A.R. Civil Code provides that "the provisions concerning the contract of employment, shall apply to the employment relationships which exist between employers and local salesmen, commercial representatives, travellers,[202] insurance agents[203] and other intermediaries, even when they are remunerated by commission or

[198] This seems to have been appreciated also in India, where it was decided in *Sardar Gulab Singh v. Punjab Zemindari Bank Ltd.* (1940) A.I.R., Lahore, 243, that a managing director is the 'servant' of the Company. It is submitted that the contrary submission of Barwell and Kar (p. 58) on this case, is wrong.

[199] *Les Commision Voyageurs*, as they are called in France. The general definition of a commercial traveller is a person, who "travels on behalf of a commercial firm for the purpose of submitting the products of this firm to customers. He is remunerated in different ways, but the most general system is a fixed salary, a commission in proportion to his turnover, and the refund of his daily travelling expenses" (I.L.R., Vol. 32, 1936, p. 209). This definition is good for the U.A.R. and Sudan.

[200] *Les représentants de Commerce*, as they are called in France. A commercial representative is a person, whose work consists of visiting "the customers in a certain area, on behalf of one or more firms. He has to conform to the instructions given by the firm or the firm represented, and therefore, he does not act on his account. He is remunerated by a commission fixed in advance, and paid solely by the firm or firms which he represents" (*Ibid.*). *Vide* the similar definition in Habeeb, p. 58; and Butros and Rajab, pp. 74–75; *vide* a similar definition of a commercial representative in *Bellet v. Planque èsqualiés* (1933), Dalloz Hebdom., 1933, 2, 77 (in I.S.D.L., Vol. 9, p. 88). This definition is good for the U.A.R. and Sudan.

[201] A local salesman is a person, who "works in the town, where the firm or firms which he represents are situated. He is under the daily supervision of the firm which employs him, and is remunerated by a fixed salary and a percentage on his turnover. He is sometimes granted a travelling allowance. There are also local salesmen, who work solely on a commission basis" (I.L.R., Vol. 32, 1936, p. 210). This definition is good for the U.A.R. and Sudan.

[202] Zaki, p. 143, states that section 676 was directly copied from the French Law (section 29 K–Y, of Book I of the French Labour Code, introduced on July 18 in 1937); and submits that a mistake was committed in copying the section. The word 'and' was omitted between 'representatives' and 'travellers,' whereas the intention was to make the description 'commercial' applicable to both. His submission seems to be correct. The said French Law of 1937, seems to have adopted the previous trend of judicial authority (*Vide* the two French decisions of 1931 and 1936, quoted in footnote 127 to this Chapter, *supra*).

[203] A commercial agent is a person, who "usually has an office independent of the firm or factory of his employer. He is engaged on a contract and organises his tours as he pleases. He generally receives a fixed allowance for his office expenses, and a percentage on his turnover" (*Ibid.*, p. 209). This definition applies to an insurance agent.

they work for more than one employer at the same time, provided that they work under the orders and control of their employers." The necessity of this express provision in the Code, concerning their contractual relationships, arose from the greater independence they enjoy in the performance of their work, and the ostensible agency powers some of them exercise on behalf of their employers. So the element of control, if existing in their contracts, attracts them into the category of workers.[204] However, if they sometimes exercise the said ostensible powers, they do so as agents and not as workers.

In England and hence in Sudan, these persons with the exception of a commercial agent, are considered 'servants,' as long as they are controlled by their 'masters.'[205] However, a commercial agent, who is a person "who undertakes to produce a specified result, employing his own means,"[206] is not controlled in his work and cannot be a 'servant.' Control is the decisive test, and not that he is almost always remunerated only by commission.

So the law in the U.A.R. and Sudan is the same in this respect though it is more clear in the former than in the latter.

(viii) Artists

Both in U.A.R. and in England and hence in Sudan, theatrical and cinema actors are workers, if they are controlled by their employers,[207] otherwise they would be independent contractors. However, it goes without saying that in both countries a painter or a sculptor engaged by some one for the production of a particular piece of art, should be

[204] *Vide* the relevant decision of the Cairo Court of Cassation in case No. 1518/35 (commercial) of 1954; the Alexandria Court of Appeal in appeal No. 88 of 1955; and the Cairo Court of Appeal in appeal No. 1102 of 1955 (all in Habeeb, pp. 198–9). *Vide* I.L.R., Vol. 32, 1936, for the similar position of the law in Belgium (p. 225), in Switzerland (p. 498) and in Germany (p. 211). It is worthy of mention that section 2(1, i) of the Iraqi Labour Code, illogically excepts the persons under discussion, from the provisions of the Code.

[205] In *R. v. Negus* (1873) L.R. 2 C.C.R., 34, the prisoner who was employed to solicit orders, was held not to be a servant, because he had complete discretion as to how and when he would seek business, despite his covenant as to exclusive service; *vide* Samuels, p. 11; and Barwell and Kar, pp. 235–6.

[206] I.L.R., Vol. 32, 1936, p. 382.

[207] Whether employers of actors technically controlled their actors or not, was dismissed by the Courts in the U.A.R., as irrelevant, as administrative control was enough: Cairo Court of Cassation in case No. 2551 of 1953 (in Badawi, K. M., p. 38 – the author was a judge in the case); Cairo Labour Court in case No. 4716 of 1957 (in Habeeb, p. 179, who quotes the French Appeal decisions Nos. 125 of 1923 and 24 of 1927, Dalloz Hebdom., as authorities to the same effect); El-Areef, p. 164, where he says that singers who celebrate a wedding, are not workers as they are not controlled by their host. In England, *Armour v. British International Pictures* (1930) 23 B. 367, decided that a cinema actor, who was engaged as a member of a crowd, at one guinea per day, was not a 'servant'; *vide* also Batt, p. 359.

an independent contractor and not a worker, unless he is employed regularly and controlled in his work, like a doctor or an advocate, in which case he will be a worker.

(ix) Kerosine distributors[208]

Judicial opinion in the U.A.R. is divided on the nature of the contracts of these persons. The weight of authority leans in favour of considering these persons as workers, if they are controlled by their employers.[209] The other opinion tends to consider them as either tradesmen or independent contractors.[210] It is submitted that the division of opinion is not real, as it mainly rests on the Court's decision in the individual case, on whether there is control or not, and the difficulty which is sometimes met in reaching this decision. Some try to find further support for considering the kerosine distributors as workers, in Law 123 of 1944 (now superseded by Law 81 of 1955), which imposes upon these persons the obligation to apply for a worker's identity card.[211] It is a fact that these distributors were requested by the Ministry of Social Affairs (now the Ministry of Labour) to apply for the said cards. But this cannot be a ground of support as aforementioned, because the Ministry's request is legal or otherwise, according to whether the distributors are workers or not.

In Sudan it is submitted that the law is similar to that in the U.A.R.[212].

(x) Drivers

In the U.A.R. a car driver can be either a worker, a partner, a trader or a domestic servant[213]. The decision on whether he is one or the other, depends on the nature of his contract with the car-owner, or even the car-user on occasion.

[208] This category of persons has been the subject of much litigation in the U.A.R., but not in England. The reason is that house-to-house retail sale of kerosine, is still an important feature of everyday life in the U.A.R. These mobile distributors, with their motorised or horse drawn transport, should of course, not be mistaken for the petroleum salesmen in shops or depots. The latter are either tradesmen or independent contractors, but can sometimes be workers, if they are legally controlled in their work.

[209] *Vide* Bandar El-Geezah District Court in case No. 949 of 1949 (in El-Fakahani, Book I, Vol. 1, p. 247); Cairo Court of Cassation in case No. 3426 of 1949; and the Council of State in case No. 667 in 1950 (in Habeeb, p. 166); *vide* also Butros and Rajab, p. 9.

[210] *Vide* Cairo Arbitration Court in disputes Nos. 245 of 1953 and 57 of 1956 (in El-Fakahani, Book I, Vol. I., pp. 244 and 247, respectively); and Cairo Labour Court in case No. 6169 of 1959 (in El-Hawwari, p. 53).

[211] *Vide* The Council of State (*vide* footnote 209, *supra*); and Faheem, p. 7.

[212] Though it has not so far been mooted in Sudan, the problem may have to be faced at any time, because kerosine distributors in Sudan, are as much a feature of everyday life as they are in the U.A.R.

[213] Domestic servants, though they fulfil the definition of workers, are expressly excepted from the Labour Code, as we shall see later.

Where a driver works on another person's car (as a taxi), under the legal control of the latter, he is a worker, even though he is remunerated by a share in the profits.[214] If the driver carries out his work without control by the car-owner, and shares the profits and losses with the latter, the driver is a partner. If he just takes the possession of the car in return for some fixed payments to the car-owner, he is a trader. If he is the private driver of a certain car-owner, he is a domestic servant.[215] However, in the latter case, if the car-owner uses it in his business and not only for his domestic purposes, the better opinion is that the driver will be a worker or a domestic servant according to the major part of his duties.[216] Finally, if any person regularly engages a driver who drives his own car, the relationship between the said person and the driver may constitute either a contract of employment or a contract for independent work, according to whether the driver is under the control of the said person or not. The fact that the car is the driver's car is not decisive.[217]

In England and hence in Sudan, the law seems to be similar to that of the U.A.R., as to the driver being a worker, a partner or an independent contractor. However, where the U.A.R. law considers the driver just a trader, the English law considers the driver a bailee of the car.[218] Finally, where a driver was considered a domestic servant in the U.A.R. only by Court decision, the definition of the domestic servant in Sudan, in section 2 of the Domestic Servants Ordinance, as we shall see later, expressly includes the driver.

So the law in both countries concerning drivers, is not in any material respect different.

[214] *Vide* Cairo Court of Cassation in case No. 37 of 1954 (in Badawi, K. M., p. 35; *vide* also Butros and Rajab, p. 12; Faheem, p. 9; and El-Hawwari, p. 19); and *vide* Cairo Labour Court in case No. 7352 of 1954; and Cairo Court of Appeal in the appeal on dispute No. 67 of 1956 (both in El-Fakahani, Book I, Vol. I, pp. 212–3). This also is the French law: Dalloz Hebdom., 1935, p. 195 (in Hebeeb, p. 187, footnote 4). It is interesting to note that out of all the Labour Codes in the Arab Countries, only the Tunisian Code expressly mentions drivers, and provides that "a driver of a Public Transport car, whether for persons or goods, is a worker, if he does not own the car or the transport licence (section 4)." Such express provision is unnecessary and productive of ambiguity.

[215] *Vide* Cairo Labour Court in cases Nos. 2459 of 1955 and 1418 of 1956 (in El-Fakahani, Book I, Vol. 1. p. 214); and Alexandria Court of Appeal in appeal No. 271 of 1959 (in El-Hawwari, p. 50).

[216] Faheem, p. 15, is of the same opinion.

[217] *Vide* footnote 74, *supra*.

[218] *Vide Venables v. Smith* (1895) 2 Q.B.D. 279; *Smith v. General Motor Cab Co. Ltd.* (1911) A.C. 188. However, The London Hackney Carriages Act, 1843, and the Town Police Clauses Act, 1847 (for the Provinces), consider the said bailment relationship, as far as the public are concerned (i.e. for the vicarious liability purposes), to be a master and servant relationship (*Keen v. Henry* (1894) 1 Q.B. 292). But there are no such legal provisions in the U.A.R.

(xi) Shoe-makers

The prevalent practice in the big shoe-making industries in the U.A.R., of engaging craftsmen who work and are remunerated on a piece-work basis, with the craftsmen sometimes providing some of the materials and equipment necessary for the work, has occasioned some difficulties in the nature of their relationship with those who engage them. But from the review of the judicial decisions,[219] it is clear that the difficulty arose from the decision on whether there was control or not, by the employer over the craftsman, in the particular case. If there is such control, the craftsman is a worker; if not, he is either an independent contractor or sometimes a partner.

Neither in England nor in Sudan does the said U.A.R. practice seem to be prevalent. But if the problem arises in Sudan, the legal position would, it is submitted, be similar to that in the U.A.R.

Certain persons expressly excepted from the definition of the worker

Having discussed the above-mentioned eleven controversial categories of persons, we now discuss the other categories of persons, who though they fulfil the definition of the worker, were for one reason or another expressly excepted[220] from the provisions of either the Labour Code or of the Sudan Ordinance, by the legislator in the U.A.R.[221]

[219] *Vide* Cairo Court of Arbitration in dispute No. 12 of 1953 (in Badawi, K. M., p. 37), which was confirmed by the High Court of Appeal on 4 april 1957 (*vide* footnote 60 to this Chapter, *supra*); *vide* also Butros and Rajab, pp. 16–18.

[220] The U.A.R. Labour Code and the Sudan Ordinance and all the Labour Laws of of the rest of the Arab Countries except Tunisia, have adopted the method of express exception to the general application of their laws, instead of enumerating the categories to whom these are applicable: *vide* sections 4,5 and 88 of the U.A.R. Labour Code (*vide* Zaki, p. 78, where he emphasises the value of express exception), 2 of the Iraqi Labour Code (*vide* El-Sa'eed, pp. 14–15, where he also points to the express exclusion method), 2 of the Kuwaiti Labour Code, 12 of the Jordanian Labour Code, 7 of the Labour Code of Lebanon, 2 of the Saudi Arabian Regulations, 3 of the Sudan Ordinance, 4 of the the Bahraini Labour Code and 21 of the Adenese Ordinance. For the enumeration method in Tunisia, *vide* sections 1 to 5 (incl.) of the Tunisian Labour Code.

[221] Section 675 of the U.A.R. Civil Code provides: "(1) the provisions of this Chapter shall only apply in so far as they do not expressly or impliedly violate the provisions of the special Labour laws, (2) the said laws shall specify the categories of workers to which the provisions of this Code shall not apply." Subsection (2), it is submitted, was badly drafted. The real intention of the legislator was intended to give a superseding effect to "the special labour laws", in as far as the application of the provisions of these laws is concerned. But it was not to empower the said laws to except any contracts, which answer to the definition of the contract in section 674 of the Civil Code (which so far is the only definition reference for these laws), from being such contracts. The correctness of the submission is illustrated by the Labour Code (and its predecessor of 1952), which expressly limit the exception to the provisions of the Code itself, and says nothing about the Civil Code provisions in sections 674 to 698, especially sections 694 and 695, re reasonable notice of termination, and compensation for the unjustifiable termination, respectively (the two

and Sudan, respectively. As we shall see presently, not all these exceptions are common to the two countries.

(A) Casual workers

Section 88 of the U.A.R. Labour Code provides:

"The provisions of this Chapter[222] shall not apply to: (a) persons engaged in casual and temporary work which owing to its nature, does not come within the scope of the employer's business and does not last for more than six months."

From this provision, we see that three conditions must be fulfilled, so as to justify the exception: (i) the work must be casual[223] and temporary, (ii) not within the scope of the employer's business, and (iii) not lasting for more than six months. The second and third conditions are clear. But the qualification 'temporary' in the first condition is not only unnecessary, so long as the duration of the work is limited in the third condition, but is also misleading. It is believed that the word 'temporary' was added simply to emphasize the casual nature of the work, although the expression is unhappy.[224] As for the limitation of the duration of work to six months, some U.A.R. writers correctly believe that it was imposed in order to limit any misuse by the employers of the exception, and thus lessen the effect of any injustice that may result to the casual worker.[225] Other writers who believe in the 'profession' restriction on the employer,[226] maintain that the limitation of the duration of work to six months and not less, aims at giving just enough time to the employer to gain the experience which will enable

sections are quoted in Chapter VI, *infra*). The U.A.R. Courts and writers seem to have taken it for granted, that section 675 could not have the above-mentioned far-reaching effect (*vide* Bandar El-Zakazeek District Court on 3 October 1952, followed by Cairo Court of Cassation in cases Nos. 2275 of 1953 and 2735 of 1953 – both reported in El-Fakahani, Book I, Vol. 1, pp. 268–270); *vide* also Murad, p. 221. The Explanatory Note to the U.A.R. Civil Code, mentions that section 675 thereof, was taken from section 446 of the Polish Code (Habeeb, p. 243).

[222] i.e. Chapter II of Book II of the Labour Code, which regulates the individual contract of employment.

[223] The Arabic word for 'casual' is *Aradhi*, which means 'not liable to be repeated.' This was the meaning adopted by the Council of State and all the U.A.R. writers; *vide*, for instance, Murad, p. 218.

[224] Badawi, K. M., p. 41, discusses the casual and temporary qualifications of the work, as if they were synonyms; and so does the Council of State (*vide The Labour Laws*, a hand-book issued by the Ministry of Social Affairs in 1954, p. 348); El-Areef, p. 375, assumes that the qualification 'temporary' refers to the third condition without comment; and so does El-Fakahani, 1959, Supplement, p. 335; Naguib and Bakr, p. 198, correctly say: "If the work by its nature comes within the scope of the employer's business, it is not casual work but temporary work, which deserves the application of the Labour Law, like seasonal work."

[225] *Vide* Habeeb, p. 219.

[226] *Vide* Section II of this Chapter, *supra*.

him to control the worker.[227] Finally, seasonal workers[228] whose work may not last for more than six months, perform work which is within the scope of the employer's business and is not causual, as it is usually repeated every season.[229]

In Sudan section 3 of the Sudan Ordinance provides:

"The following are excepted from the provisions of this Ordinance: (a) persons whose employment is of a casual nature and who are employed otherwise than for the purposes of the employer's trade or business."[230]

So the fulfilment of two conditions is required by the exception: (i) the work must be casual, and (ii) not for the purposes of the employer's business. In the first condition 'casual' work has exactly the same meaning as it has in the U.A.R.,[231] but it is not qualified or 'emphasised' by the word 'temporary,' as it is in the U.A.R. Such qualification seems, however, to be necessary, in view of the lack af ony limitation of the duration of work, like the one we saw in the third condition in the U.A.R. But a specific limitation like the U.A.R. six-months limitation, would no doubt be better, as it would define the situation not only for the worker, but also for the Courts. The second condition in Sudan is much wider than the second condition in the U.A.R. It is submitted, however, that its interpretation should be narrow, so as to limit it to the scope of the employer's business, because an exception should not be interpreted widely.

[227] *Vide*, for instance, Butros and Rajab, p. 50.

[228] Seasonal workers were expressly mentioned to be entitled to the termination gratuity, in section 71 of the Labour Code (vide Chapter VII, *infra*). However, it is believed that such an express provision was not necessary, as such entitlement follows as a matter of course, from the application of the Labour Code to seasonal workers.

[229] Section 2(f) of the Iraqi Labour Code excepts both casual and seasonal workers (*vide* El-Sa'eed, p. 18, who without making any comment on the exception of the seasonal workers, curiously attributes the exception itself to the inability of the authorities to supervise the application of the Labour Code to these persons, during the 'unstable' period of the six months prescribed by the said section); section 2(d) of the Kuwaiti Labour Code provides for the exception, subject to the fulfilment of the first and third conditions in the U.A.R.; section 1(2) of the Saudi Regulations excepts those who perform 'petty work,' which does not last for more than one week. Jordan, Libya, Lebanon and Tunisia do not make an exception of casual workers.

[230] *Vide* the similar wording of the exception, in section 4(c) of the Bahraini Labour Code, except that the employer's business is qualified by the words: "which is not conducted for profit". So the Bahraini exception is narrower. The phraseology of the exception both in Sudan and Bahrain, seems to have been copied from the English Legislation (*vide* for instance, section 3 (2,b) of the Workmen's Compensation Act, 1925). The Adenese Ordinance does not except casual workers.

[231] "casual work" is defined in Webster's Third New International Dictionary, as work "performed without regularity or at random"; and the word 'occasional' (used by the English writers sometimes, vide Diamond, p. 273), is classified in the Dictionary, as a synonym for the word "casual."

On comparison of the exceptions in the two countries, the U.A.R. law emerges as better defined, and containing a logical limitation on the duration of the work, which is lacking in Sudan.[232]

(B) Dependent members of the employer's family

Section 88 of the U.A.R. Labour Code provides:

"The provisions of this Chapter[222] shall not apply to:

(b) members of the employer's family whom he actually supports."[233]

So the exception requires the fulfilment of two conditions: (i) the worker (though he is not expressly mentioned) should be a member of the employer's family,[234] and (ii) be actually supported in his living by the employer. In the second condition the section does not specify the meaning of either the word 'actually' or the word 'supported.' A difference of opinion has occurred on whether 'actually' would or would not cover support of the family-member by the employer, by order of the Court.[235] It is submitted that the words 'actual support' should, because the provision in which they are used is an exception, be inter-

[232] It is believed that the trend of labour legislation should, for the fulfilment of social justice, be to cover casual workers by labour legislation. The fear that too many obligations would as a result be placed on the employers of casual workers, is neither realistic nor serious, because the entitlements to leaves and to the termination gratuity, for instance, are restricted by certain conditions in the relevant legislation.

[233] The Labour Code does not define 'family.' However, section 34 of the Civil Code provides: (1) A person's family consists of his relatives, (2) Relatives are persons who have a common geneology." Section 35 thereof provides: "Distant relatives are persons who have a common geneology, but are not directly related as descendants of one another." Thus 'family' in the Labour Code, includes not only the members of the immediate family of the employer, but also his distant relatives with whom he shares a common geneology (*vide* Habeeb, pp. 221–2; Zaki, pp. 79–80; Habeeb, pp. 220–1; and Faheem, p. 12). However, the Explanatory Note to Law 317 of 1952, said: "Members of the family mean the ancestors and the descendants of the employer whom he actually supports." This is narrower than the Civil Code definition. It is submitted that, although an exception should be interpreted narrowly, thus justifying the acceptance of the Explanatory Note definition, this acceptance is not legally correct, because there is a wider express definition in the Civil Code (*vide*, however, Murad, p. 222, who maintains the contrary view).

[234] Section 2(c) of the Iraqi Labour Code provides for an exception, similar to that in the U.A.R.; section 7 of the Lebanese Labour Code, and section 1(2, b) of the Saudi Regulations, except the members of the immediate family of the employer, provided also that the employer's establishment does not employ any worker who is not such family member (this is in line with the international trends, as developed by the I.L.O.: vide Butros and Rajab, p. 53); sections 1(2, b) and 2 of the Jordanian and the Libyan Labour Codes, respectively, provide for the exception of "members of the family employed in family undertakings," without the proviso we saw in the Lebanese and Saudi exceptions; Kuwait and Tunisia do not contain exception provisions.

[235] Butros and Rajab, p. 52, and Habeeb, p. 221, are of the opinion that actual support should cover support by order of the Court; Badawi, K. M., pp. 198–9; and Faheem, p. 12, adopt the contrary view, because they maintain that 'compulsory support' would do away with the close and presupposedly voluntary relationship between the members of the same family, in which the legislator did not want to interfere.

preted narrowly, so as to only include compulsory support. On the other hand, whether the word 'supported' means totally or mainly or just partially supported, is not clear. But as long as there is no specification in the provision, the logical interpretation should be 'mainly supported,' for otherwise the exception would not be really justified.[236] To be sure, however, the family member concerned is not required to reside with the employer,[237] so as to be excepted under section 88(b).

Section 3 of the Sudan Ordinance provides:

"The following are excepted from the provisions of this Ordinance:

(c) members of the employer's family residing with him and wholly or mainly dependent upon him."[238]

So the exception requires the fulfilment of three conditions: (i) the worker should be a member of the employer's family, (ii) he should reside with the employer, and (iii) should be mainly dependent upon the employer for his living. Contrary to the U.A.R. Labour Code, the Sudan Ordinance provides a definition for family,[239] and plausibly qualifies the word 'dependent' by the words 'wholly or mainly,' though the latter qualification is quite sufficient. The definition of a 'dependant, in section 2 of the Sudan Ordinance, is of course intended for another purpose.[240] On the other hand, the residence requirement in the second condition, renders the scope of the exception in Sudan narrower than it is in the U.A.R.

So the exception in Sudan is both clearer and narrower than it is in the U.A.R.[241]

[236] However, Butros and Rajab, p. 52, without comment, take the word to mean 'totally supported.'

[237] Of this opinion also, are Habeeb, p. 220; Faheem, p. 12; and El-Fakahani, 1959 Supplement, p. 336.

[238] Section 4(d) of the Bahraini Labour Code provides for the exception in identical terms. The Adenese Ordinance does not contain a relevant provision.

[239] Section 2 of the Sudan Ordinance, defines 'member of the family,' as the "wife, husband, father, mother, grandfather, grandmother, son, daughter, grandson, granddaughter, brother, sister, half-brother, half-sister, and in the case of a non-Moslem, in addition, step-father, step-mother, step-son and step-daughter." This definition exludes distant relatives. Thus section 3(c) of the Sudan Ordinance is clearer than section 88(b) of the U.A.R. Labour Code. *Vide* in this respect, the Sudan case of *Shawgi Khalil Akasha v. Heirs of Khalil Akasha* (1958), AC-APP-34 (in the S.L.J.R., 1958, p. 67).

[240] Section 2 of the Sudan Ordinance defines dependants as "those members of the family of an employed person who are wholly or in part dependent upon his earnings." This definition is intended for the purpose of the entitlement of a deceased worker's 'dependants' to his wages and termination gratuity (refer to Chapter VII, *infra*).

[241] The Explanatory Note to the U.A.R. Labour Code, justifies the exception by saying: "Family relations are stronger than legal relations." The debate in the U.A.R. Senate in 1944, which preceded the passing of the law No. 41 (which enacted in section 2(c), the exception under discussion for the first time), ran along the lines that "these persons will, because of their family relations with their employers, be treated generously." These justifications were attacked by Murad, p. 221; Zaki, p. 80; Habeeb, p. 223;

(c) Domestic servants

Section 5 of the U.A.R. Labour Code provides:

"Save as may be stipulated,[241] this Code shall not apply to domestic servants and persons who belong to their class."

Neither the Labour Code nor any other Law in the U.A.R. defines a domestic servant. The Explanatory Note to Decree Law 317 of 1952 (which provided for a similar exception), tried to justify the exception, by saying that "the nature of the work they perform, is different from the nature of the work performed by the rest of the workers. Moreover, their work is so directly close to their employer, that they can know his secrets and private life, a fact which calls for the enactment of a special law." U.A.R. Courts and writers tried to deduce a definition of a domestic servant from these words of the Explanatory Note, and from the words 'and persons who belong to their class' in the said section 5 of the Labour Code.[243] The application of the *ejusdem generis*

and El-Fakahani, 1959 Supplement, pp. 336–7, all of whom advocate the repeal of the exception. The first two correctly point out that the excepted persons would still be workers under the provisions of the Civil Code (section 674); Butros and Rajab, p. 53, attack the exception as "unsuitable for our social conditions, exept in very rare cases," without discussing the exception. It is believed that the exception should be narrowed in the U.A.R., to its scope in Sudan, and that in the U.A.R., Sudan and the rest of the Arab countries, the exception should before long, be repealed altogether, as the law should not be justified in refraining from interference (and as a result, from the extension of the benefits), when it has not done so in the more personal relationships of husband and wife, and of parent and child. However, one exception should always be made in the case of a husband being employed by his wife, as the subordinate contract relationship would contradict with the marital authority of a husband over his wife, and thus be against public policy (*vide* Badawi, Z., Vol. I, p. 29 – only impliedly); section 61 of Book I of the French Labour Code – *vide* I. S. D. L., Vol. 10, 1934–5, p. 97 – provides to the same effect, and so does the French decision in *Pautrat v. Gallo* (1934) (in the same reference). Such contradiction with marital authority, is also clear under the Moslem Law.

[242] Such an express stipulation occurs in section 160 of the Labour Code, re right to form trade unions. But no stipulation was made in Chapter II, Book II, of the Code, regulating the individual contract of employment.

Section 2(1, b) of the Iraqi Labour Code contains a similar exception (section 901(2) of the Civil Code also excepts them and leaves them to 'custom'); and so does section 2(e) of the Kuwaiti Labour Code, and section 1(2, d) of the Jordanian Labour Code. Section 2(c) of the Libyan Labour Code simply excepts domestic servants, without the *ejusdem generis* provision in the U.A.R. Neither Saudi Arabia nor Tunisia seems to except domestic servants.

[243] Zaki, p. 62, says: "Domestic servants mean persons who perform work closely and directly connected with the person of the employer or of the members of his family, like the cook or the baby-nurse; or work closely but indirectly connected as aforementioned, like the private driver or the guardsman of the employer's house" (he deduced this definition from Cairo Court of Cassation decision in case No. 1072 of 1956 – reported in El-Fakahani, Book I, Vol. 1, p. 63); El-Areef, p. 142, defines them as "those who do work in private dwellings, by helping occupants in their domestic life, whether in their food or their clothing, or in other words, private dwellings workers" (his emphasis on the dwellings, derives from the Latin word *domus*); then he refers without commitment, to the French writers who advocate leaving the definition to 'custom.' However, as appears from the Court decisions to be mentioned presently, in the cases of porters, cooks etc...,

rule (which is limited to servant and not domestic) to such persons as porters or guardsmen,[244] club-servants,[245] cooks,[246] drivers[247] and gardeners,[248] was not without some difficulty; and has produced a host of legal decisions, most of which would not have been necessary but for the lack of a statutory definition for a domestic servant. The regrettable lack of a definition of a domestic servant in the Labour Code, and of protective labour legislation for domestic servants,[249] leaves the judicial and juridical battle raging in the U.A.R. This battle had eventually been opened on whether a domestic servant is limited

the Courts have on the whole, adopted the above-mentioned justification of the exception in the Explanatory Note, as a basis of the definition of the domestic servant. But the Council of State in an opinion rendered on 24 July 1957 (vide Habeeb, p. 235), did not accept the said justification *in toto*, as it rejected the criterion of secrecy and privacy, thus widening the scope of the exception.

244 A distinction was made by the Courts, between a porter or a guardsman in the private dwelling of the employer, and the porter in a commercial housing block. The latter was held by the majority of Court decisions, not to be a domestic servant (Cairo Labour Court in case No. 2768 of 1953; and Cairo Court of Cassation in case No. 214 of 1955 – these and other relevant decisions are reported in Habeeb, pp. 235, 237 and 239 – *vide* contrary decisions in El-Fakahani, Book I, Vol. I, pp. 71–91).

245 *Vide* Cairo Court of Cassation in case No. 1481 of 1954 (in El-Fakahani, Book I, Vol. I, p. 232); and Cairo Labour Court in case No. 1034 of 1958 (in El-Hawwari, p. 15). – Cf. with Cairo Court of Arbitration in dispute No. 4 of 1954 (in Fakahani, Book I, Vol. I, p. 233).

246 *Vide* Cairo Labour Court in case No. 5683 of 1954 (a private cook); and the same Court in case No. 3611 f 1955 (an assistant private cook) – both held to be domestic servants (in El-Fakahani, Book I, Vol. I, pp. 228–9); the same Court extended the exception to a cook in a school, in case No. 2320 of 1955 (*Ibid.*, p. 221). It is submitted that the last decision is wrong; *vide* also the same Court in recent decisions, similar to the above-mentioned first two decisions in cases Nos. 2717 of 1959 and 3655 of 1955 (both in El-Hawwari, pp. 47–8).

247 *Vide* Cairo Court of Cassation in case No. 1312 of 1955 (in El-Fakahani, Book I, Vol. I, p. 215: "a driver of a businessman is not a worker, unless his work is closely connected with the business of the employer"); *vide* footnotes 225 and 226, *supra*.

248 *Vide* Cairo Labour Court in case No. 3833 of 1954 (in El-Fakahani, Book I, Vol. I, p. 67); and the same Court in case No. 2863 of 1960 (in El-Hawwari, p. 51), both of which decided that a gardener in a private house, is a domestic servant. So a gardener in any place other than a private house, would not be a domestic servant.

249 The Domestic Servants Regulations of 8 November 1916 in the U.A.R., dealt only with their identity cards. In 1948, a Bill was drafted to provide protection for domestic servants. The Bill was passed by the House of Representatives, but it was not passed by the Senate. This was understandable, because the Senate was packed with *Pashas*, who employed the greatest number of domestic servants (*vide* Butros and Rajab, p. 67). The blocking influence of these *Pashas*, seems to have extended also to the Drafting Committee of the Civil Code of 1948. Section 938 of the Draft Civil Code of 1948, contains a provision to deprive domestic servants of even the thin protection of the Civil Code and to leave them to 'custom' (*vide* section 901(2) of the Iraqi Civil Code which enacts exactly what the said section 938 contains). But what is not understandable is that no law up to the present times, had been enacted for the prupose. The legislator curiously enough, found it fit to 'promise' in express terms, the enactment of such law in section 2(g) of Law 41 of 1944; and he reiterated the promise in the Explanatory Note to Decree Law 317 of 1952. So the regulation of the employment of domestic servants was and still is, in the major part, left to 'custom' (*vide* Rashed and Hashem, p. 8).

to manual work[250] or not, or whether a person would be a domestic servant or not, if in addition he performs work which clearly falls outside his domestic service.[251] It is submitted that, pending the enactment of special legislation on domestic servants, the said judicial and juridical battle should on all its fronts be fought with the aim of limiting rather than widening the scope of the exception in section 5 of the Labour Code.[252]

In Sudan section 3 of the Sudan Ordinance provides:

"The following are excepted from the provisions of this Ordinance: (b) domestic servants as defined by the Domestic Servants Ordinance[253] or any amendment thereof."[254]

Section 3 of the Domestic Servants Ordinance of 1955, defines a domestic servant, as "any person employed either wholly or partly as cook, house servant (including bedroom and kitchen servants), waiter, butler, nurse, valet, bar boy, footman, chauffeur or washerman, or in any capacity involving the duties usually performed by whatever title the person acting in such capacity may be styled, but does not include a person so employed by the Sudan Government or by a Local Government Authority or by any catering establishment carried on for gain, or by a club, boarding-house, school, hotel, canteen, hospital, nursing home, convalescent home or other establishment, providing accommodation for aged, sick, infirm or mentally unsound persons or any establishment similar to any of them." Although this purports to be a definition, yet it is no more than an enumeration of persons falling

[250] *Vide* Zaki, p. 62, who believes that a domestic servant's work should be limited to manual work, because custom does not usually treat 'employees' as domestic servants (he presumably depends on French jurisprudence, *vide* footnote 242, *supra*); of the same opinion are El-Areef, p. 143 (though only impliedly); Badawi, K.M., p. 63; and Faheem, p. 15. Butros and Rajab, pp. 65–6; and Habeeb, p. 241–2, are of the contrary opinion. They believe that the restriction of the domestic servant's work to manual work, is not legally warranted.

[251] *Vide* Murad, p. 140; Hebeeb, pp. 237–8; Badawi, K.M., p. 63; Naguib and Bakr, p. 27; and Faheem, p. 15 (who quotes Cairo Court of Cassation on 13 November, 1952, as an authority), believe that the benefit of the doubt should be given to the servant, and thus would consider him a worker. Butros and Rajab, p. 65, on the other hand, believe that if the extra work is trivial, the original work would be the determinant factor. If it is not, they advocate the double capacity, i.e. a person being a domestic servant and a worker, at the same time.

[252] Cairo Court of Cassation in case No. 229 of 1953 (in El-Fakahani, Book I, Vol. I, p. 63): "The widening of the exception is contrary to justice, in its widest sense."

[253] The Domestic Servants Ordinance of 1921 (now repealed by the Domestic Servants Ordinance of 15 May 1955 – in *The Laws of the Sudan*, Vol. 8, Title XXII, Sub-Title 3). This Ordinance affords to domestic servants in Sudan, the protection they lack in the U.A.R.

[254] Section 5(a) of the Bahraini Labour Code, partially excludes domestic servants from the Code. In Aden there does not seem to be any special enactment for domestic servants.

under the title domestic servant. All these persons, however, seem to have one thing in common, *viz.* that their service is of "a domestic nature as to require the servant to be frequently about his master's person, or as in the case of the gardener, about his grounds."[255] The similarity between this and the U.A.R. definition (deduced as aforementioned) is clear. Another thing these persons seem to have in common, is that their work is essentially manual rather than mental. This is emphasised by the express exclusion of a nurse from the definition of a domestic servant. Thus the law in this respect in Sudan is clearer than it is in the U.A.R. However, what strikes the eye in the said definition is the word 'partly.' This word presumably means 'part-time,' in contra-distinction to 'wholly' or 'whole-time.' This part-time provision no doubt attracts a greater number of persons into the definition of domestic servants, whether their part-time employment occupies a small portion or a big portion of their working time. However, this does not preclude the double capacity of a person being a worker and a domestic servant at the same time.

On comparison of the two exceptions in the U.A.R. and Sudan, the latter emerges as better defined and the former as more limited.[256]

(d) Government officials and workers

Section 4 of the U.A.R. Labour Code provides:

"Save as may be prescribed by Presidential Decree, this Code shall not apply to workers employed by the Government or by any public establishment or administrative unit having independent legal personality.

"The extension of this Code to all or any of such workers, shall be effected gradually, without prejudice to any rights or privileges enjoyed by them, and in respect of such districts, regions and sectors, as may be determined by a Presidential Decree, issued on the proposal of the

[255] *Erle, C. J.* of England, in *Nicoll v. Greaves* (1864) 17 C.B.N.S. 27. The distinction between menial and domestic servants in England (*vide* Cooper, p. 54), is not material in Sudan.

[256] *Vide* I.L.R., Vol. 30, 1934, for an interesting article in two parts (p. 190 and 336, respectively), entitled *The Social, Economic and Legal Conditions of Domestic Servants*, by Dr. Erna Magnus. The theme of the article is that "the main aim should be to extend the improvements made during the last few decades in the living and working conditions of all workers as far as possible, to domestic servants" (p. 363). This is all the more necessary, because "for domestic servants, the individual contract of employment is the rule". *Vide*, however, *Industry and Labour* (hereinafter called I. & L.), which used to be published by the I.L.O., Vol. VI, 1951, p. 373, for an interesting attempt to make a collective agreement for domestic servants in France.

Minister of Labour after agreement with the Minister of Finance."[257]

Public establishments having independent legal personality, include mainly all those establishments created by special Presidential Decrees, issued by virtue of Law 32 of 1957 and Laws 265 and 267 of 1960, and the nationalized enterprises.[258] Administrative units having independent legal personality, include governorships, towns and villages, endowed by the legislator with such personality.[259] Some establishments and units are borderline cases, and thus were the subject of litigation.[260] Where, however, a person falling within the exception in section 4 of the Labour Code, is seconded for part-time or full-time work with a private employer, his relationship with that employer had been held not to fall within the exception.[261] The law applicable to the excepted workers, is mainly Law 210 of 1951. This Law, being an administrative law, is based on the principle that the relationship of the Government with all its officials, employees and workers is not a contractual relationship, but a relationship deriving from the sovereignty of the State, which cannot be fettered by contractual obligations, if it is to preserve and promote the interests of the public. That of course is the reason why, under the said Law, leave for instance, is a privilege and not a right.[262]

[257] Section 5 of the Order promulgating the Labour Code, made a transitional exception for Syria, where Government workers were left to the provisions of the (repealed) Syrian Labour Code of 1946, by which they used to be covered. Section 2(1, h) of the Iraqi Labour Code only excepts Government civil and military officials and employees, whereas section 2(1, g) used, before its repeal by Law 71 of 1959, to except Government workers. Section 2(c) of the Kuwaiti Labour Code excepts workers who are protected by the 1955 special Labour Code for Government Workers. Section 7 of the Lebanese Labour Code excepts all Government employees and probation or daily-paid workmen, who not being covered by the Officials Regulations, would as a special measure, be delat with separately (*vide* Order No. 7of 15 February 1961, as such special measure. Summary thereof can be referred to in I. & L., Vol. 26, 1961, pp. 376–8). Section 1 of The Jordanian Labour Code excepts Government and municipal 'officials.' Section 3 of the Libyan Labour Code excepts Government 'workers,' if they are governed by special legislation. Saudi Arabia and Tunisia impliedly except all Government workers.

[258] For the different types of these establishments (public, economic and administrative), *vide* Zaki, pp. 49–55. Section 3 of Law 265 of 1960, empowers Economic Public Establishments to form subsidiary companies and own them exclusively. The said author (in p. 54) expresses his belief that workers of such companies do not fall under the exception in section 4 of the Labour Code. It is believed that he is correct, because such companies are legal persons separate from their owning companies. This also accords with a narrow interpretation of the said exception.

[259] *Ibid.*, p. 49.

[260] *Vide* El-Hawwari, pp. 22–46, for cases which decided that the following fell within the exception: The Co-operative Agricultural Loans Bank, the Military Factories, the General Administration of the Suez Canal, the Land Reclamation Office, the Petroleum General Administration, *Kasr-El-'Ayni* Public Hospital, The *Alazhar* University and the Public Transport Administration. The National Theatre, though supported by public funds, was however, held not to fall within the exception.

[261] *Vide* Cairo Court of Appeal in appeal No. 73 of 1959 (in El-Hawwari, p. 35).

[262] *Vide* the Council of State, in its opinion No. 903 dated 26 January 1957 (in Habeeb, p. 585); and Cairo Court of Cassation in case No. 1029 of 1958 (in El-Hawwari, p. 40).

Such then is the extent of the exception in U.A.R. The wide scope of the exception has even been felt by the legislator himself, as is clear from the wording of the exception.

In Sudan section 3 of the Sudan Ordinance provides:

"The following are excepted from the provisions of this Ordinance: (e) persons who hold posts in the first or second division of the Sudan Civil Service or who are subscribers to the Provident Fund created under the Government Provident Fund Ordinance."[263]

To be sure, those who hold posts in the First and Second divisions of the Sudan Civil Service, are only a minority of persons in the service of the Sudan Government. So the scope of the exception in Sudan is narrower than it is in the U.A.R. However, the very wide powers granted to the Council of Ministers by section 3(g) of the Sudan Ordinance,[264] leaves the limitation of the exception in section 3(e) in a precarious position. It is true that these powers have not been used so far, except in the Employers and Employed Persons Rules of 15 March 1949,[265] but there is no guarantee about their future use, especially if the present development of big enterprises in which the Government participates with a controlling interest, is taken into consideration. On the other hand, the total exclusion of the Provident Fund subscribers from the Ordinance is not understandable.[266] It has widened the scope of the exception unnecessarily. The law applicable to excepted persons in the service of the Government is contained, apart from post-service benefits enactments, in the Administrative Regulations of 1934 which

[263] The Government Provident Fund Ordinance of 1 July 1930, can be referred to in *The Laws of the Sudan*, Vol. 1, Title II, Sub-Title 2. The exception from the Bahraini Labour Code, is limited in section 4(a) to "members of the Bahraini State Police, or any other security force approved by the Government of Bahrain." The definition of the employer in section 3 (h) of the Bahraini Labour Code, includes the Government and any municipality, as is the case in Sudan. Section 21 of the Adenese Ordinance excepts all those in the Government military and civil service, from the Ordinance.

[264] Section 3(g) of the Sudan Ordinance excepts from its provisions, "any class of persons whom the Council of Ministers may by order declare not to be employed persons for the purposes of the Ordinance."

[265] These rules can be referred to in *The Laws of the Sudan*, Vol. 8, p. 136. They were issued by virtue of section 34 of the Sudan Ordinance. They except from the Ordinance, "members of the Government Police Force ,Prison Officers and Warders of the Government, and Officers and Officer Cadets, non-Commissioned Officers, men and enlisted boys of the Sudan Army".

[266] The main benefit granted by the Government Provident Fund Ordinance, which is more generous than its counterpart in the Sudan Ordinance, is the 'termination gratuity,' to which the subscriber would be entitled on the termination of his service. But the Government Provident Fund is no more than the more 'generous' provident fund opereated by any employer, as envisaged by section 27 of the Sudan Ordinance (*vide* Chapter VII, *infra*). This does not justify the exception of provident fund subscribers from the Sudan Ordinance, so as to make their leave a privilege and not a right, for instance.

are based on the same principle of the above-mentioned U.A.R. Law 210 of 1951.[267]

On comparison of the two exceptions, the Sudanese emerges as more limited though open to an easy executive extension of its scope, whereas the U.A.R. exception is much wider but containing an indication of the legislator's intention to limit its scope.[268]

(e) *Apprentices*

Section 37 of the U.A.R. Labour Code defines an apprentice, as "any person concluding a contract with an employer to work for him, for the purpose of learning an occupation or trade."[269] Whether the contract of the apprentice is a contract of employment or not, has hitherto been the subject of a great conflict of opinion in the U.A.R. Contrary to expectations, this conflict was not settled by the Labour Code. Opinion was and still is divided into three directions. The first opinion considers without reservation, that the apprenticeship contract is a contract of employment, whether or not the apprentice receives wages. It considers the training of the apprentice to be remuneration in kind, for the services he renders to the employer.[270] The second opinion takes the contrary

[267] For the legal position of Crown Servants in England, *vide* Batt, pp. 34–6; Smith, p. 40; and Halsbury, pp. 449 and 483. The position there seems to be that a Crown Servant holds his office 'not during good behaviour' (i.e. not by virtue of a contract with him binding on the Crown), but 'at the pleasure of the Crown.' This position was not very much affected by the Crown Proceedings Act 1947 (10 & 11 Geo. VI, C. 44), whose main effect was that "actions in contract, which formerly could only be pursued by petition of right upon the *Fiat* of His Majesty, may now be brought against the Crown as ordinary actions of contract." (Batt, p. 36)

[268] Though it is understandable that all Governments should be unfettered by the contract of employment obligations, in their relations with certain classes of officials, they cannot be justified in extending this prerogative to all or the majority of those in their service. Differentiation between 'workers' in the Government and 'workers' of private employers, may in many cases mean the unacceptable desire of a Government to abstain from carrying the financial burdens resulting from the Labour Code, while it expects the private employers to carry them.

[269] The Explanatory Note to the Labour Code, states that "this Chapter is new in the Egyptian Region and is on the lines of what was effective in the Syrian Region." The said Chapter is Chapter I of Book II of the Labour Code, comprising sections 37 ot 41 (both incl.).

[270] Of this opinion are El-Areef, p. 81; Badawi, Z., Vol. I., p. 43; Rashed and Hashem, p. 9; and Faheem, p. 5.

Section 971 of the Draft Civil Code of 1948, contains provisions giving priority to the regulatory effect of 'custom' on the apprenticeship contract, but otherwise applies the contract of employment provisions (Law 41 of 1944, at that time), to apprenticeship. This section was not adopted in the Civil Code. However, these provisions were adopted in section 926 of the Iraqi Civil Code. Section 1(2) of the Jordanian Labour Code expressly includes apprentices in the definition of a worker. Section 21 of the Kuwaiti Labour Code, section 6 of the Saudi Regulations, and section 9 of the Libyan Labour Code, seem to limit a contract of apprenticeship to minors. Section 20 of the Lebanese Labour Code expressly excludes apprentices.

view also without reservation, irrespective of any wages or remuneration received by the apprentice. It considers the contract of apprenticeship a contract *sui generis* "although it is in some respects, similar to a contract of employment, because the main purpose of the contract, as is clear from its definition, is the learning of a certain trade.... So the provisions of the Labour Code are not applicable thereto, except in so far as there is an express provision."[271] The third opinion considers that the training of the apprentice is not remuneration in kind, and as long as remuneration is an essential in the contract of employment, the apprentice has to receive some remuneration, if his contract is to be considered a contract of employment. If the said remuneration be low, the benefit of the doubt should be given to the apprentice, and his contract be considered that of employment.[272] It is submitted that of the said three opinions, the second is the correct legal opinion, for the following reasons: (i) The Labour Code treats apprenticeship and vocational training in a Chapter separate from that regulating the individual contract of employment. (ii) The Labour Code defines an apprentice separately, after it defines the worker in section 2. (iii) Section 38 which prescribes that the apprenticeship contract should be in writing, does not contain a provision similar to that in section 43, re permissibility of proof of an oral contract by the worker.[273] So the Apprenticeship contract is a formal contract, whereas the contract of employment is not. (iv) The duration of the apprenticeship contract is not in its entirety left to the consent of the parties, as it is made by section 39 subject to limitation by an Order from the Minister of Labour,[274] whereas the duration of the contract of employment is left to the consent of the parties. (v) While the apprentice may receive remuneration, he may sometimes

[271] *Vide* Murad, p. 239; and Zaki, p. 221. Sections 7 and 160 of the Labour Code, re exemption from judicial fees and formation of trade unions, respectively, make an express reference to apprentices. Section 2 of Law 92 of 1959, re social security, expressly includes apprentices. Another advocate of the second opinion for the same reasons, is Badawi, K. M., pp. 70–1, who, however, quotes Cairo Labour Court in case No. 5517 of 1953, as an authority for the distinction, between an apprenticehsip contract and that of a student with his school. Cairo Labour Court in case No. 4433 of 1955 (in Butros and Rajab, p. 26), also supports the second opinion, and in addition, justifies it by the injustice that may result to the employer from imposing upon him the financial burdens of the Labour Code, while his return from the apprentice does not balance with these burdens. Section 569 of the *Majallah* indicates that the Moslem Law is also of the said second opinion. As we shall see later, the English Common Law is of the same opinion.

[272] El-Fakahani, Book I, Vol. I, p. 30; Habeeb, pp. 263–4; and Butros and Rajab, p. 26. These authors, however, concede that when an apprenticeship contract is a contract of employment, it is not yet completely so, except on the termination of the apprenticeship period.

[273] Section 43 of the Labour Code is quoted and discussed in Chapter II, *infra*.

[274] Order 197 of 1959 was issued by virtue of section 39, to limit the duration of the contract and deal with the other matters mentioned in the section.

have to pay a premium, whereas a worker never pays a premium. This means that the receipt of remuneration by the apprentice, is not relevant to the nature of his contract. (vi) A contract of apprenticeship is under section 40, terminable by either party, by three days notice, whereas a contract of employment is under section 72, terminable by longer periods of notice. These reasons, which cannot be dismissed as mere indications or characteristics of another type of a contract of employment, do, it is believed, rather indicate the intention of the legislator to treat the apprenticeship contract as *sui generis*, quite distinct from a contract of employment.[275]

In Sudan section 2 of the Sudan Ordinance, after it defines the 'contract of service,' expressly excludes "contracts of apprenticeship under the Apprenticeship Ordinance."[276] So like the English Common Law,[277] and contrary to the U.A.R. Law, the Sudan Law in this respect is clear.[278]

[275] *Vide* I.L.R., Vol. 84, 1961, p. 478, for an interesting Article by Dr. M. El-Arabi, entitled *A Modern Apprenticeship Scheme in the United Arab Republic.* This Article in p. 483, says: "Since the apprentice was to be considered as a trainee rather than a worker, certain stipulations had to be included in the agreement in order to safeguard his interests". E. Herz, in an Article in the I.L.R., Vol. 31, 1935, p. 849, says: "contracts of apprenticeship and the like, may also be left out of consideration here, since they belong to general social policy as part of the problem of vocational training rather than to the special case of the contract of employment." The I.L.O. *Apprenticeship Recommendation* No. 60 of 1939 (which it is believed, was one of the references for drafting Order 197 of 1959 – *vide* footnote 274, *supra*) seems to indicate the treatment of the apprenticeship contract as *sui generis*.

[276] The Apprenticeship Ordinance of 21 June 1908 (in the *Laws of the Sudan*, Vol. 8, Title XXII, Sub-Title 2), does not, however, define an apprentice. Batt, p. 421, defines an apprentice as "one who is under contract to serve a master for the purpose of learning a trade, profession or calling, the consideration for his obligation of faithful, diligent and obedient service, being the promise or duty of the master to use his best endeavours to teach the apprentice" – Note the similarity between the first part of this definition, and the definition of the apprentice in section 37 of the U.A.R. Labour Code. Section 5 of the Apprenticeship Ordinance in Sudan, makes the contracting capacity of an apprentice sixteen years and upwards, whereas the capacity of an 'employed person' to enter a 'contract of service,' was set at fifteen years by section 2 of the Sudan Ordinance. Section 5(f) of the Bahraini Labour Code, partly excludes apprentices. Section 4 of the Adenese Ordinance, excludes apprentices, in terms similar to those in Sudan.

[277] "By a contract of apprenticeship, a person is bound to another for the purpose of learning a trade or calling, the apprentice undertaking to serve the master for the purpose of being taught, and the master undertaking to teach the apprentice. Where teaching on the part of the master, or learning on the part of the other person, is not the primary but only an incidental object, the contract is one of service rather than of apprenticeship." (Halsbury, Vol. 25, p. 451); *vide* Diamond, pp. 33–5 and 57; Cooper, pp. 22, 88 and 93; Samuels, pp. 1, 3 and 4–5; Batt, pp. 424, 426, 427 and 428; and Smith, pp. 33–4 (who emphasises that the test in England, is the intention of the parties). For India, *vide* Barwell and Kar, pp. 157–83.

[278] The lack of clarity in the U.A.R. is regrettable, as it may result in the deprivation of apprentices of the protection they need. On the other hand, though the Sudan law is clear, the Apprenticeship Ordinance is long outdated and should be replaced by a new law, providing apprentices with better protection.

(f) Agricultural workers

Agricultural workers in the U.A.R. were expressly excluded from Law 41 of 1944 (section 2), even though they operated mechanical agricultural appliances and devices.[279] Section 937 of the Draft Civil Code contained a provision to exclude them from the contract of employment provisions and to leave them to custom. But the section was not adopted[280] in the Civil Code of 1948. So their contracts were covered by the Civil Code, though not by the said Law 41. Then Decree Law 317 of 1952, which superseded Law 41 of 1944, for the first time, covered agricultural workers. Decree Laws 318 and 319 of 1952, re Trade Unions and Conciliation and Arbitration, respectively, also covered them. Finally, the Labour Code of 1959 was enacted, without any exclusion of agricultural workers.[281]

In Sudan section 3 of the Sudan Ordinance provides:

"The following are excepted from the provisions of this Ordinance: (d) persons employed in agricultural undertakings, other than persons employed in the operation, repair or maintenance of mechanical appliances or devices, and other than persons employed in factories ginneries, dairies and similar establishments in which agricultural produce is processed or adapted for marketing."[282] However, a further saving from the exception may be deduced from section 5(b) of the Sudan Ordinance.[283]

Comparison of the two positions in the U.A.R. and Sudan, reveals that at least some of the agricultural workers in Sudan were covered

[279] Refer to Part I, *supra*.

[280] Section 901(1) of the Iraqi Civil Code, however, contains provisions similar to section 937 of the U.A.R. Draft Civil Code of 1948. The power of land-owners seems to have been stronger in Iraq than in the U.A.R., at that time.

[281] Section 13 of the Presidential Order promulgating the Labour Code, makes the Code applicable to "agricultural workers in the Syrian Region, in all matters not covered by (the Syrian) Law No. 134 of 1958, concerning agricultural employment relationships in the Syrian Region." The Kuwaiti Labour Code does not exclude agricultural workers. Section 1 of the Saudi Regulations expressly applies the Regulations to them. Section 2(1, a) of the Iraqi Labour Code excludes them, unless they operate mechanical agricultural appliances, or they receive cash remuneration (by virtue of Law 82 of 1958). Section 2(b) of the Libyan Labour Code excludes them, unless they work in establishments which partially or totally manufacture their agricultural produce, or they operate or maintain mechanical agricultural appliances. Sections 1(2, c) and 7(2), of the Jordanian and Lebanese Labour Codes, respectively, expressly exclude agricultural workers.

[282] Section 5(b) of the Bahraini Labour Code excepts "persons employed in agriculture, other than persons employed in the operation, repair and maintenance of mechanical appliances and devices." Note the similarity between the rest of the Sudan saving from the exception, and section 2(b) of the Libyan Labour Code (in footnote 281, *supra*).

[283] Sections 4 and 5 of the Sudan Ordinance are quoted and discussed in Chapter II, *infra*. The wording of section 5(b) of the Sudan Ordinance was copied from Article 2(1, b) of the *Contracts of Employment (Indigenous Workers) Convention* No. 86 of 1947.

by the Sudan Ordinance, four years earlier than any agricultural worker in the U.A.R. was covered by the labour legislation. However, the present commendable coverage in the U.A.R. is complete, while the Sudanese is still partial.

(g) Maritime workers

In the U.A.R. the contracts of masters and officers of ships were regulated as early as 1882, by Chapter V of the Merchant Shipping Act of 13 November 1882. This early and independent regulation of their contracts occasioned their exclusion from the Labour Law regulatory provisions, right from the start. Section 2(e) of Law 41 of 1944, which enacted such labour law regulatory provisions for the first time, expressly excluded the masters, engineers and officers of ships from the said Law. Thus the other members of the crew, who were in the lower ranks, were not excepted. Section 1(d) of Decree Law 317 of 1952, then excluded the said lower ranks from the Decree. The Explanatory Note to the said Decree said that all the above-mentioned, high or low in the ranks, were regulated by the Merchant Shipping Act of 1882. However, the exception never applied to inland water-transport workers, workers in ports or ship-building docks or to air-transport workers, because the 1882 Merchant Shipping Act did not apply to them.[284] Section 88(c) of the Labour Code provides for the exclusion of maritime workers,[285] in terms identical with those of the said section 1(d) of Law 317 of 1952. Finally, Law No. 158 of 1959 was enacted,[286] to regulate the contracts of employment of sea-farers, who work in ships of over five hundred gross registered tons, and in ships of 150 to 500 tons, if the Minister of War after consultation with the Minister of Labour, by an Order so decides. Thus the contracts of sea-farers in ships of less than 150 gross registered tons, and in ships of 150 to 500 tons (if the Minister of War does not decide as aforementioned) continue to be regulated by the 1882 Merchant Shipping Act.[287] However, the said Law 158 of 1959 leaves an avenue for the application of the

[284] *Vide* Cairo Court of Appeal in appeal No. 494 of 1955 (in El-Fakahani, Book I, Vol. I, p. 174); and *vide* Murad, p. 218.

[285] The Labour Codes in Iraq, Kuwait, Jordan and the Lebanon, do not except Maritime workers. Section 1(1, d) of the Saudi Regulations expressly covers maritime workers; and so does section 2 of the Tunisian Labour Code. Section 2(d) of the Libyan Labour Code excepts them, as "they are regulated by the Libyan Merchant Shipping Act or any other special Law."

[286] *Al-Jaridat-ul-Rasmiyyatu*, No. 158 (bis), dated 20 June 1959 (in Arabic), *vide* the reference thereto in I. & L., Vol. 23, 1960, p. 282.

[287] *Vide Al-Waseet Fi 'Akd El 'Amal El-Fardi*, by Sabbour, F. A., 1961, Cairo, in Arabic (hereinafter referred to as Sabbour), p. 570.

Civil Code and the Labour Code, as long as such application does not violate its own provisions (section 6). So those whose contracts are still regulated by the Merchant Shipping Act of 1882, can now benefit from the Civil Code and the Labour Code, so long as this does not violate the provisions of the 1882 Act. This means that the exception in section 88(c) of the Labour Code is somewhat narrowed, both in respect of those covered by Law 158 of 1959, and those still covered by the Merchant Shipping Act of 1882.

In Sudan the Sudan Ordinance does not except maritime workers. The proviso to section 14(2) of the Sudan Ordinance,[288] re periodicity of payment of wages, further emphasises the coverage of maritime workers by the Sudan Ordinance.[289] This is in line with the English Common Law.

So the contracts of maritime workers were covered by labour legislation in Sudan, earlier than they were covered in the U.A.R. However, the latter has a special law for maritime workers;[290] but the former has none.

(h) Other workers

In the U.A.R. there are no other categories of workers excluded from the Labour Code.[291]

In Sudan section 3(g) of the Sudan Ordinance empowers the Council of Ministers to declare by order, any class of persons "not to be employed persons for the purposes of this Ordinance."[292]

So the U.A.R. Law in this respect is more certain than it is in Sudan.

SUMMARY

The Labour Code in the U.A.R. does not expressly define the con-

[288] Section 14 is quoted and discussed in Chapter IV, *infra*.

[289] There is no maritime shipping legislation in Sudan. The writer has, however, taken part in the preparatory work for the enactment of such legislation, while serving as a Legal Counsel in the Ministry of Justice in Sudan. Section 5(d) of the Bahraini Labour Code expressly covers maritime workers. Section 21 of the Adenese Ordinance excludes seamen, who are covered by the "Merchant Shipping legislation in force in the Colony."

[290] This Law (Law 158 of 1959) does not grant to maritime workers any termination gratuity, whereas the Sudan Ordinance grants it to them. *Vide*, however, Sabbour, p. 572, where he submits that maritime workers in the U.A.R., would be entitled to the said gratuity, under the Labour Code.

[291] In Iraq, section 2(1, e) of the Labour Code excludes persons who work in workshops, where no mechanical power is used, and less than five persons are employed; and so does section 2(f) of the Kuwaiti Labour Code. Section 2(1, i) of the Iraqi Labour Code also excludes those whose remuneration consists of a share in the profits, or a percentage in the products or in sale or in tips (*vide* footnote 204 to this Chapter, *supra*). Sections 1(2, c) and 2(b) of the Jordan and Libyan Labour Codes, respectively, exclude shepherds. Section 1(2, c) of the Saudi Regulations excludes "compulsory work prescribed by law, for the benefit of the society."

[292] The uncommendable effect of this empowering provision, was pointed out in category (D), *supra*.

tract of employment, though a definition can be deduced from section 42 of the Code. The express definition of the contract in the Sudan Ordinance is not sufficient, as the essential element of control is not clear therein. So both in the U.A.R. and Sudan, reference to the Civil Law is necessary, when a definition of the contract is sought. In the former the reference is the Civil Code of 1948, and in the latter it is the English Common Law.

The worker's undertaking to work and the employer's undertaking to pay remuneration are in both countries, the respective obligations of the two parties to the contract.

Control as the essential element of the contract of employment, consists in the U.A.R. of the employer's power to give orders to the worker concerning the performance of the work by the latter, and the employer's power to take disciplinary measures against the worker, if he disobeys these orders. In Sudan control consists only of the power to give the said orders. The employer's power to take disciplinary measures in Sudan can only be exercised when the contract expressly authorises the employer to exercise them.

The contracting freedom is wider in Sudan than it is in the U.A.R., where more comprehensive legislation regulates this freedom.

The distinction between the contract of employment and the related contracts of independent work, agency and partnership, lies both in the U.A.R. and Sudan, in the employer's power of control.

The definition of the employer in Sudan is wider than it is in the U.A.R., as in the latter only natural or legal persons can be employers, whereas in the former unincorporated bodies of persons can also be employers. Moreover, an unsuccessful attempt at narrowing the scope of the definition of the employer, had been made in the U.A.R., by the imposition of the profession restriction on the employer. In Sudan no such attempt was made.

Neither in the U.A.R. nor in Sudan is a distinction made between a 'workman' and an 'employee,' in the definition of a worker. The controversial categories of persons who may or may not be workers, are more numerous in the U.A.R. than in Sudan. The law in this respect is generally clearer and more apprehensible in the former than in the latter.

Finally, the categories of persons excepted from the Labour Code in the U.A.R., are less than those excepted from the Sudan Ordinance. However, the excepted category of Government workers in the U.A.R. outweighs the more numerous excepted categories in Sudan.

CHAPTER II

FORMATION OF THE CONTRACT OF EMPLOYMENT

SECTION I: CAPACITY AND CONSENT OF THE PARTIES

Like other civil contracts, the contract of employment in the U.A.R. and Sudan is a consensual contract,[1] or in other words, the contract cannot be valid without the legal consent of the two parties to the contract. A valid consent presupposes that both parties are with respect to age and their mental state, capable of consenting or have a contracting capacity, on the one hand, and that there is no vitiating element like mistake, misrepresentation, fraud, coercion or undue influence, on the other hand. The non-fulfilment of one or the other of these prerequisites renders the contract voidable or void, as the case may be. Furthermore, the subject-matter of the contract must be legal and capable of performance, for otherwise the contract will be null and void.

Consent in the contract of employment is in the U.A.R. more important than in the other civil contracts. While in the latter contracts the specification of the respective rights and duties of both parties is usually necessary for the validity of the contract in addition to consent, consent on the whole is sufficient to form a valid contract of employment, "because the legislator has in the absence of specific agreement, undertaken to specify the obligations of both parties."[2] The position in Sudan is otherwise, as section 7 of the Sudan Ordinance prescribes that "every written contract shall contain in clear and unambiguous terms all that may be necessary to define the rights and obligations of the parties thereto"; and the section further proceeds to itemise what should be specified in an attested contract.[3] The reason for this different position in Sudan lies, it is believed, in the lack of comprehensiveness, which is quite distinguishable in the U.A.R. Labour Code, and in the weak development of work-rules and the general lack of collective agreements.

[1] Refer to Section I of Chapter I, *supra*, for a discussion on the consensual nature of the contract, in the U.A.R. and Sudan.

[2] Zaki, p. 220; *vide* also Habeeb, p. 254; and Badawi., Z., Vol. I, p. 48

[3] The whole section is quoted in Chapter III, *infra*.

The full contracting capacity of both parties in the U.A.R. is set at twenty-one years, by section 44 of the U.A.R. Civil Code. As minors were excluded from the scope of this study,[4] it is not proposed to deal with the provisions of Law No. 119 of 1952, concerning the capacity of those under twenty-one years, to enter into contracts of employment, whether as employers or as workers. In Sudan the full contracting capacity is also set at twenty-one years, by reference to the English Common Law.[5] The definition of the 'employed person' or worker in section 2 of the Sudan Ordinance, commences with the words "any person not under the age of fifteen years." But the capacity of workers between the age of fifteen years and the majority age of twenty-one years, also falls under the exclusion of minors.[4]

The law in the U.A.R., concerning the capacity of a corporation, i.e. a body of persons having legal personality, to enter into contracts of employment as an employer, is similar to the law in Sudan. In both countries these corporations can enter contracts as employers. Unincorporated bodies, however, can enter contracts as employers in Sudan, as was previously pointed out,[6] whereas in the U.A.R. they cannot.

Finally, categories of persons expressly excluded from the provisions of the U.A.R. Labour Code and the Sudan Ordinance,[7] are not by operation of the law, capable of entering into contracts of employment as workers, though they have a full contracting capacity under the civil law to enter other civil contracts.

SECTION II: FORM OF THE CONTRACT

Section 677 of the U.A.R. Civil Code provides that "the contract of employment shall not be required to be in any special form, save as otherwise provided by administrative laws and regulations."[8] So under the Civil Code, the contract of employment is an informal contract.[9] Section 43 of the U.A.R. Labour Code provides that "the contract of employment shall be made in writing in Arabic and in duplicate one copy for each party and if the contract is not in writing only the worker

[4] Refer to the Preface, *supra*.
[5] *Vide* Diamond, p. 39.
[6] Refer to Section II of Chapter I, *supra*.
[7] Refer to section III of Chapter I, *supra*.
[8] It is submitted that the use of the word 'administrative' in the section, is wrong. The intent might be 'special.'
[9] Cairo Court of Appeal in appeal No. 676 of 1960 (in El-Hawwari, p. 64), is to the same effect.

shall be entitled to establish his rights by all the means of proof."[10] Thus the Labour Code stopped short of changing the informal nature of the contract, for whose validity writing is not essential.[11]

The definition of the contract of service in section 2 of the Sudan Ordinance, commences with the words "any contract, whether written or oral, expressed or implied."[12] From these words, it is clear that the contract of employment in Sudan is not a formal contract. This informal nature of the contract is not affected by section 4 of the Sudan Ordinance,[13] as this section concerns the actionability and not the

[10] Similar provisions are contained in sections 15(5) and 10(3) of the Jordanian and Libyan Labour Codes, respectively. Sections 12, 1(a), 12, 2(7), and 7 of the Lebanese, Iraqi, Kuwaiti, Qatari and Tunisian Labour Codes, respectively, and section 1(3) of the Saudi Regulations, provide expressly that the contract may be oral or in writing; and so does section 436 of the *Majallah*. Section 3 of Law No. 41 of 1944 in the U.A.R., provided that the contract could be oral if the worker's wages did not exceed ten U.A.R. pounds per month; otherwise the contract had to be in writing; and the section did not contain any provision favourable to the worker, similar to that in section 43 of the 1959 Labour Code.

[11] *Vide* Murad, p. 268; Habeeb, p. 299: "An oral contract of employment is a valid contract"; Sabbour, p. 123: "Writing is not a condition for the valid formation of the contract of employment, but is only necessary for its proof"; *vide* also Butros and Rajab, pp. 28–29; El-Areef, p. 377; Rashed and Hashem. p. 11; and El-Fakahani, Book I, Vol. I, p. 9.

[12] The definition is fully quoted in Section I of Chapter I, *supra*.

[13] Section 4 of the Sudan Ordinance provides:

"(1) No action shall be brought upon any contract of service which is not to be completed within the space of six months from the making thereof unless the said contract or a sufficient memorandum thereof is in writing and signed, sealed or thumbed by the parties thereto or their agents in that behalf.

"(2) No action shall be brought by any employer upon any contract of service whereby an employed person is engaged:

(a) for employment within the Province in which he is engaged under conditions of employment which differ materially from those customary in the said Province for similar work, or

(b) for employment outside the Province in which he is engaged for a period exceeding seven days:

unless the said contract or a sufficient memorandum thereof is in writing and signed, sealed or thumbed by the employed person or his agent in that behalf."

Section 5 of the Sudan Ordinance empowers the Council of Ministers to exclude from the provisions of section 4, contracts of workers employed by an employer who employs no more than five workers, or when remuneration consists solely of the occupancy or use of land belonging to the employer. The Schedule to the Employers and Employed Persons Rules of 15 March 1949 (in the *Laws of the Sudan*, Vol. 8, pp. 136–7), contains a model form for a written contract of service.

Section 4 of the Sudan Ordinance seems to have been inspired by Aritcle 3 of the I.L.O. Convention 64 of 1939, concerning the *Regulation of Written Contracts of Employment of Indigenous Workers*. Article 3 provides:

"1. When a contract to which the Convention applies: (a) is made for a period of or exceeding six months or a number of working days equivalent to six months, or (b) stipulates conditions of employment which differ materially from those customary in the district of employment for similar work, the contract shall be made in writing."

Section 5 of the Adenese Ordinance is a copy of the said Article 3. Section 6 of the Bahraini Labour Code, which provides that "a contract of service may be written or validity of the contract.[14] On the other hand, section 4 permits the contract which is to be completed within the space of six months from the making thereof, to be oral.

As the contract in the U.A.R. and Sudan is not a formal contract, the value of writing is limited to the proof of the contract. Though evidential matters fall outside the scope of this study, the following remarks thereon seem to be necessary, as they assist in the appreciation of other relevant matters.

In the U.A.R. writing is prescribed by section 43 of the Labour Code, as the means of proof by the employer and not the worker, because the worker is thereby allowed to prove the contract by whatever means of proof he can avail himself of.[15] However, section 44 of the Labour Code, which provides that "the period of probation shall be fixed in

oral, expressed or implied," makes the writing of the contract optional at the request of the employed person, without reference to the duration of the contract.

Section 4 of the English Statute of Frauds of 1677 (repealed by the Law Reform (Enforcement of Contracts) Act, 1954), whose principles presumably applied in Sudan, before the enactment of the Sudan Ordinance, facilitated the reception of the above mentioned I.L.O. Convention. Section 4 provided that "no action shall be brought... upon any agreement that is not to be performed within the space of one year from the making thereof, unless the agreement upon which such action shall be brought or some memorandum or note thereof, shall be in writing and signed by the party to be charged therewith or some other person thereunto by him lawfully authorised."

[14] The same conclusion had been reached, on the effect of section 4 of the English Statute of Frauds. "This enactment," says Smith, p. 17, "does not render illegal or void a parol contract which does not comply with the requirements of the section. It deals merely with the evidence by which the plaintiff's cause of action on the contract is supported... Though an action cannot be brought upon the contract, it still exists." *Vide* also Cheshire and Fifoot, p. 164; and Batt, pp. 46–48.

[15] The reason for this so-called favouritism to the worker in the U.A.R., lies in the appreciation by the legislator, of the weaker position of the worker. Y. A. Sayigh, in his Article entitled *Management Labour Relations in Selected Arab Countries: Major Aspects and Determinants* (in I.L.R., Vol. 77, 1958, p. 523), correctly observes what is applicable to all the Arab countries, when he says: "Some form of verbal contract is more often drawn up between the two parties, but this is usually a form that binds the employee and leaves the employer free to act as he sees fit." For further enlightenment on the written form of the contract of employment, *vide* I.L.R., Vol. 31, 1935, pp. 854–6, and Vol. 32, 1936, p. 494.

It is generally true that, if the contract is not written, the omission is by the employer, as the worker is in most cases, not in a position to insist on a written contract, when he is about to secure his main, if not his only means of sustenance. Refusal by the employer to make a written contract, is punishable under section 221 of the Labour Code. Refusal by the worker to sign a written contract at the commencement of employment, does not present any problem, because the employer is in a position to refuse to employ him. However, the problem may arise when the contract is oral at the commencement of the employment, and the employer later on reduces it into writing, but the worker refuses to sign it. In this rare case, if the employer dismisses the worker, his dismissal will not be unjustifiable (*vide* to this effect, Cairo Labour Court in case. No 7120 of 1954, in El-Fakahani, Book I, Vol. I, p. 615). If the employer does not dismiss the worker because he needs his services, it is submitted that he can bring pressure upon him, by having him tried and punished under section 221 of the Labour Code.

the contract of employment," has occasioned some difficulty. Some writers, supported by some Court decisions, maintain that as a means of proof of the probation period, writing is not only necessary for the employer, but also for the worker.[16] It is submitted that section 44 does not affect the law as it is laid down in section 43. The word 'fixed' does not exclusively mean 'fixed in writing.' A probation clause in the contract is not more essential than the remuneration clause, and if the latter is subject to section 43, the former should likewise be subject thereto. So a probation clause, like any other, has to be in writing, in as far as proof by the employer is concerned,[17] whereas it can be oral and the worker can prove it by any means of proof, if he ever needs to.

In Sudan the two parties stand on equal footing, in respect of the necessity of writing as a means of proof of the contract. This is clear from the above-quoted provisions of the section 4(1) of the Sudan Ordinance. It is further clear from the provisions of sections 6, 7, 8 and 9 of the Sudan Ordinance, concerning the attestation of contracts.[18] However, section 4(2) affords two examples where signature by the worker is necessary, though the contract duration is less than six months. So in these two cases the two parties do not stand on equal footing. Failure to comply with sections 4, 5 and 6, renders the contract unenforceable, if the parties do not agree on its enforceability. But failure to comply with sections 7 and 8, renders the penalty under sections 36 of the Sudan Ordinance, operative.

If the contract is in writing, it has to be in Arabic in the U.A.R., by

[16] *Vide* Badawi, K. M., p. 87; Faheem, p. 23; El-Fakahani, 1959 Supplement, p. 129; and Butros and Rajab, p. 33. *Vide* also Cairo Court of Appeal in appeal 671 of 1954; and Cairo Labour Court in case No. 530 of 1956 (both in El-Fakahani, Book I, Vol. I, pp. 301 and 300, respectively). Of the contrary opinion is Badawi, Z., vol. I, p. 42; and Faheem, p. 23.

[17] *Vide* Cairo Labour Court in case No. 2020 of 1954 (in Habeeb, p. 271); and the same Court in case No. 3598 (in El-Fakahani, Book I, Vol. I, p. 397); *vide* also Rashed and Hashem, p. 13.

[18] Section 6 of the Sudan Ordinance provides:

"(1) No written contract of service shall be enforceable against any party thereto who at the time of making such contract was unable to read and understand the language in which it is written, unless it bears an attestation under the hand of a responsible person to the effect that such contract was read over and explained to such party in the presence of such responsible person and was entered into by him voluntarily and with full understanding of its meaning and effect.

(2) (Definition of the 'responsible person')."

This section seems to have been inspired by Article 6 of the I.L.O. Convention No. 64 of 1939. Section 8 of the Adenese Ordinance is an identical copy of the said article.

Section 7 of the Sudan Ordinance (quoted in Chapter III), prescribes the contents of the attested contract. Section 8 permits a single attestation for more than one contract, when these contracts bind workers by the same terms, with one and the same employer. Section 9 prescribes that an attested contract be in three copies, the first for the employer, the second for the worker and the third for the Labour Officer, to be submitted to him by the employer.

virtue of section 43 of the Labour Code.[19] The making of the contract in other languages, side by side with the Arabic text, is presumably allowed. But the exclusive use of a language other than the Arabic, is punishable under section 221 of the Labour Code, though this does not render the contract invalid.[20] As the rendering of the contract in Arabic after the infringement, is mandatory by virtue of section 43, the worker cannot disclaim it.[20] In Sudan there is no provision as to the language of the contract.[21]

SECTION III: DURATION AND RENEWAL OF THE CONTRACT

Duration of the contract

Section 678(1) of the U.A.R. Labour Code provides that "the contract of employment may be made for specific work, or for a definite or an indefinite period of time."[22] The definition of the contract in section 2 of the Sudan Ordinance, provides that the contract may be "for any period of time or for the execution of any work."[23] As the words "any period of time" in the Sudan definition denote the definite and the indefinite periods of time, the classification of the duration of the contract in the two countries is the same.

In the U.A.R. the two parties are free to expressly agree on the duration of their contract. But if they do not do so, or they agree in no clear terms, the determination of the duration of their contract depends

[19] Law No. 62 of 1942 prescribes the use of the Arabic language, in all the documents, which are subject to Governmental inspection. So the prescription of the use of the Arabic language in section 43 of the Labour Code, seems to be redundant.

Sections 15(5) and 10(3) of the Jordanian and the Libyan Labour Codes, respectively, provide like the U.A.R. Labour Code. Sections 12, 14, 48 and 15(4) of the Lebanese, Kuwaiti, Iraqi, and Qatari Labour Codes, respectively, prescribe the use of the Arabic language, but expressly permit translation into other languages. Neither the Saudi Regulations nor the Tunisian Labour Code, contains any relevant provisions.

[20] El-Areef, p. 377; Faheem, p. 18; Naguib and Bakr, p. 71, are of the same opinion.

[21] The Adenese Ordinance does not contain any relevant provision. But section 9 of the Bahraini Labour Code prescribes the writing of the contract in Arabic, if a Bahraini subject is a party thereto. The importance of using the Arabic language cannot be overlooked, for in the words of Barwell and Kar, p. 9, which are equally applicable to the Arab countries, "it is easy to see how wide may be the difference, between what the recruit thinks he is promised and what really are the benefits ultimately to be enjoyed."

[22] Sections 902(1) of the Iraqi Civil Code, and 15 of the Jordanian Labour Code, contain provisions similar to the U.A.R. provisions. Sections 13 and 17(a) of the Kuwaiti and Qatari Labour Codes, respectively, provide that duration of the contract may be for a definite or an indefinite period of time, without mention of specific work, and provisions to the same effect may be deduced from section 11 of the Saudi Regulations, and sections 13 and 17 of the Lebanese, and 17 of the Tunisian Labour Codes, respectively.

[23] The definition of the contract of service, in section 3(e) of the Bahraini Labour Code, provides in terms identical with the Sudanese. The Adenese Ordinance does not contain any relevant provision.

on their intention, which has to be ascertained from the wording of the contract, the nature of the work, custom and all the surrounding circumstances.[24] The same is true in Sudan, as can be appreciated from reference to the English Common Law.[25] The periodicity of the payment of remuneration to the worker is not relevant in the U.A.R. to the duration of the contract.[26] Though the English Common Law considers the periodicity of the payment of remuneration as a relevant circumstance,[27] it is submitted that in Sudan it is not relevant, as the above-quoted duration provision does not mention it.

As a contract for specific work and that for a definite period of time in fact fall into one category definitive in nature, duration of the contract in the U.A.R. and Sudan should better be classifid in two, instead of the three categories into which the provisions in the U.A.R. expressly, and those in the Sudan impliedly classify it. The first category which may be termed the *Limited Contract*, embraces contracts made for a definite period of time, for seasonal work, for specific work, and long-term contracts and contracts for life. The second category which may be termed the *Unlimited Contract*, embraces only one type of contract, viz. a contract made for an indefinite period of time, unlimited

[24] *Vide* El-Areef, p. 309; Zaki, pp. 192 and 193; Habeeb, pp. 201 and 207; and Sabbour, p. 107. All these writers, in addition to Badawi, K. M., p. 274, agree that a contract for a definite period, which contains a term empowering either party to terminate the contract by notice before its expiry by effluxion of time, is a contract for an indefinite period, though only in respect of termination. However, if the contract is not terminated by notice before the expiry of its period, it terminates on that expiry, without any need for notice. To this effect also are the Cairo Court of Appeal in appeal No. 876 of 1951 (in Badawi, K. M., p. 274); Cairo Court of Cassation in case No. 605 of 1955 (in El-Fakahani, Book I, Vol. I, p. 54), and the two French cases of *Journal de Valence V. Veuve Giraud-Mangin* (1936), and *Noury v. Banque Populaire Morbihannaise* (1932), both in I.S.D.L.-Vol. 13, 1939, p. 99, and Vol. 8, 1934, p. 103, respectively. Cairo Court of Appeal decision in appeal No. 857 of 1959 (in El-Hawwari, p. 82), must not be taken to be a contrary decision, because all it decides is that a contract for a definite period remains to be so, if the empowering clause of termination is really no more than the obligation of the party who does not want the renewal of the contract, to give notice to the other party one month before the effluxion of the contract. Examples of duration depending on the nature of the work, custom and all the circumstances, are the contract of an engineer employed by a contractor for the erection of a certain building (Butros and Rajab, p. 378; and Rashed and Hashem, p. 152), the contract for the demolition of a house or the digging of a canal (El-Areef, p. 326), or the contract for the temporary replacement of a worker called to military service (Suez Court of Cassation in case No. 119 of 1954 – in Habeeb, p. 201).

[25] *Vide* Diamond, p. 173: "Duration of a contract of service depends upon the intention of the parties" (*vide* the authorities he quotes in footnote 1). He also quotes *Edwards Ltd., V. Comber*, 42 T.L.R., 247, as authority that "the intention may be implied from a well known custom." *Vide* also Barwell and Kar, p. 70, who say that "in a contract of service, the duration actually agreed upon may be implied from the surrounding circumstances"; and *vide* Batt, p. 55.

[26] *Vide* Alexandria Court of Appeal in appeal No. 1319 of 1958 (in El-Fakahani, Book I, Vol. I, p. 50); *vide* also Sabbour, p. 107; Zaki, p. 197; and El-Areef, p. 309.

[27] *Vide* Diamond, p. 175; and Smith, pp. 38–39.

by the work to be performed or the season during which it is to be performed. We shall now proceed to discuss these two categories, respectively.

(a) The limited contract

(i) Contract for a definite period of time.[28] In the U.A.R. this contract was defined as "a contract whose expiry is determined by the occurrence of a certain future incident, which is independent of the will of either party, as when the parties appoint a future date for the expiry of the contract, or agree on a certain period of time for its effectiveness."[29] However, such appointment of a future date or agreement on a certain period of time may not be sufficient to make a contract one for a definite period of time for all purposes, if the contract contains some other condition which indicates that the parties' intention is to make an unlimited contract. An example of this possibility is when the contract contains a clause empowering either party to terminate the contract by notice, before the occurrence of the said future incident, as we have seen above.[30] If this clause empowers only one party to so terminate the contract, the contract will be unlimited with respect to him only and limited with respect to the other party.[31] Some difficulty has arisen in the so-called 'retirement cases.' It frequently happens that an employer appoints a retirement age for his workers, who are bound to him by unlimited contracts. Some plaintiff workers maintained that, through the said action of the employer taken by him subsequent to the making of the contract, the contract becomes a contract for a definite period

[28] *Contrat à dureé Déterminée*, as it is called in France.

[29] Zaki, p. 192. The parties are free to limit their contract by any length of time, subject to the provisions concerning long-term contracts and contracts for life. One interesting device, which the French Courts held to be a limitation on the contract duration, is illustrated by *Sabatier v. Cheysson Administrator of the Concarcio Alamgrera* (1932), Gaz. du Palais, 1933, 1, 567 (in I.S.D.L., Vol. 9, 1935, p. 78). There the duration of the contract was not fixed, but it was agreed that the party making use of the right to rescind before a certain date, shall pay compensation to the other party. It was held that the contract was one for a definite period up to the said date.

It is interesting to note that of all the Arab Countries, the only two that set a limit to the duration of a 'contract for a definite period of time,' are Kuwait and Qatar. Sections 13 and 17(a) of their Labour Codes, respectively, set the limit at five years, renewable as many times as the parties choose. But a contract expressly providing for a longer duration, is null and void. This of course does not mean that unlimited contracts cannot be made. It is believed that the said provisions in these two countries, were enacted because the vast majority of their workers are foreigners, and the authorities do not want to be 'tied up' with them for many years, so as to be precluded from replacing them with their own nationals at large expense.

[30] *Vide* footnote 24, *supra*.

[31] *Vide* El-Areef, p. 309; and Habeeb, pp. 207–208, who quotes the French decision of 11 December 1933 (Gaz. du Palais, 1934, 1, 129), as an authority to the same effect

of time, viz. the attainment by the worker of his retirement age. But the Court decisions have unanimously rejected this contention. They ruled that the said action of the employer is no more than an administrative action, which falls within the managerial powers of the employer, and thus does not change the unlimited nature of the contract, so as to preclude either party from terminating the contract by notice at any time before the worker attains his retirement age.[32] However, there is nothing to preclude the worker and the employer from agreeing either in the contract or in the work-rules, that the contract be limited by the worker's attainment of a certain retirement age.[33] In such cases the contract will be a contract for a definite period of time; and the employer cannot change the retirement age without the consent of the worker, as the fixing of that age is a condition in the contract and not a mere administrative action.[34] Another difficulty has arisen in the case of a 'pobationary contract,' or a contract which contains a probationary condition.[35] It is submitted that a mere probationary condition in a contract does not change a limited contract to an unlimited contract and *vice versa*.[36]

In Sudan the parties are free to define the duration of their contracts without any time-limitation, as is clear from the definition of the

[32] *Vide* the High Court of Appeal in appeal No. 332 of 1960; Cairo Court of Appeal in appeal No. 273 of 1960; and Cairo Labour Court in case No. 77 of 1960 (in El-Hawwari, pp. 293, 294 and 300, respectively); and to the same effect is the French decision in *Picot et Prunier v. Steam Pacific* (1933) Dalloz Hebdom., 1933, 2,29 (in I.S.D.L., Vol. 9, 1935, p. 84), which decided that "fixing a retirement age at 61 or 65 years in a pension fund by the employer, after the making of an indefinite contract, does not change the contract to a contract for a definite period." Writers also support the Court decisions: *vide* Habeeb, p. 205; Butros and Rajab, p. 379; and Badawi, K. M., p. 281. However, Court decisions and writers agree that the appointment of a retirement age permits the employer to terminate the worker's service by notice, without further justification: *vide* Alexandria Court of Cassation in case No. 757 of 1959, and Cairo Labour Court in case No. 744 of 1960 (in El-Hawwari, pp. 299, 296, respectively) – *vide* section II, B of Chapter VI, *infra*, for the justification of the dismissal by the employer.

[33] *Vide* the High Court of Appeal in appeal No. 248 of 1959 (in El-Hawwari, p. 291).

[34] *Vide* Cairo Court of Appeal in appeal No. 1145 of 1959 (in El-Hawwari, p. 296).

[35] Section 44 of the U.A.R. Labour Code provides that "the probation period shall be fixed in the contract, and the worker shall not be employed on probation for a period exceeding three months, or more than once by the same employer." Refer to Section II of Chapter VI, *infra*, for the termination of these contracts.

[36] *Vide* Cairo Court of Cassation in (an unnumbered) case decided on 17 December 1953 (in Badawi, K. M., p. 91). In this case, the Court rejected the contention that the probation contract is *sui generis*, or that the probationary condition is a suspending condition; *vide* also the same Court in case No. 35 of 1958 (in El-Hawwari, p. 72). Those who support the same opinion, are Murad, p. 250; El-Areef, p. 330; Badawi, K. M., p. 223; Zaki, p. 224; Sabbour, p. 118; Butros and Rajab, p. 34; Badawi, Z., Vol. II, p. 42; and Hebeeb, p. 265. Consequently, the probation period forms a part of the contract duration: *vide* Habeeb, p. 266; and the French decision in *Société Frères v. Lapointe* (1934), Dalloz Hebdom, 1934, 484 (in I.S.D.L., Vol. 10, 1936, p. 87).

contract.[37] If a contract for a definite period of time contains a clause empowering either or only one of the parties to terminate it by notice, at any time before it is terminated by the effluxion of time, it is submitted that the law in Sudan would treat the contract as the law in the U.A.R. treats it.[38] It is further submitted that the law in Sudan is also similar to that in the U.A.R., concerning the effect of appointing a retirement age for the worker on the contract.[39] Finally, it is submitted that the law in Sudan is also similar to the law in the U.A.R., concerning the effect of a probationary condition on the nature of the contract.

(ii) Contract for seasonal work. The limitation of the duration of a seasonal contract arises from "the work being dependent on a certain agricultural crop, or an agricultural, industrial or commercial season, or a certain season of the year, e.g. the cotton crop, the seed-crushing or the fruit-drying season, or the touring season. In these cases, there is no need for the express time-limitation of the contract, as the contract duration is impliedly limited by the nature of the work, or the specification of the purpose of the work."[40] This contract should be distinguished from the contract for casual work, which is excepted from the U.A.R. Labour Code and the Sudan Ordinance.[41]

[37] Sudan has thus followed in the footsteps of the English Common Law, and rejected the time-limits set by the I.L.O. Convention No. 86, concerning the *Maximum Length of Contracts of Employment of Indigenous Workers* of 1947, and the previous I.L.O. Recommendation (of the same title) of 1939; and so did Bahrain. However, Aden has adopted the I.L.O. principles ,as is clear from section 6 of the Adenese Ordinance.

[38] The English Common Law, as stated by Smith, pp. 37–38, to the effect that the empowering clause in a yearly hiring, "will not render it the less a hiring for a year," does not preclude the above submission, because all it amounts to is that the contract will expire by the effluxion of the year, if it is not terminated before then, by virtue of the said empowering clause. The position is the same in the U.A.R. – vide footnote 24, *supra*.

[39] *Vide* in support, the interesting Canadian Court of Appeal decision of 16 December 1960, reported in the Labour Gazette (Ottawa) of 31 July 1961, p. 687. A collective agreement contained provisions for payment of pensions "whenever the Company retires an employee because of old age and/or sickness which renders him physically unfit or unqualified for the job." The Company subsequently fixed the age of compulsory retirement at 65 years. The union challenged the Company's action as a unilateral departure from the collective agreement. It was held that the fixing of a compulsory retirement age fell within the management functions, which were not restricted by the collective agreement. In India the Supreme Court on 14 November 1960 (Labour Law Journal (Madras), 1960, Vol. II, pp. 716–720), without, it seems, denying the employer's managerial powers to fix a retirement age, interfered so as to examine the fair exercise of these powers by the employer.

[40] Rashed and Hashem, pp. 152–153. This is equally applicable in the U.A.R. and Sudan. *Vide* El-Fakahani, Book I, Vol. I, p. 496 *et seq.*; and Habeeb, p. 202.

[41] Refer to 'Casual Workers,' in section III of Chapter I, *supra*; *vide* Faheem, p. 11; and Sabbour, pp. 109–110.

(iii) Contract for specific work. "One of the forms of a limited contract is where an employer contracts with a worker, for the performance of a specific work, so that the contract expires when the specific work agreed upon is completed."[42] The duration of the contract is impliedly limited by the time necessary for the performance of the specific work agreed upon. This contract should be distinguished from a contract for piece-work, which is generally unlimited. The completion of every piece of work is usually relevant to the periodicity of the payment of remuneration, and is of no relevance to the duration of the contract, unless the contract is for one piece of work only, when it is more properly called a contract for specific work.[43]

In Sudan the legislator envisages two categories of contracts for specific work, one with reference to time and the other without reference to time, as can be deduced from the provisions of section 10(1) of the Sudan Ordinance, re termination of the contract by notice.[44] It is submitted that this classification contains a redundancy. If the contract is for specific work with reference to time, it still is a contract for a definite period of time, with whose effluxion it terminates, exactly as any other contract whose time-duration is expressly limited, without mentioning the work to be performed thereunder. So there is no necessity for the creation of this separate category, especially since it produces ambiguity. The contract for specific work without reference to time, is the exact counterpart of the contract for specific work in the U.A.R. Finally, it is submitted that the Sudanese legislator does not intend the contract for specific work without reference to time, to be the same as a piece-work contract, because he uses the term 'piece-work' in section 15 of the Ordinance, with respect to payment of wages,[45] in the same sense it is given in the U.A.R. Labour Code.

(iv) Long-term contracts and contracts for life. Section 678(2) of the U.A.R. Civil Code provides that, "where the contract is made for the life-time of the worker or of the employer or for more than five years, the worker may after the lapse of five years, terminate the contract by

[42] Cairo Labour Court in case No. 5285 of 1959 (in El-Hawwari, p. 78); *vide* also Cairo Court of Cassation in case No. 3553 of 1953 (in Habeeb, p. 200).

[43] *Vide* Sabbour, p. 109; and Zaki, p. 197.

[44] The section is quoted in Section II, A, 2, of Chapter VI, *infra*. Section 12 of the Bahraini Labour Code, and section 6 of the Adenese Ordinance, impliedly make the same classification. The English Common Law is clearer in this respect. Under it, a contract for specific work is called an 'entire' or 'indivisible' contract, as distinguished from a piece-work contract, which is called a 'divisible' contract: *vide* Macdonell, p. 153; and Cheshire and Fifoot, p. 445.

[45] Section 15 of the Sudan Ordinance is quoted in Section III, C, of Chapter IV, *infra*.

serving six months' notice upon the employer, without paying to him any compensation."[46] So a contract for life is not null and void, as it used to be under the 1883 Civil Code.[47] The new development aims at "the fulfilment of two purposes which are seemingly contradictory, viz. the freedom of work and the desire to protect the two parties (especially the worker), by providing the contract with some stability."[48] The protection of the worker, which is afforded by granting him alone the right to terminate the contract by notice,[49] is the subject of much criticism in the U.A.R. Some writers advocate the amendment of the law, so as to give the right of termination to both parties,[50] or make the contract an unlimited contract terminable by ordinary and not six months' notice, by either party.[51]

In Sudan there is no express legislative provision equivalent to the U.A.R. provision. But the words "any period of time" in the definition of the contract in Section 2 of the Sudan Ordinance, impliedly permit the making of long-term contracts or contracts for life. This is in line with the English Common Law.[52] So long-term contracts or contracts for life are not void. There is no five years limitation, as we

[46] Section 902(2) of the Iraqi Civil Code provides in identical terms. Section 1639 V of the Netherlands Civil Code, as amended in 1953, provides in similar terms.

[47] Section 402 of the 1883 Civil Code provided that persons could not be employed, except for a certain period of time or for specified work; *vide* Sabbour, p. 108; and Zaki, pp. 194–5. Section 11 of the Lebanese Labour Code still considers a contract for life null and void. Sections 13 and 17(a) of the Kuwaiti and Qatari Labour Codes, respectively, which set the duration of a limited contract at five years, in mandatory terms, impliedly consider contracts for life or for more than five years null and void. Section 16(2) of the Qatari Labour Code expressly provides to this effect. The Jordan, Libyan and Tunisian Labour Codes do not contain any relevant provisions, nor do the Saudi Arabian Regulations.

[48] *The Preparatory Work for the U.A.R. Civil Code of 1948*, Vol. 5, p. 120, wherein it is stated that the five years limitation was copied from the German legislation, but that the Polish and Swiss legislation set the limit at three and ten years, respectively.

[49] The German and the Polish legislation likewise, grant the right of termination to the worker, but the Swiss legislation grants it to both parties. The U.A.R. legislator adopted the former "as long as the real object is the protection of the worker." (*Ibid.*)

[50] *Vide* El-Areef, p. 328, who says that "sometimes the employer is weaker than the worker, as when he is a sick person, a foreigner or a woman"; *vide* also Habeeb, p. 207.

[51] *Vide* Zaki, p. 195. If the law should be amended, it is believed that the sense of fairness to the worker, who is the weaker party of the contract, calls for the requirement from the employer, of a notice appreciably longer than the notice required from the worker; *vide* section 1639 J of the Netherlands Civil Code.

[52] *Vide* Smith, p. 67: "A contract to serve another during the contractor's life, is not invalid"; Batt, p. 51: "The length of a contract of service... may be any period from an hour or a day to a year, or even the lives of the contracting parties, since there seems no doubt that an agreement to serve for life is perfectly valid in the absence of any vitiating elements, such as fraud, undue influence or undue restriction of trade"; *vide* also Cooper, p. 39; Macdonell, p. 31; and Halsbury, Vol. 25, p. 455. The classical English case on the subject is *Wallis v. Day* (1837), 2 M. & W. 273, where the Court upheld the contract of the defendant, who sold his carrier's business to the plaintiff, and agreed to serve him for the rest of his life.

have seen in the U.A.R. The contract is not ordinarily terminable by notice,[53] and the law treats the two perties on equal footing, and does not provide any special protection to the worker.

(b) The unlimited contract[54]

This is the most prevalent form of contract. This form of the contract, which is sanctioned by section 678(1) of the U.A.R. Civil Code, has been defined as "a contract which is not limited by time or by the nature of the work to be performed thereunder."[55] The contract may be of this form in one of three eventualities:

(i) When the parties do not limit the duration of their contract either expressly or by implication. The contract is impliedly limited, when it is made for specific or seasonal work.

(ii) When the contract, though limited, contains a clause empowering either or one of the parties to terminate it, before its termination by the effluxion of time, as we have seen above.[56]

(iii) When the parties continue with the contract after the expiry of its term.[57] However, an exception is made in the case of contracts for specific work.[58]

Finally, we have already seen in the so-called 'retirement cases' that an unlimited contract is not changed to a limited contract, by the employer's managerial appointment of a retirement age for the worker, subsequent to the making of the contract.[59]

In Sudan an unlimited contract is sanctioned by the contract definition in section 2 of the Sudan Ordinance. The contract can be in this form in Sudan, in eventualities (i) and (ii) of the U.A.R. However, eventuality (iii) is not totally applicable, because in the absence of any legislative provisions,[60] reference to the English Common Law does not totally warrant it. The position in this respect seems to depend on the wording of the contract.[61]

[53] *Vide* Halsbury, Vol. 25, p. 520.
[54] *Contrat à durée indéterminée*, as it is called in France.
[55] Zaki, p. 195; *vide* also Habeeb, p. 207.
[56] *Vide* Footnote 24, *supra*.
[57] *Vide* section 679 of the U.A.R. Civil Code, which is quoted in footnote 64, *infra*.
[58] *Vide* section 680 of the U.A.R. Civil Code, which is quoted in footnote 65, *infra*.
[59] *Vide* footnote 32, *supra*.
[60] The Sudanese legislator, however, found it fit to provide for the temporary extension and not the renewal of the contract, in certain exceptional circumstances, as is clear from the provisions of section 11 of the Sudan Ordinance, quoted in footnote 71, *infra*.
[61] *Vide* footnote 70, *infra*.

The classification of the contract into limited and unlimited contracts, is important for the termination of the contract both in the U.A.R. and the Sudan,[62] and for the termination gratuity in Sudan.[63]

Renewal of the contract

Renewal of the contract in the U.A.R. may either be tacit or express. The contract is tacitly renewed, where the parties continue with the contract after the expiry of its period. Section 679(2) of the U.A.R. Civil Code deems the contract when it is tacitly renewed, to have changed to an unlimited contract.[64] Section 71 of the Labour Code provides that "a contract made for a definite period shall be deemed to have been renewed for an indefinite period, if both parties continue to abide by it after the date of its expiry." However, section 680(2) of the Code preserves the limited character of the contract on tacit renewal, when it is for specific work, which by its nature is capable of renewal.[65]

[62] Refer to section II of Chapter VI, *infra.*

[63] Refer to Chapter VII, *infra.*

[64] Section 679(2) of the U.A.R. Civil Code provides:

"If the parties continue with the contract after the expiry of its period, the parties shall be deemed to have renewed the contract for an indefinite period."

The provisions of the Civil Code follow the German and Polish provisions, as is expressly stated in p. 122, of *The Preparatory Work for the U.A.R. Civil Code, 1948,* and reject the Swiss Law which preserves the limited nature of the contract on renewal. The Netherlands Civil Code provides in section 1639 F, as the Swiss Law does, except that the time-limitation for renewal is set at one year. The Moroccan Law is similar to the Netherlands Law (*vide* the *Labour Survey of North Africa,* p. 210). Section 915(2) of the Iraqi Civil Code provides in terms identical with the U.A.R. Civil Code provisions. Sections 58, 53, 17(b) and 17 of the Lebanese, Kuwaiti, Qatari and Tunisian Labour Codes, respectively, and section 11 of the Saudi Regulations, provide to the same effect. The Jordanian and Libyan Codes are silent on the subject.

[65] Section 680(2) of the U.A.R. Civil Code provides:

"If the work is by its nature capable of being repeated, and the contract continues after the work is completed, the contract shall be deemed to have been tacitly renewed for the period required for the completion of the specific work another time."

The Explanatory Note to the Code curiously states that "the section is applicable to the teachers of private schools and other similar institutions." Most writers have passed this without comment: *vide,* for instance, Murad, p. 258; Rashed and Hashem, p. 157; Butros and Rajab, p. 379; and Badawi, K. M., p. 269. Some Court decisions have followed suit: *vide* Cairo Court of Cassation in case No. 1079 of 1959; and Cairo Labour Court in case No. 4384 of 1959 (both in El-Hawwari, pp. 79 ad 80, respectively). Habeeb, p. 204, submits that teachers' contracts are for definite periods of time, viz. the school year, and not for specific work, so the renewal of their contracts falls under section 679(2) and not section 680(2) of the Civil Code. Sabbour, p. 121, makes the artificial distincton between a teacher's contract for the school year, with reference to the work and that without reference to the work. He then applies section 680(2) to the former, and section 679(2) to the latter. It is submitted that Habeeb's opinion is the correct one, as it is more logical, and it gives the benefit of the doubt to the weaker party, viz. the teacher.

Section 916 of the Iraqi Civil Code provides in terms identical with the U.A.R. Civil Code. But none of the Labour Codes of the other Arab countries, contains any provisions on the subject.

When it is not so capable of renewal, there is no question of its continuation after its expiry,[66] and so is the case when the contract is for seasonal work.[67] Express renewal of the contract may be effected, in either of two ways. The first is where the parties expressly agree anew, whenever they want to renew the contract; and in this case the contract remains a limited contract, in fulfilment of the express will of the parties.[68] The second is where the parties provide in their contract that it is renewable for further similar periods, if neither party notifies the other of his intention not to renew. In this case the Courts deem the contract to have changed to an unlimited contract, or in other words they treat it like contracts tacitly renewed.[69] However, the judicial tendency seems to lean in favour of applying this, only when the contract period is fairly short.[69]

In Sudan there is no legislative provision on the renewal of the contracts, and that brings into operation the rules of the English Common Law. The position under the said Law, is still contractual. If the employment is for a period certain, any continuation after the expiry of the period, renews the contract for a similar period only, or in other

[66] This is contrary to Rashed and Hashem, p. 155, who, it seems, reach their conclusion by the simple inversion method, without any reasoning.

[67] The contrary view of Rashed and Hashem, p. 157, follows from their view concerning the contract for specific work: *vide* the preceding footnote.

[68] Cairo Court of Appeal in the two appeals Nos. 987 and 1000 of 1960 (both in El-Hawwari, p. 75); Cairo Court of Cassation in case No. 1323 of 1954 (in Habeeb, p. 203); and Beni Sweif District Court in case No. 37 of 1954 (in Badawi, K. M., p. 271). The same Court in a decision on May 11 of 1951 (vide Faheem, p. 21), refused to consider the contract a limited contract though expressly renewed, because renewal came several months after the expiry of the first contract.

[69] *Vide* Cairo Court of Cassation in case No. 3844 of 1954 (in Badawi, K. M., p. 274). The Court quoted the French decision of 22 June 1949 (Dalloz Hebdom., 1949, p. 598), in support. Another French decision in support, is *Petit v. Chemins de fer Paris–Orléans* (1931), Dalloz Hebdom., 1931, p. 533 (in I.S.D.L., Vol. 7, 1933, p.123), concerning a contract for one day, renewable for an unlimited number of times. El-Areef, p. 310, quotes in additional support, the decisions of the Mixed Courts in the U.A.R., of 27 January 1937 and of 4 June 1947. The *raison d'être* of the French and U.A.R. decisions, is that the employers, by providing for the renewal of short-term contracts, aim at ridding themselves of the notices they are required to serve, in order to terminate the unlimited contracts. In other words, they camouflage an unlimited contract by a limited form, so as to get the better of the two worlds, while they are seemingly legal in their actions. "Experience has proved in France, that the other solution may facilitate the escape from the notice obligations, by entering into a renewable one-day contract, which can be terminated without responsibility": *The Preparatory Work of the U.A.R. Civil Code*, 1948, p. 122. Again, "the device in question is the conclusion of a limited contract for a limited and usually short period of time, and its prolongation successively from time to time. In practice, this is really a contract for an indefinite period, and must therefore be treated as such": I.R.L., Vol. 32, 1936, p. 199. *Vide* section 1639 K of the Netherlands Civil Code. This commendable reasoning obliges the employers to expressly renew the contract, however short, every time they want to renew it. Such tedious task, which not many employers are prepared to undertake, almost annihilates the danger of termination of the contract without notice.

words, the contract remains a limited contract. If on the other hand, the contract provides that it is terminable by a certain notice, in case it is continued after the expiry of the initial period of the contract, the contract becomes an unlimited contract, like the contract in the U.A.R. in the same circumstances.[70] It is submitted that the law in the U.A.R. is clearer and the law in Sudan, in addition to being ambiguous, is productive of much unnecessary litigation.

Temporary extension of the contract, as distinguished from its renewal, is expressly provided for in the Sudan Ordinance, but not in the U.A.R. Civil or Labour Codes.[71]

SECTION IV: NOVATION AND VICARIOUS PERFORMANCE OF THE CONTRACT[72]

Section 685(a) of the U.A.R. Civil Code provides that "the worker shall perform the work himself." By analogy it can be concluded from

[70] Batt, pp. 53–54, illustrates this distinction under the English Common Law, by the two cases of *Langton v. Carleton* (1873), 9 Ex. 57, and *Castigan v. Gray Bovier* (1925), 41 T. L.R., 372.

Neither the Bahraini Labour Code nor the Adenese Ordinance, provides for the renewal of the contract. Presumably, the English Common Law is applicable in both countries.

[71] Section 11 of the Sudan Ordinance provides:

"If while the employed person is engaged in any journey or voyage connected with his employer's business, the period of duration of his service shall expire or he shall give due notice to his employer to determine his contract of service, the employer may, for the purpose of compelling the employed person to complete such journey or voyage, extend the period of service for a period not exceeding one month from the date at which such contract would otherwise have terminated: Provided that in every such case the employed person shall be entitled to recover for the period of such extended service wages at the rate of one-fourth more than the rate of wages stipulated in the contract."

The circumstances peculiar to Sudan which, it is believed, called for the enactment of such provision, are the vast geographical expanse of the Country, the lack of ready transportation and the difficult task of replacement of the employed person. Neither the Bahraini nor the Adenese Labour Codes provide for the temporary extension of the contract. In the U.A.R. such temporary extension of the contract is only possible by the agreement of the parties: *vide* El-Areef, p. 337; and Zaki, p. 384. This is presumably the case in the rest of the Arab countries.

[72] "Novation is a transaction by which, with the consent of all the parties concerned, a new contract is substituted for the one that has already been made. The new contract may be between the original parties, e.g. where a written agreement is later incorporated in a deed, or between different parties, e.g. where a new person is substituted for the original debtor or creditor" (Cheshire and Fifoot, p. 430); *Vide Tolhurst v. Associated Portland Cement Manufacturers (1900), Ltd.*, (1902), 2 K.B. 660. "The assignment of a debt... operates as an effective transfer without the consent or the collaboration of the debtor" (*Idem*). "The only way then in which an obligation can be effectively assigned, so as completely to transfer liability for its performance from one person to another is by novation" (*Ibid.*, p. 434); *vide* also Barwell and Kar, p. 31.

The distinction between assignment and novation of the contract in the U.A.R., can be deduced from sections 323 and 208 of the U.A.R. Civil Code. Section 323 provides that, "subject to the provisions of section 208, performance of the contract can be effected by the debtor, his representative, or by any other interested person. Performance can this provision, that "the worker can refuse the substitution of another employer or his own temporary transfer to another employer."[73] The position in Sudan is the same, as is clear from reference to the English Common Law. It is a rule that "vicarious performance of a personal contract, is not performance in the eyes of the law."[74] So both in the U.A.R. and the Sudan, the only way of substituting either party of the contract by a third party, is novation.

Exceptions to the said rule concerning the vicarious performance of the contract, are expressly provided for in section 85 of the U.A.R. Labour Code, in the cases of the unauthorised closing down of an establishment, or its amalgamation or transfer. The section provides that in these incidents, the contracts of workers of the establishment subsist, in spite of the change of parties involved.[75] These exceptions were

also be effected by an uninterested person, even without the previous consent or knowledge of the debtor, provided that the creditor may refuse performance by any person other than the debtor, if the latter notifies the creditor of his objection to such performance." Section 208 provides that "the creditor may refuse performance by any person other than the debtor, if the contract expressly provides that it shall be personally performed by the debtor or the nature of the work requires personal performance."

[73] Badawi, Z., p. 51; *vide* also Zaki, p. 241; and El-Areef, p. 200; and *vide* section 146 of the U.A.R. Civil Code.

[74] Cheshire and Fifoot, p. 436; *vide* also Diamond, pp. 220–221: "A performance therefore, by a third person cannot be relied upon as a performance of the contract"; Macdonell, p. 242: "Contracts of hiring and service cannot be transferred or assigned, without consent of the parties thereto"; Cooper, pp. 2–3 and 46–47, who quotes *Lord Atkin* on the issue of the transfer of a worker, in *Nokes v. Doncaster Amalgamated Collieries, Ltd.*, (1940), A.C. 1014 at p. 1026: "I confess it appears to me astonishing that, apart from overriding questions of public welfare, power should be given to a Court or to any one else to transfer a man without his knowledge and against his will, from the service of one person to the service of another"; and Barwell and Kar, pp. 72–73, who quote the same case.

[75] Section 85 of the U.A.R. Labour Code provides:

"The dissolution of an establishment its winding up closing down bankruptcy amalgamation or its transfer by inheritance, will gift sale or assignment or any other way, shall not constitute a bar to the fulfilment of all obligations.

"Save in the cases of winding up, bankruptcy and authorised final closing down, the contracts of employment of the workers of the establishment shall remain in force.

"The successor shall be jointly liable with the previous employers for the fulfilment of the said obligations."

Vide Alexandria Court of Appeal in appeal No. 305 of 1955 (in Habeeb, p. 417); Cairo Court of Cassation in case No. 157 of 1959 (in El-Hawwari, p. 205); Cairo Court of Appeal in Appeal No. 182 of 1958 (*Ibid.*, p. 164), on amalgamation of the establishment; and Cairo Court of Cassation in case No. 299 of 1960 (*Ibid.*, p. 204), on the dissolution of the establishment. The exact French counterpart of this section, is section 23 of Book I of the French Labour Code (*vide* I.S.D.L., vol. 8, 1934, p. 101). In Italy, "the worker contracts with the undertaking, so that the cession of the undertaking also entails the transfer of the juridical relations resulting from the hire of services: *Cagnoni and others v. Rognoni* (1925), Giuv. Lav., 1925, p. 356" (from I.S.D.L., Vol. 2, 1926, p. 228); *vide* I.L.R., Vol. 32, 1936, p. 197, where the importance of the worker's relationship with the undertaking and not personally with the employer is emphasised, and the tendency to adopt the Italian view is stated to gain ground in many countries.

Section 127 of the Iraqi Labour Code provides in terms, similar to the provisoins of the first paragraph of section 85 of the U.A.R. Labour Code. Section 924 of the Iraqi Civil justified "by the public welfare, which requires economic stability and the combatting of unemployment."[76] The section is applicable when the establishment is merely leased.[77] On the other hand, the compulsory transfer of the establishment by public auction, was held to fall outside the scope of the section.[78] This was also held in the cases of the taking and retaking by the Government, of establishments running public amenities.[79]

Opinion in the U.A.R. is unanimous in supporting the view that the effect of section 85 is not limited to the employer, but also operates to oblige the worker to continue with the contract, when the incidents mentioned in the said section occur.[80] It is submitted that this interpretation is the correct one, because the continuity of the contract as prescribed in the section, presumably means continuity by both parties to the contract, and not by one without the other[81].

Finally, the exceptional provisions of section 85 should be distinguished from the provisions of section 53 of the U.A.R. Labour Code,[82]

Code is the counterpart of the second paragraph of the said section 85 (this was copied from section 969 of the U.A.R. Draft Civil Code of 1948, which was not adopted). Cf. the provisions in sections 15(4), 10(2) and 15, of the Jordanian, Libyan and Tunisian Labour Codes, respectively. Section 60 of the Kuwaiti Labour Code makes continuation of the contract dependent on the agreement of the worker and the new employer. Section 60 of the Lebanese Labour Code expressly makes the continuation of the contract, obligatory not only on the employer, but on the worker as well. The Qatari Labour Code and Saudi Regulations do not contain any relevant provisions.

[76] Cairo Labour Court in case No. 4921 of 1959, in El-Hawwari, p. 206.

[77] *Vide* Cairo Court of Appeal in appeal No. 563 of 1955 (in Butros and Rajab, p. 424); and the same Court in appeal No. 222 of 1955 (in El-Fakahani, Book I, Vol. III, p. 444); *vide* the contrary decision of the Cairo Court of Arbitration in dispute No. 244 of 1954 (*Ibid.*, p. 446), which seems to be the only contrary decision. It is of no serious concern, as it is earlier than the above decisions of superior Courts. *Vide* also Habeeb, pp. 411 *et seq.*

[78] *Vide* Cairo Labour Court in case No. 7010 of 1955 (*Ibid.*, p. 443); *vide* also Sabbour, p. 423.

[79] *Vide* decisions quoted by El-Fakahani, (Book I, Vol. III, pp. 452–458); and Cairo Court of Appeal in appeal No. 807 of 1959 (in El-Hawwari, p. 209); *vide* also Habeeb, p. 413. Naguib and Bakr, p. 193, maintain otherwise, without reasoning.

[80] *Vide* Cairo Labour Court in case No. 4921 of 1959 (in El-Hawwari, p. 206); Rashed and Hashem, p. 324; Habeeb, pp. 412 and 418; Faheem, p. 120; Butros and Rajab, pp. 425–426; Badawi, K. M., p. 429; and *Da'irdt-ul-Ma'aref El-Ummaliyyatu*, by Husseini, M. H., and El-Hawwari, I., 1961, Cairo, in Arabic (hereinafter called Husseini and Hawwari), p. 334.

[81] This submission is not affected by section 146 of the U.A.R. Civil Code, which provides that, "if the contract creates personal rights and obligations related to a certain thing, these rights and obligations devolve to the transferee of the thing, if it is essential to it and the transferee knew of them at the time of the transfer." The contracts of employment are personal to the employer, and not to the establishment.

[82] Section 53 provides that, "if an employer entrusts another employer with the performance of any of his operations or any part thereof within the same area the second employer shall maintain complete equality of all rights as between his own workers and those of the first employer and the latter shall in this respect be jointly liable with the former." Sections 15(3) and 6 of the Jordanian Labour Code, 11 and 16 of the Libyan and Kuwaiti Labour Codes, respectively, and 2 of the Saudi Regulations, provide to a similar effect. Cf. sections 28 to 30 of the Tunisian Labour Code. Iraq, Qatar and Lebanon do not have any relevant provisions.

concerning the so-called sub-contractors. The latter section has nothing to do with the vicarious performance of the contract, and is only applicable after novation is effected.[83]

In Sudan the rule concerning the vicarious performance of the contract, is strictly applied.[84] There are no exceptions in the Sudan Ordinance or any other enactment, similar to the exceptions in section 85 of the U.A.R. Labour Code. Rules of the English Common Law applicable in Sudan, absolutely block the way to any such exceptions,[85] as the said Law is very jealous of the voluntary nature of the contract of employment.[86]

SECTION V: TERMS OF THE CONTRACT

Section 147 of the U.A.R. Civil Code provides that "the contract is the 'law' of the parties." In other words, the parties are free to agree on any terms they like. This freedom of contract is not absolute, however, especially in the making of the contract of employment.[87] The

[83] When it is applicable, it provides additional protection to the wroker, which the rules of the general law deny. For enlightenment on the effect of section 53 of the U.A.R. Labour Code, *vide* Cairo Court of Appeal in appeal No. 63 of 1958; and Cairo Labour Court in case No. 6261 of 1959 (both in El-Hawwari, pp. 163 and 164, respectively); Badawi, K. M., pp. 170–171; Butros and Rajab, pp. 41–45; Faheem, p. 29; and Naguib and Bakr, p. 84.

[84] An interesting example of such strict application, is afforded by the Expatriate Officials Compensation Ordinance of 15 August 1954 (in the *Laws of the Sudan*, Vol. 1, Title II: Sub-Tittle 2). By virtue of this Ordinance, contracts of all expatriate officials with the Condominium Government of Sudan, had to be terminated; and those officials whose stay was needed by the Sudan Government after independence (in 1956), had to enter new contracts with the new Government. Novation of the contracts was resorted to, and vicarious performance of the contract was rejected.

Section 17(b) of the Bahraini Labour Code provides that, "on the transfer of a business, the contract of service shall continue with the new owner, unless the new owner or the employed person wishes to terminate it." The influence of the U.A.R. legislation is apparent. In Aden section 10 of the Adenese Ordinance, copies Article 10 of the I.L.O. Convention No. 64, which not only requires the consent of the worker to any transfer of the contract, but also prescribes the necessity of "endorsement of the transfer upon the contract by a public Officer accredited for the purpose."

[85] *Vide* the words of *Lord Atkin*, in footnote 74, *supra*; *vide* also Cooper, p. 47; Diamond, p. 114, who mentions the case of *Collier v. Sunday Referee Publishing Co.* (1940), 2 K.B. 647, in which the contract of a chief sub-editor was held to be broken, when the newspaper he worked for, was sold during the currency of his contract; and *vide* the same author, in pp. 219–221; *vide* also Batt, p. 86, who mentions the case of *Nokes v. Doncaster etc. Collieries Ltd.* (1940) A.C. 1014, in which it was held that an amalgamation of two companies, relieved the succeeding company of the contracts of service of the old company's servants; Cheshire and Fifoot, p. 437; and Barwell and Kar, p. 62.

[86] It is believed that the development of big industrial establishments, calls for a way out from the strict rule of vicarious performance, apart from novation; *vide* footnote 75, *supra*, for the international tendency in favour of such a way out.

[87] Refer to the discussion on the consensual nature of the contract, in Section I of Chapter I, *supra*.

parties in the making thereof, are bound by section 6 of the U.A.R. Labour Code, which provides:

"Any term conflicting with the provisions of this Code, shall be null and void even where it is made before the coming into force of the Code.[88]

"Exception is, however, made in respect of the provisions of Chapter II of Book II of this Code[89] if the term is more favourable to the worker.[90]

"Any compromise or disclaimer of the rights deriving from the contract of employment, while the contract is effective, or within one month after its termination, shall be null and void, if it conflicts with the provisions of this Code."[91]

The term is deemed null and void by virtue of the first paragraph of section 6, whether it is "embodied in an individual or collective contract of employment, or in the work-rules of the establishment, or is prescribed by custom."[92] If the contract contains a term or terms, some of which without the others, are in conflict with the provisions of the U.A.R. Labour Code, only such conflicting term or terms are null and void. Subject to the provisions in the second paragraph of section 6, the said conflicting terms are automatically replaced by the relevant provisions of the Labour Code; and the validity of the contract is thus preserved.[93] If, however, the conflicting term is, so to say, mixed in its provisions, so as to accord in one part, a more favourable treatment than that accorded

[88] Section 83(b) of the Iraqi Labour Code provides in similar terms; *vide* also sections 917(2) and 920(2) of the Iraqi Civil Code. Sections 7(1), 96, 77, 3 and 128, of the Jordanian, Libyan, Kuwaiti, Qatari and Tunisian Labour Codes, respectively, and section 43 of the Saudi Regulations, also provide similarly only in respect of leaves and wages. Sections 1639 R, V, and W, of the Netherlands Civil Code, also provide to the same effect, in respect of the payment in lieu of the notice, the right to terminate long-term contracts or contracts for life, and the right to request the Judge to dissolve a contract in certain circumstances, respectively.

[89] This is the Chapter which mainly regulates the individual contract of employment.

[90] Sections 133, 77, 3, 7(1), 96 and 126, of the Iraqi, Kuwaiti, Qatari, Jordanian, Libyan, and Tunisian Labour Codes, respectively, provide to the same effect. Section 43 of the Lebanese Labour Code provides in similar terms, only in respect of leaves. *Vide* also section 1639 R of the Netherlands Civil Code.

[91] None of the Arab Labour Codes contains similar provisions, except the Qatari Code, whose section 4 makes any compromise or disclaimer absolutely void.

[92] Rashed and Hashem, p. 333; *vide* also Murad, p. 212; and *vide* sections 96 and 97 of the U.A.R. Labour Code, concerning terms in the collective contracts of employment; *vide* also to this effect, the French decision in *Société Pharmacie Centre du Nord v. Dame Eysseric* (1937), D.H., 1937, p. 512 (in I.S.D.L., Vol. 13, 1939, p. 73).

[93] *Vide* Cairo Court of Appeal in appeal No. 764 of 1951; and Alexandria Court of Appeal in appeal No. 97 of 1954 (both in Habeeb, pp. 216 and 214, respectively); *vide* also Badawi, K.M., p. 18; Zaki, p. 66; Naguib and Bakr, pp. 28–30; Butros and Rajab, p. 32; and Rashed and Hashem, p. 334. *Vide* examples of the nullity of such terms in Badawi, K. M., p. 181 (deductions from wages bigger than those authorised by the Labour Code), and p. 436 (disentitlement of the worker to the certificate of service, guaranteed to him by the Labour Code).

by the Labour Code, the over-all effect of the term is the measure of its validity. If this effect is more generous to the worker than the Labour Code provisions, the term is valid, and if it is less generous, it is invalid.[94] However, the term cannot be held valid in part, and invalid in the other part, or in other words, the worker cannot have the better of the two worlds.[95]

The provisions in the second paragraph of section 6 were enacted as a saving from the sweeping provisions in the first paragraph, because of the legislator's fear that the worker would without this saving, be deprived of any benefits more favourable to him than those in the Labour Code, which he had acquired or may acquire. In other words, the legislator emphasises by the said provisions, that the Labour Code provisions are no more than the minimum standards, below which no contract can provide.[96] If a term in the contract is more favourable to the worker than the relevant minimum standard in the Labour Code, the term is binding, and the provisions of section 6 do not entitle the employer to reduce the term so as to comply with the Labour Code, unless the worker agrees thereto.[97]

The use of the word disclaimer in the third paragraph of the section, illustrates the case of the extreme denial of the protection afforded by the Labour Code. This the section seeks to prohibit. The nullity or compromise arises from the fact that they are signed by the worker, while he is in a state of need.[98] As this state of need is deemed by the legislator to cease, at the expiry of one month from the termination of

[94] *Vide* the High Court of Appeal in appeal No. 441 of 1960 (in El-Hawwari, p. 354); Cairo Court of Appeal in appeal No. 25 of 1953 (in Rashed and Hashem, p. 334); and Tanta Court of Cassation in case No. 280/66 of 1952 (Ibid., p. 335); *vide* also El-Areef, p. 420; Murad, p. 213; and Faheem, p. 32.

[95] *Vide* the High Court of Appeal in appeal No. 367 of 1954; the Alexandria Court of Appeal in appeal No. 116 of 1955 (both in Habeeb, p. 217); the Cairo Court of Cassation in case No. 1201 of 1959; and Cairo Court of Appeal in appeal No. 40 of 1959 (both in El-Hawwari, pp. 363 and 135, respectively); *vide* also the arbitration cases quoted in Butros and Rajab, pp. 32–33; Naguib and Bakr, p. 29; Rashed and Hashem, pp. 93–4 and 189, and El-Fakahani, 1959 supplement, p. 172.

[96] *Vide* Habeeb, p. 215; and Zaki, p. 67. For the application of the provisions in the second paragraph of section 6, *vide* the Alexandria Court of Appeal in appeal No. 362 of 1959 (in El-Hawwari, p. 361), re the termination gratuity; the Cairo Court of Cassation in case No. 265 of 1956 (*Ibid.*, p. 122), re annual leave; *vide* also Badawi, K. M., p. 284; El-Fakahani, 1959 Supplement, p. 132; Butros and Rajab, pp. 381 and 421; and Faheem, p. 45 and pp. 122–123.

[97] *Vide* Cairo Court of Appeal in the appeal on dispute No. 1 of 1959 (in El-Hawwari p. 136); and Cairo Court of Arbitration in dispute No. 277 of 1953 (in El-Fakahani, Book I, Vol. II, p. 199). *Vide* also Badawi, K. M., pp. 425–426; Butros and Rajab, pp. 104–105; and Faheem, p. 62.

[98] *Vide* Cairo Labour Court in case No. 5654 of 1959 (in El-Hawwari, p. 386); and Cairo Court of Cassation in case No. 157 of 1959 (*Ibid.*, p. 380); and *vide* Murad, p. 214.

the contract, any compromise or disclaimer made thereafter is valid.[99] If it contains a list of sums of money related to certain rights of the worker, it is valid only in respect of the said rights, even though it contains in addition a provision of a general compromising or disclaiming effect, as the case may be.[100]

Amendment of the contract terms in the U.A.R. is also subject to the limitations prescribed by section 6 of the Labour Code. This is sanctioned by section 147 of the Civil Code, which provides that "the contract cannot be amended, except by agreement of the parties or by the operation of the law."

Finally, ambiguous terms of the contract have to be interpreted "in the interests of the debtor. However, ambiguous terms shall not be interpreted so as to prejudice the interests of the adhering party."[101] Section 100 of the Civil Code provides that "acceptance in the contracts of adhesion, is limited to the acceptance of conditions already determined by a party who refuses to negotiate thereon." Though the contract of employment in the U.A.R. has some adhesive nature,[102] it cannot safely be denominated a 'contract of adhesion.' If, however it can be so denominated, the adhering party is more often than not, the worker and not the employer .In such a case, the interpretation of ambiguous terms in the contract has to be in favour of the worker, whether he is the 'debtor' or the 'creditor.' Support for such a proposition, when the ambiguity of a term in the contract arises from an ambiguity in the Labour Code itself, is afforded by the *Cairo Court of Appeal in appeal No. 98 of 1959*, which said that "the rules of interpretation of the labour laws especially lean in favour of what is more beneficial to the worker, whenever there is an ambiguity."[103] The proposition is supported by some writers, on the ground that labour legislation has the protection of the worker as its goal; and the achievement of this goal requires the interpretation of the said legislation to be in favour of the worker.[104]

[99] *Vide* Cairo Court of Appeal in appeal No. 5 of 1956 (in Habeeb, p. 546); and the cases quoted in El-Hawwari, pp. 379–384; *vide* also, to a similar effect, the French decision in *Jomard v. Omnium Automobile* (1934), Gaz. du Palais, 1934, 2, 633 (in I.S.D.L., Vol. 10, 1936, pp. 89–90); *vide* also Badawi, K. M., pp. 153–154; El-Areef, p. 347; Murad, pp. 213–4 (who adds that the provisions of section 6(3) constitute a departure from the rules of the general law); El-Fakahani, 1959 Supplement, p. 67; *vide* the I.L.O. 1961 Report No. VII (1), on the *Termination of Employment*, pp. 28–29, for enlightenment on how some other countries view the matter under discussion.

[100] *Vide* Cairo Court of Appeal in appeals Nos. 1000 and 987 of 1960 (in El-Hawwari, pp. 384–385); *vide* also El-Areef, p. 347.

[101] Section 151 of the U.A.R. Civil Code.

[102] Refer to Section I of Chapter I, *supra*.

[103] The case is reported in El-Hawwari, pp. 58–61.

[104] *Vide* Sabbour, pp. 7–8; Habeeb, pp. 237 and 329; Naguib and Bakr, p. 104.

Other writers oppose the proposition, on the ground that the interpretation should be guided by the public interest and not the interests of either party to the contract.[105] One writer advocates a middle course, by saying that interpretation in favour of the worker, is tenable only if the legislator's intention preponderantly supports such interpretation, while not losing sight of the public interest.[106] It is submitted that, as long as the contract of employment is not expressly declared by the legislator to be a contract of adhesion, the interpretation of the ambiguous terms of the contract in favour of the worker always, is not legally warranted. However, without declaring as aforesaid, the legislator can achieve the same end by expressly sanctioning the said favourable interpretation, in the Labour Code. It is believed that such sanction is required by the weaker position of the worker, and will preclude any employer's attempt to take advantage of ambiguities.

In Sudan the parties are also free to agree on the terms of their contract, as they choose. However, section 35 of the Sudan Ordinance provides that "nothing in this Oridnance shall be construed as preventing an employer from paying wages and providing other benefits to any employed person which are more favourable to such employed person than the wages and other benefits prescribed under the provisions of this Ordinance."[107] This is the equivalent of the second paragraph of section 6 of the U.A.R. Labour Code. There are no equivalents of the provisions in the first and third paragraphs of section 6. However, such provisions can be implied from the said section 35, without the one month's limitation mentioned in the third paragraph of section 6. So any term in the contract, conflicting with the provisions of the Sudan Ordinance, or any compromise or disclaimer of the rights due to the worker by virtue of the contract, unless made after the termination of the contract, will be held null and void.[108] Consequently, the limitation of nullity to the conflicting term of the contract, and the treatment of the so-called mixed terms would, it is submitted, be the same as in the U.A.R.

[105] *Vide* Badawi, K. M., pp. 14–15, who quotes in support, the Cairo Court of Appeal in the appeal on dispute No. 54 of 1953; and Butros and Rajab, p. 65. El-Areef, p. 7, opposes the proposition on the same grounds, but in p. 151, supports it by depending on section 151 of the U.A.R. Civil Code.

[106] *Vide* Zaki, p. 15.

[107] Section 23 of the Sudan Ordinance redundantly provides to the same effect, in respect of the annual and sick leaves. This section seems to have been inspired by Article 9 of the I.L.O. *Holidays With Pay Convention* No. 52 of 1936. *Vide* section 34 of the Bahraini Labour Code, which provides in terms similar to section 35 of the Sudan Ordinance; *vide* also section 18 of the Bahraini Code.

[108] *Vide* the express provision in section 72(b) of the Bahraini Labour Code.

Amendment of the contract terms in the Sudan is also subject to the above-mentioned limitations, prescribed by section 35 of the Sudan Ordinance and the inferences therefrom.

Ambiguous terms of the contract are interpreted in accordance with "the ordinary canons of construction which are applicable to contracts generally."[109] So there is no question of interpretation in favour of the worker, as was raised in the U.A.R.[110]

SUMMARY

Consent of the parties without the specification of their rights and obligations in the contract, is sufficient in the U.A.R., to make a valid contract, whereas in the Sudan this is not always the case. Unincorporated bodies in Sudan are capable of entering contracts of employment as employers, but in the U.A.R. they are not. Both countries exclude otherwise capable persons from entering contracts of employment as workers.

The contract in the U.A.R. and Sudan is an informal contract. Writing is prescribed only for the proof of the contract. In the U.A.R. the employer alone is required to so prove the contract. But in Sudan both the employer and the worker are so required. When the contract is in writing, it has to be in the Arabic language in the U.A.R., whereas in the Sudan there is no such requirement.

The law in Sudan, concerning the duration of a contract for a definite period of time or for seasonal work, is similar to the law in the U.A.R., though it is clearer in the latter than in the former. Though similarity of the law in the two countries is true in respect of contracts for specific work, the Sudan Law makes an unnecessary artificial distinction which is prone to ambiguity, between contracts for specific work with reference to time, and those without reference to time. Contracts for life and long-term contracts are valid in the two countries. However, termination of such contracts in the U.A.R. is permitted only for the worker by six months notice after five years of service, but neither party in Sudan has such a right. A contract for an indefinite period of time is accorded a similar, but not a totally similar treatment in the U.A.R. and Sudan. In Sudan whether a contract for a definite period of time becomes a contract for an indefinite period, if it is

[109] Smith, p. 60.

[110] It is believed that a provision to permit such interpretation in favour of the worker, should be introduced in the Sudan Ordinance, for the same reason previously mentioned in the case of the U.A.R.

continued after the expiry of its period, depends on the terms of the original contract. In the U.A.R. the change takes place automatically by operation of the law, even though the parties expressly provide otherwise in their first contract, unless the contract is for specific work which by its nature is renewable, in which case, the contract preserves its limited nature on continuation. In both countries the parties are free to renew their contract for another period, every time the contract expires; and the contract in this case preserves its limited nature. The law concerning the renewal of the contract, is clearer in the U.A.R. than in the Sudan. Temporary extension of the contract is expressly provided for in Sudan, but there is no relevant provision in the U.A.R.

Vicarious performance of the contract of employment is, as a rule, no proper performance of the contract, both in the U.A.R. and Sudan. Novation of the contract is, as it were, the only way out in both countries. However, there are some wide statutory exceptions to the said rule in the U.A.R., but none in the Sudan.

Both in the U.A.R. and Sudan the parties can choose the terms of their contract. However, in the making and amendment of these terms, the parties are bound expressly in the U.A.R. and impliedly in the Sudan, to abide by the minimum standards prescribed in favour of the worker, by the U.A.R. Labour Code or by the Sudan Ordinance, as the case may be. These minimum standards are more extensive in the former than in the latter. Compromises or disclaimers of rights deriving from the contract, are invalid in the U.A.R., if they are made before or during the effectiveness of the contract, or within one month after its termination. In Sudan they are invalid, only if they are made before or during the effectiveness of the contract. Finally, the law in the U.A.R. and Sudan denies any favouritism to either party in the interpretation of ambiguous terms of the contract or of any ambiguous labour legislation provisions. However, there is some judicial tendency in the U.A.R. towards favouring the worker.

CHAPTER III

RIGHTS AND OBLIGATIONS OF THE PARTIES

Rights and obligations of the parties to the contract of employment emanate both in the U.A.R. and Sudan, from the contract itself. In other words, the parties are supposed to agree on these rights and obligations in the contract. However, the regulation of the contract in the U.A.R. by the Labour and Civil Codes, releases the parties of most of their obligations to specify their rights and obligations in the contract,[1] with the exception of the probation period.[2] Though the same should be expected in Sudan,[3] section 7 of the Sudan Ordinance prescribes the specification of these rights and obligations in every written contract, and furthermore itemises what shoud be specified thereon in the attested contracts.[4] However, both in the U.A.R. and Sudan, custom of the

[1] *Vide* footnote 2 to Chapter II, *supra*; *vide* also section 689 of the U.A.R. Civil Code, which provides that "the worker shall in addition to the obligations prescribed in the preceding sections, be bound by the obligations prescribed in the special laws"; and *vide* section 693 of the Code, which provides in similar terms, in respect of the obligations of the employer. The special laws referred to in these two sections, presumably mean the labour laws, in the first instance.

[2] Section 44 of the U.A.R. Civil Code provides that "the period of probation shall be fixed in the contract of employment." *Vide* Cairo Labour Court in case No. 4029 of 1956 (in El-Hawwari, p. 73), in which it was held that a worker cannot be said to have been appointed under probation, unless that is fixed in writing (though only for the sake of proof by the employer – *vide* Section II of Chapter II, *supra*); *vide* also the same Court in case No. 2087 of 1960 (in *Ibid.*); and *vide* section 939(1) of the Draft Civil Code, which contained an express provision as these cases decided, but was not adopted; *vide* also Badawi, K. M., p. 86; Habeeb, p. 270; and Faheem, p. 23.

[3] "...In the relationship of master and servant, ... express contractual terms are often absent, or prescribe inadequately the reciprocal rights and duties of the parties": Cheshire and Fifoot, p. 141.

[4] Section 7 of the Sudan Ordinance provides:

"Every written contract shall contain in clear and unambiguous terms all that may be necessary to define the rights and obligations of the parties thereto and, without prejudice to the generality of the foregoing, a responsible person shall not attest any contract of service unless it specifies as accurately as may be:

(a) the name of the employer and of the undertaking and of the place of employment;
(b) the name of the employed person and any other particulars necessary for his identification;
(c) the nature of the service to be performed;
(d) the place or limits within which such service is to be performed;
(e) the wages to be paid and the manner and periodicity of payments of wages;
(f) the appropriate period of notice to be given by the party wishing to terminate the contract, due regard being had to the provisions of section 10;
(g) any special conditions of the contract."

locality and trade is considered as a source of reference, spelling out the rights and obligations of the parties, but only if there is nothing in the contract to expressly or impliedly preclude such reference.[5]

Statutory regulation of the contract of employment in the U.A.R. and Sudan looms large in the regulation of the rights and obligations of the parties. These can be divided into two groups. The first consists of the rights and obligations arising at the commencement of and during employment; and the second comprises those that arise on and after the termination of employment. We shall now discuss some important selected rights and obligations, in these two groups, respectively.

SECTION I: RIGHTS AND OBLIGATIONS OF THE PARTIES ARISING AT THE COMMENCEMENT OF AND DURING EMPLOYMENT[6]

(a) Transportation

Section 55 of the U.A.R. Labour Code provides that "the employer shall be liable for the expenses of transporting his workers from the place wherefrom he requests them to come to the place of work, unless they leave their work without justification before the expiry of its period."[7] Section 64 of the Code further provides that "the employer who employs workers in places where the normal means of transport do not reach, shall provide for them the appropriate means of transport."[8]

These two sections prescribe the obligation on the employer to provide transportation for his worker, at the commencement of and during employment, respectively.

The employer's obligation under section 55, does not necessarily extend to the transportation of the worker from the latter's ordinary place of residence. The Explanatory Note to the Civil Code suggests

Section 8 of the Bahraini Labour Code, and section 6 of the Adenese Ordinance provide in similar terms. These provisions in Sudan, Bahrain and Aden, seem to have been inspired by Article 5 of the I.L.O. Convention No. 64 of 1939. *Vide* Section II of Chapter II, *supra*, re attested contracts.

[5] *Vide* section 682 of the U.A.R. Civil Code, in Section II of Chapter I, *supra*. For Sudan, *vide* Cheshire and Fifoot, pp. 122–124; and Batt, p. 154.

[6] The rights of the worker to receive wages and take holidays and leaves, and the obligations of the employer to pay wages to the worker, and grant him his holidays and leaves, are discussed in Chapters IV and V, *infra*.

[7] The Libyan Labour Code (section 13(d)), is the only one in the other Arab countries, which prescribes the said obligation, but without the saving provision in the U.A.R.

[8] Sections 46, 57(a) and 132(a), of the Kuwaiti, Qatari and Iraqi Labour Codes, respectively, provide to the same effect. Some writers advocate that the means of transport should be appropriate to the position of the worker: *vide* Butros and Rajab, p. 270; El-Fakahani, 1959 Supplement, pp. 147–8; and Faheem, p. 53. *Vide* Section I, F, of this Chapter, infra, for the transportation of sick workers.

that the relevant place is the place of recruitment.[9] It is submitted that the section leaves the appointment of the place to the agreement of the parties, provided that they cannot legally agree to make the employer's obligation to transport the worker for a distance shorter than that from the place of recruitment to the place of work. The employer's obligation does not extend to the transportation of the worker's family.[10] Finally, the section provides in effect, for the reimbursement of the employer by the worker, if the latter leaves the work before the expiry of its period. This presumably applies to the limited contract workers.[11] However, the same rule should be applicable to the unlimited contract workers,[11] when the worker unjustifiably[12] terminates the contract.[13]

The normal means of transport mentioned in section 64, are the public means of transport.[14] The situation of the worker's residence is immaterial.[15] Opinion is divided on who bears the cost of the said transportation. Some writers believe that the employer should bear these expenses, because if the legislator intended otherwise, he would have imposed a ceiling on the charges to the workers, as he has done in the case of housing and meals,[16] so as to put a limit on the exploitation of the worker by the employer.[17] Other writers believe that the worker

[9] Habeeb, p. 360; and El-Fakahani, 1959 Supplement, p. 146, accept the view in the Explanatory Note, without comment.

[10] *Vide* Alexandria Court of Cassation in case No. 1098 of 1953 (in Habeeb, p. 362); and *vide* El-Fakahani, 1959 Supplement, p. 147. It is believed that the section should be amended, so as to add this obligation, at least on the basis of sharing the expenses between the employer and the Government, and up to the place in which the worker is to live with his family, which is not necessarily the place of work. Such a suggestion is in line with the employer's obligation to provide housing for married workers, in certain circumstances (*vide* Section I, G, of this Chapter, *infra*).

[11] Refer to Section III of Chapter II, *supra*, for the definition and classification of the limited and unlimited contracts.

[12] Refer to Section II, B, of Chapter VI, *infra*.

[13] Badawi, K. M., pp. 184–5; Butros and Rajab, p. 270; Faheem, p. 54; and Habeeb, p. 361, are of the same opinion.

[14] Murad, p. 328; Zaki, p. 294; Naguib and Bakr, p. 103; Habeeb, p. 362; Rashed and Hashem, p. 101; and Faheem, p. 61, are of the same opinion.

[15] *Vide* El-Fakahani, 1959 Supplement, p. 178; and Naguib and Bakr, p. 103. However, if the employer is obliged to provide housing for his workers (*vide* Section I, G, of this Chapter, *infra*), and the worker refuses to take the employer's housing, Butros and Rajab, p. 291; Badawi, K. M., pp. 188–189; and Sabbour, p. 220, correctly submit that the employer should be relieved of the transportation obligation, prescribed by section 64. Faheem, p. 63, maintains otherwise, on the ground that there is no obligation on the worker, to accept the employer's housing.

[16] *Vide* Section I, G, of this Chapter, *infra*.

[17] *Vide* Zaki, p. 294, who quotes the Explanatory note to the U.A.R. Labour Code, in implied support. The said Note says that "section 64 is enacted to meet the worker's complaint that their far-placed establishments do not provide for them means of transport, so that the workers are obliged as a result, to wake up early, in order to avoid late arrival and the disciplinary penalty involved. As the worker is usually obliged to make a walking journey, the legislator obliges the said employers to provide the means of

should bear these expenses, for if the legislator intended otherwise, he would have expressly said so, as he did in section 55 of the U.A.R. Labour Code. They add that the charges to the worker should not exceed the actual cost.[18] It is submitted that the second opinion is the correct opinion, because *prima facie* the worker should pay for his own transport, and this is not changed by the provisions of section 64 of the Code.[19] However, there is no difference in opinion, concerning the right the worker acquires to free transport, if the employer provides the same and continues to do so for some time. This is considered to be a binding implied term of the contract, and the employer cannot withdraw therefrom.[20]

In Sudan there is no provision in the Sudan Ordinance or any other enactment, equivalent to the U.A.R. Labour Code provisions.[21] Any liability of the employer for transportation is purely contractual.

(b) Provision of work by the employer, and personal and exclusive service by the worker

(i) Provision of work by the employer

Both in the U.A.R. and Sudan the worker is obliged to make himself available for the service of the employer, in accordance with the contract of employment binding him with the employer; and the employer is obliged to accept the worker and enable him to serve in accordance with the contract.[22]

Whether the said obligation of the employer entails an obligation to provide work for the worker, seems to be doubtful in the U.A.R.[23]

transport, in order to prevent the worker's fatigue and the employer's loss from the said fatigue"; *vide* also Naguib and Bakr, p. 104 (who quote (an unnumbered) Cairo Court of Arbitration decision of 9 January 1955, in support); Habeeb, p. 363; and Faheem, p. 62.

[18] *Vide* Murad, p. 328; Badawi, K. M., p. 188; Butros and Rajab, p. 290; Badawi, Z., Vol. 2, p. 173; and Rashed and Hashem, p. 101.

[19] However, it is believed that the section should be amended, so as to expressly oblige the employer to bear the transport expenses, because the worker is expected in any case, to bear the cost of transport, from his residence to the place from which he can take the employer's transport, on the one hand, and because the worker sacrifices his own time in transportation, on the other hand. This belief is supported by the Explanatory Note to the Labour Code (*vide* footnote 17, *supra*) which adds: "at least from the place where the ordinary means of transport stop, to the place of work."

[20] *Vide* Cairo Court of Arbitration in dispute No. 72 of 1953 (in Naguib and Bakr, p. 104); *vide* also Rashed and Hashem, p. 102; and Butros and Rajab, p. 290.

[21] This is particularly regrettable in Sudan, because of the long distances involved.

[22] *Vide* Habeeb, p. 12; and Sabbour, p. 169. For Sudan refer to Smith, pp. 69 and 117; and Macdonell, pp. 7 and 8.

[23] *Vide* El-Areef, p. 201, who says that "the payment of wages without the provision of work, is not sufficient, because the worker may sometimes feel that he is undignified

It is, however, submitted that the employer's obligation in the U.A.R. is fulfilled by the payment of wages to the worker. This is supported by the definition of the contract of employment, which only mentions the employer's obligation to pay wages, in return for the worker's undertaking to work.[24] In Sudan the definition of the contract does not imply any obligation on the employer to provide work.[24] Under the English Common Law, it is a rule that "a master commits no breach of contract, in refusing to give his servant any work to do, so long as he pays the agreed wages."[25] The doubts arising in relation to this point in the U.A.R., do not arise in Sudan.

However, opinion in the U.A.R. favours the obligation of the employer to provide work, in the case of piece-work.[26] This should also apply to commission-work, unless a fixed salary is payable in addition to a small variable commission, and to the particular types of contracts whose nature demands the provision of work, like some theatrical contracts. In Sudan reference to the English Common Law reveals that the obligation of the employer to provide work in the case of piece-work, depends on the terms of the contract and the circumstances of the case.[27] However, if "a minimum piece-work rate is laid down by the Wages Council, the employer cannot avoid this by not supplying sufficient work to enable a worker to earn it."[28] In the case of commission-work without payment of a fixed salary, the Courts are more inclined to imply a term obliging the employer to provide work, than in the case of piece-work, though the circumstances of the case are

by what looks like charity or lack of confidence, and because the worker may thereby be deprived of experience, and thus be prejudiced in his chances of getting better employment with other employers"; *vide* also Zaki, p. 254.

[24] Refer to the definition of the contract, in Section I of Chapter I, *supra*. Zaki, p. 254, expressly submits to the same effect, subject to what is mentioned in the preceding footnote; Habeeb, p. 32, impliedly suggests the same opinion.

[25] Batt, p. 169, who quotes *Turner v. Sawdon & Co.* (1901), 2 K.B., 653, as the authority for this statement of the law in England; again, "the mere relation of employer and employee does not cast upon the employer the duty of providing work" (*Ibid.*, p. 43); this case is also an authority for the rejection of the experience issue raised by the plaintiff (*vide* footnote 22, *supra*); *vide* Cooper, pp. 58–59; Smith, pp. 45–46 and p. 47, where he says: "The word 'employ' is capable of more than one meaning, but the use of this word in a contract of hiring, does not necessarily bind the master to find work for the servant during the continuance of the contract"; *vide* the words of *Lawrence*, L. J., in similar terms, in *Marbe V.G. Edwardes (Daily's Theatre)*, (1928), I, K.B., 269; and *vide* also Macdonell, p. 130; and Halsbury, Vol. 25, p. 458.

[26] *Vide* El-Areef, p. 201; and Badawi, Z., Vol. 1, p. 52; *vide* also Zaki, p. 254; and *vide* to the same effect the implication from section 1639 Q (5) of the Netherlands Civil Code.

[27] Cf. Smith, pp. 48 and 50, with Batt, p. 169; and *vide* Cooper, p. 58; Barwell and Kar, p. 123; and Halsbury, Vol. 25, pp. 467–8.

[28] Samuels, p. 39, who quotes as an authority, *Nathan v. Gulkoff & Levy, Ltd.* (1933) Ch., 809. This is also the law in the U.A.R.

also examined.[29] In the case of theatrical and other contracts of a particular nature, there is plenty of authority in favour of implying the said obligation on the employer, as this is considered to be a part of the consideration in the contract.[30]

Comparison of the law in the U.A.R. and Sudan reveals that the exceptions to the rule that the employer is not obliged to provide work, are basically the same exceptions.

(ii) Personal service of the worker:

Section 685(a) of the U.A.R. Civil Code provides that "the worker shall perform the work himself."[31] This personal obligation of the worker is all the more emphasised by the provisions of section 697, which deem the contract terminated on the death of the worker.[32] The rule that vicarious performance of the contract by the worker is not proper performance, emanates from the said personal obligation of the worker.[33] Though a similar obligation on the employer logically follows from the worker's obligation, the employer's obligation does not seem to be as strict as it is in the case of the worker. This can be concluded from the provisions of the said section 697, which save the contract from termination on the death of the employer, unless the employer's personal qualities were of material consideration at the time of making the contract. Moreover, except in small establishments, the employer usually performs his part of the contract by delegation, without consulting the worker, whereas the worker cannot, without the permission of the employer, delegate his duties to another nor can he without such permission, even bring a 'helper.'[34] The contract in the case of authorised delegation, is novated either temporarily or permanently, as the case may be.[33] But in the so-called helper's case the contract subsists, and the worker continues to be responsible for the actions of the helper.[33]

[29] *Vide Turner v. Goldsmith* (1891), I. Q.B., 544; and cf. *Turner v. Sawdon & Co.* (1901), 2 K.B., 653; *vide* also Cooper, pp. 170 and 42–43; Smith, pp. 45–6; and Samuels, p. 18.

[30] *Vide Bunning v. Lyric Theatre, Ltd.*, 71 L.T. 396 (a case of a musical director of an orchestra, who was not permitted to conduct the orchestra, though his salary was paid); and *Clayton v. Waller* (1830), A.C. 209 (loss of a theatrical role, though salary was paid); *vide* also Cooper, pp. 58–9; Batt, pp. 43 and 170; and Smith, p. 48.

[31] Section 909(a) of the Iraqi Civil Code provides in identical terms; the German, Swiss and Polish Laws contain similar provisions (*vide* El-Areef, p. 190); sections 571 and 572 of the *Majallah* provide in similar terms.

[32] Section 697 of the U.A.R. Civil Code is quoted in Section I, F, of Chapter VI, *infra*.

[33] Refer to Section IV of Chapter II, *supra*, for a discussion on the vicarious performance and novation of the contract.

[34] *Vide* Sabbour, p. 275; Murad, p. 356; and El-Areef, p. 190; *vide* also I.L.R., Vol. 32, 1936, p. 61; and *vide* Habeeb, p. 308, re delegation.

In Sudan the personal obligation of the worker is likewise very clear.[33] Unlike the position in the U.A.R., the personal obligation of the employer is emphasized by the provisions of section 12 of the Sudan Ordinance,[35] which deem the contract terminated on the death of the employer. The personal obligations of the two parties are more or less parallel.[36] This is, however, somewhat mitigated in the case of the employer, by the permissibility of performance by delegation, similar to that open to the employer in the U.A.R. The law concerning delegation by the worker and the bringing by him of a helper, is similar to the law in the U.A.R.[37]

So the personal performance of the contract by the worker is as mandatory both in the U.A.R. and Sudan. However, personal performance by the employer seems to be more strictly required in the latter than in the former.

(iii) Exclusive service by the worker:

Section 676 of the U.A.R. Civil Code applies the provisions concerning the contract of employment to "local salesmen, commercial representatives, travellers, insurance agents and other intermediaries.... even when they work for different employers at the same time."[38] This is an express provision against the imposition of an obligation on the worker to exclusively serve an employer. On the other hand, there is no prohibition against the worker's occupation of his spare time with other work for another employer, unless the other work prejudices the interests of the employer.[39] "If, however, the other work is different in its nature, from the employer's work, and no custom prohibits the doing of other work, or if the contract with the employer does not contain such a prohibition, the worker does not commit a breach of his essential obligations by doing the said other work."[40]

[35] Section 12 of the Sudan Ordinance is quoted in Section I, F and G, of Chapter VI, *infra*.

[36] "A contract of service, unless there be specific agreement to the contrary, is performable only by the parties thereto, so that neither party can assign the contract": Cooper, p. 46.

[37] "A servant cannot perform his duties by deputy unless the contract so provides, for the essence of the contract is personal service by the servant" (Batt, p. 154); *vide* section 40 of the Indian Contract Act; and *vide* the discussion on *Badlis*, which in India, is another word for Helpers, in Barwell and Kar, p. 63.

[38] Section 676 of the U.A.R. Civil Code is fully quoted in Section III of Chapter I, *supra*. Refer to category (vii), of certain persons discussed in the said Section. *Vide* also Cairo Court of Appeal in appeal No. 655 of 1960 (in Habeeb, p. 191).

[39] *Vide*, however, Cairo District Court in case No. 16 of 1945 (in Rashed and Hashem, p. 269).

[40] Sabbour, p. 276, who quotes a Cairo Court of Appeal decision (unnumbered) taken on 27 April 1952, as an authority for the said statement of the law; *vide* also a decision of the same Court in appeal No. 300 of 1955 (in Butros and Rajab, p. 409), in support of

In England and hence in Sudan, a "person may be a servant of different masters."[41] On the other hand, "it would seem that, in the ordinary case, the earnings of a workman in his spare time belong to him, though where he works in competition with his master, his conduct may amount to bad faith and constitute a breach of the contract."[42] If the parties agree in the contract, to the effect that "the master secures the whole time of his servant during the period of service," the agreement is valid,[43] though it would be invalid "if and in so far as there are attached to it any servile incidents, as, for example, severe restraints on personal freedom of action."[44] However, "there is no term of necessary implication in a contract of service, that the servant will take no other employment during its currency."[45]

Comparison of the law in the U.A.R. and Sudan reveals no differences between them.

(c) Faithful service of the worker and the bona fides of both parties

(i) The care of a reasonable man in the performance of the work:

Section 685(a) of the U.A.R. Civil Code, after prescribing that the worker should perform the work personally, provides that "he shall in the performance of the work use the care of the reasonable man."[46] This is presumably the case, unless the contract expressly or impliedly provides for a higher degree of care, or the circumstances require such care or even permit a lower degree of care.[47] There is no similar statutory provision in Sudan; but similar rules apply, through reference to the English Common Law.[48]

the same statement; and *vide* Zaki, p. 243; El-Areef, p. 193; and Badawi, Z., Vol. 1, p. 59; and I.L.R., Vol. 32, 1936, p. 65. The problem of the occupation of the worker's spare time has caught the attention of the I.L.O., which has issued Recommendation No. 21 of 1924, concerning the *Development of Facilities for the Utilization of Workers' Spare Time*, whose main gist is the improvement of the worker's conditions of service, so as to "prevent workers from having recourse to additional paid work."

[41] Halsbury, Vol. 25, p. 448; *vide* also *Lord Russell of Killowen*, in *Jones v. Scullard* (1898) 2 Q.B., 565. Refer to category (vii), in Section III of Chapter I, *supra*, concerning commercial representatives etc.

[42] Batt, pp. 159–160; *vide* also the relevant words of *Lord Greene*, M.R., in *Hivac Ltd. v. Park Royal Scientific Instruments Ltd.* (1946), Ch. 169.

[43] Halsbury, Vol. 25, p. 461; *vide* also Smith, p. 66; and Batt, pp. 98–99.

[44] Halsbury, Vol. 25, p. 461.

[45] Barwell and Kar, p. 127; *vide* also *Lloyd v. Midland Railway Co.* (1914), 30 T.L.R., 247.

[46] Section 909(1, a) of the Iraqi Civil Code provides in identical terms; *vide* El-Areef, p. 191; and Murad, p. 356.

[47] A lower degree of care is usually deemed to be permitted, when an employer knowingly accepts an unexperienced worker.

[48] *vide Liste v. Romford Ice and Cold Storage Co., Ltd.* (1957) A.C. 555, where *Viscount Simonds* said it is an implied term in the contract, that the workman should "perform his duties with proper care"; *vide* also Diamond, p. 104; Cheshire and Fifoot, p. 142; Barwell and Kar, p. 367; and Macdonell, p. 209.

(ii) The employer's orders

Section 685(b) of the U.A.R. Civil Code provides that the worker "shall obey the employer's orders concerning the performance of the work agreed upon or the work falling within the duties of the worker's position, provided that these orders do not violate the contract terms or the provisions of the law or the public morality, and provided that the obedience to these orders does not endanger the worker's safety."[49] Obedience to the employer's orders is the backbone of his control of the worker which, as we have previously seen, constitutes the most essential element of the contract of employment.[50] Section 10(2) of the Sudan Ordinance provides that an employer may dismiss an employed person without notice, "for wilful disobedience of a lawful order."[51] So by inference, the worker in Sudan is bound to obey the employer's lawful orders. The legality of the orders in Sudan includes legality by virtue of the law and of the contract itself. In this respect, the statutory provisions in the U.A.R. are similar.[52] Reference to the English Common Law in Sudan shows similarity in the worker's right to refuse to obey an order endangering his safety.[53]

In the U.A.R. the worker is obliged to obey the employer's orders, as prescribed in the said section 685(a), "whether the orders are oral or written, whether issued by the employer himself or his representative, or whether contained in the disciplinary rules or the work rules."[54] It is submitted that the same applies in Sudan.

[49] Section 909 (1, c) of the Iraqi Civil Code provides in identical terms; *vide* also similar provisions in section 608 of the *Majallah.*

[50] *Vide* Cairo Court of Cassation in case No. 216 of 1958 (in El-Hawwari, p. 245); *vide* also El-Areef, p. 198; Murad, pp. 357–8; Zaki, p. 242; and Habeeb, pp. 309–310. *Vide* Section I of Chapter I, *supra,* for the element of control in the contract.

[51] *Vide* similar provisions in section 13(a) of the Bahraini Labour Code. Section 10 of the Sudan Ordinance is fully quoted and discussed in Section II of Chapter VI, *infra.*

[52] In this respect, the Sudan provision is also similar to the English Common Law: *vide* Diamond, p. 102; Batt, pp. 61, 154 and 155; Cooper, pp. 73–74; Smith, p. 81; Macdonell, p. 205; Halsbury, Vol. 25, p. 462; and Barwell and Kar, pp. 77–78 and 368.

[53] *Vide* Diamond, p. 102; Batt, p. 61; Cooper, pp. 73–74; Macdonell, p. 205; and Barwell and Kar, p. 77. This rule in England, is strictly limited to the safety of the worker himself, and is not extended to an immediate danger to the life of a close relative, even if he be one of the parents of the worker; *vide* in this respect, the surprising decision in *Turner v. Mason* (1845), 14, M. & W. 112, where a housemaid was held to be rightly dismissed, after she absented herself for one day to see her dying mother, in defiance of her employer's refusal to let her go. It is submitted that such a dismissal will be held unjustifiable in the U.A.R. It is also submitted that the application of 'justice, equity and good conscience' in Sudan, should preclude the holding of the said dismissal as rightful. Refer to Section IV of Chapter V, *infra,* for the emergency leave prescribed in some countries, purposely to preclude the happening of the awkward situation which happened in *Turner's* case.

[54] Habeeb, p. 310; *vide* also Murad, p. 358; El-Areef, pp. 197–198; Rashed and Hashem p. 260; and El-Fakahani, Vol. II, Book I, p. 114.

The right of the worker to disobey the employer's orders which violate the contract terms, emanates from the basic principle in the law of contract that no contract can be amended by the will of either party, without the consent of the other.[55] The said violating orders amount to an amendment of the contract by one party only. In the U.A.R. and Sudan such violating orders amount to a breach of the contract.[56]

To this rule there are some exceptions in the U.A.R. These are contained in the Labour and Civil Codes. Section 57 of the Labour Code provides that "the employer shall not violate the terms of the contract or request the worker to perform work not agreed upon except for the necessary prevention of an accident or the repair of the damage resulting therefrom or in the case of *force majeure*, provided that such violation or performance shall be temporary. The employer shall be entitled to request the worker to perform[57] work other than the work agreed upon, if it is not essentially different therefrom."[58] There is an essential difference "between the new work and the work agreed upon, when the change involves a change in the nature of the original work, and a change in the social or legal status of the worker."[59] When the work is changed in accordance with the said section, no reduction of the worker's wages is permitted.[60] Section 696(2) of the U.A.R. Civil Code provides that "the transfer of the worker to a less advantageous or less suitable position for no wrong committed by him shall not be considered as an unjustifiable dismissal in an indirect manner if such transfer is required by the interests of work, but it shall be so considered

[55] Section 147 of the U.A.R. Civil Code provides that "the contract is the 'law' of the parties, and may not be renunciated or amended without the consent of both parties." The same principle applies in Sudan: *vide* Barwell and Kar, p. 51, where they say that "the terms of the contract can not be varied unilaterally."

[56] Zaki, pp. 329–330; and Habeeb, p. 421, maintain that the breach results only in limited contracts. In unlimited contracts, they maintain that the violating orders amount to a notice of termination, because either party has a right to terminate such contracts by notice. Cairo Court of Cassation in case No. 1976 of 1959 (in El-Hawwari, p. 161), supports their view. It is submitted, however, that they are wrong, simply because the notice of termination, prescribed by section 72 of the U.A.R. Labour Code, should be in writing (*vide* Chapter VI, Section II, A, 2, *infra*).

[57] The intent in this case, is "to temporarily or permanently perform."

[58] Of all the Labour Codes of the Arab countries, only the Libyan Labour Code (section 14(d)), and the Saudi Regulations (section 10(3 and 4)), contain provisions similar to the U.A.R. provisions.

[59] Cairo Court of Cassation in case No. 1976 of 1959 (in El-Hawwari, p. 161); *vide* also Cairo Court of Appeal in appeal No. 444 of 1954 (in Habeeb, p. 422). Rashed and Hashem, p. 69; and Faheem, p. 60, say that an essential change occurs, when the worker is transferred from mental to manual work; *vide* I.L.R., Vol. 32, p. 62.

[60] *Vide* Faheem, p. 60.

if the intention is to injure the interests of the worker."[61] This section should be read subject to the abovementioned section 57 of the U.A.R. Labour Code.[62] Both sections were enacted, in order to enable the employer to exercise his managerial powers of control in the best interests of the work.[63] No reduction of the worker's wages is permitted, when the status is lowered by virtue of section 696(2) of the Civil Code.[64] Finally, the provisions of section 56 of the U.A.R. Labour Code[65] do not form any exception to the general rule that a contract can not be altered unilaterally.[66]

In Sudan there is no statutory provision equivalent to section 57

[61] Section 921(2) of the Iraqi Civil Code provides in identical terms. The burden of proof lies on the worker: Cairo Court of Appeal in appeal No. 35 of 1955 (in El-Fakahani, Vol. II, Book I, p. 82).

[62] *Vide* section 675(1) of the U.A.R. Civil Code, quoted in footnote 42 to the Introduction, *supra*; *vide* also Badawi, K. M., pp. 197 and 201. However, Butros and Rajab, p. 280, deny the apparent conflict between the two sections.

[63] *Vide* Alexandria Court of Appeal in appeal No. 321 of 1956 (in Habeeb, p. 423); *vide* also El-Areef, p. 203, who adds that the converse case of promotion of workers also falls within the employer's managerial powers.

[64] *Vide* El-Fakahani, 1959 Supplement, p. 153.

[65] Section 56 of the U.A.R. Labour Code provides that "the employer shall not without the worker's written consent transfer him from the monthly-paid to the daily or weekly-paid category of workers or to that paid on a piece-work basisor by the hour, and the worker when he so consents shall retain all the rights he acquired by virtue of sections 58, 61, 71, 72, 73, 78 and 81, during the period he was paid by the month." Zaki, pp. 330–331; and Habeeb, p. 621, correctly point out that the said enumeration of the seven sections in section 56, is surprising, because monthly-paid and other workers are, with the exception of section 72 (concerning the length of the notice of termination of the contract: *vide* Section II, A, 2, of Chapter VI, *infra*), equally treated under the other six sections, in respect of the annual leave (sections 58 and 61: *vide* Section I of Chapter V, infra), the termination gratuity (sections 73, 71 and 78: *vide* Chapters VII and VI, *infra*), and the authorised absence on sickness (section 81: *vide* Section I, A, of Chapter VI, *infra*).

Section 10(2) of the Saudi Regulations provides in similar terms. Section 30(2) of the Kuwaiti Labour Code also provides similarly, except that there is no provision concerning the saving of acquired rights.

[66] *Vide* El-Fakahani, 1959 Supplement, p. 149; Zaki, p. 330, correctly points out, however, that the requirement of the worker's consent to be in writing, is a departure from the general rules of the law.

Though the same general rule should apply to the reverse case of a transfer of a worker, from piece-rate, hourly, daily or weekly pay, to monthly pay, and to the so-called parallel transfer from piece-rate to daily pay and *vice versa*, the Courts have ruled otherwise, and writers have rallied in support, on the grounds that such transfers are usually dictated by the interests of the work, and are usually in the interests of the worker. They also agree that any transfer should not involve a reduction of the worker's wages: *vide* Cairo Court of Appeal in the appeal on dispute No. 25 of 1959 (in El-Hawwari, p. 153); Alexandria Court of Arbitration in disputes 9 and 10 of 1953 (in Habeeb, p. 427); and Cairo Court of Appeal in appeal No. 1244 of 1955 (in El-Fakahani, Vol. II, Book I, p. 111) – These three cases illustrate the said judicial view on the transfer from a daily to a monthly pay, from piece-rate to daily pay and *vice versa*, respectively; *vide* also Habeeb, pp. 424–427; Rashed and Hashem, p. 67; Naguib and Bakr, pp. 90–92; Faheem, pp. 58 and 60; Badawi, Z., Vol. 1, pp. 153–154; Butros and Rajab, pp. 275–277; and Badawi, K.M., pp. 150–151 and 195.

of the U.A.R. Labour Code,[67] providing for express exceptions from the general law. "Servants may not be dismissed, if they refuse to perform services of a kind which they did not undertake to perform."[68] The application of this rule of the general law is subject to the particular circumstances of every individual case. It is, however submitted that the Courts will easily presume a duty on the worker to assist in the prevention of an accident, or the repairing of a damage resulting therefrom. It is further submitted that they will also hold a transfer by the employer of the worker from one work to another, to be rightful, if both types of work are not essentially different, and the change does not involve any pecuniary loss to the worker. However, any change of the worker's status will not give the worker any so-called right of protest, as the worker has in the U.A.R. by virtue of section 696(2) of the Civil Code, because the doctrine of the justification of dismissal[69] is not applicable in England and Sudan. Finally, any change in the worker's category of pay (for which section 56 of the U.A.R. Labour Code partially provides), should be subject to the said application of the general rules of the law,[70] and all the rights acquired before the said change, should be preserved for the worker, by virtue of section 35 of the Sudan Ordinance.[71]

Both in the U.A.R. and England particular attention, both judicial and juridical, is directed to whether or not a worker is bound to obey an order from his employer involving the change of the place of work. The law in both countries rules that the determination of the question depends on the express or implied terms of the contract and on the custom of the trade.[72] There is direct authority in England that the said rule of the law is subject to the qualification that the worker is not bound in any case to obey the said order, if it involves a personal danger which he has not contracted for.[72] Such qualification in the U.A.R. is contained in the above-quoted section 685(b) of the Civil Code.

[67] Neither is there any such statutory provision in Aden or Bahrain. However, *vide* the second item in the third Schedule to the Bahraini Labour Code, which lists among the disputes on which parties may be required to enter arbitration, "any dispute relating to the assignment of an employed person to work which he is not normally required to perform or which is not directly related to his normal work."

[68] Macdonell, p. 205; *vide* also Barwell and Kar, pp. 50–51; and Clark, p. 229.

[69] Refer to Section II, B, of Chapter VI, *infra*.

[70] The Industrial Court in England, ruled in *L.M.S. Railway v. National Union of Railwaymen* (award No. 1602 on 13 November 1934), that the employer is entitled to transfer the workers from piece-work to time-rate, as long as the work remains the same (*vide* I.S.D.L., Vol. 10, 1936, p. 30).

[71] Section 35 of the Sudan Ordinance is quoted in Section V of Chapter II, *supra*.

[72] For the U.A.R., *vide* Abdin District Court in case No. 3718 of 1950 (in Badawi, K.M., p. 202); and Cairo Labour Court in case No. 989 of 1960 (in El-Hawwari, p. 149); *vide*

(iii) Care for the work materials and equipment

Section 685(c) of the U.A.R. Civil Code provides that the worker "shall take good care of the things entrusted to him for the performance of his work."[73] The liability of the worker under this section, is contractual.[74] The degree of care required of the worker in this case, is the care of the reasonable man.[75] Section 54 of the U.A.R. Labour Code provides that, "where a worker, through his own fault, causes the loss, damage or destruction of equipment, machinery or products belonging to or in the custody of the employer, he shall pay the requisite amount in compensation."[76] As the liability under this section is purely tortious,[77] it is submitted that there is no need for such an express provision, which is already enacted in the Civil Code.[78] This tortious liability is excused in one instance peculiar to certain workers. This is when there is a custom in the trade making an allowance, as it were, for the worker. The custom is known in such businesses as cafés, restaurants, bars, etc., where a reasonable loss of china forms a part of the ordinary risk of the business.[79] However, responsibility for the loss which results from the incompetence of the worker only, is another thing, for that responsibility is contractual and depends on whether the employer

also El-Áreef, p. 202; Habeeb, pp. 423–424 (who also quotes Cairo Court of Appeal in appeal No. 35 of 1955, as authority for the correct proposition, that the employer's right of transferring the worker to another place, is also subject to section 696(2) of the U.A.R. Civil Code); Badawi, K. M., pp. 198–199; Rashed and Hashem, pp. 69–70; Butros and Rajab, pp. 279–280; El-Fakahani, 1959 Supplement, pp. 154–155; and Faheem, pp. 59–60. *Vide* also the two French decisions in *Weick v. Société générale et Banque française de Syrie* (1932), Gaz. du Palais, 1932, 140, and *Lamiot v. Poiret* (1927), Gaz. du Palais, 1927, 1, 457, (both in I.S.D.L., Vol. 8, 1934, p. 106, and Vol. 3, 1928, p. 96, respectively).

For England and hence for Sudan, *vide* and compare the two cases of *The Ottoman Bank v. Chakarian* (1930) A.C. 277; and *Bouzourou v. Ottoman Bank* (1930) A.C. 271; *vide* also Diamond, p. 102; Cooper, p. 56; Barwell and Kar, p. 72, 77–78 and 341; and Batt, p. 89, who shows that the same rule applies, in the case of a transfer of the employer's business itself to another place, thus involving a change of the worker's place of work by necessity.

[73] *Vide* the Cairo Labour Court in case No. 4534 (in El-Hawwari, p. 253). Section 909 (1, d) of the Iraqi Civil Code provides in the same terms, and adds that the worker is by law, a bailee of the said things; *vide* also section 609 of the *Majallah*.

[74] *Vide* El-Areef, p. 196. Presumably, this means the contract of bailment.

[75] *Vide* section 211 of the U.A.R. Civil Code; and *vide* Murad, p. 358.

[76] Sections 44, 14(b), 69–70 and 10–14 of the Iraqi, Lebanese and Tunisian Labour Codes, respectively, and section 8 of the Saudi Regulations contain similar provisions. *Vide* section 76(3) of the U.A.R. Labour Code (in Section II, A, 4, of Chapter VI, *infra*). *Vide* also the I.L.O. *Protection of Wages Convention No. 95 of 1949.*

[77] *Vide* El-Areef, p. 196; and Rashed and Hashem, pp. 62–63.

[78] *Vide* sections 4,5, 163 and 164 of the U.A.R. Civil Code.

[79] *Vide* Murad, p. 359; El-Areef, p. 196; Rashed and Hashem, pp. 62–63; El-Fakahani, 1959 Supplement, p. 144; Badawi, Z., Vol. 1, p. 72; Naguib and Bakr, p. 87; Faheem, p. 48; and Badawi, K. M., p. 182.

knew of the worker's incompetence, at the time of making the contract or not.[80]

In Sudan there is no equivalent to the said section 54 of the U.A.R. However, section 10(2) of the Sudan Ordinance provides that an employer may dismiss an employed person without notice, "for serious negligence or wilful misconduct calculated seriously to injure the employer's business."[81] From this provision and the rules of the English Common Law,[82] the worker's contractual and tortious liabilities like those obtaining in the U.A.R., can be deduced. It is submitted that the excusal of the worker's tortious liability on the ground of custom, is also applicable in Sudan. As for the responsibility for the loss which results from the worker's incompetence, it is also contractual in Sudan.[83]

(iv) Preservation of professional secrets

Section 685(d) of the U.A.R. Civil Code provides that the worker "shall preserve the industrial and commercial secrets of the work."[84] Section 76(7) of the U.A.R. Labour Code empowers the employer to dismiss the worker without notice, if the latter reveals "the secrets of the establishment." So the latter section is wider in scope than the former, in respect of the definition of secrets. These secrets include "all the information, which concerns the commerce or industry and whose disclosure will undermine the confidence in the merchant or industrialist, and all the information which by custom is usually kept confidential."[85] The reason behind the imposition of this obligation on the worker, is the safeguarding of the employer's interests by precluding competition with the employer in his trade, whether by the worker himself or

[80] *Idem. Vide* also Section II, A, 3, of Chapter VI, *infra*, for the employer's power to dismiss the worker, for misrepresentation.

[81] *Vide* similar provisions, in section 13(a) of the Bahraini Labour Code. Sections 18(c) and 21(1) of Ordinance 33 of 1945 in Aden, expressly provide in terms, similar to section 54 of the U.A.R. *Vide* Batt, p. 128, for a mention of the worker's obligation to compensate the employer for damaged goods, similar to the obligation in the U.A.R.; and *vide* section 2 of the English Truck Act of 1896, to the same effect; *vide* also section 7 of the Indian Payment of Wages Act, No. IV of 1936.

[82] *Vide* Batt, pp. 157–8; Cooper, p. 68; Smith, pp. 72–3; Macdonell, p. 209; and Barwell and Kar, p. 374.

[83] *Vide* Batt, pp. 157–8: "Presumably the servant would be liable in an action for breach of contract for having failed to possess and apply that skill which by entering his engagement of service he contracted to possess and apply, unless the master knew of his servant's lack of skill, when the master would have only himself to blame"; *vide* also Barwell and Kar, p. 366.

[84] Section 909 (1, e) of the Iraqi Civil Code provides in identical terms.

[85] Cairo Court of Appeal in appeal No. 401 of 1960 (in El-Hawwari, p. 255). Murad, p. 360, correctly points out that the faithful service of the worker also imposes on the agricultural worker, the duty not to disclose his employer's secrets.

by those to whom the worker discloses the employer's secrets.[86]

In Sudan section 10(2) of the Sudan Ordinance provides that the employer may dismiss an employed person without notice, "for gross misconduct in or connected with his employment... or wilful misconduct calculated seriously to injure the employer's business." From this provision and from the rules of the English Common Law, an obligation of the worker not to disclose the trade secrets can be deduced.[87] The same reasons for the imposition of this obligation obtain in Sudan, as can be inferred from the English Common Law.[88]

(v) The bona fides of the parties

The general law of contracts, both in the U.A.R. and Sudan, prescribes that the parties to the contract should show *bona fides* in the performance of their contractual duties.[89]

The *bona fides* of the worker or his duty of fidelity towards his employer, is in both countries, manifested mainly by the worker's honesty as regards his employer's property,[90] by not receiving a secret commission related to the business of his employer, and if such commission or other monies are received while working for the employer, by accounting therefor,[91] by good behaviour towards the employer and his

[86] *Vide* Cairo Labour Court in case No. 5322 of 1959; and Cairo Court of Appeal in appeal No. 486 of 1960 (El-Hawwari, pp. 257 and 256, respectively); *vide* Butros and Rajab, p. 346; Zaki, pp. 242–243; Habeeb, pp. 312–313; El-Areef, pp. 193–195; Rashed and Hashem, pp. 268–271; and Badawi, Z., Vol. 1., p59; *vide* also I.L.R., Vol. 32, 136, p. 64.

[87] *Vide Helmore v. Smith* (1886), 35 C.D. 449; *vide* also Batt, pp. 63–64, and p. 160, where he says: "How far a servant must observe silence in regard to his master's affairs must presumably depend upon all the circumstances. No liability could attach for revealing the frauds or malpractices of his master, indeed he may be under a public duty to disclose these"; and *vide East Anglican Railways Co. v. Lythgoe* (1851) 20 L.J.C.P. 841; and *Triplex Safety Glass Co. v. Scorah* (1938) Ch. 211; *vide* also Diamond, p. 105; and Cooper, p. 40.

[88] *Vide Hivac Ltd. v. Park Royal Scientific Instruments, Ltd.*, (1946), Ch. 169; and *Pearce V. Foster* (1886), 17 Q.B.D. 536; *vide* also Batt, p. 156; Macdonell, p. 210; Diamond, pp. 65 and 78–80; Cooper, pp. 63–64 and 65; and Smith, p. 66.

[89] *Vide* section 148 of the U.A.R. Civil Code. For Sudan *vide* Diamond, p. 105; Smith, p. 71; and Macdonell, p. 209.

[90] For the U.A.R., *vide* Cairo Court of Appeal in appeal No. 655 of 1960; and Alexandria Court of Cassation in case No. 126 of 1959 (both in El-Hawwari, pp. 240 and 241, respectively); and *vide* Murad, p. 359. For Sudan, *vide Cunningham v. Fonblanque* (1883), 6C & P 44 N.P., quoted by Barwell and Kar, p. 376, where they correctly add that "the conduct of the servant during his employment is alone material." It is submitted that the same applies in the U.A.R.

[91] For the U.A.R., *vide* Alexandria Court of Appeal in appeal No. 288 of 1957 (in Habeeb, p. 309); Cairo Court of Cassation in case No. 2158 (in El-Hawwari, p. 251); *vide* also El-Areef, p. 193; and *vide* the French case of *Société Chaleur et Froid* (1931), Gaz. du Palais, 1931 ,2, 659, (in I.S.D.L., Vol. 7, 1933, p. 122). However, tips received by workers in cafés, restaurants and bars, are not such secret commissions, as it is customary to accept tips in the said places; section 684 of the U.A.R. Civil Code (*vide* Chapter IV, Section I, *infra*), provides for the partial or exclusive remunerative function of

representatives and towards colleagues and customers,[92] and by not lowering the production in a disguised manner.[93] As for the worker's obligation to disclose any dishonesty connected with and committed by him during employment, the law in England and hence in Sudan, is settled to the effect that "a servant need not inform against himself, that would be the standard of saints and angels."[94] Nor is the worker obliged to disclose his past dishonesties committed before the commencement of the employment, unless "by some special term of the contract disclosure of any previous conduct is incumbent on the servant."[95] Moreover, the worker is not obliged to disclose any dishonesties connected with his employment, when they are committed by his fellow-workers, unless the terms of the contract otherwise provide.[96] In the U.A.R. it is submitted that the law would be similar to England and Sudan, in respect of disclosure by the worker of his own dishonesties. However, as the employer's powers of dismissal are fettered by his obligation to justify the dismissal,[97] the worker's *bona fides* in the U.A.R. would impose upon him an obligation to disclose the dishonesties of his fellow-workers.

The *bona fides* of the employer in the U.A.R. and Sudan is mainly manifested by the good treatment of the worker,[98] and by his protection

these tips. For Sudan, *vide Boston Fishing Co. v. Ansell* (1888) 39 C.D. 399; and *Morison v. Thompson* (1874) L.R. 9 Q.B. 48; *vide* also Diamond, pp. 108 and 110; Smith, pp. 71–72; Halsbury, Vol. 25, p. 462; Batt, pp. 64 and 158–160; Cooper, p. 68; and Barwell and Kar, pp. 81–82. However, "in many classes of service the receipt of tips is fully recognized by the employers, or it is so notorious a practice that they cannot complain of it. In many employments the fact that the servants will obtain tips regulates the wages they are paid": Batt, p. 156; *vide* also Cooper, p. 69.

[92] For the U.A.R., *vide* Cairo Court of Cassation in cases No. 672 of 1958, and No. 1339 of 1959 (both in El-Hawwari, pp. 255 and 248, respectively); Cairo Court of Appeal in appeal No. 1185 of 1960 (*Ibidem*, p. 260); *vide* also Murad, p. 360; El-Areef, pp. 193-194; Rashed and Hashem, p. 256; and Habeeb, p. 309. For Sudan, *vide* the Indian case of *Middleton v. Playfair* (1925) A.I.R. Cal. 87; and the English case of *Lacy v. Osbaldiston (1837)*, 8 C. & P. 80, both quoted by Barwell and Kar, in pp. 77 and 373, respectively; *vide* also Batt, p. 63, and Macdonell, p. 213.

[93] *Grève perlée*, as it is called in France; *vide* El-Areef, p. 192; Habeeb, pp. 308–309; Butros and Rajab, p. 338. It is submitted that the same applies in Sudan.

[94] Batt, p. 155 – vide *Bell v. Lever* (1932) A.C. 161: In the course of his judgement, *Lord Atkin* said: "The servant owes a duty not to steal, but, having stolen, is there a superadded duty to confess that he has stolen? I am satisfied that to imply such a duty would be a departure from the well-established usage of mankind and would be to create obligations outside the normal contemplation of the parties concerned"; *vide* also Barwell and Kar, pp. 79 and 369.

[95] Barwell and Kar, p. 376 – *vide Baster v. London and County Printing Works* (1899) I.Q.B. 901.

[96] *Vide Swain v. West (Butchers) Ltd.* (1936) 3 A.E.R. 261; *vide* also Batt, p. 155; Cooper, p. 37; and Barwell and Kar, pp. 372–373.

[97] *Vide* Section II, B, of Chapter VI, *infra*.

[98] Apart from the deduction of this obligation of the employer from section 148 of the Civil Code, the obligation can also be deduced from section 696(1) of the Code, which

from dangers at work.[99] Before the statutory obligation was first imposed on the employer (by law 41 of 1944), to give his worker a certificate of service at the termination of the service, the Courts held that such obligation existed in any case, as it was required by the *bona fides* of the employer.[100] In Sudan there is no such statutory obligation, nor is there any such obligation on the employer under the English Common Law, unless the contract prescribes it. However, if the employer chooses to give a testimonial to the worker, he should not state anything therein, unless he *bona fide* believes it to be true. The question of the employer's responsibility for the loss of or damage to the worker's personal property, does not seem to have been mooted in the U.A.R. However, it is submitted that, apart from the employer's liability as a bailee of the said property, when there is a contract of bailment between him and the worker,[101] the liability iso therwise tortious and is decided accordingly.[102] In England and hence in Sudan, the law is similar to the said submission concerning the law in the U.A.R.[103]

(d) Work rules

Section 68 of the U.A.R. Labour Code provides that "every employer who employs fifteen or more workers shall display in a prominent place in his establishment the basic rules of the work and shall deposit them

gives the worker a right to leave his employment, on account of 'unjust treatment' (*vide* Section II, A, 3, of Chapter VI, *infra*, and *vide* therein section 76(3 & 4) of the U.A.R. Labour Code); *vide* also El-Areef, pp. 200 and 203; and Habeeb, p. 317. For Sudan, *vide* Barwell and Kar, p. 77, who quote in support, the Indian case of *Middleton v. Playfair* (1925) A.I.R. Cal. 87: "The judgement went on to say that the master, by necessary implication had, under a contract of personal service, the duty of protection and of the exercise of gentleness and moderation in his bearing towards his servants."

[99] *Vide* Section I, F, of this Chapter, *infra*.

[100] *Vide* The High Court of Appeal in two (unnumbered) appeals decided on 18 May 1950 and 11 February 1954 (El-Areef, p. 365); *vide* also Habeeb, p. 318; Zaki, p. 254; and Rashed and Hashem, p. 331; refer to Section II, B, of this Chapter, *infra*.

[101] *Vide* sections 720–728 of the U.A.R. Civil Code.

[102] *Vide* sections 163 and 174 of the U.A.R. Civil Code; El-Areef, pp. 203– 206, submits similarly, and quotes some old French decisions in support – *vide*, however, the two French Decisions of *Société d'apprêts et teintureries roannaises v. Vernisse* (1933), Dalloz Hebdom., 1933, 553, and *Société d'Electricité Ouest-Lumière v. Moulin* (1931), Gaz. du Palais, 1931, 1, 134, (both in I.S.D.L., Vol. 9, 1935, p. 76, and Vol. 7, 1933, p. 124, respectively) – these two cases show the judicial trend in France, in favour of implying a contract of bailment from the employment relationship; *vide* also the German decision of 10 November 1961, reported in I.L.R., Vol. 87, 1963.

[103] *Vide Deyong v. Shenburn* (1946) I A.E.R. 226; *vide* also Cheshire and Fifoot, p. 143. Barwell and Kar, p. 119, correctly submit that, "in instances where it is a term of a contract that the servant shall perform his services in a prescribed costume, there would be a duty in the master to provide a reasonably secure method of safe custody for such garments. This is not to say that the master thereby becomes either a bailee of such property or an insurer of them." It is submitted that this would be the case in the U.A.R.

with the competent administrative authority."[104] This section seemingly prescribes as an obligation on the employer, what *prima facie* is first and foremost a right of the employer,[105] in securing the smooth operation of the work. Work rules have been defined "as the rules for the regulation of the work, and the treatment of the workers."[106] Accordingly, these rules are supposed to be limited to all the employer's executive orders, concerning the performance of the work. With this limitation, it can easily be appreciated that the employer's power to make the work rules, emanates from his power of control over his workers. In other words, the so-called administrative nature of these rules is quite apprehensible. However, work rules sometimes contain some regulation of the rights and obligations of both parties, especially those of the worker. This has given rise to a controversy as to the contractual nature of work rules. Opinion in this respect is divided into three directions. The first considers that the work rules are administrative, and they are binding on the worker as long as "they do not violate the provisions of the law."[107] The second considers that the work rules are contractual, and thus can not be amended unilaterally.[108] The third takes the middle course between the two, and considers that work rules are of a mixed

[104] The Labour Office, within whose jurisdiction the place of work is situated, is designated as the competent authority, by Order No. 134 of 25 August 1959 (*Al-Jaridat-ul-Rasmiyyatu* No. 72 of 14 September 1959). The work rules must be in the Arabic language, by virtue of Law No. 62 of 1942.

The limitation of the number of workers to fifteen (it was fifty under Law 317 of 1952), is because of the para-familial ties, between the employers and their workers when they are so few, and to the employer's ability to issue his orders to the workers orally (*vide* Habeeb, p. 282; Badawi, Z., Vol. 1, p. 155; Butros and Rajab, p. 320; and Murad, p. 322).

Sections 15, 50, 66 and 86 of the Saudi Regulations, and the Kuwaiti, Lebanese and Libyan Labour Codes, respectively, provide in terms similar to section 68 of the U.A.R. Labour Code, though with different limits of the number of workers; and so does section 22 of Book I of the French Labour Code. Section 43(1) of the Iraqi Labour Code obliges the employer to make work rules, irrespective of the number of his workers.

[105] "The conditions of work in the modern factory, where a large number of workers are employed and must cooperate smoothly among themselves and under a common management, require that the work done in common shall be regulated by general provisions. This is the object of rules of employment": I.L.R., Vol. 31, 1935, p. 856; *vide* also to the same effect, Zaki, pp. 228, 229 and 230; and Badawi, K. M., p. 247.

[106] The High Court of Appeal in appeal No. 362 of 1957 (in El-Hawwari, p. 141). *Vide* also Zaki, p. 228; and Naguib and Bakr, p. 124.

[107] *Vide* Cairo Court of Appeal in appeal No. 768 of 1958; and the appeal on dispute No. 100 of 1958, (both in El-Hawwari, pp. 144 and 142, respectively); *vide* also Zaki, pp. 230 and 231.

[108] *Vide* Sabbour, p. 138; Butros and Rajab, pp. 319 and 312; and Naguib and Bakr, pp. 124–125; *vide* also the two French decisions of *Société Faux et Lafon v. Padovani* (1935), Sirey, 1935, 1, 45, and of the Cour de Cass., Ch. Civ., on 23 April 1929, Gaz. du Palais, 1930, 1,853 (sub-note (b)), (both in I.S.D.L., Vol. 11, 1935–1936, p. 105 and Vol. 6, 1931, p. 84, respectively); cf. the decision on 28 June 1909, Dalloz Hebdom., 1910, 1,21 (quoted by El-Areef, p. 215); and *vide* section 98 of the U.A.R. Civil Code; *vide* also I.L.R., Vol. 31, 1935, p. 858.

nature, contractual in as far as they regulate the rights and obligations of the parties, and administrative otherwise.[109] It is submitted that the first opinion is the correct opinion, and the regulation of the rights and obligations of the parties in the work rules does not change the so-called administrative nature of these rules. Whether the said regulation of the rights and obligations does or does not bind the worker, depends on the terms of the contract between the worker and the employer. If the work rules are binding on the worker, it is because the contract itself has made them binding by their incorporation as binding terms in the contract, and not by virtue of any independent superimposed contractual nature of their own.[110] Furthermore, the freedom allowed to the employer by the said section 68 of the Labour Code, to make or not to make any work rules, if he employs less than fifteen workers,[111] emphasises the administrative nature of the work rules.[112] It is further submitted that the obligation of the employer to display the work rules, prescribed by the said section 68, does not of itself give these rules a contractual nature. When the regulation of the rights and obligations of the parties in the work rules is binding, it is immaterial whether the rules are displayed or not. The real reason behind the requirement to display the rules, is to preclude the worker from claiming that he did not know of the orders of the employer, and consequently should not be penalised for any disobedience to these orders.[113] Finally, the highest tribunal in the U.A.R. twice rejected the contention that the employer is by virtue of section 68 of the Labour Code, obliged to include a cadre for the classification and promotion of his workers, "because the section is limited to organisational matters, and does not deal with the monetary rights of the workers."[114] It is quite clear that, had it not been for the administrative function of the work rules, no work rules would be necessary, for any collective regulation of the rights and obligations of the parties has a handy and a distinctly contractual

[109] *Vide* Badawi, K. M., pp. 248–249; Habeeb, pp. 284–285; El-Areef, pp. 213 and 216; El-Fakahani, 1959 Supplement, p. 197; Rashed and Hashem, pp. 140 and 141; and Faheem, p. 69.

[110] Section 682 of the U.A.R. Civil Code (quoted in Section II of Chapter IV, *infra*), which mentions the fixing of wages and the defining of obligations, in work rules, does not contradict with the said submission.

[111] *Vide* footnote 104, *supra*, and Section I, E, of this Chapter, *infra*.

[112] Zaki, p. 232, however, tries to conclude from the said limitation, a contractual nature for the work rules, if they are made voluntarily by an employer, who employs less than fifteen workers. It is submitted that he is wrong.

[113] *Vide* C, (ii), of Section I of this Chapter, *supra*, re orders.

[114] *Vide* The High Court of Appeal in appeals Nos. 283 and 362 of 1957 (both in Habeeb, p. 283); vide also Murad, pp. 323–4; and footnote 41 to Chapter IV, *infra*.

vehicle, viz. the collective contracts which automatically bind a new worker.

In Sudan there is no legislative provision on work rules.[115] The English Common Law has not plunged into the controversy we saw in the U.A.R., concerning the administrative or contractual nature of the work rules. The law is quite settled in England to the effect that any regulation of the rights and obligations of the parties in the work rules is not binding except by implication as terms in the contract,[116] much the same as is the binding effect of collective agreements.

(e) Disciplinary rules and measures

The element of control in the contract of employment in the U.A.R. includes, as was previously mentioned, the employer's power to take disciplinary measures against the worker, "if the latter neglects or fails to carry out the prescribed work, or to abide by the terms of the contract or the work rules or the provisions of the law."[117] So the employer's power to take disciplinary measures arises automatically with the making of the contract, and does not need any further contractual authorisation from the worker – "The disciplinary power is based on the employer's right of management and control."[118]

In Sudan the employer, cannot illogically,[119] exercise any power of discipline, unless he is so authorised by the contract. So this power does not arise automatically with the making of the contract, contrary to the position in the U.A.R.[120]

[115] There are no provisions in Bahrain and Aden. However, India has a provision in the Industrial Employment (Standing Orders) Act, 1946 – *vide* L.S., 1946 (Ind. 2).

[116] *Vide* Batt, p. 51 (footnote 3); O. Kahn-Freund in Flanders and Clegg, p. 49; and Clark, p. 3.

[117] Refer to Section I of Chapter I, *supra*. *Vide* also the Council of State's opinion No. 13919/11/51 delivered on 30 December 1951, (in Rashed and Hashem, p. 142; and El-Areef, p. 199), to the same effect.

[118] Zaki, p. 256; *vide* also Murad, p. 364; Badawi, K. M., pp. 29, 32 and 236; Rashed and Hashem, pp. 115 and 141–142; El-Fakahani, 1959 Supplement, pp. 184 and 198; Naguib and Bakr, p. 111; and I.L.R., Vol. 32, 1936, p. 60.

[119] The illogicality is apparent from the insistence on the employer's power of control, in England and Sudan. "There can be no management in public or private enterprise without disciplinary power. The relation between employer and employee is one of subordination. The law, however, considers that the disciplinary power of the employer rests on the contract of employment. By entering into that contract, the employee submits to that power in so far as this is customary or expressly agreed": O. Kahn-Freund, in Flanders and Clegg, p. 49 – These words are a witness of a commendable attempt at the injection of Continental ideas in England.

[120] This is by virtue of reference to the English Common Law: *vide* Cooper, p. 117: "The permissibility of the practice of imposing fines on workmen or shop assistants depends upon the making of a contract between the employer and employee"; *vide* also Samuels, p. 45; Batt, p. 127; and Macdonell, pp. 32 and 33. The position in Aden, is

The exercise by the employer of his contractual power of dismissal in Sudan, is governed by the contract between the employer and the worker. 'Justice, equity and good conscience' presumably renders applicable in Sudan, the principles of section 1 of the English 1896 Truck Act.[121] By virtue of this section, no fine can be imposed upon a workman, unless the contract specifies the eventualities justifying the imposition of fines, provided that these should be eventualities in which the employer's business is likely to be damaged or hindered. The section further provides that the contract should specify the amounts and the basis of the calculation of fines, provided that the amounts of the fines should be reasonable in the circumstances.[122] "Such fines may be imposed under these provisions for general misconduct or breaches of good order and decorum."[123] On the other hand, "where under the contract of service forfeiture or deduction of wages is provided for as the penalty of absence or breach of rules, anything the servant may wish to say should be heard by the employer before the forfeiture or deduction is effected."[124]

Government workers in Sudan, who are covered by the Sudan Ordinance, are by virtue of an implied term in their contract, bound by the Officials Discipline Ordinance of 1927. Section 7 of this Ordinance enumerates the disciplinary penalties as reprimand, "fine not exceeding the amount of fifteen days pay," "stoppage of pay for a period not exceeding thirty days," "suspension from duty with loss of pay for a period not exceeding ninety days," "reduction of pay or of grading, or of both," "retardation of promotion or increase of pay," dismissal and "partial or total forfeiture of... gratuity" (which by virtue of section 8 of the Ordinance "may only be passed in conjunction with a sentence of dismissal for misconduct, insubordination or neglect of duty"). It can be deduced from section 7 that the Government's power to dismiss workers without notice, by virtue of section 10(2) of the Sudan Ordinance, and the resultant deprivation of the worker of his

similar to Sudan – *vide* Section 19 of the Adenese Ordinance. In Bahrain, however, section 38 of the Labour Code grants the disciplinary power to the employer, and considers it as a 'management right.' The influence of the U.A.R. in this respect, is clear.

[121] 59 and 60 Vict., C. 44.

[122] In India statutory limitations on the employer's disciplinary powers, are contained in the Industrial Employment (Standing Orders) Act of 1946 (*vide* L.S., 1946 Ind. 2), which provides for the making of disciplinary rules by the employer; and in the Payment of Wages Act No. IV 1936, which provides for disciplinary fines.

[123] Batt, pp. 127–128, who quotes as authority, *Squire v. Bayer & Co.* (1901), 2 K.B. 299 (dancing during meal hours and raising dust injurious to machines); *vide* also Cooper, p 118, who adds that "the most usual offence for which a fine is levied, is for lateness in arriving at the workshop or factory."

[124] Halsbury, Vol. 25, p. 480.

gratuity by virtue of section 25 of that Ordinance, cannot be exercised without the holding of a disciplinary trial for the worker, in accordance with the Officials Discipline Ordinance. On the other hand, the Government's power to inflict the penalty of the reduction of pay or of grading amounts to the reduction of the worker's contractual rights. This violates the provisions of section 35 of the Sudan Ordinance in the case of workers covered by the Ordinance, because this section impliedly prohibits giving to the workers any rights less than those guaranteed for them by the Ordinance. It is, therefore, submitted that the penalty of reduction cannot be inflicted on these workers. The Officials Discipline Ordinance further proceeds in Part III thereof, to provide for the constitution of the boards of discipline and their powers, and in Part IV, to provide for the procedure which guarantees the right of defence for the worker.

In the U.A.R. the automatic bestowal of the disciplinary power upon the employer necessitated the legislator's interference, so as to curb the said power and preclude any misuse thereof. This interference is witnesed by the provisions in sections 68, 66, 69 and 70 of the U.A.R. Labour Code, and by Orders 147, 148 and 149 issued in 1959, under sections 66, 68 and 70, respectively.

Section 68 of the Code provides that "every employer who employs fifteen or more workers shall display in a prominent place in his establishment... the disciplinary rules and conditions of their application. These rules and any amendments thereof shall not be applicable except with the approval of the competent authority within 45 days of their submission thereto. The Minister of Labour may by order issue model discilinary rules for the different types of work for the guidance of the employers in making their rules."[125] The limitation of the obligation to the employers who employ fifteen workers or more, seemingly leaves those who employ less than fifteen workers, free to discipline their workers as they choose. It is, however, submitted that they are bound by the provisions re fines and suspension in section 66 of the Labour Code, and re disposition of fines in section 70 of the Code.[126] The sub-

[125] What is mentioned in footnote 104 to this Chapter, *supra*, re the competent authority, the limitation of the number of workers to fifteen and the language (*vide* also section 8 of Order 147 of 1959, which provides that disciplinary rules should be written in a form understandable to the workers), equally applies to disciplinary rules.

Sections 43(1), 51 & 52, 72, 25(2), 66 & 67 and 25(3), of the Iraqi, Kuwaiti, Qatari, Jordanian, Lebanese and Libyan Labour Codes, respectively, and section 15 of the Saudi Regulations, prescribe an obligation on the employer to make disciplinary rules, and so does section 22 of Book I of the French Labour Code.

[126] Murad, p. 365; and Rashed and Hashem, pp. 116 and 140, are of the same opinion.

mission to the competent authority is necessary to ascertain whether or not the rules violate the provisions of the law. The authority's approval may be express or tacit by the non-objection of the authority to the disciplinary rules within the said 45 days.[127] If the employer differs with the authority, he can appeal to the Council of State, which is competent to examine the validity of an administrative decision like the decision of the authority in this case.[128] The right to amend the disciplinary rules belongs to the employer and not to the worker.[129] Model disciplinary rules were issued by Order 148 of 1959, dealing mainly with non-observation of the working hours, infringements of the work rules and the worker's conduct.

Section 66 of the Labour Code provides:

"No employer shall for a single offence inflict upon the worker a fine exceeding five days' wages, or subject him to a disciplinary suspension from work for more than five days, provided that no deduction from the worker's wages in satisfaction of fines shall exceed five days' wages nor shall any suspension exceed five days in any one month.

"No worker shall be charged with an offence if more than fifteen days have elapsed since the discovery of the offence.

"No disciplinary penalty shall be inflicted if more than thirty days have elapsed since the commission of the offence by a monthly-paid worker has been proved or more than fifteen days have elapsed in the case of other workers.

"Disciplinary penalties regulations and procedures shall be specified in an order from the Minister of Labour."[130]

The Minister of Labour accordingly, issued his Order 147 of 1959. Section 1 of this Order specifies the penalties as: warning, fine, sus-

[127] Murad, p. 366, maintains that the competent authority's non-objection amounts to a refusal, without reasoning.

[128] El-Fakahani, 1959 Supplement, p. 198; *vide* also Rashed and Hashem, p. 145; Butros and Rajab, p. 324; Habeeb, pp. 321-2; and Naguib and Bakr, p. 127.

[129] *Vide* Cairo Court of Arbitration in dispute No. 265 of 1953, (in Habeeb, p. 323); and the Council of State's opinion quoted in footnote 117, *supra*. The reason for the said decision and opinion, is that the power of discipline belongs to the employer. It is submitted that this reason precludes any right for the workers to request the amendment of the disciplinary rules – this is contrary to what Murad, p. 366; Butros and Rajab, p. 325; and Faheem, p. 70, maintain. But this does not mean that any rules or amendment of the rules are binding on the worker, if they violate the provisions of the law, for therein lies the worker's guarantee.

[130] Cf. sections 43(3), 52, 72, 25(2), 68 & 70, 25(3), of the Iraqi, Kuwaiti, Qatari, Jordanian, Lebanese and Libyan Labour Codes, respectively; cf. also section 22 of Book I of the French Labour Code (*vide* Zaki, p. 259); *vide* the *Labour Survey of North Africa*, for the position in Morocco, Algeria and Tunisia – France and the three North African countries do not permit the use of a fine as a penalty, except for the infraction of safety rules.

pension from work, and dismissal from service without deprivation from the termination gratuity. This enumeration gave rise to the question as to whether it is exclusive or not. Sections 6 and 11 of the Order[131] further gave rise to the said question, particularly as to whether the summary dismissal of the worker by the employer by virtue of section 76 of the Labour Code,[132] should or should not be a disciplinary dismissal.[133] Opinion was and is still divided into two directions. The first answers the question in the affirmative, mainly because it could not accept that the said serious measure of summary dismissal could be taken without a disciplinary trial, whereas minor offences punishable by less far-reaching penalties, could only be punished after the holding of such trial.[134] The second answers the question in the negative, mainly because section 76 of the Labour Code includes the employer's power of summarily dismissing the worker during the probation period, presumably on account of the worker's incompetence and not any wrong he commits. Furthermore, the worker has by virtue of section 77 of the Code, the right to leave his service instantly in certain eventualities mentioned therein;[132] and it is unthinkable that, before the worker exercises this right, he should take a disciplinary measure against the employer.[135] There is no doubt that it is advisable for the interests of

[131] Section 6 of the Order prohibits the disciplinary punishment of the worker, "for anything he commits outside the place of work, unless it concerns the work, the employer or his authorised representative, without prejudice to the provisions of section 76 of the Labour Code." Section 11 of the Order provides that a disciplinary penalty "shall not be executed before the lapse of three days after the worker is informed of the penalty in writing except in the case of summary dismissal by virtue of section 76 of the Labour Code."

[132] Sections 76 and 77 are quoted in Section II, A, 3 and 4, of Chapter VI, *infra*.

[133] Section 5 of the Order provides that "the worker shall not be suspended from work during the disciplinary investigation except in the circumstances specified in section 67 of the Labour Code." The said section provides for the employer's right to suspend the worker, for the commission of certain criminal offences, while they are being investigated by the authorities (refer for the section to Section I, C, of Chapter VI, *infra*). It is clear that the reference to section 67 ,does not make the suspension thereunder a disciplinary suspension. So the reference to section 76 of the Labour Code, in sections 6 and 11 of Order 147, does not necessarily render the summary dismissal thereunder, a disciplinary dismissal either.

[134] *Vide* the judicial decisions in El-Hawwari, pp. 124–150, 153, 176–183 and 261. *Vide* also El-Areef, p. 512 (refer to Faheem, p. 97) – *vide*, however, pp. 393–394 and footnote 1 to page 395; El-Fakahani,Vol. III, Book I ,pp. 156–158, and the 1959 Supplement, pp. 192 and 194; Rashed and Hashem, p. 126 – *vide*, however, pp. 221 and 244, where they impliedly slip into the contrary view unwittingly; Butros and Rajab, pp. 351, 352 and 367 – *vide*, however, pp. 372 and 423; Badawi, K. M., pp. 89 and 249 – *vide*, however, pp. 246 and 248; Sabbour, pp. 309–12; and Murad, p. 368.

[135] *Vide* the High Court of Appeal in appeal No. 131 of 1956 (in Zaki, p. 365); and the judicial decisions in El-Hawwari, pp. 150-153 and 261. *Vide* also Zaki, pp. 262–3 and 364; Habeeb, pp. 331–333; Badawi, Z., Vol. I, p. 95; and footnote 127 and the related text in this Chapter, *supra*. Habeeb, p. 344, who quotes the High Court of Appeal in appeal No. 202 of 1957, correctly adds that the employer's dismissal of the worker, by

the employer, to hold a disciplinary trial, before he summarily dismisses his worker by virtue of section 76 of the Labour Code, and such a trial will secure for the worker some fair treatment, by affording him a chance of explaining and justifying his deeds.[136] However, it is submitted that, though the employer on the whole does hold such trial in order to help avoid the charge of unjustifiable dismissal, he is not obliged to do so by law. "Though the dismissal of an absenting worker may be considered a disciplinary penalty before whose infliction a disciplinary trial should be held, the omission to hold the said trial does not mean that... the dismissal is unjustifiable, the Court will hold the dismissal to be justifiable if the continuous absence which is a ground of dismissal[137] is proved."[138] The Labour Code provides for the disciplinary penalties in section 66, and separately provides for the summary dismissal in section 76. So the Minister of Labour, who is requested or authorised by the former section to specify the disciplinary penalties, cannot by his order, subject, as it were, the latter section to the former section – any such attempt is *ultra vires.*[139] Indeed the inclusion of the penalty of dismissal without deprivation from the termination gratuity, in section 1 of the Order, is also *ultra vires*,[138] because such dismissal is subject to the employer's obligation by virtue of sections 74 and 75 of the Labour Code, to justify the dismissal in Court.[140] As for the reduction of the worker's wages and the lowering of his contractual position, it is submitted that the employer cannot employ them as disciplinary penalties, because each involves an unwarranted prejudice to the worker's contractual rights.[141]

Section 2 of Order 147 of 1959, prohibits the imposition of two penal-

virtue of his powers under the said section 76, does not preclude him from making the compensatory deduction from the worker's wages by virtue of section 54 of the Labour Code (*vide* the section quoted in Section III of Chapter IV, *infra*, and mentioned in Section I, C, of this Chapter, *supra*). Presumably, he cannot do this, by virtue of section 2 of Order 147 of 1959 (to be presently mentioned), if the summary dismissal under section 76, is a disciplinary dismissal.

[136] *Vide* sections 5 and 4 of Order 147 of 1959, which provide for a fair trial and execution, respectively.

[137] This is one of the grounds of summary dismissal, by virtue of section 76(5) of the Labour Code – *vide* Section II, A, 4, of Chapter VI, *infra*.

[138] The High Court of Appeal in (an unnumbered) decision taken on 22 November 1956 (*vide* Naguib and Bakr, p. 168).

[139] Zaki, p. 263; Habeeb, p. 330; and Faheem, p. 7, also hold the same view.

[140] *Vide* sections 74 and 75 in Section II, B, of Chapter VI, *infra*.

[141] *Vide* Butros and Rajab, p. 352 – *vide*, however, p. 355; Habeeb, p. 329; Naguib and Bakr, p. 113; and Faheem, p. 96. Though El-Areef, p. 395; and Rashed and Hashem, pp. 122, 125 and 126, agree that the reduction of wages cannot be used as a disciplinary penalty, they maintain that the lowering of the worker's position can – Refer to section 696(2) of the U.A.R. Civil Code, and section 56 of the Labour Code, in this Chapter *supra*.

ties for one offence, and the imposition of a penalty together with the deduction from the worker's wages by virtue of section 54 of the Labour Code, for the damage to the employer's materials, machinery and products.[142] Section 9 of the Order provides that "the disciplinary rules shall not prescribe a heavier penalty for the repetition of the offence if more than six months have elapsed after the preceding offence." Section 10 of the Order provides that the worker should be informed of the penalty in writing, unless the penalty does not exceed three days' wages or suspension or is just a warning,[143] when the posting on the notice-board in the establishment is sufficient. Section 3 of the Order provides that "the average wages of the piece-rate worker during the fifteen days preceding the commission of the offence," should be the basis of calculation of the amount of a fine. This provision is *ultra vires*, because it conflicts with section 9 of the Labour Code, which for the purposes of the Code, bases the average on "the sums received by the worker in respect of actual days worked during the preceding year." On the other hand, whether the calculation of the suspension days includes or excludes the weekly or other rest-days, which may happen to fall within the suspension period, is not settled;[144] nor is it settled whether the worker can take other work or not during suspension[145]. It is, however, submitted that the weekly or other rest-days should be included in the suspension period, because the purpose of the penalty is not the enrichment of the employer; and that the worker should be free to take other work, unless the contract otherwise provides.

Finally, section 70 of the U.A.R. Labour Code provides that "fines imposed on the workers shall be recorded in a special register showing the reasons thereof the worker's name and the amount of his wages, and such fines shall accrue to a special account which shall be used according to what the Minister of Labour by order prescribes."[146] The Minister accordingly issued his Order 149 of 1959, which provides for

[142] *Vide* section 54 quoted in Section I, C, of this Chapter, *supra*. *Vide* Zaki, p. 265; Habeeb, p. 319; Rashed and Hashem, p. 120; *vide*, however, Butros and Rajab, pp. 356–357.

[143] Zaki, pp. 257–8; and Habeeb, p. 326, however, maintain that a warning can be served orally. It is submitted that they are wrong, because the section is clear.

[144] Butros and Rajab, p. 359, advocate the inclusion of the weekly or other rest-days, because they maintain that the purpose of suspension is to remove the worker from work.

[145] Faheem, p. 93, maintains that the contract is temporarily suspended during suspension, so the worker is legally free to take other work. Rashed and Hashem, p. 125, maintain that the said work will do away with the purpose of the penalty altogether.

[146] Cf. the some what similar provisions in sections 45, 25 (2), 71 & 73 and 25 (3), of the Iraqi, Jordanian, Lebanese and Libyan Labour Codes, respectively. The Kuwaiti Labour Code and the Saudi Regulations do not provide for the disposition of fines.

the disposition of the fines by a committee, composed of one representative of the employer and two of the workers, to promote the social welfare of the workers. Thus no monetary or compensatory interest accrues to the employer, and therein lies some further protection for the workers. This protection is further afforded by section 9 of the Order, which provides that "on the closing of the establishment, the fines in the account shall be equally distributed among the then workers of the establishment."

(f) Medical treatment and protection from dangers at work

Section 65 of the U.A.R. Labour Code provides:

"The employer shall provide for his workers means of medical aid in the establishment and if the number of his workers in any one place or one town or within an area which is fifteen kilometers in diameter exceeds one hundred he shall employ a special experienced nurse to administer such medical aid and shall appoint a doctor to attend and treat the workers in a place specially provided by the employer and shall supply his workers with the required medicines, provided that all the above shall be free of charge.

"If the number of the workers as aforementioned exceeds five hundred the employer shall in addition provide them free of charge with all the means necessary for treatment by specialists, surgical operations and other treatment and with the required medicines.

"If the worker is treated as prescribed in the two preceding subsections in a Government or Philanthropic hospital the employer shall reimburse the hospital with the costs of treatment, medicines and residence.

"The fixing of the costs mentioned in the preceding subsection and the application of all the foregoing provisions shall be in accordance with the rules which shall be contained in an order from the Minister of Labour after he agrees thereon with the Minister of Health."[147]

So by virtue of this section, the employer's obligation to provide medical treatment for his workers is a compulsory term in the contract of employment. There is, however, nothing to preclude the employer

[147] Accordingly, the Minister of Labour issued his Order No. 58 of 1960. *Vide* and cf. the provisions concerning the medical treatment, in sections 913(1, a) and 129 (together with Order 13 of 1958 issued thereunder), of the Iraqi Civil and Labour Codes, respectively, and in sections 32, 12–6 and 28, of the Jordanian, Lebanese (*vide* also Decree No. 6341 of 24 October 1951), and the Libyan Labour Codes, respectively, and section 15(3) of the Saudi Regulations.

from providing a more generous treatment.[148] This obligation is limited to the workers and does not extend to their families, unless the contract provides otherwise.[149] On the other hand, whether the obligation extends to all kinds of sickness is not settled;[150] nor is it settled whether treatment includes the provision of eye-glasses, false teeth and artificial eyes and limbs,[151] or X-rays and laboratory analysis.[152] However, it is submitted that the basis of the employer's contractual obligation is the effect of the sickness on the worker in his work.[153] This should be the measure of the applicability of the obligation in the above-mentioned cases, without adding any super-imposed limitations. It is further submitted that section 65 does not exclude the so-called preventive medicine.[154] If the worker chooses to be treated by other than the doctor of his employer, he cannot call upon the employer to pay the costs of the treatment and the medicines.[155] Section 2 of Order 58 provides that the place in which medical treatment is to be dispensed, should be as near as can be to the employer's establishment. Section 3 of the Order provides that the worker should bear the cost of his own transport to the said place. If that place is situated unreasonably far from the establishment, the employer should presumably bear the cost of transport, at least from the establishment to the said place.[156]

The obligation of the employer to protect his workers from dangers

[148] *Vide* section 12 of Order 58 of 1950, which expressly provides to the same effect.

[149] *Vide* the High Court of Appeal in appeal No. 269 of 1959 (in El-Hawwari, p. 156); *vide* also section 8 of Order 58 of 1960.

[150] Murad, p. 336; Zaki, p. 297; Habeeb, p. 373; Rashed and Hashem, pp. 108–109; Naguib and Bakr, p. 108; and Faheem, p. 66, all favour the extension of the obligation to all kinds of sickness, whatever is the cause or degree of the sickness. This includes venereal diseases, and long-term sickness like diabetes. Butros and Rajab, pp. 297–298, believe otherwise.

[151] El-Fakahani, 1959 Supplement, p. 182; Habeeb, p. 375 (who quotes the Council of State's opinion delivered on 18 May 1954, in support); Rashed and Hashem, p. 66; and Badawi, K. M., p. 230, all agree that the obligation does not extend thereto.

[152] Habeeb, p. 375, maintains that the obligation in these two cases, depends on the nature of the sickness; and he quotes the Council of State's opinion (mentioned in the preceding footnote), in support.

[153] Any other social and humanitarian justification of the obligation, belongs to the field of Social Security – *vide* in this respect, section 8 of Order 58 of 1960, and Law No. 92 of 1959, re Social Security; *vide*, however, the Council of State's (undated) opinion (in Naguib and Bakr, p. 109), which says that "the basis of this obligation is the *moral* and legal obligation of the employer to provide full medical treatment for his workers, if his capabilities have reached a certain enabling standard"; and cf. this with another opinion of the Council, dated 23 March 1953 (in Rashed and Hashem, p. 111), which expressly says, that the basis of the obligation is the employer's *financial ability*.

[154] Rashed and Hashem, p. 109, maintain otherwise, as to preventive treatment.

[155] *Vide* Cairo Court of Cassation in case No. 1851 of 1954 (in Badawi, K. M., p. 233); and the same Court in case No. 832 of 1955 (in Habeeb, p. 374); section 7 of Order 58 of 1959, relieves the employer of the costs of any medicines not prescribed by his doctor.

[156] Badawi, K. M., p. 231, submits to the same effect; and Habeeb, p. 379, agrees with him.

at work, is deducible from the employer's liability under the law of tort.[157] So the legislator unnecessarily provides for the same in section 108 of the Labour Code, though he properly places it outside the contract of employment provisions in the Code.[158] However, the commencement of section 65 of the Code speaks of medical aid and an experienced nurse. These are mainly related to protection from dangers at work, rather than medical treatment as such,[159] or in other words, they are related to the tortious rather than the contractual liability of the employer. It is submitted that a further clarification is due from the legislator.

In Sudan the employer's obligation to provide medical treatment for his workers, is purely contractual.[160] Thus the law in Sudan follows in the footsteps of the English Common Law. "Apart from any statute, and apart from any special provision in the contract of service, the master is not bound, in the case of a domestic servant or *a fortiori* in the case of other servants, to provide medicines or medical attendance during the illness of his servant."[161] However, if the employer voluntarily provides medical treatment and medicines, he has no right of reimbursement from the worker, and the employer remains liable, if he permits his servant to request such medical treatment and medicines as his agent, or subsequently adopts the action of his servant.[162]

The employer's obligation in Sudan to protect the worker from dangers at work, is deducible from his tortious liability, as it is in the U.A.R. "In matters of personal safety, it is not the law of contract, but the law of tort which provides the legal framework of industrial relations."[163]

[157] *Vide* section 163 of the U.A.R. Civil Code; *vide* El-Areef, p. 380; Rashed and Hashem, p. 99; and El-Fakahani, 1959 Supplement, p. 356.

[158] Sections 42–88 (Chapter II of Book II) of the Code. The Labour Code thus corrected the position under Law 317 of 1952, whose section 26 is the predecessor of section 108 of the Labour Code. On the other hand, the Explanatory Note to Law 317, states that the enactment of section 26 thereof, was needed until a Factory Law could be enacted.

[159] This is how most of the writers interpret it: *vide* El-Fakahani, 1959 Supplement, p. 181; Rashed and Hashem, p. 107; Butros and Rajab, p. 295; and Faheem, p. 65.

[160] *Vide* paragraph 4 in the Form of Written Contract of Service (contained in the Schedule to The Employers and Employed Persons Rules), for the specification of the employer's obligation to provide medical treatment or food rations, if any.

[161] Halsbury, Vol. 25, p. 466; *vide* also Diamond, p. 117; Cooper, p. 115; Samuels, p. 46; Smith, pp. 150–151; and Barwell and Kar, pp. 119 and 122. For the statutory obligations in England, *vide* Batt, pp. 136 and 143; and Smith, p. 152.

At one time in England, authority existed (*Scarman v. Castell* (1795) I Esp. 270), for the proposition that the master was liable for the care of his servant "in sickness and in health." But this was finally rejected in *Wennall v. Adney* (1802), B & P, 247.

[162] *Vide Cooper v. Philips* (1831) 4 C. & P. 581; *vide* also Batt, pp. 167–168; and Cooper, p. 57.

[163] O. Kahn-Freund, in Flanders and Clegg, p. 52. Again, "the development in the courts of the tort of negligence has also imposed duties of care both on masters and ser-

Comparison of the law in the U.A.R. and Sudan reveals that, though the employer's obligation to provide medical attendance to his workers is contractual, the contracting freedom in the former is regulated by statute with penal sanctions, whereas in the latter the parties are still free to agree as they choose.[164] On the other hand, the employer's obligation to protect his workers from dangers at work, emanates in both countries from the employer's tortious liability to compensate the worker for the injury he suffers.

(g) Housing and food

Section 64 of the U.A.R. Labour Code provides that "the employer who employs workers in places far from inhabited areas which shall be specified in an order from the Minister of Labour shall provide them with suitable housing some of which shall be allotted to married workers[165] and shall also provide food at not more than one third of the costs provided that the worker shall not be charged for one meal more than twenty Egyptian millemes in the Egyptian Region or twenty Syrian piastres in the Syrian Region.[166] The conditions and specifications of housing and the kinds and quantities of food to be provided for every worker shall be specified in orders from the Minister of Labour in agreement with the Minister concerned."[167] So the housing and food obligations as prescribed in this section, are compulsory implied terms in the contract of employment.

vants, and has provided a remedy for either if injury occurs as a result of the other's negligence": Cooper, p. 56; *vide* also Barwell and Kar, p. 83. *Vide* the two Sudanese decisions of *Hamad El Nur v. Modern Aluminium Works* (1958) HC–CS–603; and *Ali El Hag Mansour v. El Hag Ahmed Abu Zeid and Mohamed Tewfik Hussein* (1959) HC–CS–214, (both in the *Sudan Law Journal and Reports*, 1960, pp. 129 and 179, respectively). The Sudanese Workshops and Factories Ordinance of 31 December 1949, and the Workshops and Factories Regulations of 1 August 1952 (both in *The Laws of Sudan*, Vol. 8, Title XXII, Sub-Title 5), impose on the employer the obligations related to his tortious liability. In this respect, the Sudan is better off than the U.A.R., which is still to enact a Factory Law (*vide* footnote 158 to this Chapter, *supra*). Sections 37(a) and 89(g) of the Bahraini Labour Code also provide for such obligations. For Aden, *vide* section 8 (1, b, v) of the Adenese Ordinance.

[164] The precarious position of the worker in Sudan, in this respect, is very clear.

[165] This is the first provision in the U.A.R., prescribing housing for families.

[166] The U.A.R. Labour Code was enacted in 1959, for both Egypt and Syria, of which the U.A.R. was then composed, *vide* Section II of the Introduction, *supra*.

[167] For the housing obligation, *vide* and cf. sections 132(b) & 33, 47, 57(a), 25 (3, e) and 29(a), of the Iraqi, Kuwaiti, Qatari, Jordanian, and Libyan Labour codes, respectively, and sections 10(6) & 20(4) of the Saudi Regulations. For the food obligation, *vide* and cf. sections 129 (15), 57(c) ad 29(b), of the Iraqi, Qatari and Libyan Labour Codes, respectively, which are the only three of the above-mentioned Labour Codes, which contain some relevant provisions.

The Minister of Labour accordingly issued his Orders 145 of 1959, in which he specified "places far from inhabited areas,"[168] 146 of 1959, in which he specified "the kinds and quantities of food to be provided for every worker," and 195 of 1960, in which he specified "the conditions and specifications of housing."[169]

The wording of the section has occasioned a controversy as to whether the prescribed housing is to be provided free of charge to the worker,[170] or at one third of the costs as is the case in the provision of food,[171] or as agreed upon between the parties.[172] It is submitted that the reference in section 64 to one third of the price is limited to food and has nothing to do with housing.[173] If this is the case, and since the worker should *prima facie* pay for his own housing, the clear conclusion is whether he should so pay, and if so how much, or he should not pay at all, should depend on the agreement of the parties. However, the worker should not pay more than the actual cost of housing, because the benefit intended by the section would be lost, if the employer is allowed to make a profitable enterprise out of his obligation under the section.

[168] These areas were specified, as "the Red Sea, Sinae, West and South *Muhafazat* (Governorships), and places of work which are at least fifteen kilometers away from the borders of the nearest town or village." An old war-time Order No. 469 of 28 February 1944, however, imposes an obligation to provide the lunch meal in every working day, to every worker (at not more than half of the costs, and provided that the worker should not be charged more than fifteen millemes), on those in Kena and Aswan Governorships, who employ fifty or more workers in commerce or industry, or those who own more than two hundred acres of agricultural land. Thus the Order does not make it a condition, that the place of work should be "far from inhabited areas." This Order, which was also extended to the Red Sea Governorship, by Order 522 of 1944 (*vide* Badawi, K. M., p. 191), is still operative in Kena, Aswan and the Red Sea Governorships, together with the obligation under section 64 of the Labour Code: *vide* the High Court of Appeal in appeal No. 27 of 1959 (in El-Hawwari, p. 158); and Asyout Court of Arbitration in dispute No. 12 of 1954 (in Habeeb, p. 148); Sabbour, pp. 219–220; Butros and Rajab, pp. 292–294 (they compare and differentiate the obligations under Order 469 of 1944 and section 64 of the Labour Code); *vide* Also Zaki, pp. 166–167; but only El-Areef, p. 33, says that Order 469 of 1944 is no more effective, thus overlooking Order 102 of 1945, which saved it from the repeal of all war-time orders.

[169] The "suitable housing" was described by the Explanatory Note to Law 317 of 1952 (whose section 27 is the predecessor of section 64 of the Labour Code), as housing "in which the health and sanitary requirements are satisfied."

[170] The only writer who advocates this view, is Zaki, p. 295. He maintains that, if the legislator intended that the worker should pay anything, he would have provided an upper ceiling, as he did in the case of food.

[171] Cairo Court of Appeal in the appeal on dispute No. 30 of 1957 (in El-Hawwari, p. 160); El-Areef, p. 381; Rashed and Hashem, p. 102; and Faheem, p. 62, support this view.

[172] The High Court of Appeal in appeal No. 362 of 1957 (in Habeeb, p. 365); and the Council of State's opinion delivered on 5 July 1958 (*Ibidem*, p. 367); Murad, p. 333; Badawi, K. M., p. 188; Sabbour, p. 220; and Butros and Rajab, p. 291, support this view.

[173] The Arabic text of section 64 is, in this respect, clearer than that of section 27 of Law 317 of 1952, which is its predecessor. This may be the reason of the view, which advocates the payment for housing, at not more than one third of the costs (*vide* footnote 171, *supra*).

Furthermore, the allotment of some housing to married workers supports the said conclusion, because if the legislator intends that the employer should supply free housing to the worker's family, he should have said so.

Opinion differs as to whether the employer can without the agreement of the worker, substitute his housing obligation under section 64, by the provision of transportation for his workers from the place of work to where they can rent their own housing, even though the place of work be "far from inhabited areas," or by the payment of a compensatory allowance to the worker.[174] It is submitted that it is open for the parties to agree on the said substitution, but if the employer carries out his obligation by providing housing, the worker cannot insist on the said substitution, though he is of course free to provide his own housing and transportation. Finally, it goes without saying that the worker's occupation of the employer's housing should end with the termination of his service.[175]

The employer's food obligation under section 64 is limited to the worker and is not extended to his family, even if it resides with him.[176] The number of subsidised meals depends on the worker.[177] On the other hand, if the worker chooses not to take the meals, he is free to agree with the employer on any monetary compensation therefor, but he cannot insist on it.[178]

[174] The Council of State's opinion (mentioned in footnote 172, *supra*), answers the question in the negative, because the employer's housing obligation is mandatory. Faheem, p. 63, illogically adds that the worker can insist on having transportation, as an alternative to housing (*vide* footnote 15, *supra*).

[175] Section 948 of the Draft Civil Code of 1948, provides to the same effect; *vide* also El-Areef, p. 165; Badawi, K. M., p. 188; Butros and Rajab, p. 291; Sabbour, p. 220; and Naguib and Bakr, p. 106. However, it is believed that a provision should be made, so as to give the worker a chance to stay on in the employer's housing, in order that he may find other housing, especially when he is married and his family redises with him. On the other hand, the employer's housing obligation could and should be replaced by joint Government-Employer housing schemes. The U.A.R. and Iraq have in this respect, achieved some progress. *Vide* Article III of the I.L.O. Recommendation No. 21 of 1924.

[176] *Vide* the Council of State's opinion delivered on 20 September 1954 (in Habeeb, p. 366); *vide* also Butros and Rajab, p. 292. This limitation is not logically consonant with the allotment of some housing to married workers.

[177] *Vide* the Council of State's opinion, mentioned in the preceding footnote.

[178] *Vide* Asyout Arbitration Court in dispute No. 14 of 1954 (in El-Fakahani, Book I, Vol. I, p. 41); Zaki, pp. 184–185, maintains that it is not open for the parties to agree as above-mentioned, because the provision is mandatory, and he cites section 155(b) of the U.A.R. Labour Code, in support. This section expressly prohibits such agreement, in the case of mine and quarry workers. It is submitted that the non-inclusion of a similar express provision in section 64 of the Code, is sufficient ground to maintain the contrary view. The express provision in section 155(b) is understandable, because of the health protection relationship, between food and the peculiar nature of the work of mine and quarry workers.

In Sudan there is no obligation on the employer to provide any housing or food for his workers. So the position there is purely contractual,[179] as it is in England. "In the absence of express or implied agreement to the contrary, a master is under no liability to provide board and lodging for his servants."[180] But "where such agreement exists, the liability continues during the illness of the servant."[181] On the other hand, by virtue of section 17 of the Sudan Ordinance, no employer can deduct anything from the worker's wages, unless he is authorised to do so in the contract of service. This means that, if the worker accepts any housing or food voluntarily supplied to him by his employer, without any mention thereof in the contract, the worker should not be liable to pay therefor. On the other hand, any temporary despatch of the worker by the employer on the latter's business, will render the employer liable for the food and lodging of his worker.[182]

(h) The worker's inventions

"The right of the worker to any inventions he may make in the course of his employment, has become of utmost importance, after the development of society and the improvement in the means of production, to the extent that science and industry are so well connected, and research has become an integral part of the industiral processes."[183]

The first statutory regulation of the worker's rights in his inventions

[179] *Vide* footnote 160 to this Chapter, *supra*. The position is the same in Bahrain and Aden. It is regrettable that the legislator has not yet interfered in Sudan, so as to impose some housing and food obligations, especially because housing is not easily secured by the workers, and the food costs are comparatively high.

[180] Diamond, p. 116; *vide* also Cooper, p. 57; Batt, p. 167; Smith, p 149; and Halsbury, Vol. 25, p. 466.

[181] Diamond, p. 116.

[182] Batt, p. 167, submits to the same effect in England.

[183] Zaki, p. 244; *vide* also I.L.R., Vol. 83, 1961, p. 36: "Today, when independent inventors are tending to become steadily rarer and a growing majority of inventors are salaried employees in public or private service, the question is even of greater importance." This problem has caught the attention of the I.L.O., over the last thirty years. The Advisory Committees on Professional Workers and Salaried Employees, discussed the problem, and adopted resolutions Nos. 62 G.B. 160 and 197, in 1929 and 1931, respectively, (*vide* the texts of these resolutions in pp. 243–244, of Vol. 2, of *The International Labour Code*, 1951, I.L.O., Geneva, 1952). Unfortunately, however, the matter was not followed up by the I.L.O., until "the Committee set up by the International Labour Conference at its 43rd session in 1959, to study the problems of non-manual workers called upon the I.L.O. to make the necessary studies, with a view to convening a committee of experts to consider the problems of salaried inventors." *Vide* in this connection, the illuminating article called *Employees' Rights in Their Inventions – A Comparison of National Laws*, by F. Newmeyer, (in I.L.R., Vol. 83, 1961, pp. 36–64), but this remains to be the only contribution so far made.

in the U.A.R.[184] came in section 688 of the Civil Code, and this was followed by the Patent Law No. 132 of 1949.

Section 688 of the U.A.R. Civil Code provides:

"If a worker makes a new invention while employed by an employer, the latter shall have no right in the invention, even though the worker may have made the invention in connection with any work which he performed for the employer.

"However, any inventions made by the worker in the course of his work shall be the property of the employer, if the nature of the work which the worker has contracted to perform requires him to devote himself to inventing or if the employer had expressly stipulated in the contract that he would have the property in any inventions his worker may make.

"If the invention is of real economic value the worker may in the cases mentioned in the preceding subsection claim special return which shall be fixed in accordance with the rules of equity provided that any assistance which the worker had drawn from the employer and his use of the employer's outfit shall be taken into consideration."[185]

Section 7 of Law 132 of 1949 provides:

"If a person requests another to make a particular invention, all the rights in the invention shall be the property of the former.

"All the rights in the inventions made by a workman or an employee whilst in the employ of another shall likewise be the property of the employer if the inventive work is within the contract terms or the employment relationship. The name of the inventor shall be mentioned in the patent and he shall in all cases be entitled to remuneration for the invention.

"If no agreement on the said remuneration is made the inventor shall be entitled to a fair compensation from the person who requested him to make the invention or from the employer."[186]

[184] It is interesting to note that in France, there is no statutory regulation of the worker's inventions, and that the insufficient regulation by collective agreements, is employed there for the purpose (*Ibid.*, p. 38).

[185] *Vide* identical provisions in section 912 of the Iraqi Civil Code; *vide* also similar provisions in section 343 of the Swiss Civil Code (I.L.R., Vol. 83, 1961, p. 49); cf. the somewhat similar provisions *in* sections 10 and 12 A of the Netherlands Patents Act of 1910, as amended up to 1957 (*Ibidem*, p. 42).

[186] *Vide* similar provisions in section 23 of the Italian patent law of 1939 (*Ibidem*, p. 43). However, the employer's proprietary rights in his worker's inventions "are original and are not in any way assigned to him" (*Idem*); but this is not so in the U.A.R., as can be deduced from section 9 of Law 132 of 1949, to be quoted presently. The concept of "company inventions" does not exist, either in the U.A.R. or in Italy. This concept, which gives the right in the invention to the employer, when it is made by the cooperation of several workers and it is impossible to identify the inventors, exists in Denmark (*Ibidem*, p. 54).

Section 8 of Law 132 of 1949 provides:

"In the cases other than those mentioned in the preceding section and when the invention is within the scope of the business of the public or private establishment in which the inventor works the employer shall have the right to choose between the exploitation of the invention or the purchase of the patent in return of fair compensation which he shall pay to the inventor provided that he shall exercise his choice within three months after he is notified of the taking out of the patent."[187]

Section 9 of Law 132 of 1949 provides:

"Any application by the inventor for the taking out of a patent for an invention within one year of his (the inventor's) leaving of the public or private establishment shall be deemed to have been made during the effectiveness of the contract or the subsistence of the employment relationship and both the inventor and the employer shall have the rights mentioned in the two preceding sections as the case may be."

As the said provisions of Law 132 of 1949 deal with the same subject as does section 688 of the Civil Code, and were enacted after the said Code, they have an overriding effect thereon, in as far as there is any conflict between them.[188] Comparison of the two reveals that the absolute ownership of the invention guaranteed for the inventor by the provisions in section 688(1), is qualified by the employer's pre-emption rights granted to him by section 8 of Law 132, jointly read with section 9 of the said Law.[198] On the other hand, section 7 of the said Law does not derogate from the provisions in subsections 2 and 3 of section 688, but adds thereto the token of the worker's right in having his name mentioned in the patent of his invention; and more important still, it expressly provides for the inventor's right to demand a remuneration, irrespective of whether the invention has or does not have a "real economic value." However, the said section 7 does not mention the express relinquishment in the contract, by the worker of his rights in his inventions, as is mentioned in section 688. This leaves the worker in such eventuality to a fair compensation, only when the invention has a "real economic value."[190]

In Sudan there is no patent law or any other statutory enactment dealing with inventions, not to mention workers' inventions. So the

[187] *Vide* similar provisions in section 24 of the Italian patent law of 1939 (*Ibid.*, p. 43).

[188] This is by virtue of section 2 of the U.A.R. Civil Code.

[189] Zaki, p. 245, correctly criticises the said section 7 of Law 132, because "the inventive power of the worker is the basic cause of the invention, and much more so than the chances afforded to him by his work in the establishment."

[190] Zaki, pp. 245–246, correctly points out that this contractual relinquishment by the worker, is not for a real return or to use the English term, not for a real consideration.

law in this respect is governed by the English Common Law, as modified by Statute. Under the said law, "the mere relation of master and servant does not make the master the first and true inventor, nor prevent a servant from taking out a patent, although he has used his employer's time, servants and materials."[191] If, however, the servant is just a mere tool in, or contributes to a very minor extent to the discovery of an invention, the invention will belong to the master.[192] On the other hand, there may be an agreement between the parties; but "whether there is agreement or not, the benefits of the discovery will, at common law, accrue to the employer, wherever it would be contrary to good faith for the discoverer to take these benefits."[193] This doctrine of good faith, adopted by the force of equity, made the inventor a trustee of the invention for his master.[194]

Comparison of the law in the U.A.R. and England and hence in Sudan, reveals that the inapplicability of the doctrine of good faith of the worker, in respect of his inventions *vis a vis* his employer in the U.A.R., renders the grounds of the employer's entitlement to his worker's inventions, narrower than they are in England and Sudan. On the other hand, the U.A.R. Law guarantees for the worker-inventor a return, or in some cases an equitable compensation for his invention, whereas there are no such rights in England and Sudan.

[191] *Vide* Diamond, p. 107, who together with Batt, p. 161, quote *Saxby v. Gloucester Wagon Co.* (1883), Griffin's Patent Cases, 1888, pp. 54 and 56, as authority for this statement of the law.

[192] *Vide* Diamond, p. 107, who quotes *Bloxam v. Elsee* (1825), I C. & P. 558, and *Allen v. Rawson* (1845), 1 C.B. 551, as authorities for the two parts of this statement of the law, respectively.

[193] *Vide* Cooper, p. 66, who quotes *British Reinforced Concrete Engineering Co. v. Lind* (1917), 86 L.J. (Ch.), 486 as authority; *vide* also *British Celanese, Ltd. v. Moncrieff* (1948), Ch. 564. This doctrine of good faith in relation to inventions, is not applicable in the U.A.R.

[194] "If the servant makes an invention or discovery in the course of his employment, he is normally, by virtue of an implied term in his contract of service, a trustee of that invention or discovery for his employer": Halsbury, Vol. 25, pp. 462–3; *vide* also *Triplex Safety Glass Co. Ltd. v. Scorah* (1938), 54, T.L.R. 90. By virtue of section 1 of the English Patents Act of 1907, only the "true and first inventor of an invention" could take out the patent, and he had under the said doctrine of good faith, to assign the patent to his employer. But by virtue of section 1(1) of the Patents Act of 1949, the patent can now be taken out by the employer himself, after the servant-inventor assigns to him the invention. Section 56 of this Act gives to the servant and the master the right to refer any dispute between them, to the Comptroller General of Patents for determination.

SECTION II: RIGHTS AND OBLIGATIONS OF THE PARTIES ARISING ON AND AFTER THE TERMINATION OF EMPLOYMENT[195]

(a) Transportation

Section 55 of the U.A.R. Labour Code provides that the employer "shall within a period of seven days after the cessation of the work or the termination of the contract for any of the reasons specified in sections 72, 78 and 81, be liable for the expenses of transporting them back to the said place wherefrom he requested them to come[196] unless the worker refuses in writing to return within the said period and if the employer fails to transport the worker or to pay the costs thereof the administrative authorities shall if so requested by the worker on the expiry of the said period transport him at the employer's expense and may recover the expenses incurred by way of administrative attachment."[197]

This obligation of the employer is limited to the worker and does not apply to the members of his family, unless the contract otherwise provides.[198] Furthermore, it goes without saying that the obligation is not applicable if the employer had recruited the worker locally, even if the ordinary residence of the worker be in a different place.[199] On the other hand, the section limits the employer's obligation to the cases where the work is stopped or the contract is terminated, for certain reasons specified in section 72 (the desire of either party to terminate the relationship by notice), section 78 (the worker's right to leave the service without notice in certain circumstances,[200]) and section 81 (the disso-

[195] The obligation of either party to give a notice, when he wants to terminate the contract is discussed in Section II, A, 2, of Chapter VI, *infra*, and so is the worker's right to time-off during the notice period, in order to look for another job. The worker's rights in the arrears of the wages on the termination of his contract, and in the final leave and the termination gratuity, are discussed in Chapters IV, V and VII, respectively.

[196] *Vide* Section I, A, of this Chapter, *supra*, for the commencing provisions of section 55; and *vide* there the meaning of the "place wherefrom he requested them to come."

[197] *Vide* the somewhat similar provisions, but without any provision for the interference of the administrative authorities, in sections 94 and 913(d), of the Iraqi Labour and Civil Codes, respectively, in section 23 of the Qatari Labour Code, and in section 10(1) of the Saudi Regulations – Transportation should be provided to the worker within 15, 15 and 28 days, after the termination of the contract, in Iraq, Qatar and Saudi Arabia, respectively. Kuwait, Jordan, Libya and Tunisia do not have any provisions on the subject; *vide* the *Labour Survey of North Africa*, p. 240, for the absence of any relevant provisions in Libya, Tunisia, Algeria and Morocco.

[198] *Vide* Alexandria Court of Cassation in case No. 1098 of 1953 (in Habeeb, p. 362); *vide* also Badawi, K. M., p. 186; Sabbour, p. 218; and Butros and Rajab, p. 273.

[199] Badawi, K. M., p. 185–6; and Sabbour, p. 218, are of the same opinion.

[200] *Vide* also section 696(1) of the U.A.R. Civil Code (in Section II, B, of Chapter VI, *infra*), by virtue of which the worker is entitled to compensation, when he is compelled to leave the service by the employer's conduct, though he is not actually dismissed by the employer.

lution of the contract by the worker's prolonged illness or death[201]). This limitation has given rise to the questions, whether the employer's transportation obligation applies, (a) when a limited contract[202] ordinarily expires, or (b) when the contract becomes impossible of performance, or (c) when the employer believes that the worker had terminated the contract unjustifiably, though he had served the notice of termination in accordance with section 72 of the Labour Code, or (d) in the converse case of the employer's termination of the contract for justifiable cause, by virtue of section 76 of the Labour Code. It is submitted that the answer to the first question should be in the affirmative, because the employer is obliged by virtue of section 55, to transport limited contract workers to the place of work in the beginning of service,[196] and the legislator cannot be taken to mean the freeing of the employer from the transportation obligation at the expiry of the contract.[203] The answer to the second question should be in the negative, because the legislator has, by reference to section 81 of the Labour Code, impliedly limited the application of the transportation obligation, to only two cases of impossibility of performance, viz. the worker's prolonged illness and his death.[204] The answer to the third question should be in the affirmative, because this case should be equated with the ordinary case of termination by notice, until the lack of justification of the worker's termination is proved in Court; and if it is so proved, the employer can then claim a refund of the transportation costs.[205] Finally, the answer to the fourth question should be in the affirmative, because the employer cannot be the party and the judge in his own cause, and it is the Court which will decide on this issue.[206]

The wording of section 55 gives to the employer the choice between

[201] *Vide* sections 72, 76, 77 and 78 in Section II, A, 3 & 4 of Chapter VI, *infra*, and section 81 in Section I, A, of the same chapter.

[202] *Vide* Section III of Chapter II, *supra*, for the definition of a limited contract.

[203] Sabbour, p. 217, gives the same answer – though for a wrong reason, it is submitted, as he misinterprets the words "after the cessation of the work," in section 55 of the Code, to mean "the performance of the work"; Badawi, K. M., p. 184; Butros and Rajab, p. 271; and Habeeb, p. 361, also give an affirmative answer, but without reasoning. On the other hand, Badawi, Z., Vol. 1, p. 114, answers the question in the negative, because he maintains that no obligation can be imposed without express provision.

[204] Badawi, K. M., p. 184, gives an affirmative answer, without reasoning.

[205] All the writers mentioned in footnote 203, *supra*, give a negative answer which they deduce from the entitlement of the worker to transportation, when he justifiably terminates the contract for the reasons mentioned in section 78 of the Code (actually the reasons are listed in section 77 of the Code, and a reference only is made thereto in section 78 – this, it is submitted, is bad drafting).

[206] All the writers mentioned in footnote 203, *supra*, together with Murad, p. 329, give a negative answer, depending on the deduction mentioned in the preceding footnote.

the provision of the means of transport and the costs thereof.[207] But opinion differs as to whether the worker can travel at his own expense, and subsequently claim reimbursement of the costs from the employer. It is submitted that the worker has no such right. He has to wait for the employer's decision, and cannot oblige the employer to exercise his said choice, before the expiry of the seven days.[208] On the other hand, the worker's right to request transportation by the administrative authorities,[209] should be made 'on the expiry' of the seven days. It is submitted that the legislator should have specified a time-limit for the exercise of this right by the worker, in order that the worker, the administrative authorities and the employer may know the limits to their rights and obligations, in this respect.

Finally, section 81 of the Labour Code, which is mentioned in section 55 thereof, does not only mention prolonged illness as a reason for the dissolution of the contract, but also mentions the worker's death as another reason. So it is submitted that the employer's obligation under section 55, to transport the worker at the termination of the contract, extends to the transportation of the worker's body, if he dies. However, the employer's obligation for such return transportation does not, by virtue of the said section, extend beyond the place wherefrom he requested the worker to come, at the beginning of the service. So pending a further clarification from the legislator, any extra transportation costs should be borne by the worker's relatives who request his body.[210]

In Sudan section 12 of the Sudan Ordinance speaks of "any stipulation" in the contract of service, "to return the employed person to the place of his engagement."[211] So the employer's obligation for the return transportation of his worker is purely contractual.[212] In this the legis-

[207] These costs are fixed according to custom; *vide* Murad, p. 330; Badawi, K. M., p. 186; and Sabbour, p. 218, who are of the same opinion.

[208] Habeeb, p. 361; and Sabbour, p. 218, submit to the same effect. Butros and Rajab, pp. 272–3, however, maintain that the worker has such a right, provided that he should claim reimbursement within the seven days. Faheem, p. 55, also maintains that the worker has the said right, provided that he can only exercise it, if the employer refuses to give him transportation, in "the day following his request."

[209] These are the Police Authorities: *vide* Butros and Rajab, p. 272; Badawi, Z., Vol. 1, p. 114; Naguib, and Bakr, p. 89; and Faheem, p. 55.

[210] The legislator may as well substitute the burial costs for the transportation of the worker's body, where the worker had already chosen to be buried near the place of work, or where his relatives otherwise so decide.

[211] The section is quoted and discussed in Section I, F and G, of Chapter VI, *infra*; section 17(a) of the Bahraini Labour Code speaks in the same terms.

[212] In Aden the position is otherwise, and is very similar to that in the U.A.R., including the pre-condition that the obligation is applicable, only if the worker has originally "been brought to the place of employment by the employer": section 13 of the Aden Ordinance – *vide* also sections 14, 15, 16, 17 and 19 thereof, for the complete picture of the obligation. These provisions are inspired by Article 13 of the I.L.O. Convention 64 of 1939.

lator followed in the footsteps of the English Common Law. "The question of railway fare home on the termination of the contract of a domestic or other servant is not free from difficulty on the authorities, but it would appear that there is a right to such fare where the terms of the agreement express or implied, secure it to the servant."[213] However, "if the servant is wrongfully dismissed, it would appear that the fare is part of the general damages."[214] This means that it is open for the Courts to grant such fare, but for the worker it is not an automatic right which follows from wrongful dismissal.

Comparison of the law in the U.A.R. and Sudan, reveals that the position is still purely contractual in the latter, whereas the contractual freedom in the former, is to a great extent regulated by statute with penal sanctions.

(b) Certificate of service[215] and return of the worker's papers

Section 86 of the U.A.R. Labour Code provides:

"The employer shall on the termination of the worker's contract give him if he so requests a certificate free of charge showing the dates of the worker's commencement and termination of service and the nature of his work and showing in addition if the worker so requests his wages and other remuneration and the nature of the privileges enjoyed by him if any.[216]

[213] Batt, p. 168. However, in Sudan domestic servants are within certain conditions, entitled to return transportation to the place of engagement, even though they were not initially transported therefrom, at the employer's expense (*vide* section 13(d) of The Domestic Servants Ordinance of 1955). It is somehow illogical to deny such right to other workers, and to leave them to the contract terms, as is clear from the Sudan Ordinance.

[214] Batt, p. 169, who quotes *Gordon v. Potter* (1859), I. F. & F. 644, as authority for this proposition -- he quotes *French v. Brooks* (1830), 6 Bing. 354, as a contrary authority. However, it is submitted that the latter case is not a case of wrongful dismissal, and was decided on the contract terms.

[215] In England the much wider term of *character* is used. This includes, besides the certificate of service, any other testimonial which the employer may give to a person other than the worker, re the latter's service. We are, however, only concerned with the certificate of service.

[216] *Vide* footnote 100 to this Chapter, *supra*, and the relevant text, for the *bona fide* duty of the employer to give such certificate, even before it became a statutory duty. The *bona fides* of the employer also requires him to write the certificate in an acceptable form: *vide* El-Areef, pp. 366–7; Rashed and Hashem, p. 330; Naguib and Bakr, p. 196; and Badawi, Z., Vol. 1, p. 115. The certificate has, by virtue of Law 62 of 1942, to be written in the Arabic language. So it is submitted that El-Areef, p. 367, is wrong in adding "or any other language understood in Egypt." Presumably, however, a translation into any other language is permitted, but it cannot be a substitute for the Arabic text – *vide* Rashed and Hashem, p. 330.

Sections 16(3), 21 and 27, of the Jordanian, Libyan and Tunisian Labour Codes, respectively, and section 10(5) of the Saudi Regulations, contain provisions similar to those

"The employer shall return to the worker any documents or certificates or tools which the latter may have previously deposited with him."[217]

The section prescribes the obligation to give the certificate, on the termination of the contract, without any further condition. This in the first place, means that the manner of the termination of the contract, and whether the contract is terminated by the employer or the worker, is irrelevant to the obligation.[218] So any denial by the employer of the granting of the certificate, gives the worker a right to claim the damages, which he may suffer as a result.[219] In the second place, the employer is not obliged to give to the worker any certificate before the contract is terminated, or to give any testimonial to any other person, concerning the worker, whether during or after the termination of the service.[220] On the other hand, the employer is not obliged to give the certificate, as is prescribed by section 86 of the Labour Code, unless the worker first requests it.[221] The making of the request can be oral as well as in

in section 86 of the U.A.R. Labour Code; and the same applies in Algeria and Morocco (*vide* the *Labour Survey of North Africa*, p. 240) – section 24 of the French Labour Code also provides to the same effect (*vide* I.L.R., Vol. 79, 1959, p. 633). Section 913(e) of the Iraqi Civil Code (copied from section 956 of the Draft Civil Code of 1948 in the U.A.R.), and sections 93, 61, and 22 of the Iraqi, Kuwaiti and Qatari Labour Codes, respectively, prescribe the granting of the certificate to the worker, without a request from him.

[217] Section 43 of the U.A.R. Labour Code, provides that "the worker shall be given a receipt for the documents and certificates he deposits with the employer."

Provisions similar to those in subsection 2 of section 86 of the U.A.R. Labour Code, are contained in sections 913(f) of the Iraqi Civil Code (copied from section 956 of the Draft Civil Code of 1948 in the U.A.R.), and sections 61, 22, 16(3) and 21, of the Kuwaiti, Qatari, Jordanian and Libyan Labour Codes, respectively, and section 10(5) of the Saudi Regulations.

[218] *Vide* Cairo Court of Cassation in case No. 1284 of 1954 (in Habeeb, p. 389); and the same Court in case No. 1467 of 1956 (in El-Hawwari, p. 388); *vide* also Murad, p. 409; El-Areef, p. 366; Faheem, p. 71; and Sabbour, p. 517. Badawi, K.M., p. 435; and Rashed and Hashem, p.327, correctly add that the denial of the certificate to the worker cannot be made a penalty in the Disciplinary Rules (*vide* Section I, E, of this Chapter, *supra*).

The reasoning behind the view, concerning the irrelevance of the manner of termination of the contract or who terminates it, is the combatting of unemployment; *vide* the second case and all the writers mentioned above; and *vide* the I.L.O. Report VII (1) (*Termination of Employment*), 1961, p. 62, which says: "The grant to a dismissed worker of the right to receive from his employer a certificate specifying the dates of his engagement and termination is a further widespread method of facilitating re-employment"; *vide* also I.L.R., Vol. 32, 1936, p. 195.

[219] *Vide* Alexandria Court of Cassation in case No. 171 of 1959 (in El-Hawwari, pp. 389–90); *vide* also Cairo Court of Appeal in appeal No. 580 of 1954 (in Badawi, K. M., p. 437), which decided that the damages are not any "periodical payments until the worker finally secures another work"; *vide* also the first case quoted in the preceding footnote. Section 24 of Book I of the French Labour Code, expressly prescribes the employer's obligation to give the certificate, "on pain of damages" (*Vide* I.L.R., Vol. 79, p. 633).

[220] The employer's responsibilities resulting from his voluntary provision of such other certificate or testimonial, are governed by the rules of the law concerning defamation and deceit, much the same as is the case in England, and hence in Sudan.

[221] *Vide* Cairo Court of Cassation in case No. 1240 of 1955 (in Habeeb, p. 389); and the same Court in case No. 1844 of 1957 (in Sabbour, p. 517); *vide* also the two cases

writing.[222] The section does not specify a time-limit beyond which the worker cannot make the request,[223] nor does the section prescribe the time-limit for the fulfilment by the employer of his obligation.[224] It is believed that the legislator should have specified these time-limits. The place of delivery of the certificate is not specified by the section. But it had been judicially decided that the depositing by the employer of the certificate in the worker's service-file, is sufficient.[225] Whether the employer can request the worker to sign a receipt for the certificate, is not settled.[226] So it is believed that these two issues of the place of delivery of, and the receipt for the certificate, need further clarification from the legislator. As for the contents of the certificate, the section exclusively defines the obligatory items which have to be stated therein; and the section does the same with the other items, which the employer is obliged to mention, if the worker so requests.[227] So the inclusion of any further items is left for the agreement of the parties, as neither party can oblige the other to agree to such inclusion.[228]

quoted in the next coming footnote; *vide* El-Areef, p. 366; Murad, p. 409; Rashed and Hashem, p. 327; Butros and Rajab, p. 326; and Faheem, p. 72.

[222] *Vide* all the writers mentioned in the preceding footnote, who add that it is on the worker to prove that he had made the request – El-Fakahani, 1959 Supplement, p. 332, however, illogically differs therefrom. *Vide* the Cairo Court of Appeal in the two appeals Nos. 987 and 1000 of 1960 (in El-Hawwari, p. 387), which decided that the requirement in section 86 is satisfied, if the worker makes his request in a statement of claim, which he lodges in the Court against the employer.

[223] Badawi, K. M., p. 435; Murad, p. 410; Rashed and Hashem, p. 326; Habeeb, p. 389; and Faheem, p. 72 – all correctly submit that the time-limit is one year, by virtue of the prescription provisions in section 698(1) of the U.A.R. Civil Code.

[224] Murad, p. 410; Sabbour, p. 517; Rashed and Hashem, p. 327; and Faheem, p. 72, submit that the employer should carry out his obligation within a reasonable time.

[225] *Vide* Cairo Court of Cassation in case No. 1116 of 1957 (in El-Hawwari, p. 391); *vide* also Rashed and Hashem, p. 327; and El-Areef, p. 366 (who quotes the French decision of 18 August 1934, Dalloz. Hebdom., 1934, pl. 557, as authority for the charging to the worker of the postage costs, if the employer mails the certificate to the worker's residence) – *vide* in this connection, *Mouclin v. Consorno* (1934), Dalloz. Hebdom., 1934, p. 326, as authority for the lack of any obligation on the employer, to send the certificate to the worker (I.S.D.L., Vol. 10, 1936, p. 92).

[226] El-Areef, p. 366; Badawi, Z., Vol. 1, p. 115; Rashed and Hashem, p. 327; Naguib and Bakr, p. 195; and Faheem, p. 72, all submit that the employer can request such a receipt, so that the worker should not deny receiving the certificate. It is submitted that the worker's *bona fides* requires him to sign the said receipt.

[227] The Cairo Labour Court in case No. 2150 of 1958 (in El-Hawwari, p. 390), held that a Court judgement in favour of the worker uttered after the termination of the contract, is a good substitution for the certificate of service, and so it is a relief for the employer from his obligation to give the certificate, if the judgement contains the obligatory items prescribed by section 86. It is submitted that the decision is wrong, because its effect deprives the worker of his right to request the inclusion of the other items specified in the section. Faheem, p. 74, criticises the decision, for the reason that the worker would be prejudiced in his chances of getting further employment, if he has to produce a court judgement against his ex-employer.

[228] *Vide* Murad, p. 410; Zaki, p. 301; *vide* also Abdin District Court in case No. 1397, which ruled to the effect that "any comment on the worker's competence will prejudice

Finally, the certificate of service is not the so-called 'free of charge certificate,' or in other words, it is not concerned with the final settlement of the rights of the parties.[229] So the employer has no right of lien on the certificate, even if the worker does not return to him any property he had bailed with him.[230]

The return to the worker of his documents, certificates and tools, as prescribed by section 86, "is also prescribed by the general law, though the special provision thereon (in the Labour Code), renders the failure to carry it out subject to the mischief of the Code, in addition to the remedies of specific performance or of damages, as the case may be."[231]

In Sudan there is no statutory provision, equivalent to section 86 of the U.A.R. Labour Code.[232] So there is no obligation on the employer to give a certificate of service to the worker, on the termination of his contract, much the same as is the case under the Common Law in England. Under this Law, "a master is under no duty to give his servant or former servant a character."[233] But if the employer chooses to give

him in getting further employment, if it is unfavourable, and if unfavourable comment is disallowed without disallowing a favourable comment, a similar prejudice to the worker will result from the employer's failure to make the favourable comment" (*vide* Habeeb, p. 391, footnote 1) – Butros and Rajab, p. 327, state that this reasoning is drawn from the French jurisprudence. Badawi, K. M., p. 436, submits what amounts to a criticism of the said decision and jurisprudence, on the ground that there is nothing to prevent the employer from giving to the worker another testimonial containing favourable comment; so presumably, he could do the same in the certificate of service. It is submitted that he is correct, provided that the worker agrees with the wording of the employer's comment – *vide* in line with Badawi's submission, the I.L.O. proposed recommendation No. 10, in para 37 of Report V(1) of 1962, entitled *Termination of Employment at the Initiative of the Employer*.

[229] *Vide* section V of Chapter II, *supra*, re "compromise or disclaimer of the rights deriving from the contract of employment"; *vide* also Alexandria Labour Court in case No. 2014 of 1953 (in Rashed and Hashem, p. 329); and the second case quoted in footnote 218 to this Chapter, *supra*; and *vide* section 24 of Book I of the French Labour Code (I.L.R., Vol. 79, 1959, p. 633).

[230] *Vide* of the same opinion, Murad, p. 409; Butros and Rajab, p. 328; Habeeb, p. 368; Sabbour, p. 517; and Faheem, p. 72. However, Rashed and Hashem, p. 330, submit to the contrary. It is submitted that they are wrong, because the statutory right of the worker in the certificate of service, should not with its function of a public character (viz. the combatting of unemployment), be subject to the right of lien.

[231] Zaki, p. 301.

[232] Nor is there any in Aden. However, section 22 of the Bahraini Labour Code contains provisions identical with the U.A.R. provisions. So the influence of the U.A.R. in this respect, is clear. In India every permanent employee is entitled to the certificate, on dismissal from service, by virtue of the Model Standing Orders, issued under the Industrial Employment (Standing Orders) Act of 1946, as modified up to 31 October 1954 (*vide* I.L.R., Vol. 80, 1959, pp. 451, 444 and 442).

[233] Diamond, p. 118, who together with most other writers, quotes as an authority the case of *Carrol v. Bird* (1800), 3 Esp. 201, N.O.; *vide* also Cooper, p. 59; Batt, p. 172; Samuels, p. 19; Smith, p. 296; Macdonell, p. 185; and Halsbury, Vol. 25, pp. 470–1. *Vide* these writers for the other rule of the law, that the employer is not obliged either to answer questions from any other interested person, concerning the worker, whether during or after the termination of service. If the employer volunteers to answer the said

the worker a certificate, it becomes the property of the worker, and must be returned to him intact by any other employer to whom he presents it.[234] On the other hand, the rules of the law of bailment apply to the return of the said certificate and of all the other documents and tools, which the worker may have deposited with his employer.[235]

(c) The worker's competition with the employer after the termination of the contract

In the U.A.R. the worker is, by virtue of section 685(d) of the Civil Code, precluded from disclosing the secrets of the employer, after the termination of the contract.[236] So this obligation on the worker follows automatically from the employment relationship, and does not for its application, pre-suppose a previous specific agreement between the employer and the worker. But if the parties make an agreement, in respect of the said obligation and of the worker's post-service competition with his employer, section 686 of the Civil Code[237] interferes, as

questions, or to give a certificate to the servant, his liability therefor is mainly tortious and belongs to the field of deceit or defamation, which for the present study, are not our concern (*vide* footnotes 215 and 220, *supra* – for enlightenment on these topics); refer to Cooper, pp. 59 *et seq.*; Batt, pp. 173 *et seq.*; Smith pp. 296 *et seq.*; and Barwell and Kar, pp. 128 *et seq.* On the other hand, the employer ,by giving a testimonial, whether to the servant himself or to the other interested parties, may bring himself within the mischief of the Servants' Characters Act 1892 (32 Geo. III, Ch. 56), if he enters falsehoods in the testimonial.

[234] *Vide Wennhak v. Morgan* (1888), 20 Q.B.D. 635; cf. the older case of *Taylor v. Rowan* (1835), 7 C. & P. 70, in which it was held that "no action lay against a master who had endorsed on the character of his employee his reasons for dismissing him"; *vide* also Cooper, p. 59; Batt, p. 179; Halsbury, Vol. 25, p. 471; and Barwell and Kar, p. 128.

[235] *Vide* Batt, p. 173 – footnote 1, for the employer's obligation under the pain of a penalty by virtue of the Insurance Acts, to return to the servant his insurance cards; and he quotes the case of *Price v. Webb* (1913), 2 K.B. 367, as an authority that the employer is not liable for damages, if the neglects to return the secards – cf. this with the employer's liability for damages in the U.A.R. (*vide* footnote 231, *supra*, and the relevant text).

[236] *Vide* section 685(d) quoted in Section I, C, (iv), of this Chapter, *suptra*; and *vide* therein the wider meaning of secrets by virtue of section 76(7) of the Labour Code. It is submitted that the same applies here, because the workers' obligation in both cases, emanates from the same provision.

[237] Section 686 of the Civil Code provides:

"If the work requested of the worker allows him to know the employer's customers or his business secrets, the parties may agree that the worker shall not after the termination of the contract compete with the employer or take part in any undertaking competitive with him: Provided that the agreement shall be valid only if:

(a) the worker be of full contracting age at the time of making the contract,

(b) the restriction be limited in respect of the time, place and the nature of the work to what is necessary for the protection of the lawful interests of the employer.

"The employer shall not be entitled to insist on the agreement if he without being justifed by the worker's actions terminates the contract or refuses to renew it, or if his own actions justify the termination of the contract by the worker."

it were, to regulate such agreement.[238] In the first instance, the section does not, it is submitted, amount to a prohibition against the worker precluding him from the benefit he draws from his experience with the employer, for his experience and skill is the worker's property, of which no one can deprive him.[239] The section, in the second place, imposes two conditions, for the validity of the agreement. The first is in respect of the worker's age, which has to be the full contracting age; and this is more stringent than the capacity to make a contract of employment.[240] The second limits the agreement, or to use the English term, the covenant, to "what is necessary for the protection of the employer's lawful interests."[241] The legality of these interests is determined by reference to the provisions of the law, including those relating to the public order and morality. On the other hand, the said second condition provides for a triangular basis, beyond whose limits the protection of the lawful interests of the employer should not extend. "It is well settled juridically and judicially, that a covenant is null and void if the worker thereby binds himself not to do a similar work in any other place without limitation, because this amounts to an infringement of his freedom of work, and if the worker does not abide by the said cove-

Vide similar provisions, in section 910 of the Iraqi Civil Code. *Vide* for the U.A.R. and Iraqi sections, the similar provisions in sections 356, 357 and 360 of the Swiss *Code de Obligations* – section 359 of this Code properly provides that "no prohibition to compete shall be valid unless the agreement is in writing" (*vide* I.L.R., Vol. 32, 1936, pp. 498–9); but neither the U.A.R. nor the Iraqi Civil Code contains similar provisions (*vide* the resolution adopted by the Advisory Committee on Professional Workers in May 1931, in *The International Labour Code*, Vol. II, pp. 245–6, to the same effect).

[238] "The regulation is for the balancing, between the employer's interests and the worker's freedom of work": Zaki, p. 248, who in p. 249, adds that, on the worker's side, the reason for the regulation is "the protection of the worker after the termination of his contract, from a heavy restriction on his freedom, which does not have an adequate return, so that his covenant not to compete is not based on any return; and on the other hand, the preclusion of any scheming by the employer, who might briefly employ a worker whose competition he fears, in order to burden him with a covenant not to compete." This writer speaks of the lack of the adequate return, and in one breath, identifies it with the lack of a return. It is submitted that the return for the covenant in the U.A.R., if any, is found in the employment itself, for otherwise, the legislator would have provided for a compensation for the worker, in section 686 of the Civil Code. Butros and Rajab, p.346, add that the "provisions of section 686(1) are a limitation on the right guaranteed for the worker by section 678(2), so the legislator did not leave this limitation without regulation" (*vide* section 678(2), quoted in Section III, a, (iv), of Chapter II, *supra*).

[239] El-Areef, pp. 195-196, says: "In any case, the duty to preserve the secrets does not preclude the worker from benefitting therefrom, after the termination of the contract, so long as the secret is not a registered right like a patent right or a personal family secret," and he speaks in similar terms in p.370. This observation is correct, although one can scarcely call a patent a secret.

[240] *Vide* Section I of Chapter II, *supra*, re capacity.

[241] Zaki, p. 248, correctly adds that these interests must not be imaginary. It is submitted that they also should not be unforeseen future interests.

nant, he should not be liable to pay any compensation therefor. However, if the worker's covenant precludes him from work in a certain area or place, or in any place for a certain period of time, the covenant is valid."[242] From these words it can be concluded that the limitations as to the time, place and nature of the work, are not only for the protection of the employer, but also for that of the worker. They provide the basis of determination of the reasonability of the covenant, in respect of the two parties. Though the public interest is partly involved in the interests of the employers and the workers, nothing is mentioned thereon in section 686 of the Civil Code. This section, in the third place, relieves the worker of the covenant, if (i) the employer unjustifiably terminates his worker's contract of employment,[243] or conversely, if by his own conduct causes the worker to justifiably terminate the contract,[244] or (ii) the employer refuses to renew the contract, without being afforded a reason therefor by the worker.

Section 687 of the U.A.R. Civil Code,[245] in the fourth place, comes

[242] Cairo Court of Appeal in (an unnumbered) appeal decided on 21 July 1930, (in Rashed and Hashem, p.272); *vide* Habeeb, p. 313; Zaki, p. 249; and Sabbour, p. 318; *vide* also the French case of *Société Carbel v. Société Cranion fils et Compagnie et Ragon* (1936), Dalloz Hebdom., 1936, p. 380, (in I.S.D.L., Vol. 12, 1938, p. 86).

[243] *Vide* Section II, B, of Chapter VI, *infra*, for the doctrine of justification of the termination of the contract by either party. Zaki, p. 249, criticises this provision by saying: "However, the deprivation of the employer of the right to benefit from the covenant, is not consonant with the principles of equity, if he is obliged to terminate the contract for urgent economic reasons." Vide the French cases of *Société lyonnaise des cafés Torredo v. Ramus* (1936), Gaz. du Palais, 29–30 March 1936, and the *Cour D'Appel de Rennes, O. & B. v. Mr. and Mrs. Ch.* (1935), Gaz. du Palais, 1936, 1, note (a), 642 (both in I.S.D.L., Vol. 12, 1938, p. 87 and Vol. 11, 1937, p. 90, respectively) – and cf. the first mentioned case, with the extreme case of *Société Frères v. Lapointe* (1934), Dalloz Hebdom., 1934, 484, (in I.S.D.L., Vol. 10, 1936, p.87), where it was held that a three years' covenant was binding on a probationary worker, even if his contract was terminated during the probationary period. *Vide* also the resolution adopted by the Advisory Committee on Salaried Employees, in April 1931 (in the *International Labour Code*, Vol. II, p.247).

[244] *Vide* section 696(1) of the U.A.R. Civil Code (quoted in Section II, B, of Chapter VI, *infra*); and *vide* footnote 200, *supra*.

[245] Section 687 provides: "If a penalty clause for the violation of the covenant not to compete is agreed upon and the amount of the penalty is exaggerated so as to oblige the worker to remain in the service of the employer for a period longer than the stipulated period the said clause together with the whole covenant shall be null and void." It is submitted that the same is applicable, if the contract is for an unlimited period, and the penalty clause prejudices the worker's right to terminate it by notice (as he is entitled to do so, by virtue of section 72 of the Labour Code), with the result that he is obliged to stay in the service of the employer, more than he chooses.

This section replaces the relevant section of the Draft Civil Code of 1948, which reads:

"If the covenant not to compete contains a penalty clause the worker may relieve himself of the covenant by paying the agreed penalty, unless it is ascertained from the provisions of the agreement that the parties intended the penalty to be a fair estimate of the compensation for the damage.

"If the intention is otherwise the employer may claim a supplementary compensation to the aid of the worker so as to relieve him of the whole covenant, if by means of a penalty therein on the worker, it amounts to the prolongation of the stipulated duration of the contract. This goes further than the provisions of the general law, which subject any liquidated damages agreed upon by the parties, to the overriding power of the Court to lower the amount of these damages, if it is in excess of the damage actually suffered.[246]

In Sudan there are no statutory provisions, equivalent to those in the U.A.R. So the rules of the law there, are determined by reference to the English Common Law.[247] This Law calls the agreement under discussion, a covenant or a contract in restraint of trade. This was defined as "a contract whereby a restraint is imposed upon the liberty of an individual to earn his living or exercise his calling."[248] Though the Common Law rejected any such restraint, as early as the year 1300, it had, with the development in the fields of employment and trade, to gradually and partially allow the restraint,[249] until the present position of the law was finally reviewed and recast, at the end of the nineteenth century. The review and recasting came from the House of Lords, in *Nordenfelt v. Maxim-Nordenfelt.*[250] The Lords in this case, uttered the criterion of reasonableness, with regards to the interests of the parties and the public, as the basis of determination of the validity of the covenant.[251] Moreover, "the Lords held that a restrictive covenant was not of necessity void because it was world wide or unlimited in time; these were only important factors in deciding whether the covenant in all

for the damage over and above the agreed penalty, and he may in addition request the stoppage of the violation if his damaged interests and the worker's violation justify such request."

Vide section 359 of the Swiss *Code des Obligations*, from which the said draft provision seems to have been inspired (*vide* I.L.R., Vol. 32, 1936, p. 499).

[246] *Vide* Section 224 of the U.A.R. Civil Code; *vide* also Badawi, K.M., p. 319; Zaki, p.250; Sabbour, p. 319; and Faheem, p. 78. *Vide* and cf. in this respect, the resolution adopted by the Advisory Committee on Professional Workers, in May 1931 (in the *International Labour Code*, Vol.II, p.247).

[247] The rules of the English Common Law similarly apply, in Bahrain and Aden.

[248] *Eve*, J., in *Hepworth Manufacturing Co. v. Ryot* (1920), 1 Ch.1, at p. 33.

[249] *Vide* for the history of this development: Smith, pp. 53–55; and Batt, pp. 97–98.

[250] (1894) A.C. 535.

[251] In that case, *Lord Macnaghten* said: "Restraints of trade and interference with individual liberty of action may be justifed by the special circumstances of a particular case. It is a sufficient justification and indeed the only justification, if the restriction is reasonable – reasonable, that is, in reference to the interests of the parties concerned and is reasonable in reference to the interest of the public, so framed and so guarded as to afford adequate protection to the party in whose favour it is imposed, while at the same time it is in no way injurious to the public." *Lord Herschell*, in the same case said: "A covenant entered into by an employee must be valid when any covenant less wide would not adequately protect those interests in respect of which the employer is entitled to protection, namely, trade secrets and trade connections." *Vide* Samuels, p. 20.

the circumstances of the case was reasonable."[252] The interest of the public is manifested by the protection of "the master... in his trade secrets, and his clientele is assured to him, and he is thereby emboldened to employ servants in confidential capacities, so that employment is increased and the interests of the covenantee and of the public are served."[253] On the other hand, the Common Law allows severability of the void from the valid parts of the covenant, if these parts are in reality independent covenants; otherwise the whole covenant is invalid.[254] Another requirement for the validity of the covenant, is that it should be for consideration, even if the covenant be under seal, though consideration need not be adequate.[255]

If the employer wrongfully terminates the contract, or the contract becomes impossible of performance, the worker is relieved of the covenant.[256] But infancy is no relief from the covenant, if the contract

[252] Batt, p.102, and *vide* p.105; *vide* also Diamond, p. 66. Other factors in deciding the reasonableness of the covenant, are the nature of the employer's business, the practice or the usage of the business, the position held by the worker and the particular circumstances of the case: *vide* Batt, pp.106–10; and Cooper, pp. 41–3.

[253] Diamond, pp.73–74; cf. this with the words of Batt, in pp. 109–110, which are in effect a criticism of the legal decisions including *Nordenfelt's* case, in respect of public interest – he says: "... it is difficult to imagine cases where the public interest would suffer, if the restraining is reasonable having regard to the interests of the parties, and, indeed, there is no reported case where a covenant otherwise reasonable has been held unreasonable as against public interest; a restriction on the work of a scientific or literary genius, however, favourable to him as regards consideration, might conceivably be held against public interest, but such a case has not arisen and is not likely to arise" – these words can easily be pleaded, in defence of the lack of any mention of the public interest, in section 686 of the U.A.R. Civil Code.

[254] *Vide Attwood v. Lamont* (1920), 3 K.B.; 571, this is the so-called *blue pencil doctrine of severance*; *vide* also Diamond, p. 76; Cooper, pp. 43 and 44; Smith, p. 56; Samuels, pp. 22 and 23; Batt, p. 113; Cheshire and Fifoot, pp. 324 and 326–9; and Halsbury, Vol. 25, p. 460. It is submitted that the same applies in the U.A.R.

[255] *Vide Gravely V. Barnard* (1874) 18 L.R.Eq. 518; and *Morris v. Saxelby* (1916) 1 A.C., 688; *vide* also Diamond, p. 68; Samuels, p. 20; Macdonell, p.138; and Halsbury, Vol. 25, p. 460. Batt, p.110, says that "there is no direct modern authority where such restraint had been held invalid for the absence of consideration, nor is it easy to imagine how the point can arise, since by the very nature of the case the employment supplies the consideration" – *vide* footnote 238, for the position in the U.A.R. On the other hand, Batt (*Idem*) submits that "it is difficult, if not impossible, to see how a restriction in respect of which the consideration was inadequate could ever be rightly held to be unreasonable as regards the interests of the covenantor." It is submitted that he is correct, in as far as all the circumstances of the case, including the said consideration of 'employment,' have to be considered, in order to determine the reasonableness of the covenant – *vide* footnote 252, *supra*.

[256] *Vide General Billposting Co. Ltd. v. Atkinson* (1909) A.C., 118 – (wrongful dismissal) – *vide* Section II, B, of Chapter VI, *infra*, for the definition of wrongful dismissal; *Konski v. Peet* (1951) 1 Ch. 530; and *Measures Bros., Ltd. v. Measures* (1910) 2 Ch. 248 – (a receiver and manager appointed – resulting impossibility of performance – defendant relieved of covenant, even if he was given notice); *vide* also Batt, p. 119; Samuels, p.24; Diamond, p. 78; Cooper, p.48; Cheshire and Fifoot, p. 445; and Barwell and Kar, p. 398.

as a whole including the covenant, is for the benefit of the infant.[257] Nor is there any relief for the worker, if the ex-employer sells or assigns his business, for the covenant "forms a part of the goodwill of the business and passes to the purchaser of that good will and of the beneficial interest, who thereupon has a right of action in the event of breach."[258]

If the covenant contains a stipulation that the worker should pay a certain sum of money if he fails in abiding by it, the Court will not hold the covenant void, even if it be *in terrorem* so as to compel performance, or in other words, compel the worker to specifically perform the contract.[259] But the Court will ascertain the intention of the parties, as to whether the said sum is in reality, liquidated damages agreed upon between the parties, or a penalty over the head of the worker.[260] If it is liquidated damages, the Court will award it; but if it is a penalty, the full sum is not necessarily recoverable, for the "covenantee will be able to revover as damages only the actual loss which he can prove he sustained through the breach in question."[261]

Finally, apart from any covenant entered into by the worker, the worker is, under the Common Law, bound by his duty of fidelity which he owes to his ex-employer, to preserve the latter's secrets.[262] Subject to the said covenant and duty of fidelity, the worker is free to benefit from his experience and skill of which no one can deprive him, even if he gained them during his service with his ex-employer. "Trade secrets, the names of customers, all such things which in sound philosophical language are denominated objective knowledge – these may not be given away by a servant ... On the other hand, a man's aptitudes, his skill, his dexterity, his manual and mental ability – all those things

[257] *Vide Bromley v. Smith* (1909) 2 K.B., 235; *vide* also Diamond, pp. 41 and 43; Batt, pp.98–99; Cooper, p.31; and Samuels, pp.8 and 23.

[258] Samuels, p. 23, who quotes *Jacoby v. Whitmore* (1883), 49 L.T., 335, as an authority; *vide* also Diamond, pp.70–1; and Batt, p.63. Smith, p.63, says: "But such a covenant, on its true contruction, must not be merely a personal one so as to come within the rule as to the non-assignability of personal contracts." It is submitted that, if the covenant should have consideration, and this consideration be no more than the employment itself, as we have seen above (*vide* footnote 255, *supra*), then the covenant should end with the passing of the business from the ex-employer to any other person and by whatever manner, because that other person did not employ the worker, and thus provided no consideration. It is submitted that the same should also apply in the U.A.R.

[259] *Vide* in this respect, the resolution adopted by the Advisory Committee on Professional Workers in May 1931 (in the *International Labour Code*, Vol.II, p.247), which, it is believed, was adopted mainly by the influence of the Committee members, brought up under the influence of the English Common Law.

[260] *Vide Law v. Redditch Local Board* (1892) 1 Q.B. 127; *vide* also Batt, p. 120; and Smith, p.65.

[261] Batt, p.119; *vide* also Smith, p.66.

[262] *Vide* Cooper, pp. 64 and 65; Batt, p.180; and Barwell andKar, p. 79. This is equivalent to the duty of the worker in the U.A.R., under section 685(d) of the Civil Code.

which in sound philosophical language are not objective, but subjective – they may, and they ought not to be relinquished by a servant, they are not his master's property, they are his own property, they are himself."[263]

Comparison of the law in the U.A.R. and Sudan, reveals the following grounds of similarity and difference:

(i) Both laws impose a general obligation on the worker, not to reveal his ex-employer's secrets, after the termination of his contract.

(ii) Infancy invalidates the covenant in the U.A.R., whereas the infant is bound thereby in the Sudan, if the contract of employment as a whole is for his benefit.

(iii) The covenant should be reasonable, in respect of the interests of the two parties in the U.A.R.; whereas in the Sudan, the public interest is added.

(iv) In the Sudan the covenant falls with the employer's wrongful termination of the contract and with the contract's impossibility of performance. In the U.A.R. the covenant falls with the employer's unjustified termination of the contract, the worker's justified termination of the contract and the employer's refusal without proper cause, to renew the contract.

(v) In the Sudan the covenant must be for consideration, which is almost always the employment itself. In the U.A.R. there is no mention of the necessity of a return though if it is required, it is also the employment. The rule that the covenant can pass to a successor of the covenantee-employer, in the former, is not consonant with the requirement of consideration. There is no such rule in the latter.

(vi) Severability of the valid from the invalid parts of a covenant, is permitted within certain conditions in Sudan. The same should apply in the U.A.R.

(vii) In the U.A.R. the whole covenant falls with any penalty clause therein, if its effect is to prolong the duration of the contract. In the Sudan such a penalty clause affects the determination of the damages, payable by the worker for his violation of the covenant, but does not affect the validity of the covenant itself.

(viii) Subject to his duty to preserve the employer's secrets, and to any restrictive covenant, the worker both in the U.A.R. and Sudan, is entitled to benefit from his personal experience and skill.

[263] Per *Lord Shaw*, in *Morris v. Saxelby* (1916) 1 A.C., 688; *vide* also Cooper, pp. 40–42 and 64; Smith, pp. 63 and 64; Batt, pp. 100, 104, 107, 156–7, 179 and 181; Samuels, p. 21; Halsbury, Vol. 25, p. 465; and Barwell and Kar, pp. 80–81.

SUMMARY

Statutory regulation of the contract of employment in the U.A.R. and Sudan, looms large in the regulation of the rights and obligations of the parties, but more so in the former than in the latter.

It is a statutory compulsory term of the contract in the U.A.R., that the employer is bound at the commencement of employment, to pay the expenses of transporting his workers to the place of work, except in certain circumstances. He is also bound to provide them with transportation during employment, if the normal means of transport do not reach to the place of work. In Sudan the transportation of the workers at the commencement of or during employment, is still purely a contractual matter between them and the employer.

The employer both in the U.A.R. and Sudan, is not obliged to provide work for the worker, and the payment of remuneration by him is sufficient, except in certain cases which on the whole are the same in the two countries. On the other hand, the worker is obliged to serve the employer personally in both countries, but personal performance by the employer, is more mandatory in the Sudan than in the U.A.R. The rules governing the exclusive or non-exclusive service by the worker in both countries, are similar.

The worker should in the performance of the work, exercise the care of the reasonable man, in both countries. He is also bound to obey the lawful orders of the employer, provided that his safety is not thereby endangered. Orders in violation of the contract constitute a breach of the contract in the U.A.R. and Sudan; but there are statutory exceptions to this rule in the former, though not in the latter. The contractual and tortious liabilities of the worker for the employer's property entrusted to him or otherwise, are similar in both countries. The worker is in both countries, obliged to preserve the employer's business secrets, and to avoid any injurious competition with his employer. The worker's duty of fidelity towards his employer, is basically the same in the U.A.R. and Sudan. However, his duty of disclosure is in one respect, wider in the former than in the latter. The employer's *bona fides* is the same, in both countries.

The work rules are to a considerable extent, regulated by statute in the U.A.R., but not at all in the Sudan. A controversy as to the contractual or administrative nature of these rules, has arisen in the former but not in the latter.

The employer's power of discipline in the U.A.R., arises automatically with the making of the contract of employment. Due to the danger that flows from this automatic power of discipline, the legislator has interfered in order to limit it. In Sudan such power of discipline only arises from a contractual authorisation by the worker, and this is not consonant with the element of control in the contract. Due to this, the legislator has not so far interfered in order to regulate the said power, except in the case of Government workers.

It is a statutory compulsory term in the contract in the U.A.R., that the employer should, subject to certain conditions, provide medical treatment, medicines, housing and food to his workers. In Sudan the provision thereof is still purely contractual. The employer's duty to protect his workers from the dangers at work, is in both countries, deducible from the employer's tortious liability for negligence.

The grounds of entitlement of the employer to his worker's inventions, are narrower in the U.A.R. than in Sudan. The worker is guaranteed in the former but not in the latter, a special return or equitable compensation, if his invention is of real economic value.

At the termination of the contract, the employer in the U.A.R. is bound to provide return transportation for his worker, except in some specified cases. In Sudan any such obligation is purely contractual. On the other hand, the employer in the U.A.R. is bound by statute to give a certificate of service to his worker, whereas in Sudan such provision of the said certificate is purely voluntary. However, the employer in both countries, is bound to return to the worker, at the termination of the contract, any such certificate and all other documents and tools, which the worker has deposited with the employer. Such duty of the employer has a penal sanction in the U.A.R., but is purely civil in the Sudan.

Finally, the law concerning post-service competition by the worker with his employer, is similar in both countries, in as far as the worker is obliged to preserve his employer's business secrets. They are also similar as concerns the worker's right to benefit from his experience and skill, subject to the terms of any valid restrictive covenant, into which the worker may have entered. The law concerning such covenants is also similar in both countries, in respect of the severability of the valid from the invalid parts of the covenant and in the worker's relief from the covenant, when the contract is wrongfully terminated in the Sudan, and unjustifiably terminated in the U.A.R. However, the laws in the two countries, are different in other respects, in such a way as to afford a ground of relief for the worker from the covenant, wider in scope in the U.A.R. than in Sudan.

CHAPTER IV

WAGES[1]

SECTION I: DEFINITION AND KINDS OF WAGES

Section 3 of the U.A.R. Labour Code provides:

"Wages shall for the purposes of this Code mean all that is given to the worker including all kinds of allowances in return for his work irrespective of its nature and particularly the following:

1. the commission paid to local salesmen, commercial representatives (and) travellers,[2]
2. the privileges in kind and the cost of living and family allowances paid to them,[3]
3. any bonus or other sums given to the worker over and above his wages as a reward for his honesty or efficiency and the like if these sums are provided for in the individual or collective contracts of employment or in the work rules or if the payment thereof has grown into a custom so that the workers consider them a part of the wages and not mere ex-gratia payments.

"Tips shall not be considered a part of the wages unless their payment has grown into a custom and their amounts can be assessed by fixed rules.

"In certain classes of business such as hotels restaurants cafés and bars it shall be permissible that the worker's wages consist only of the tips he receives and the food he eats provided that the value thereof can be assessed by rules fixed in the contract of employment."[4]

The definition of wages in the first paragraph of this section, is not

[1] The word 'remuneration' is sometimes used, instead of 'wages.' These two words are synonymous. The word 'wages' was preferred, because it is more familiar.

[2] It is submitted that the word 'and,' between the words 'representatives' and 'travellers,' was omitted by oversight, as is the case in section 676 of the Civil Code (*vide* footnote 202 to Chapter I, *supra*); and that the omission of the 'insurance agents' in section 3, is also an oversight, because they are mentioned in the said section 676, by which the provisions of section 3 are partly inspired – the supplementary inspiration coming from sections 683 and 684 (*vide* Zaki, p. 103).

[3] It is submitted that the word 'privileges' is not the proper word, because the intent is 'benefits,' nor is the word 'them,' because the intent is 'him,' referring to the worker in the commencing provisions of the section.

[4] *Vide* and cf. the definitions in sections 29, 2(6), 2(8) and 1, of the Kuwaiti, Qatari, Jordanian and Libyan Labour Codes, respectively. The Saudi Regulations, and the Iraqi, Lebanese and Tunisian Labour Codes do not contain any express definitions; and the reference therefor, should be made to the definitions of the contract of employment, the employer or the worker (refer to Chapter I, *supra*), as the case may be.

complete, without reference to the definition of the worker in section 2 of the Labour Code.[5] By such reference, wages emerge better defined as all that the worker receives, in return for the work which he performs for and under the control of another person called the employer.[6] This brings out of the definition all ex-gratia payments.[7] It also brings out any payment for work, when the contract of employment is invalid, in which case the payment is considered a debt, which is payable under the rules of unjust enrichment.[8]

In Sudan section 2 of the Sudan Ordinance defines wages, as "the aggregate of basic pay[9] and all other forms of remuneration payable to an employed person by an employer, and includes the value of any food, fuel or quarters supplied to the employed person by the employer, and any overtime payments or other special remuneration for the work done, whether by way of bonus, cost of living allowance or otherwise, but shall not include any ex-gratia payment or gift or the value of a travelling allowance or concession, or a contribution paid by the employer of an employed person towards any provident fund, pension or life assurance fund, or a sum paid to an employed person to cover any special expenses entailed on him by the nature of his employment."[10]

This definition of wages is also not complete, without reference to the definition of the *contract of service*, in the same section of the Ordinance,[11] and to the English Common Law. Such reference renders a definition of wages basically similar to that ascertained in the U.A.R. Ex-gratia payments are accordingly out of the definition, as indeed is expressly provided in the said section 2. The counterpart in Sudan, for a payment under the rules of unjust enrichment in the U.A.R., is the payment of a *quantum meruit*.[12]

[5] *Vide* the definition of the worker, in Section II of Chapter I, *supra*.

[6] Once wages are so defined, it is not of any relevant importance that wages are time or piece-work wages, or a combination of both (*vide* El-Areef, pp. 261 and 294–7).

[7] Express reference to ex-gratia payments, is made in the said section 3 of the Labour Code, in respect of bonuses; *vide* the discussion on remuneration in Section I of Chapter I, *supra*.

[8] *Vide* section 179 of the U.A.R. Civil Code, for the provisions on unjust enrichment, *L'enrichissement sans cause*, as it is called in French; *vide* also Cairo Court of Cassation (Commercial) in case No. 2353 of 1953 (in Habeeb, pp. 36–7); and *vide* El-Areef, p. 260; and Murad, pp. 270–1.

[9] Basic pay is defined in the same section, as the "basic rate of remuneration payable to an employed person by an employer but excludes all other remuneration."

[10] *Vide* a similar definition in section 3(9), read with section 3(b) of the Bahraini Labour Code. The Adenese Ordinance does not contain any definition; but section 12 of the Minimum wage and Wages Regulations, bears some similarity to the Sudan definition, though not as much as the Bahraini definition. The definitions in Sudan, Bahrain and Aden, seem to have been inspired by Article 1 of the I.L.O. *Protection of Wages Convention* No. 95 of 1949.

[11] *Vide* the definition of the contract, in Section I of Chapter I, *supra*.

[12] *Vide* footnote 26 to Chapter I, *supra*, and the related text.

So the elements of the definition of wages are in the U.A.R., basically the same as those in Sudan. Though this means that the law should in the two countries, readily give the same answers, as to whether certain payments or givings to the workers, are wages or not, we shall presently see that the task of eliciting such similar answers is not an easy task. These answers are important for the calculation of the worker's benefits, and for the protection of wages.[13]

The definition in the U.A.R., permits wages to be in kind as well as in money.[14] The benefits in kind are all the benefits whose value can be estimated in money.[15] Those of particular importance of the said benefits, are housing, food and clothing.[16] They are considered as wages, as long as their provision is not casual.[17] Housing, however, is not wages, even if it is provided free of charge, when the provision thereof is necessitated by, and is made for the better performance of the work.[18] Otherwise, whether the value of any total or partial free housing is or is not wages, depends on the agreement between the parties.[19] The same applies to the provision of food and clothing.[20]

[13] The worker's benefits are mainly his leaves (*vide* Chapter V, *infra*), his payment in lieu of the notice of the termination of the contract, and compensation for the unjustifiable or wrongful dismissal (*vide* Section II of Chapter VI, *infra*), and his termination gratuity (*vide* Chapter VII, *infra*). For the protection of wages, *vide* Section II of this Chapter, *infra*.

[14] This was the first recognition of the permissibility of the wages to be in kind, in the Labour law (*vide* Habeeb, p. 572). However, the U.A.R. Civil Code made an earlier recognition of the same, generally in section 350, and particularly in section 684, which permits the provision of food to be wages in certain classes of business. The said permissibility is what distinguishes wages from a selling price, which has to be in money by virtue of section 418 of the Civil Code; *vide*, however, section 463 of the *Majallha*, which permits any thing which is good as a selling price, to be good as wages.

[15] *Vide* Badawi, K.M., p. 95; *vide* also Zaki, p. 87; and Habeeb, pp. 51 and 52, both of whom say that the use of a land can also be wages in kind.

[16] *Vide* the Alexandria Court of Appeal in the appeal on dispute No. 210 of 1950 (Rashed and Hashem, p. 30); and Cairo Labour Court in case No. 4958 of 1959 (in El-Hawwari, p. 104); *vide* also Zaki, p. 88; and Habeeb, p. 52. Section 948 of the Draft Civil Code of 1948, which was not adopted, contains an express mention of food and housing as kinds of wages; *vide* the French case of *Martin v. Limonsis* (1931), Sirey, 1931, 1, 175 (in I.S.D.L., Vol. 7, 1933, p. 126).

[17] *Vide* Cairo Court of Appeal in appeal No. 374 of 1958 (in El-Hawwari, p. 103); *vide* also El-Areef, pp. 262–3 (who quotes in support, a French decision taken on 4 November 1937, Dalloz Hebdom, 1938, p. 50); Murad, p. 298; Habeeb, pp. 53–6; and El-Fakahani, 1959 Supplement, p. 54. Butros and Rajab, p. 93, say the same thing impliedly, adding that the circumstances of every case should be discussed separately, so as to determine whether the worker has come to depend on housing, food and clothing, as part of his wages.

[18] *Vide* Cairo Court of Cassation in case No. 1287 of 1954 (in Habeeb, p. 56). It is submitted that Faheem, p. 63, is without saying more, wrong in stating that the value of free housing is wages.

[19] This is also applicable to any such provision of housing, by virtue of section 64 of the U.A.R. Labour Code (*vide* Section I, G, of Chapter III, *supra*).

[20] *Vide* the Cairo Court of Arbitration in dispute No. 111 of 1954; the Alexandria Court of Arbitration in dispute No. 14 of 1955; and Zakazeek Court of Arbitration in

In Sudan the definition of wages permits remuneration in kind, and expressly mentions thereunder, housing and food.[21] What was mentioned above, concerning housing, food and clothing, is also applicable in Sudan,[22] together with the submission made thereon. As we shall see later, the permissibility of remuneration in kind, is less in Sudan than in the U.A.R.

The commission payable to commercial representatives and travellers, and the percentages payable to some workers in commercial establishments, are wages, both in the U.A.R. and Sudan.[23] The worker's remuneration may in both countries, consist of a share in the profits.[24]

dispute No. 29 of 1954, (all three in Habeeb, pp. 54–5); *vide* also Murad, p. 298; Butros and Rajab, p. 73; and Faheem, p. 42.

[21] Subject to the provisions of the Truck Act 1831, re workmen (*vide* footnote 89, *infra*), the same applies in England: *vide* Cooper, p. 36, who quotes some authorities, to the effect that "the grant of food and lodging may amount to consideration"; *vide* also Smith, p. 135; and Barwell and Kar, p. 235. However, the Adenese provisions (*vide* footnote 10, *supra*), expressly exclude housing and food, from the definition of wages. *Vide* Article 4 of the I.L.O. *Protection of Wages Convention* No. 95 of 1949, which permits, but puts limitations on the remuneration in kind; *vide* also Article 15(7) of the *Social Policy (Non-Metropolitan Territories) Convention* No. 83 of 1947.

[22] *Vide Hughes v. The Overseers of the Parish of Chatham* (1843), 5 Man & G. 54, in which it was said: "A master may pay his servant by conferring on him an interest in real property... But it may be, that a servant may occupy a tenement of his master's, not by way of payment for services, but for the purpose of performing them." *Vide* section 16 of the Sudan Ordinance, in Section III, A, of this Chapter, *infra*. This section also permits the tillage of the land, to be wages in kind (*vide* footnote 15, *supra*, for comparison with the U.A.R.).

[23] Section 683 of the U.A.R. Civil Code expressly provides that "commissions payable to local salesmen and commercial travellers and representatives," and "the sale-percentages payable to the workers of commercial establishments," shall each be "an integral part of the wages"; this can also be deduced from the provisions of section 676 of the Code (*vide* the section quoted in Section III of Chapter I, *supra*, and Section III of the present Chapter, *infra*); *vide* also Cairo Court of Cassation in case No. 430 of 1960, on commissions; and Cairo Labour Court in case No. 568 og 1960, on percentages, (both in El-Hawwari, p. 100); and Cairo Court of Appeal in appeal No. 132 of 1948, on percentages, (in Naguib and Bakr, p. 11); and *vide* El-Areef, pp. 268 and 269; Murad, p. 296; Zaki, p. 99; Habeeb, p. 61; and Faheem, pp. 37 and 38, where he distinguishes between commissions and percentages; section 64 of Book I of the French Labour Code, considers commissions as wages (*vide* I.L.R., Vol. 32, 1936, p. 337).

For Sudan, *vide* in addition to the definition of wages (which permits this kind of remuneration by implication): Cooper, p. 13; Macdonell, pp. 41–2; and Barwell and Kar, pp. 235–6.

[24] *Vide* Habeeb, p. 127; Zaki, p. 97 (who adds in p. 99, that the share of the profits is wages, even though it is prescribed by law, and he mentions in p. 122, Law No. 26 of 1954, as an example); and Butros and Rajab, p. 114, who also list the dates of the introduction of the profit-sharing in France, England and the U.S.A., as 1820, 1860 and 1869, respectively.

For Sudan, *vide* in addition to the definition of wages (which permits this kind of remuneration by implication): Smith, p. 33; Macdonell, pp. 41–2; and Barwell and Kar, p. 236.

Section 691 of the U.A.R. Civil Code obliges the employer to "furnish the worker after each stock-taking with an account of what he owes to him"; and for the purpose of verification, the employer should also give the necessary information to, and permit the inspection of his accounting books by the worker, or any other trusted person, appointed

The growing of the payment of a bonus (*gratifications*) and also of a reward (which is covered thereunder) into a custom, has provoked in the U.A.R., a great deal of judicial and juridical discussion, because section 3 of the U.A.R. Labour Code mentions custom, without defining how a custom is established.[25] The weight of authority leans in favour of the fulfilment of three conditions, before a custom is established. These are continuity (*la constance*), comprehensiveness (*la généralité*) and non-variability (*la fixité*).[26] However, it is submitted that these three conditions are not warranted by the section, because they restrict the right of the worker in the bonus or reward, while the section itself makes the test more subjective than objective, as concerns the worker.[27] Continuity and comprehensiveness should be sufficient to establish a custom, for the entitlement to the bonus; and continuity alone should be sufficient, in the case of the reward. As for the non-variability it should, provided there is an ascertained minimum, be relevant only in the determination of the payable amount of the bonus or reward.[28]

for the purpose, either by the two parties or by the Judge. In Sudan there is no such statutory provision. But reference to the English Common Law reveals almost identical obligations on the employer: *vide Harrington v. Churchward*, 29, L.J. Ch. 521; *Rishton v. Grissell*, 5 Eq. 326; and *Turner v. Bayley*, 4 De G.J. & Sm. 332, as authorities to the effect in question.

[25] Nor does section 683 of the U.A.R. Civil Code, from which the relevant provisions of section 3 of the Labour Code, are inspired. Section 683 provides that "every bonus given to the worker over and above his wages and sums given to him as a reward for his honesty or for his increased family responsibilities and other similar sums," shall be considered as integral parts of the wages, "if they are provided for in the individual or collective contracts or in the work rules or their grant has grown into a custom so that the workers consider them a part of the wages and not mere ex-gratia payments provided that the amounts thereof shall be ascertained before the attachment."

[26] *Vide* the High Court of Appeal in two appeals decided on 28 November 1957 and 11 February 1960 (both in Zaki, p. 95); Alexandria Court of Appeal in an appeal decided on 6 January 1953 (in Faheem, p. 40); Cairo Court of Arbritation in dispute No. 221 of 1954, (in Habeeb, p. 110); Cairo Court of Cassation in case No. 1591 of 1957, (in El-Hawwari, p. 94); and Cairo Court of Appeal in the two appeals Nos. 64 and 81 of 1959 (*Ibid.*, pp. 93 and 95), respectively; *vide* also Murad, p. 302; Naguib and Bakr, pp. 14–5, and the above-mentioned references Zaki, Faheem and Habeeb; all this seems to be inspired by the French Law: *vide* Zaki, pp. 93–4, who, however, believes that the word 'custom' in the U.A.R. legislation, is not the same as that in France, because the former amounts to no more than a 'permanent usage.'

[27] Zaki, p. 94, criticises this subjective test as being wrong, because *prima facie* a bonus or reward is voluntary, and it is the employer's intention which should be ascertained. However, it is submitted that the intent of the two parties should be ascertained, with a special leaning towards the worker, because he is the taker and not the giver of the bonus or reward.

[28] El-Fakahani, 1959 Supplement, pp. 56–7, submits to the same effect, re the bonus, but comprehensiveness stays with him as a pre-requisite also for the reward; Rashed and Hashem, pp. 22 and 25, submit that continuity and non-variability are sufficient, both for the bonus and the reward; Badawi, K.M., p. 96, insists that non-variability is a pre-requisite for both. Those who insist on the non-variability, concede that a non-variable minimum is sufficient to satisfy the requirements: *vide* Rashed and Hashem, pp. 22–3; Habeeb, p. 114, where he quotes in support, the Cairo Court of Arbitration in disputes

·Once the bonus or reward becomes wages, it becomes contractually due to the worker, and is entered in the calculation of his other benefits, and cannot be denied because the employer does not realize any profits or even incurs a loss in a certain year.[29] This also justifies the entitlement of a worker to a proportion of the bonus or reward, distributed at the termination of the year, during which his services were terminated.[30]

In Sudan the definition of wages expressly considers the bonus as a wage,[31] without prescribing any conditions similar to those in the U.A.R. Presumably, the bonus is a wage, where the contract between the worker and the employer so provides. It is submitted that the bonus can also be a wage, by virtue of an established custom. "An employer may, of course, give a present to an employee..., but if such presents become so habitual that the employee came to regard (them) as a right, the question of their legality would immediately arise."[32] On the other hand, "the custom must be reasonable, in its terms, and must be proved by evidence to be uniform, certain, of reasonable antiquity and so notorious that persons would contract on the basis of its existence."[33] When this is applied to the payment of a bonus or a reward, it means that the payment must fulfil the three conditions necessary for the establishment of a custom in the U.A.R., and must in addition, be both reasonable and notorious in the trade or the establishment. The noto-

Nos. 78 and 118 of 1953; and the Alexandria Court of Arbitration in dispute No. 25 of 1954; another decision in support, is the Cairo Court of Arbitration in dispute No. 189 of 1954 (in El-Fakahani, Book I, Vol. I, p. 543); *vide* also Faheem, p. 40.

[29] Cairo Court of Appeal in the appeal on dispute No. 193 of 1953 (El-Fakahani, Book I, Vol I, p. 550); and the same Court in the appeal on dispute No. 99 of 1957 (in El-Hawwari, p. 98); Cairo Court of Arbitration in dispute No. 78 of 1953; and the Alexandria Court of Arbitration in dispute No. 57 of 1956 (both in Habeeb, p. 115); *vide* also Murad, pp. 302–3; El-Fakahani, 1959 Supplement, p. 59; Butros and Rajab, p. 98; Naguib and Bakr, p. 15; and Faheem, p. 40. Rashed and Hashem, p. 28, however, believe otherwise; and they in page 27, quote in support, Alexandria Court of Cassation in case No. 159 of 1950. It is submitted that they and the said decision are wrong.

[30] *Vide* Cairo Labour Court in case No. 1339 of 1953 (in Faheem, p. 41); Alexandria Court of Appeal in appeal No. 143 of 1954, (in Habeeb, p. 117); and the Cairo Court of Cassation in case No. 1083 of 1955 (Ibid., p. 118). Contrary decisions are the Cairo Court of Cassation in case No. 2490 of 1953 (in El-Fakahani, Book I, Vol. I, p. 552), and the appeal thereon No. 1104, decided by the Cairo Court of Appeal on June 14, 1955 (*Ibid.*, p. 553). It is submitted that these contrary decisions are wrong. *Vide* also Murad, p. 303; El-Areef, p. 279; Naguib and Bakr, p. 16; El-Fakahani, 1959 Supplement, p. 58; Butros and Rajab, p. 98; and Badawi, K.M., p. 105.

[31] In England "the bonus is not wages": Batt, p. 128, and he quotes *Deane v. Wilson* (1906), 2 T.R. 405, as an authority. It is, however, submitted that this does not preclude the bonus from being wages, by virtue of the contract of service, or by virtue of a custom.

[32] Samuels, p. 42.

[33] Diamond, pp. 181–2, who quotes *Foxall v. International Land Credit Co.* (1867), 16 L.T. 673; and *Devonald v. Rosser* (1906) 2 K.B. 728, as authorities; *vide* also Samuels, p. 10.

riety can only be ascertained, after the examination of all the surrounding circumstances, and with the aid of the doctrine of constructive knowledge. In the U.A.R. reasonability of the usage is irrelevant to the establishment of a custom. Notoriety though not mentioned, should be taken for granted in the U.A.R., as a condition necessary for the establishment of a custom. Once the bonus or reward becomes wages, it is submitted that the law concerning the entitlement thereto, even if there be no profits or there is a loss, and the worker's entitlement to his due proportion of the bonus or reward, would in Sudan, be the same as in the U.A.R.

The cost of living and family allowances are expressly considered as wages, in section 3 of the U.A.R. Labour Code.[34] In Sudan the definition of wages expressly considers the cost of living allowance, as a wage. It is submitted that the family allowance would, under the *ejusdem generis* rule, also be a wage.

Tips (*le pourboire*) are wages in the U.A.R., by virtue of the definition in section 3 of the Labour Code, if their payment in any business has grown into a custom. Section 684 of the Civil Code provides in its first paragraph, that "no tips shall be considered wages except in the industrial or commercial business in which the payment of tips has grown into a custom and unless the amounts thereof can be assessed by fixed rules." It is clear that these are the provisions, from which the relevant provisions in section 3 of the Labour Code were copied almost identically. In its second paragraph, section 684 provides that "tips

[34] Section 683 of the U.A.R. Civil Code also considers them wages (*vide* footnotes 22 and 24, *supra*); *vide* also Cairo Court of Cassation in case No. 842 of 1959 (in El-Hawwari, p. 95). Zaki, p. 96, points out that the definition of wages in the Labour Code, classifies the said allowances as wages, without any condition, whereas the Civil Code wrongly subjects the entitlement to the family allowances, to the custom mentioned in section 683 thereof. It is submitted that he is correct, and that section 3 of the Labour Code supersedes in this respect, the provisions of section 683 of the Civil Code.

Before the Civil Code, the wartime Military Order No. 358 of 1942 (*vide Al-Jaridat-ul-Rasmiyyatu* No. 221 dated 9 December 1942), which was the first enactment to prescribe the payment of the cost of living allowance and the family allowances, to workers in commercial and industrial establishments, classified them as wages – This Order was renewed yearly, and has since 1950, been kept effective, by Order No. 99 of 1950 (*Ibid.*, No. 32 *bis*, dated 21 February 1950), and in due course, by section 4 of the Presidential Order issuing the U.A.R. Labour Code (*Ibid.*, No. 71 *bis* B, p.1 dated 7 April 1959) – *vide* Cairo Court of Appeal in an appeal decided on 18 January 1948 (in Badawi, K.M., p. 293).

In France it was held in *Mercier v. Chemins de fer de l'Est*, on 26 March 1935, (Gaz. du Palais, 1935, 1, 933), that the family allowances, prescribed by the Act of 11 March 1932 (section 74 *et seq.* of Book I of the French Labour Code), were as much wages, as those which were voluntarily granted before the said Act; cf. this with the decision in *Vernet v. Compagnie d'assurances La Préservatrice*, on 25 December 1935, (Gaz. du Palais, 1935 20, 12), in which it was held that the said family allowances were not wages for work done, but statutory payments for the benefit of the worker's family – *vide* these two decisions in I.S.D.L., Vol. 11, 1937, pp. 125 and 123, respectively.

shall be considered as a part of the wages if any sums paid as tips by the customers to the employees of one and the same commercial establishment are collected in a common fund to be subsequently divided among the said employees by the employer or under his supervision." *Zaki*, p. 102, correctly criticises the imposition of the custom and assessment conditions, for the tips to be wages. But he wrongly submits that the coupling of the two conditions produces an anomalous or contradictory provision. The flaw in his argument can be detected from his presumption that a sure assessment can only be made, by the specification of a percentage in the contract of employment. It is clear here that he is mixing up the provisions of the first paragraph of section 684, with the provisions of the last paragraph in section 3 of the U.A.R. Labour Code. On the other hand, *Zaki*, p. 103, submits that the provisions in the second paragraph of section 684, supersede the provisions of the first paragraph thereof, and their counterpart in section 3 of the Labour Code, with the result that the proof of a custom as is required therein, can be dispensed with, when there is the common fund. It is submitted that he is wrong, because the said common fund provision is no more than a substitute for the assessment by fixed rules; otherwise the section would, as it were, be pulling the strings and loosening them at the same time.[35] On the other hand, tips are wages, if in hotels, bars, cafés and restaurants and the like, their amounts are ascertainable by rules fixed in the contract of employment.[36] This brings out of the definition

[35] *Vide* Murad, pp. 306–7, where he confirms that the common fund provision is no more than a substitute for the assessment by fixed rules.

[36] This ascertainment provision is a novelty, as it does not exist in the last paragraph of section 684 of the Civil Code, from which the relevant provisions of section 3 of the Labour Code were copied.

Whether these tips are wages for, and can be distributed among the workers, in the said classes of business (whether they are in direct contact with the customers or not), is not finally settled. Section 951 of the Draft Civil Code (which was copied from section 42 of Book I of the French Labour Code: *vide* Habeeb, p. 103); expressly excluded the workers, who were not in direct contact with the customers. The non-adoption of the said section 951 led some Courts and writers to take the same, as a tacit approval of the contrary view: *vide* Cairo Court of Arbitration in dispute No. 291 of 1954 – in Habeeb, p. 102; and Cairo Labour Court in case No. 1572 of 1960 – in El-Hawwari, p. 102; *vide* also Badawi, K.M., p. 176; and Butros and Rajab, p.18. Others stick to the view in the said unadopted section 951, because they maintain without further detail, that the provisions of the general law demand this view: *vide* Cairo Court of Arbitration in dispute No. 57 of 1953 – in Habeeb, p. 102; and the same Court in dispute No. 206 of 1954 – in Butros and Rajab, p. 18; *vide* also Rashed and Hashem, pp. 29–30; Zaki, p. 104; and Habeeb, p. 102. It is submitted that the answer to the question, depends in the first instance, on any agreement on the matter, between the employer and the workers (*vide* Cairo Court of Appeal in the appeal on dispute No. 50 of 1959 – in El-Hawwari, p. 103); and failing such agreement, the circumstances of every case should be examined, while keeping in mind that those in contact with customers, depend in earning the tips, not only on their skill, but also on the cooperation of the other workers.

of wages, any casual tips paid by the customers.[37] It is not settled whether the employer can agree with his workers (a) to take the wage-tips and pay them fixed wages in lieu, or (b) to deduct for himself a part of these tips, in compensation for the breakage of china. It is submitted that an agreement as mentioned in (a) is legal, because section 3 of the Labour Code prescribes the conditions, under which tips can be considered wages, but does not prohibit their substitution by fixed wages.[38] However, it is submitted that an agreement as mentioned in (b), is illegal, because thereby the employer would be entitled to make an unwarranted deduction from wages, on the one hand, and he would exercise such right, even without the occurrence of the breakage of china, which gives rise to the tortious liability of the worker, and to his resultant liability to compensate the employer, on the other hand.[39]

In Sudan there is no mention of tips, in the definition of wages. If tips are paid irregularly, it is submitted that they would fall under the exclusion of ex-gratia payments. If, on the other hand, they are habitually paid in a certain class of business, so as to constitute a custom, it is submitted that a term would be implied in the contract of employment, so as to consider them wages.[40] In this respect, there is some similarity to the law in the U.A.R., without the string of ascertainment attached thereto by the latter law.

Overtime payments are expressly stated to be wages, in the Sudan definition. In the U.A.R. it is submitted that the definition of wages

[37] *Vide* Cairo Court of Appeal in appeal No. 329 of 1960, (in El-Hawwari, p. 102); *vide* also Habeeb, p. 106; and Naguib and Bakr, p. 17.

[38] *Vide* Murad, p. 308; Badawi, K.M., p. 175; and El-Areef, p. 280, all of whom adopt the same view, without reasoning; and Butros and Rajab, p. 19, who likewise adopt the same view, because the said agreement "is no more than an agreement to determine the amount of wages." On the other hand, Zaki, p. 105, submits (and Habeeb, pp. 103–5, agrees with him), that the said agreement is illegal, because it violates the provisions of section 6 of the U.A.R. Labour Code (quoted in Section V of Chapter II, *supra*). It is submitted that the only case, where Zaki's submission would not be wrong, is when the said agreement is made after the assessment of the tips, and the agreement in effect substitutes a fixed wage less than the said assessed tips.

[39] For the said tortious liability, *vide* Section I, C, iii, of Chapter III, *supra*.

Zaki, p. 105; and Habeeb, pp. 103–5, give the same answer, but they depend on the said section 6, as aforementioned; El-Areef, p. 281, gives the same answer impliedly, because the "legislator did not interfere," so as to prohibit such agreement, as did the French legislator in section 42 of Book I of the French Labour Code. However, Butros and Rajab, p. 20, submit to the contrary, and they quote the Cairo Court of Arbitration in dispute No. 291 of 1954, in support. It is submitted that they and the said decision are wrong.

[40] Reference to the English Common Law, assists in reaching the same conclusion: *vide Manubesn v. Leon* (1919), 1 K.B. 208, as an authority for such said implication, in the hair-dressing business; *vide* also Barwell and Kar, p. 239.

also covers overtime payments, because they are payments for work done.[41]

Wage increases are voluntary on the employer in the U.A.R.[42] But when they are granted, they add to the contractual wages.[43] In Sudan it is submitted that the same will apply, by virtue of the general principles of the law of contract.

Expenses incidental to the performance of the work, are expressly excepted from the definition of wages in Sudan. In the U.A.R. it is submitted that these expenses would be excepted from the definition, because they are not for work done.[44]

Whether the termination gratuity in the U.A.R. is a wage for all purposes, is not finally settled. However, the weight of authority heavily leans in favour of not considering it a wage.[45] It is submitted that for

[41] El-Areef, p. 260; and Zaki, p. 92, both hold the same view; Murad, p. 419, agrees with the proviso that the overtime payments should be regular. However, Rashed and Hashem, pp. 172–3, maintain otherwise, because these payments "do not constitute an element in the contract... and the worker's dependence thereon is not guaranteed, for (overtime work) depends on the will of the employer." It is submitted that they are wrong, because the constituion by the said payments, of an element in the contract, depends on whether they are wages or not, and because the said guarantee for the worker is irrelevant, not only in as far as these payments are concerned, but also in respect of the ordinary wages.

[42] There is no obligation on the employer to provide a wage-cadre, for the classification and promotion of his workers: *vide* the two cases quoted in footnote 114 to Chapter III, *supra*; and *vide* El-Mansourah Court of Appeal in the appeal on dispute No. 17 of 1954 (in El-Fakahani, Book I, Vol. I, p. 521); Cairo Court of Arbitration in dispute No. 63 of 1953, (*Ibid.*, p. 528); and the same Court in dispute No. 139 of 1953 (El-Areef, p. 284); Alexandria Court of Arbitration in dispute No. 12 of 1956 (in Habeeb, p. 121); and Cairo Court of Appeal in the appeals on disputes Nos. 99 of 1957 and 23 of 1959 (both in El-Hawwari, p. 91); *vide* also El-Areef, p. 283; Murad, pp. 308–9; and Naguib and Bakr, p. 12.

[43] *Vide* Alexandria Court of Arbitration in dispute No. 57 of 1953 (in Habeeb, p. 120); Cairo Court of Arbitration in dispute No. 54 of 1953 (in El-Fakahani, Book I, Vol. I, p. 522); Cairo Court of Cassation in cases Nos. 631 of 1955, and 479 of 1956 (*Ibid.*, pp. 524 and 526, respectively); *vide* also Zaki, p. 96; and Habeeb, p. 119.

[44] *Vide* Cairo Court of Appeal in the appeal on dispute No. 14 of 1960; and the Alexandria Court of Appeal in appeal No. 322 of 1959 (both in El-Hawwari, p. 105); and *vide* El-Areef, pp. 260 and 261; Murad, p. 296; El-Fakahani, 1959 Supplement, p. 54; Butros and Rajab, p. 441; Zaki, p. 92; Habeeb, pp. 38–9 and 56–8; and Faheem, pp. 42 and 63; *vide* also the two French decisions of the Cour de Cass., Ch. Civ., Ch. des Requêtes (1930), Gaz. du Palais, 1930, 2, 61, (both in I.S.D.L., Vol. 7, 1933, p. 137, and Vol. 6, 1931, p. 89, respectively).

[45] *Vide* Cairo Court of Appeal in appeal No. 61 of 1955 (in Habeeb, p. 536); Cairo Court of Cassation in case No. 734 of 1958, (in El-Hawwari, p. 353); and the same Court in case No. 1878 of 1958, (*Ibid.*, p. 99); Cairo Labour Court in case No. 6242 of 1959, (*Ibid.*, p. 351); Cairo Court of Appeal in appeals Nos. 223 and 283 of 1960, (*Ibid.*, pp. 350 and 352, respectively); *vide* also El-Areef, p. 409; Badawi, K.M., p. 339 (though impliedly); Sabbour, p. 512; Badawi, Z., Vol. I, p. 89; and Habeeb, p. 40. However, Rashed and Hashem, p. 293, maintain that the gratuity is a wage, "whose payment is postponed" to the time of the termination of the contract; *vide* Murad, p. 248; and Zaki, p. 313, who are of the same opinion. It is submitted that they and those who hold their view, are wrong, mainly because the termination gratuity can be denied in certain circumstances, by virtue of section 76 of the U.A.R. Labour Code (*vide* Chapter VI, *infra*), whereas wages cannot be denied: *vide*, in this respect, the Cairo Labour Court decision (*supra*).

the purposes of calculating the worker's benefits, the termination gratuity is not a wage.[46] In Sudan it has been judicially held that a claim for the termination gratuity, was a claim for wages.[47] However, it is submitted that this does not mean that it is a wage for all purposes, and that it cannot be entered in the calculation of the worker's benefits, like the sickness or annual leave.[48]

Whether the payments for the sickness and annual leaves are wages or not, is not settled in the U.A.R.[49] It is submitted that, though the legislator had to interfere so as to prescribe the said leaves by way of an exception to the rule that remuneration is the return for work,[50] the payments for these leaves were by the said interference itself made wages.[50] If this is not the case, the legislator would have applied the

[46] *Vide* Chapter VII, *infra*, for the termination gratuity and for section 82 of the Labour Code, which by providing for special rules for the distribution of the gratuity contrary to the ordinary (Moslem *Shari'a*) rules of succession (applicable to the distribution of wages), is yet another proof that the termination gratuity is not wages.

[47] *Vide Yousif Abdel Razig v. Heirs of John Pothitos* (1960), AC-Revision-394-1960, (in the S.L.J.R., 1960, p. 274). This decision held that a claim for the termination gratuity was a claim for wages, so the action thereon was statute-barred after one year, by virtue of the Prescription and Limitation Ordinance of 1928 (*The Sudan Laws*, Vol. 10, Title XXVI, Sub-Title 4), on the ground that the gratuity was not excluded from the definition of wages, in section 2 of the Sudan Ordinance. The decision also depended on Halsbury, Vol. 22, paragraph 226, to the effect that "the opportunity of earning a gratuity at the end of the period of service may be good as part of the consideration of the contract" – *vide* also in this respect, Smith, p. 135, where he quotes *Lake v. Campbell*, 5 L.T. (N.S.) 582, as authority to the effect, that "no action will lie for a gratuity promised at the end of the year, unless it were promised as part of the wages." On these authorities, it is submitted that the Sudan decision is wrong, and in any case should be limited to the barring of actions on the gratuity.

In the U.A.R. section 698 of the Civil Code better provides that "actions arising from the contract of employment shall be barred by limitation at the end of one year after the termination of the contract," without saying that the termination gratuity is a wage. Section 52 of the U.A.R. Labour Code, re attachment of wages, (*vide* Section III of this Chapter, *infra*), applies its provisions to the termination gratuity, only by special mention. It is clear that the legislator would not have done so, if he intended the gratuity to be a wage.

[48] This is mainly because of the employer's right to deny the gratuity to the worker, by virtue of section 10(2) of the Sudan Ordinance (*vide* Section II, A, of Chapter VI, *infra*), whereas wages cannot be denied (*vide*, Batt p. 199).

[49] Habeeb, pp. 49–50, maintains that the payment in lieu of the leave, is not a wage; and he quotes in support, Alexandria Court of Appeal in appeal No. 369 of 1955; and Cairo Court of Appeal in appeal No. 1244 of 1955. El-Areef, p. 260, takes the opposite view, "because wages have a general nature, so that they may be spread not only over the working days, but also over the rest-days which are by virtue of the contract or the provisions of the law considered as (contracted) days." Badawi, K.M., p. 205–6; and El-Fakahani, Book I, Vol. II, p. 191, also take the said opposite view, and so they, in pp. 208 and 193, respectively, advocate the right of the heirs of a deceased worker, in his annual leave payment, after this death – *vide*, however, Cairo Labour Court, in the two dissenting decisions No. 5755 of 1959 (in El-Hawwari, p. 125), and No. 5597 of 1954 (in El-Fakahani, Book I, Vol. II, pp. 215–6).

[50] *Vide* footnote 38 to Chapter I and the relevant text, *supra*. *Vide* section 60 of the Labour Code (in Section I of Chapter V, *infra*), which entitles the employer to stop or

wage-attachment provisions of section 52 of the Labour Code to the said leave payments, by special mention, as he did in the case of the termination gratuity.[51] In Sudan it is submitted that, through reference to the English Common Law, the said leave payments would also be held to be wages.[52]

Payment in lieu of notice of the termination of the contract of employment, is not a wage in the U.A.R., as can be understood from section 72 of the Labour Code, which by allowing the said payment in lieu, does away with the requirement that the worker should be available for work during the notice period.[53] The above-mentioned section 52 of the Labour Code, which also applies its provisions to the said payment in lieu only by special mention, is yet another indication that it is not a wage. In Sudan it is submitted that such payment in lieu would easily be held to be a wage, in so far as the barring of an action thereon is concerned.[54] However, reference to the English Common Law reveals that, "in the absence of an obligation to provide work he commits no breach of contract by paying wages in lieu of notice."[55] This leads to the conclusion in Sudan that such payment in lieu is not a wage, as is the verdict of the law in the U.A.R.

Payments given to the worker in the U.A.R., for any inventions he

otherwise recover the worker's wages, if the latter works for another during his annual leave. *Vide* also section 61 of the Code, which reserves for the worker his right in the final leave, irrespective of the manner of termination of the contract, contrary to the entitlement to the termination gratuity. These two sections are indications that the payment for the annual leave, is a wage. *Vide* Rashed and Hashem, pp. 72–3; and Badawi, K.M., p. 206.

[51] *Vide* footnote 46, *supra*.

[52] As long as the contract is not suspended or terminated, because of the sickness, "the right to wages... will continue until express termination": Cooper, pp. 97–8. *Vide* also Barwell and Kar, pp. 252–3.

Further support for the submission, may be drawn from section 14(2) of the Sudan Ordinance (as amended in 1963), which provides that, "when wages are payable at a daily, weekly, fortnightly or monthly rate the employed person shall, in the absence of any agreement to the contrary, be deemed to have contracted to work for his employer for six days out of every seven during the period of his angegement and shall be entitled to receive full wages." This provision, which considers the payment for the weekly rest-day to be wages, is by analogy, applicable to the leaves under discussion, which are also statutory rest – periods. *Vide* also section 20 of the Sudan Ordinance, in Section III of this Chapter, *infra*.

[53] This is also emphasised by the provisions of section 695 of the Civil Code (*vide* this section and the said section 72, in Section II,A,2, of Chapter VI, *infra*); *vide* also Cairo Court of Appeal in appeal No. 61 of 1955 (in Habeeb, p. 536); and *vide* El-Areef, p. 343; Badawi, K.M., p. 285; and Habeeb, p. 40; *vide* also the French decision in *Keller-Dorian v. Chrétien* (1937), Gaz. du Palais, 1937, I, p. 408 (in I.S.D.L., Vol. 13, 1939, p. 99).

[54] *Vide* the Sudan decision, in footnote 47, *supra*. The barring by limitation, by virtue of section 698 of the U.A.R. Civil Code (mentioned in the said footnote), also applies to the payment in lieu of the notice.

[55] Diamond, p. 112, who quotes *Konski v. Peet* (1915) 1 Ch. 530, as an authority.

makes whilst in the employment of another, are not wages, whether they are provided for in the contract of employment, or are prescribed by law.[56] In Sudan no such payments are prescribed by law. If, however, they are provided for in the contract, they would not be wages.

Finally, it goes without saying that any compensation paid for the unjustifiable termination of the contract of employment in the U.A.R., or the wrongful termination in the Sudan, is not a wage.[57]

SECTION II: AGREEMENT ON WAGES

The amount of the wages and any alteration thereof are in the U.A.R., left to the agreement of the parties, by virtue of the general law.[58] This rule is the reason why the reduction of wages cannot be used as a disciplinary penalty,[59] and why there is no obligation on the employer to provide in his work rules, for a wage-cadre for the classification and promotion of his workers.[60] If the parties do not agree on the amount of wages, section 682 of the U.A.R. Civil Code[61] comes to their aid, so as to fix the wages, provided that the work is not gratitous, or is not out of the scope of the profession of the person who performs it.[62] If the parties agree on the payable wages, their contracting freedom

[56] *Vide* Section I, H, of Chapter III, *supra*; *vide* also El-Areef, p. 282.

[57] For the U.A.R., *vide* section 75 of the Labour Code, and Cairo Court of Cassation in case No. 931 of 1959 (in El-Hawwari, p. 425); *vide* also El-Areef, pp. 357 and 405; Murad, p. 428 (*vide*, however, p. 445); Habeeb, pp. 40, 534 and 635; Faheem, p. 31; and Rashed and Hashem, p. 228.

For the Sudan, *vide* Smith, pp. 121–122: "In this action... the servant seeks compensation, not for services he has rendered previous to his discharge, but for the injury he has sustained by such discharge in not being allowed to serve and earn the wages agreed upon.'

[58] *Vide* section 147 of the U.A.R. Civil Code, which provides that the contract is the 'law' of the two parties, without whose consent the contract cannot be altered. The agreement on wages may be contained, either in the individual or collective contract of employment, or in the work rules of the establishment. *Vide* Cairo Court of Arbitration in dispute No. 181 of 1954, (in Habeeb, p. 130); *vide* also Zaki, p. 87; Habeeb, pp. 130–1; Butros and Rajab, pp. 100 and 102; Sabbour, p. 171; and *vide* Section V of Chapter II, *supra*.

[59] *Vide* footnote 141 to Chapter III, *supra*, and the relevant text.

[60] *Vide* footnote 114 to Chapter III, *supra*, and the relevant text; *vide* also footnote 41, *supra*.

[61] Section 682 of the U.A.R. Civil Code provides that, "if the individual or collective contract or the work rules do not specify the wages payable by the employer, wages shall be determined on the basis of the estimated wages for the same kind of work if any, otherwise they should be determined in accordance with the custom of the trade and the locality, and in default the Judge shall fix them according to equity." *Vide* Cairo Labour Court in case No. 472 of 1960, (in El-Hawwari, p. 84), which decided that "the non-fixing of the wages in the contract, does not (necessarily) preclude the employment relationship, and the fixing of wages in such a case, will be in accordance with the custom of the trade, or with the Judge's decision on the grounds of equity."

[62] *Vide* section 681 of the U.A.R. Civil Code, quoted in Section I of Chapter I, *supra*; *vide* also Habeeb, p. 139.

in this respect, is limited in two ways, one peculiar to all contracts generally,[63] and the other peculiar to the contracts of employment. The latter is manifested by the statutory imposition of minimum wages,[64] below which the parties cannot agree. If, however, they so agree, the statutory minimum automatically replaces the wage agreed upon;[65] and the criminal court "shall also order the offender to pay the difference in wages."[66] A second manifestation of statutory interference in the contracting freedom of the parties, is clear from section 53 of the U.A.R. Labour Code, which prescribes equality in rights (presumably including wages) between the workers of an employer and those of his sub-contractor.[67] A third manifestation is afforded by the legislation which grants a share of the profits to the workers, like Law No. 26 of 1954.[68] A fourth manifestation is afforded by the overtime pay-

[63] Section 129 of the U.A.R. Civil Code empowers the Judge to reduce the obligations of either party to the contract, or even to hold the contract void, if the other party's obligations are far less, and the said other party has taken advantage of the rashness of the first mentioned party. Section 147 of the Code empowers the Judge to reduce the remuneration, if general unforeseen circumstances cause the debtor (here the employer) to incur a great loss, in carrying out his obligations. Section 566 of the *Majallah* authorizes the reduction of remuneration, if it is very much exaggerated.

[64] *Vide* foornote 34, *supra*, for Order No. 358, and its legislative development. This Order also prescribed minimum wages, for workers in the commercial and industrial establishments; and this was the first statutory prescription of minimum wages in the U.A.R. Its successor, Order No. 99 of 1950, was kept alive, by section 4 of the Presidential Order issuing the Labour Code, "until the decisions of the committees set up under section 156 of this Code become effective"; *vide* sections 156–159 of the Code, for the provisions on these wage-fixing committees, which are also the first provisions of their kind in the U.A.R. For agricultural employees, Order No. 468 of 1944 (*Al-Jaridat-ul-Rasmiyyatu No. 23* of 28 February 1944), was the first enactment, to prescribe minimum wages. This was superseded by Law No. 178 of 1952, which was amended by Law No. 241 of 1953 (*Ibid.*, No.40 *bis* of 14 May 1953). The above-mentioned new provisions of the Labour Code are also applicable to agricultural workers. Presumably, Law 178 of 1952 should still be effective, however, until the decisions of the Labour Code Committees also become effective, though the said section 4 of the Presidential Order issuing the Labour Code, should have said so, as it did in respect of Order 99 of 1950.

Vide and cf. the minimum wage statutory provisions, in sections 35–40 and 106(2) of the Iraqi Labour Code, and sections 44–6, 24, 24, and 132, of the Lebanese, Jordanian, Libyan and Tunisian Labour Codes, respectively; *vide* the *Labour Survey of North Africa*, pp. 188 and 189, for similar provisions in Algeria and Morocco, respectively. Section 28 of the Qatari Labour Code, expressly leaves the matter to the *Emir*. Neither the Kuwaiti Labour Code nor the Saudi Regulations contain any relevant provisions. In Saudi Arabia, however, the writer knows that the Government used to consult with the Arabian American Oil Co., the biggest single employer in the country, so as to fix the minimum wages of the Company's workers.

[65] *Vide* footnote 93 to Chapter II, *supra*, and the relevant text; *vide* also Cairo Court of Appeal in the appeal on dispute No. 22 of 1958 (in El-Hawwari, p. 86); Asyout Court of Arbitration in dispute No. 8 of 1954; and Cairo Court of Arbitration in dispute No. 286 of 1954 (both in Habeeb, p. 132).

[66] Section 228 of the U.A.R. Labour Code.

[67] *Vide* the section quoted in footnote 82 to Chapter II, *supra*.

[68] *Vide* footnote 23, *supra*.

ments, prescribed for work over and above the ordinary contractual work.[69]

In Sudan the parties are also under the general law, free to agree on wages, as they choose;[70] and this rule has the same results which we saw in the U.A.R. Unlike the U.A.R., section 7 of the Sudan Ordinance prescribes that every attested contract should specify the "wages to be paid."[71] This section in addition generally provides that every written contract should "define the rights and obligations of the parties." Thus all written contracts should presumably, specify the payable wages. However, it is submitted that the parties to such contracts can always agree that the payable wages should be as fixed from time to time in a collective agreement or the work rules of the establishment; or they may expressly leave the matter to the prevailing custom. In this respect, there is some similarity with section 682 of the U.A.R. Civil Code. In oral contracts in Sudan, the said similarity is clearer, for the parties thereto do not have to agree on the specific amount of the payable wages. In this case, reference to the English Common Law warrants the application of rules, similar to those deducible from the said section 682 of the U.A.R., provided also that the work is not gratitous.[72] If the parties agree on the payable wages, reference to the English Common Law reveals that the Courts are not prepared to interfere with the wages or to avoid the contract, as by virtue of section 129 of the Civil Code, the U.A.R. Courts are authorised to do.[73] On the other hand, the

[69] *Vide* section 121 of the U.A.R. Labour Code.

[70] *Vide* Section V of Chapter II, *supra*; *vide* also Samuels, p. 35: "The questions how much salary or wages an employer is to pay his employee, and how the salary is to be paid are, in general, matters to be settled by agreement between the parties."

[71] *Vide* the section, quoted in footnote 4 to Chapter II, *supra*.

[72] *Vide* O. Kahn-Freund, in Flanders and Clegg, p. 48; *vide* also Diamond, pp. 81 and 82; Barwell and Kar, pp. 116–7; and Clark, pp. 3 and 47. Note should, however, be taken of the difference between the U.A.R. and the Sudan, concerning the effect of a collective contract and a collective agreement, in these two countries, respectively. The effect of the former on the individual contract of employment is automatic, whereas the effect of the latter is only by the express or implied consent of the parties.

[73] *Vide* Cheshire and Fifoot, p. 69: "The Courts... will not seek to measure the comparative value of the defendant's promise and of the act or promise given by the plaintiff in exchange for it, nor will they denounce an agreement merely because it seems to be unfair... The parties are presumed to be capable of appreciating their own interests and of reaching their own equilibrium." Barwell and Kar, p. 254, add that "it is now well settled in England that Courts of Law will not inquire as to the adequacy of an employed person's remuneration, unless the disparity between remuneration and labour be so great as to fall within the doctrine whereby complete want of mutuality vitiates the contract." It is submitted that this last-mentioned statement of the law is somehow misleading, because if there is a complete want of mutuality, the proper enquiry of the Courts will be into the validity of the contract itself, and not into the adequacy of the consideration completely wanting on the side of the employer. On the other hand, the insanity and not the rashness of the party in question, is what renders the contract void (*vide* Cheshire and Fifoot, p. 354).

freedom of the parties is affected by the statutory minimum wages which can be imposed in Sudan,[74] and below which the parties cannot agree. If, however, they do so, the minimum wages will replace the lower wages agreed upon; and the Court "shall order the employer to pay to the worker the difference" over the last three years.[75] A second manifestation of statutory interference, is the increase of wages, in the circumstances mentioned in section 11 of the Sudan Ordinance.[76] A third manifestation is afforded by the overtime payments, prescribed for extra work, as in the U.A.R.[77]

Comparison of the law in the U.A.R. with that in the Sudan, reveals that the parties have in respect of wages, more contracting freedom in the latter than in the former.

SECTION III: PROTECTION OF WAGES[78]

Both in the U.A.R.[79] and Sudan,[80] wages should be paid to the worker personally. However, payment to another person, properly authorized by the worker to receive the wages, is expressly permitted in Sudan.[80] In the U.A.R., section 49 of the Labour Code prescribes that "the Minister of Labour shall specify the conditions and procedure

[74] *Vide* the Wages Tribunals Ordinance of 15 February 1952 (in the *Laws of the Sudan*, Vol. 8, Title XXII, Sub-Title 7), and the two Orders issued thereunder, on 15 August 1958, one for shop-assistants, and the other for the Arabic clerical workers in commercial houses (*Idem*).

Vide and cf. section 89 of the Bahraini Labour Code, and sections 5, 9, 10 and 11 of Ordinance No. 33 of 1945, in Aden.

[75] Section 11 of the Wages Tribunals Ordinance, *supra*; and *vide* Section V of Chapter II, *supra*; and especially section 35 of the Sudan Ordinance, quoted therein; *vide* also Samuels, p. 38: "Rates fixed by a Wage Regulation Order are the statutory minimum that may be paid. Terms of service contracts providing for the payment of less rates take effect as if they were replaced by the statutory minimum rates."

[76] *Vide* the section, quoted in footnote 71 to Chapter II, *supra*.

[77] *Vide* section 13 of the Sudan Ordinance.

[78] "Measures relating to the protection of wages comprise the legal provisions which exist to ensure the elimination of abuses in connection with the medium and manner of payment of wages and to enable the worker freely to dispose of them": *Labour Survey of North Africa*, p. 190; *vide* also E. Herz in I.L.R., Vol. 32, 1936, p. 68.

For the worker's entitlement to remuneration, *vide* Section I of Chapter I, *supra*, and especially footnote 10 thereto.

[79] This is deducible from the provisions of section 46 of the U.A.R. Labour Code, which deem payment to a worker to be in full discharge of the employer's liability, even when the worker has attained the age of fourteen years only.

[80] Section 17 of the Sudan Ordinance expressly provides that "wages shall be paid to the employed person personally or to any person authorized by him in that behalf in writing"; *vide* also Samuels, pp. 47–8: "There is nothing to prevent an employee asking his employer to pay his wages or part of them to someone else. He may give authority for one particular occasion or for a particular period, or as holding good until he revokes it, provided that the authority is in writing so as to be his written agreement."

which shall be complied with in the proof of the receipt of wages."[81] It is submitted that since Order 141 is limited to the proof of the receipt of wages, it cannot oust the law of agency,[82] so as to preclude the worker from properly authorizing another person to receive his wages. If he so authorizes another, signature by that other as prescribed by the said order, should, it is submitted, be as good as the signature of the worker, when he receives the wages personally. On the other hand, the employer is not either in the U.A.R. or in Sudan, obliged to personally pay the wages to the worker.[83]

Apart from the worker's right to receive his wages personally, his wages are legally protected from abuses by the employer, by third parties and by the worker himself, as follows:

(a) Payment of wages in legal tender

Section 45 of the U.A.R. Labour Code provides that "wages and all other sums due to the worker shall be paid in legal tender."[84] This is correctly interpreted by writers to be subject to the proviso, that it is applicable only when the wages are not originally agreed upon to be in kind, as the remuneration in kind is sanctioned by the law.[85] Payment by cheque with the consent of the worker, is also correctly held by some writers to be no infringement of

[81] The Minister accordingly, issued his Order No. 141 of 1959, which provides that the employer "shall not be discharged of (his liability to pay) the worker's wages, unless the worker signs on the wage-register or the wage-list or on the recepit especially prepared therefor, in the establishments which use machines for the preparation of wages."

Vide footnote 24, *supra,* re employer's accounting obligations to profit-sharing workers.

[82] *Vide* Section I of Chapter I, *supra,* re agency.

[83] *Vide* footnote 35 to Chapter I, *supra,* and the related text; and *vide* Section I,B,*ii*, of Chapter III, *supra,* for the delegation by the employer, of his obligations towards the worker.

[84] *Vide* similar provisions in sections 31, 29(1), 47 of the Iraqi, Qatari and Lebanese Labour Codes, respectively, and section 7 of the Saudi Regulations; *vide* also the *Labour Survey of North Africa,* p. 191, for similar provisions in Tunisia, Algeria and Morocco. The Kuwaiti, Jordanian and Libyan Labour Codes do not contain relevant provisions.

Section 43 of B I of the French Labour Code also prescribes payment of wages in legal tender (*vide* El-Areef, p. 301).

[85] *Vide* Section I of this Chapter, *supra,* for the remuneration in kind; *vide* also Zaki, p. 275; and Habeeb, p. 337. Sabbour, p. 172, submits that when wages are not agreed upon, they should always be paid in legal tender. It is submitted that he is wrong, because custom may in accordance with section 682 (in footnote 61, *supra*), show that the wages are payable in kind, in a certain business (*vide* section 3 of the Labour Code in Section I of this Chapter, *supra*). *Vide* E. Herz in I.L.R., Vol. 32, 1936, p. 74.

the said section.[86] Any payment contrary to the section, is void.[87]

In Sudan section 16 of the Sudan Ordinance provides:

"The wages other than the value of any food, fuel or quarters of an employed person shall be paid in money unless:

(a) there is an agreement to the contrary, which ,subject to the provisions of sections 4 and 5, shall be in writing,[88] or

(b) there is an oral agreement for the use of land for tillage or other similar benefits in lieu of wages to the employed person."[89]

So the payment of wages in kind is expressly sanctioned in this section, whereas in the U.A.R., this cannot be maintained except by reference to other legislation permitting remuneration in kind. On the other hand, the categories of wages which are free from the obligation to pay in money, are in Sudan less than those in the U.A.R., where there is no requirement to make an agreement, as is mentioned in the said section 16 of Sudan. Payment of wages by cheque with the consent of the worker is, it is submitted, a good payment in money, as it is in the U.A.R.[90] Payment in other than the Sudanese money is, it is submitted, an infringement of the said section 16, because the section is enacted for Sudan, and should not be taken to mean any other money. Payment otherwise than in accordance with the said section, is void, as is the case in the U.A.R.[91]

[86] *Vide* Butros and Rajab, p. 123; and Faheem, p. 43. *Vide* section 29(3) of the Qatari Labour Code, which expressly permits the said payment.

Payment in legal tender, other than that of the U.A.R., does not satisfy the section: *Vide* the Explanatory Note to Law 317 of 1952, whose section 5 is the predecessor of the said section 45 of the Labour Code. However, the Note attributes the reason of the enactment of the section, to the loss the worker incurs in changing his wages into the U.A.R. currency, if he is paid in foreign legal tender. It is submitted that the real reasons are the enablement of the worker to easily benefit from his wages, and the preclusion of the employer from paying in kind, after he agrees with the worker to pay him in money.

[87] *Vide* Zaki, p. 275, where he says that "the employer cannot claim reimbursement from the worker... except under the rules of unjust enrichment."

[88] *Vide* these sections in Section II of Chapter II, *supra*.

[89] *Vide* almost identical provisions, in section 26 of the Bahraini Labour Code; and cf. some similar provisions in section 14 of Ordinance 33 of 1945 in Aden, section 6 of the Payment of Wages Act (IV) of 1936 in India, and section 11 of the English Truck Act of 1831 (for the workmen specified in section 19 thereof, only: *vide* Batt, p. 129, who says that "it cannot be too often pointed out that the Truck Acts have only a limited application, in particular, that, where the employee is not a workman..., the parties may make any arrangement as to payment of wages, deductions and the like").

[90] The Payment of Wages Act 1960 in England (8 and 9 Eliz. II Ch. 37), permits such payment by cheque or postal or money order, with a written request from the worker. Section 8 of the Truck Act of 1831, was not as permissive, and its scope in that behalf, was more limited.

[91] Section 4 of the English Truck Act of 1831, entitles the workman to recover any wages, paid otherwise than in the 'coin of the realm.' However, it is submitted that such would not be the case in Sudan, because the Sudan Ordinance in this respect, is not as mandatory as is the said Truck Act, and because section 1 of the latter, does not permit the agreement sanctioned by section 16 of the former.

(b) The worker's freedom of purchase

Section 50 of the U.A.R. Labour Code provides that "the worker shall not be obliged to buy food or goods from particular establishments or from the employer's products."[92]

The reason behind this provision lies in the legislator's fear of any attempt by the employer, to reduce the contractual value of the worker's wages, by obliging him to buy the food or goods at high prices.[93] But the section does not preclude the worker from buying from the employer, or from any particular establishment, if he chooses to do so.[94] On the other hand, the purchase of goods covers the purchase of services, like the entertainment services.[95]

In Sudan there is no similar provision. However, it is submitted that the principles of section 2 of the 1831 English Truck Act,[96] similar to those in section 50 of the U.A.R., would, through the aid of 'justice, equity and good conscience,' be held applicable in Sudan, on the ground of public policy. The English section has behind it the same reason mentioned for the U.A.R.[97] The provision does not prevent the worker from voluntarily buying from the employer or from a particular shop.[98]

[92] *Vide* similar provisions in sections 33(2), 31 and 32 of the Iraqi, Kuwaiti and Qatari Labour Codes, respectively; *vide* the *Labour Survey of North Africa*, p. 191, for similar provisions in Tunisia, Algeria and Morocco. Saudi Arabia, Jordan, Lebanon and Libya do not have relevant provisions.

[93] *Vide* El-Fakahani, 1959 Supplement, pp. 67–8; Zaki, p. 275; Rashed and Hashem, p. 37; and Faheem, p. 46. On the other hand, the provisions in the section, may be taken to indicate the legislator's desire to limit the scope of remuneration in kind.

The Explanatory Note to Law 317 of 1952, whose section 9 is the predecessor of section 50 of the Labour Code, states that the section was enacted, in order that the workers "may have their freedom of choice, and that they would not be overburdened," presumably with debts; Zaki, pp. 274–5, correctly adds that the overburdening of the worker with debts, may oblige him to stay in his employer's service, more than he wants to. Another reason for the provision in the section, lies in the protection of the worker's health, from the injurious goods of the employer, as when they are alcoholic goods: *vide* El-Fakahani, 1959 Supplement, pp. 67–8; and Faheem p. 46. But this reason is not so much related to the protection of wages, as it is related to the protection of the worker's health.

[94] *Vide* El-Areef, p. 384; Badawi, K.M., pp. 95–6; Butros and Rajab, p. 123; Habeeb, p. 338; Faheem, p. 46; and Naguib and Bakr, p. 80.

[95] Butros and Rajab, p. 124; and Faheem, p. 46, are of the same view.

[96] This section deems any contract illegal, if it contains any stipulation, concerning the manner and place of spending the wages: *vide Wilson v. Cookson* (1863), 13 C.B.(N.S.) 496, where it was held that it was an offence under the Act, for the employer to supply goods to the workman from his shop, and to deduct the cost thereof, from the latter's wages; and *Athersmith v. Drury* (1857), 7 W.R. 14, where it was held that it was an offence under the Act, for the employer to give a note on a certain shop, even though he had no interest in the shop.

[97] *Vide* Cooper, p. 112, who says that, "by placing a fictitious value upon the services rendered or the goods supplied an unscrupulous employer had a ready means of reducing his labour costs."

[98] *Vide* Batt, p. 128, who says: "If a workman, having been paid his wages, then spends them, or part of them, in his employer's shop, there is no offence under the Acts."

If he buys on credit, section 18 of the Sudan Ordinance entitles the employer to claim their value, but only before the expiry of the contract.[99] Finally, it is submitted that the purchase of goods also covers the purchase of services in Sudan.

(c) Time, place and periodicity of payment of wages during employment

Section 690 of the U.A.R. Civil Code provides that "the employer shall subject to the provisions of special laws pay the worker his wages at the time and place specified in the contract or as determined by custom."[100]

Section 47 of the Labour Code provides:

"Wages shall be paid on a working day at the place of work[101] provided that:

(a) workers engaged with monthly wages shall be paid at least once per month,

(b) if wages are payable per piece and the work lasts longer than two weeks the worker shall be paid an advance every week, proportionate to the work completed and shall be paid the full balance of his wages within the week following the delivery of the work contracted upon,

(c) wages shall otherwise than in the aforementioned cases be paid to workers at least once per week or if the workers so agree in writing they may be paid once per every fortnight or once per month."[102]

Payment on a working day does not necessarily mean payment during

[99] Section 18 provides that "no claims by an employer against an employed person for or on account of advances made or goods supplied by the employer during the period of the contract of service shall be enforceable in any Court after the expiration of such contract." Section 5 of the English Truck Act 1887, precludes such claim by the employer, whether during or after the expiry of the contract.

[100] *Vide* similar provisions, in section 904 of the Iraqi Civil Code.

[101] *Vide* the Explanatory Note to Law 41 of 1944 (whose section 12(1) is the first predecessor of the said section 47), which states that the provision was enacted, "in order that the workers may not be deprived of their rest-day, if they were obliged to go and get their wages in any other than a working day," and "in order that the employer may not resort to payment in a place where the workers may be tempted to spend a part of their wages unprofitably."

Sections 32, 29(3) and 47, of the Iraqi, Qatari and Lebanese Labour Codes, respectively, and section 7 of the Saudi Regulations, also prescribe the payment of wages on a working day, and at the place of work. Section 465 of the *Majallah* prescribes payment in the place of work.

[102] Cf. the somewhat similar provisions, in sections 32, 29(2) and 47 of the Iraqi, Qatari and Lebanese Labour Codes, respectively, and section 7 of the Saudi Regulations; Sections 25(1) and 25(1) of the Jordanian and Libyan Labour Codes, respectively, only prescribe that wages should be paid, within seven days after which they become due. Section 476 of the *Majallah* leaves the periodicity of the payment of wages to the contracting parties. *Vide* also Article 12 of the I.L.O. *Protection of Wages Convention*, No. 95

the working hours.[103] Payment at other than the working place, is not invalid, though the employer would thereby bring himself within the mischief of the Labour Code.[104] However, it is submitted that payment to a bank, with the consent of the worker, is a valid payment,[105] because this cannot offend the legislator's intention. On the other hand, section 6 of the Labour Code[106] saves the validity of any contract term, which is more favourable to the worker than the minimum terms prescribed by the Code. So any term to pay the wages to the worker, at shorter periods than those prescribed in the said section 47, is presumably valid.[107] However, the provision in section 47(c) is an express exception to this rule.[108]

In Sudan section 15 of the Sudan Ordinance provides that "all wages whether payable at a daily, weekly, fortnightly or monthly rate or payable for piece-work shall, in the absence of any written agreement to the contrary be paid not later than five days after they become due at such intervals, not being longer than one month, as may be agreed between the employer and the employed person."

So contrary to the U.A.R., there is no provision to prescribe payment on a working day[109] and at the place of work.[110] However, it is submitted

of 1949, and paragraph 4 of the *Protection of Wages Recommendation* No. 85 of 1949. For the reason behind the enactment of these provisions, *vide* E. Herz, in I.L.R., Vol. 32, 1936, who says: "While it is important that definite dates should be fixed for the payment of wages, so that the worker shall not suffer from irregular payment, the protection this is intended to afford may become illusory if the dates so fixed are too far apart."

Vide Section 10 of the U.A.R. Labour Code which provides that, "unless otherwise expressly provided a year shall for the purpose of this Code consist of 365 days and a month shall consist of 30 days."

[103] Naguib and Bakr, p. 78, are of the same opinion.

[104] *Vide* section 221 of the Labour Code; and *vide* Sabbour, pp. 172–3, who is of the same opinion. On the other hand, Cairo Court of Appeal in the appeal on dispute No. 67 of 1959 (in El-Hawwari, p. 88), decided that non-payment of wages in the place of the work, is no infringement of section 47 of the Labour Code, if the payment thereof is otherwise prohibited by law. The place in question was the airport, wherein the Exchange Control Regulations preclude the entry of the local currency.

[105] Sabbour, p. 173, is of the same opinion; and so is Habeeb, p. 346.

[106] *Vide* the section, quoted in Section V of Chapter II, *supra*.

[107] *Vide* Cairo Court of Arbitration in dispute No. 231 of 1953 (in El-Fakahani, Book I, Vol. I, p. 360); *vide* also Sabbour, p. 173; and Habeeb, pp. 345–6.

[108] Butros and Rajab, p. 117, explain this provision by the prevalent custom of the worker's payment of his major living expenses, once per month. They correctly add that the monthly payment of wages to a worker engaged on daily pay, if he consents as is prescribed by section 47(c), does not make him a monthly-paid worker; or in other words, it does not entitle him to the greater statutory benefits of the latter.

[109] Section 87(a) of the Bahraini Labour Code expressly provides that payment should be made on a working day, and so do sections 17(3) of Ordinance 33 of 1945, in Aden, and 5(4) of the Payment of Wages Act (IV) of 1936, in India. It is submitted that 'justice, equity and good conscience,' renders such a provision applicable in Sudan, on the ground of public policy.

[110] Section 27(a) of the Bahraini Labour Code provides that payment should be made

that 'justice, equity and good conscience,' will render applicable in Sudan, the relevant Indian Law to the effect that, "unless the contract otherwise provides, payment is to be made at the place where the service is usually rendered."[111] Payment of wages to a bank with the consent of the worker, is valid.[112] On the other hand, the section leaves a contracting freedom to the parties in Sudan, re periodicity of payment of wages, wider in scope, than section 47 of the Labour Code in the U.A.R. The Sudanese provision also permits a five-days respite, whereas the U.A.R. provision permits none. This does not render the provisions of section 35 of the Sudan Ordinance[113] applicable, so as to invalidate any agreement, except when the agreement makes the wages payable at intervals each longer than one month. Contrary to the U.A.R., there is no exception to this rule.

(d) Payment of wages at the termination of the contract

In addition to the general provisions of the U.A.R. Civil Code,[114] section 48 of the Labour Code provides that "when the worker's service is terminated his due wages shall be paid to him immediately unless he himself leaves the service in which case the employer shall pay the due wages within seven days of the date the worker so leaves."[115]

The prescription of the immediate payment in the section, is for the protection of the worker from "delaying wage-payment to him, in order to compel him to return what may have been bailed with him, or in order to gain time for a probable winning of damages from him."[116] On the other hand, the respite of one week, granted to the employer by the section, shows "the legislator's care to protect the employer from surprise... Moreover, the worker who leaves service, is not usually pressed for his wages immediately on the leaving of service,

in a recognized pay centre, in the employment area. Neither Aden nor India has a relevant provision.

[111] Barwell and Kar, pp. 230–1, who quote as authorities, the two Indian cases of *Beg Mohammed V. Kavasji* (1900) 2 Bomb.L.R. 514; and *Seshagiri Row v. Nawab Askur Jung* (1907) 30 Mad. 438.

[112] The personal payment, prescribed by section 17 of the Sudan Ordinance (*vide* the section quoted in footnote 80 to this Chapter, *supra*), does not, it is submitted, preclude such payment to a bank, for such payment can also be personal payment.

[113] *Vide* the section quoted in Section V of Chapter II, *supra*.

[114] *Vide* section 690, quoted in part (C) of the present Section in this Chapter, *supra*.

[115] *Vide* the same provisions, in sections 15(4) of the Libyan Code, and 7 of the Saudi Regulations. Cf. the somewhat similar provisions, in sections 99 and 30, of the Iraqi and Qatari Labour Codes, respectively. Section 25(1) of the Jordanian Labour Code, prescribes payment within one week after the termination of service, in either case. *Vide* Article 12 of the I.L.O. *Protection of Wages Convention*, No. 95 of 1949.

[116] Butros and Rajab, p. 119.

because it is he who has chosen the leaving-time convenient to his circumstances."[117] It is submitted that the week's respite is also due to the employer, even if the worker justifiably terminates the contract by virtue of section 77 of the Labour Code or section 696 of the Civil Code,[118] because at the time of termination, the said justification is not yet ascertained. On the other hand, section 47(b) of the Labour Code,[119] re piece-work, gives one week's respite to the employer, even though it is not the worker who terminates the contract. Finally, the termination of the contract by the worker's death, does not amount to a leaving of the service by the worker, for then the deceased worker's wages will be payable through the Court,[120] and this may take more than one week.

Section 676(2) of the U.A.R. Civil Code provides that, "when the services of the commercial representative or of the traveller[121] terminate even by way of expiry of the contract period, they shall be entitled to receive by way of wages the agreed or customary commission on any orders of which the employer had no notice except after the said representative or traveller had left service provided that the said orders were the direct results of their representations to the customers while they were still in service and provided that they shall not be entitled to claim the said right except during the customary period of time in the trade concerned."[122]

If the representative or traveller lodges the claim for the commission, "within the customary period of time in the trade concerned,"[123] the employer should pay the commission within a reasonable time of lodging the claim. The same applies to a worker's claim for the pro-

[117] Naguib and Bakr, p. 79.

[118] *Vide* the two sections, quoted in Section II,A, of Chapter VI, *infra*.

On the other hand, Butros and Rajab, p. 119, submit that the employer should not benefit from the week's respite, if the worker serves a notice of termination of the contract, in accordance with section 72 of the Labour Code (*vide* Chapter VI, *infra*). It is submitted that they are wrong, because the section does not make any distinction, between the manners of termination. Faheem, p. 45, submits that the employer should pay the wages, even before the expiry of the week's respite, if the usual pay-day in the establishment falls during the said week. It is submitted that he and the other authors he mentions, are wrong, because no such restriction as they try to impose, can be read in the section. The futility of the submission is clear, from the probability that the said pay-day may fall, only one or two days after the worker leaves the service.

[119] *Vide* the section, quoted in part C of the present Section in this Chapter, *supra*.

[120] *Vide* Butros and Rajab, p. 119.

[121] *Vide* footnote 202 to Chapter I, *supra*, and the related text.

[122] Cf. section 29 (K & R) of Book I of the French Labour Code (*vide* I.L.R., Vol. 79, 1959, pp. 639–40); and the Belgian Act of 7 August 1922 (*vide* I.L.R., Vol. 32, 1936, p. 226).

[123] This customary period should not, by virtue of the limitation provision in section 698 of the Civil Code, exceed one year from the termination of the contract.

portionate part of the bonus or reward, which would be due to him, if he leaves the service before the bonus or reward is distributed.[124]

In Sudan section 15 of the Sudan Ordinance provides that, "if the employer terminates the contract of service he shall pay to the employed person all wages due to him under such contract within two days of the termination thereof."[125]

Thus in Sudan, whether the worker leaves the service or not, is irrelevant to the length of time within which wages should be paid, on the termination of service. On the other hand, there is no equivalent in Sudan, to section 47(b) of the U.A.R. Labour Code, re piece-work. However, it is submitted that, by analogy, no more than the two days, which are prescribed by the said section 15, should be allowed to the employer, because there is no real justification to differentiate this case from the case where the employer terminates the contract.

There is also no provision in Sudan, equivalent to section 676(2) of the U.A.R. Civil Code. However, some similar rules can be deduced from reference to the English Common Law.[126] On the other hand, the claim to the commission or bonus or reward should also be made within the period of time customary in the trade,[127] and the employer should pay it within a reasonable time.

(e) Deductions from wages

In the U.A.R. the parties have no freedom of contracting on deductions from wages, as this freedom is completely regulated by statute, mainly by the Labour Code, as we shall presently see. In Sudan section 17 of the Sudan Ordinance, after it prescribes the personal payment of wages to the worker, further provides that the payment should be made, "without any deduction whatsoever except such deduction as may be specially authorised by the contract under which the wages are payable or by this Ordinance or as may be otherwise authorized by

[124] *Vide* footnote 30, *supra*, and the related text.

[125] *Vide* almost identical provisions, in section 17(2) of Ordinance 33 of 1945, in Aden; and cf. similar provisions, in section 27(b & c) of the Bahraini Labour Code, and section 5(2) of the Payment of Wages Act (IV) of 1936, in India.

[126] *Vide Sellers v. London Counties Newspapers* (1951) I A.E.R., 544, where the plaintiff-appellant, who was employed as a canvasser for advertisements in the defendant's newspapers, was remunerated partly by commission, which was not payable until after the advertisements obtained by him had actually appeared in the newspapers. It was held that he was entitled to the commission, even though the advertisements had not so appeared, until after he left the service of the defendants.

[127] This is also subject to the one year limitation prescribed by the Prescription and Limitation Ordinance of 1928 (in *The Laws of the Sudan*, Vol. 10, Title XXVI, Sub-Title 4)

law."[128] So the freedom of the parties in Sudan, concerning agreement on deductions, is curtailed only to a very limited extent.

The main deductions from wages can be conveniently discussed, under the following headings:

(i) *Disciplinary deductions*

Section 66 of the U.A.R. Labour Code[129] limits deductions from wages, in satisfaction of disciplinary fines, to five days' wages in any one month. This limitation should be read, together with the proviso that the worker should have worked one full month. In other words, the five days should be taken to mean one sixth of the days actually worked in any one month or in any one wage-period; otherwise, the protection intended by the legislator may be lost. In Sudan the deduction and the amount of the deduction for fines, depend on the terms of the contract between the worker and the employer, as can be deduced from the above-quoted provisions of section 17 of the Sudan Ordinance. However, the said amount should be fair and reasonable.[130]

(ii) *Compensatory deductions*

Section 54 of the U.A.R. Labour Code, which entitles the employer to compensation from the worker, for the loss resulting to "the equipment, machinery or products belonging to or in the custody of the employer,"[131] further provides that "the employer shall be entitled to start deducting the said compensation from the worker's wages provided that no such deduction shall exceed five days' wages in any one month."[132] It is to be noted that the entitlement of the employer to deduct as authorized in the section, is limited to the cases where the worker does not cause the said loss on purpose, for otherwise the worker

[128] *Vide* identical provisions, in section 28 of the Bahraini Labour Code. In Aden, section 18 of Ordinance 33 of 1945, authorizes the employer to make certain deductions, without authorization in the contract. Section 7 of the Payment of Wages Act (IV) of 1936, in India, forbids any deduction from wages, except the deductions authorized by the Act.

[129] *Vide* the section quoted in Section I,E, of Chapter III, *supra*, and footnote 130 thereto; *vide* also section 70 of the Labour Code, quoted in the said Section.

[130] This submission is based on section 1 of the English Truck Act of 1896. Section 19(1,d) of Ordinance 33 of 1945, in Aden, expressly provides to the same effect.

[131] *Vide* the section, partly quoted in Section I,C,iii of Chapter III, *supra*

[132] The same submission, re one sixth of the worker's wages, for the purposes of section 66, *supra*, should likewise be applicable for the purposes of section 54; *vide* Badawi, K.M., p. 181; Butros and Rajab, p. 128; Habeeb, p. 343; Naguib and Bakr, p. 86; and Sabbour, p. 184. *Vide* also footnote 142 to Chapter III, *supra*, and the related text, for the express prohibition of deducting by virtue of section 54, when any disciplinary penalty is imposed.

thereby commits a criminal offence;[133] and the employer cannot then start deducting the compensation, but will have to claim it under the general law.[134] On the other hand, the worker cannot authorize the employer to deduct more than one sixth of the wages in any one wage-period, because this will violate the provisions of section 6 of the Labour Code.[135] However, there is nothing to preclude the worker from repaying the said compensation with more than one sixth of his wages, after he receives his wages.[136]

In Sudan[137] the said compensatory deduction and the amount thereof, depend on the terms of the contract between the worker and the employer.[138] This amount should, however, be fair and reasonable.[139]

(iii) *Deductions in satisfaction of loans*

Section 51 of the U.A.R. Labour Code provides that "the employer shall not deduct more than ten percent of the worker's wages in satisfaction of any loans which he may have made to him nor shall he charge any interest thereon."[140] The wages mentioned in the section, should be the actual wages earned by the worker, and not the nominal wages,[141] for otherwise the legislator's protective goal will not be fully achieved. On the other hand, any agreement authorising the deduction of more than ten per cent of the wages, is void, by virtue of section 6 of the

[133] *Vide* section 361 of the U.A.R. Penal Law; *vide* also Badawi, K.M., p. 179; Habeeb, p. 342; and Naguib and Bakr, p. 86.

[134] Sabbour, p. 184, is of the same opinion.

[135] *Vide* the section quoted in Section V of Chapter II, *supra.*

[136] *Vide* Badawi, K.M., p. 181; Habeeb, p. 342; and Naguib and Bakr, p. 86, who are of the same opinion.

[137] *Vide* footnotes 81 and 82 to Chapter III, *supra,* and the related text, for the worker's tortious liability, similar to that in the U.A.R., under section 54 of the Labour Code.

[138] *Vide* section 17 of the Sudan Ordinance, quoted in the present Section of this Chapter, *supra.*

[139] This submission is based on section 2 of the English Truck Act of 1896.

[140] This provision was taken from section 51 of Book I of the French Labour Code (*vide* Zaki, p. 278).

Vide similar provisions, in sections 32 and 25(2, b) of the Kuwaiti and Libyan Labour Codes, respectively, and in Order No. 21 of 1959, which was issued by virtue of section 129(10) of the Iraqi Labour Code. Section 33(c) of the Qatari Labour Code prohibits interest on loans, but allows deduction up to thirty five per cent of the wages. Section 9 of the Saudi Regulations limits deduction to ten per cent, but does not mention anything about interest, presumably because the Moslem *Shari'a* Law applied in Saudi Arabia, prohibits interest. Section 25(3,a) of the Jordanian Labour Code authorises the deduction of loans, without limitation. Section 144(3) of the Tunisian Labour Code limits the deduction for loans, only to the loans for the purchase by the worker of tools and equipment. Section 145 thereof limits the deduction to ten per cent of the wages, but there is no prohibition of the charging of interest. *Vide* Article 17(2) of the I.L.O. *Social Policy (Non-Metropolitan Territories) Convention* No. 82 of 1947.

[141] Butros and Rajab, pp. 125–6; Habeeb, p. 341; Faheem, p. 46; and Naguib and Bakr, p. 80, are of the same opinion.

U.A.R. Labour Code.[135] But there is no percentage limit on the repayment of loans by the worker, after he had received his wages. Finally, some writers[142] submit that advances on wages, made in anticipation of the regular payment-date thereof, are not loans within the meaning of section 51, and so could be deducted from the next coming payment, even though the amount be in excess of ten per cent of the wages. It is submitted that the correctness of their opinion is not absolute, and the validity of the said deduction should depend on the circumstances of every case, for what is called an advance on wages may sometimes be a camouflaged loan transaction. The charging of interest on the said advances on wages, should also be illegal, by way of analogy with loans. This in itself calls for the careful scrutiny of the circumstances of every case, in order to decide whether a certain transaction is a loan or an advance on wages.

In Sudan there is no provision on loans, equivalent to section 51 of the U.A.R. Labour Code.[143] The deduction from wages for the satisfaction of loans, and the charging and the amount of interest thereon, should therefore depend on the agreement of the parties.[144] On the other hand, section 19 of the Sudan Ordinance provides that "no employer shall make any deduction by way of discount, interest or any similar charge on account of any advance of wages made to any employed person in anticipation of the regular date of payment of such wages."[144]

(iv) *Other deductions*

In the Sudan section 17 of the Sudan Ordinance[145] expressly sanctions the deductions "otherwise authorized by law."[146] In the U.A.R. there is no such express provision. However, it goes without saying that deductions, authorized either by the Labour Code in other than the pro-

[142] Zaki, pp. 278–9; and Habeeb, p. 341.

[143] Cf. section 24 of the English Truck Act of 1831, which permits loans for certain limited purposes.

[144] *Vide* section 18 of the Sudan Ordinance, quoted in footnote 99, *supra*, re the non-enforcibility in Court, of any claim on advances, after the expiration of the contract. *Vide* provisions similar to those in section 19 of the Sudan Ordinance, in section 29 of the Bahraini Labour Code (which, however, expressly authorizes the charging of interest on loans from the monetary scheme mentioned in section 21 thereof); and cf. the provisions in section 18(f & i) of Ordinance 33 of 1945, in Aden, and section 7 of the Payment of Wages Act (IV) of 1936, in India.

[145] *Vide* the section quoted in the present Section of this Chapter, *supra*.

[146] It is interesting to note from the provisions of section 27 of the Sudan Ordinance (quoted in Section II of Chapter VII, *infra*), re approved Provident Funds or similar schemes, that the employer cannot deduct the worker's subscription to such scheme, unless the worker has accepted entry into the scheme, which does not seem to be absolutely obligatory.

visions on the individual contract of employment,[147] or by any other law,[148] are all legally valid deductions.

On the other hand, section 20 of the Sudan Ordinance authorizes deductions for the worker's absence from work, proportional to the length of the absence.[149] It is, however, submitted that this so-called deduction is not a deduction in the real sense of the word, because presumably the employer has not contracted to pay any wages for the days not worked by the worker. The same should also apply in the U.A.R.

(f) *Attachment and assignment of wages*

Section 52 of the U.A.R. Labour Code provides:

"No more than one quarter of the first three Egyptian pounds or the first thirty Syrian pounds of the monthly wages or the first ten Egyptian piastres or the first Syrian pound[150] of the daily wages shall be attached or assigned for the payment of an alimony or the costs of food or clothing supplied to the worker and his dependants and the balance may be assigned or attached up to one quarter for the satisfaction of any other debt provided that the alimony debts shall be satisfied before the costs of the food and clothing.

"These provisions shall also apply to all the sums due to the worker by virtue of sections 72, 73, 78, 79, 80 and 81 and in the event of any deduction from the worker's wages by virtue of this Chapter[151] the part liable to assignment or attachment shall be calculated in proportion to the balance of the wages remaining after deductions."[152]

[147] *Vide* section 172, which authorizes the employer to deduct the worker's subscription to a trade union, at the written request of the trade union, without further authorization from the worker. *Vide* section 108, which prohibits any deduction for the worker's protection from the dangers at work.

[148] *Vide* section 56 of Law No. 92 of 1959, re Social Security, which authorizes the deduction of five per cent of the worker's wages, as a subscription for pension; and vide sections 61 and 63 of Law No. 14 of 1939, re Income Tax, which authorize the deduction of the worker's tax.

[149] Sections 30 of the Bahraini Labour Code, and 18(2,b) of Ordinance 33 of 1945, in Aden, provide to the same effect; and so does section 25(2,d) of the Libyan Labour Code.

[150] One Egyptian pound is supposed to be equal to ten Syrian pounds, and each of these pounds is divided into a hundred piastres. One Egyptian pound is supposed to be equal to one sterling pound or ten Dutch guilders.

[151] That is Chapter II of Book II of the Labour Code, on the Individual Contract of Employment. The sum referred to in section 72, is the payment in lieu of the notice of termination of the contract of employment, by either party (*vide* Chapter VI, Section II, A,2, *infra*); and the sums referred to in the other mentioned sections, are all one, viz. the termination gratuity, payable on the termination of the contract (*vide* Chapter VII, *infra*).

[152] *Vide* the Explanatory Note to Law 317 of 1952, whose section 11 is the predecessor of section 52 of the Labour Code, which says that the section was enacted, in order that

Whether the alimony mentioned in the section, means the alimony granted by order of the Court to a spouse or relative, or any alimony voluntarily incurred on these persons, is not settled. It is submitted that the former is the correct opinion, because the latter is wider in its effect on the worker's wages, and a protective provision like that in section 52, should be interpreted narrowly.[153] On the other hand, the food and clothing mentioned in the section, cannot be qualified by any condition of essentiality to the worker.[154] Finally the deductions mentioned in the section, are limited to the deductions by virtue of sections 51, 54 and 66 of the Labour Code.[155]

In Sudan there is no provision equivalent to section 52 of the U.A.R. Labour Code.[156] However, section 201(1, f) of the 1929 Civil Justice Ordinance,[157] precludes altogether the attachment of "the wages of labourers and domestic servants whether payable in money or in kind." The word *labourer* is not defined in the said Ordinance, nor in any earlier or subsequent enactment. This word has, however, been limited in England to those who perform manual work, thus making the term *labourer* a synonym for the term *workman*.[158] The conclusion which can be drawn therefrom, is that not every employed person as defined in

"the means of living will be secured (for the worker), and the work will not be disturbed."

Vide and cf. the provisions, in sections 33, 33(b), 25(4), 25(2,c) and 146 & 147, of the Kuwaiti, Qatari, Jordanian Libyan and Tunisian Labour Code, respectively; *vide* also sections 61 and 62 of Book I of the French Labour Code (*vide* I.S.D.L., Vol. 1, 1925, p. 114).

[153] Habeeb, p. 339; Faheem, p. 49; and Naguib and Bakr, p. 81, are of the same opinion, though without reasoning; Butros and Rajab, p. 131, maintain the contrary opinion, also without reasoning.

[154] Section 15 of Law 41 of 1944, the first predecessor of section 52 of the Labour Code, contained such qualification. Section 11 of Law 317 of 1952, its second predecessor, dropped the qualification. Butros and Rajab, p. 132, still advocate the qualification, and illogically submit that the legislator did not mean to forego the protection behind the qualification, even though he dropped it.

[155] This means the exclusion of the Loan deductions, and the Compensatory and Disciplinary deductions, respectively, discussed in (iii) and (i) of Section III, E, of this Chapter, and the exclusion of the other deductions mentioned in (iv), therein.

[156] Nor is there any in Bahrain or Aden.

[157] *The Laws of the Sudan*, Vol. 10, Title XXVI, Sub-Title 1, Cf. this Sudanese provision, with section 1 of the English Wages Attachment Abolition Act of 1870 (35 and 34 Vict. 30), which provides that, "after the passing of this Act, no order for the attachment of the wages of any servant, labourer or workman shall be made by the judge of any Court of Record or inferior Court."

[158] *Vide* for instance, section 10 of the English Employers and Workmen Act of 1875 (38 & 39 Vict. c. 90), which starts the definition of a *workman*, with the words: "any person who, being a labourer, ... engaged in manual Labour." The express exclusion of a domestic servant from this definition, explains the express inclusion of domestic servants, in the said section 201(1,f) of the Sudan Ordinance, for the word *labourer* did not satisfy the Sudanese legislator's intention of bestowing protection also on the domestic servants. Thus the legal connotation of the word *labourer* in Sudan, should be the same as that of the word *workman* in England, defined as aforementioned.

section 2 of the Sudan Ordinance,[159] will be covered by the said section 201 (1, f). On the other hand, reference to the English Common Law reveals that the worker can assign his wages to any creditor,[160] except his employer.[161] However, "though an assignment of salary may be valid, it will not be so when its effect may be to deprive the assignor of his means of support."[162]

(g) Priority of wages

Section 8 of the U.A.R. Labour Code provides that "the sums due to the worker or those entitled after him by virtue of the provisions of this Code shall have priority over the movable and immovable property of the debtor and shall be paid directly after the judicial costs the sums due to the Treasury and the expenses for maintenance and repair."[163] This is wider in scope, than the provisions of section 1141 of the U.A.R. Civil Code.[164] Section 1141 limits the priority of wages to the six months preceding the debtor's (here the employer's) insolvency which should be declared by a judicial order,[165] and equates the wages and the alimony adjudged to the employer's relatives on the one hand, and the costs of food and clothing supplied to the employer and his dependants, on the other hand. As for the priority, it is not limited to the worker, but it extends to the rights of those who become entitled after the death of the worker.[166] On the other hand, the Labour Code is silent, and properly so, about the distribution of the worker's wages among his heirs or next-of-kin, as this distribution belongs to the Moslem *Shari'a* Law.[166]

The Sudan Ordinance does not contain any provision, similar to section 8 of the U.A.R. Labour Code, nor is there in the other enactments any general provision similar to section 1141 of the U.A.R. Civil Code.

[159] *Vide* the section quoted in Section III of Chapter I, *supra*; *vide* therein also, the mention that the definitions in Sudan and in the U.A.R., do not make a distinction between a *workman* and an *employee*.

[160] *Vide Russel v. Austin Fryers* (1909), 25 T.L.R., 414; and *Re Mirams* (1891) I Q.B. 594.

[161] *Vide Penman v. Fife Coal Co.* (1936) A.C. 45; *vide* also Batt, p. 130; and Samuels, p. 48.

[162] *Vide King v. Michael Faraday and Partners*, Ltd. (1939) 2 K.B. 753.

[163] *Vide* and cf. the similar provisions, in sections 34(1), 7 and 48, of the Iraqi, Qatari and Lebanese Labour Codes, respectively.

[164] Contrary to section 8 of the Labour Code, this section gives priority only to wages, and does not mention any other sums to which the worker may be entitled, like the payment in lieu of the notice of termination of the contract, and the termination gratuity.

[165] El-Areef, p. 304, is of the same opinion.

[166] Cf. this with the provisions in section 82 of the Labour Code, re distribution of the termination gratuity, which is not a wage (*vide* Section III of Chapter VII, *infra*).

However, section 221 of the 1925 Companies Ordinance[157] gives in the winding up of a company, second and third priorities to the salaries of employees and to the wages of labourers, respectively, for the services they rendered to the company during the six months preceding the date of the winding up order or the commencement of the winding up, as the case may be. These priorities are, however, limited to the value of fifty Sudanese pounds[168] only. The priorities do not extend to the dependants of the deceased worker, to whom the wages may devolve by virtue of section 33 of the Sudan Ordinance and the schedule attached thereto. Contrary to the U.A.R., the heirs do not, by virtue of the said section 33, seem to be entitled to share in the wages of the deceased worker. This drastic exclusion of the Moslem *Shari'a* Law should have been made by express provision, and should not be left to implication from section 33.[169]

SUMMARY

The definition of wages in the U.A.R. is not complete, without reference to the definition of the worker in the Labour Code. The definition of wages in Sudan is not complete, without reference to the definition of the contract in the Sudan Ordinance. The said references reveal basically similar definitions in both countries. Remuneration in kind is recognized by both laws, though to a wider extent by the former than by the latter. Both laws consider to be wages, the commission of a commercial representative or traveller, the percentages paid to workers in commercial establishments, and the share of profits given to the worker. The bonus and reward are wages under both laws, though if they are payable by virtue of a custom, the rules thereof are somewhat more strict in Sudan than in the U.A.R. The cost of living and the family allowances are wages, under both laws. Tips are wages in both countries, whether they are payable by virtue of the contract, or by virtue of a custom. However, there are some statutory restrictions thereon in the

[167] The *Laws of the Sudan*, Vol 4, Title XII, Sub-Title 5.

[168] One Sudanese pound is equal to about one pound sterling or ten Dutch guilders.

[169] As such exclusion is not juridically justifiable, the writer, while serving as a Legal Counsel to the Sudan Government, recommended in 1960, the amendment of the said section 33, so as to expressly provide for the distribution of wages, in accordance with the *Shari'a* Law. *Vide* Section III of Chapter VII, *infra*, for what is stated about the distribution of the termination gratuity. *Vide* section 36 of the Bahraini Labour Code, which expressly prescribes that the distribution of the wages and all other payments due to the worker, presumably including the termination gratuity, should be in accordance with the *Shari'a* Law. *Vide* also Article 11(2) of the *Contracts of Employment (Indigenous workers) Convention*, No. 64, of 1939.

U.A.R., but none in the Sudan. Overtime payments and wage increases are wages in both countries, but not the expenses incidental to the performance of the work. The termination gratuity is not a wage in either country, at least for the purposes of calculating the worker's benefits. Leave payments are wages in both countries. The payment in lieu of the notice of termination of the contract, is not a wage in either country, nor is the compensation payable for the unjustifiable termination of the contract in the U.A.R., or for the wrongful termination in the Sudan.

In the U.A.R. and Sudan, the parties are left to agree on the wages and the alteration thereof. The parties have in certain cases, to fix the amount of wages in the contract in the latter, whereas they do not have any such obligation in the former. If the parties do not agree on the said amount, similar but not totally similar rules of the law, are applied for the ascertainment thereof. If they agree on the said amount, their freedom to do so is more limited in the U.A.R. than in Sudan.

Legal provisions for the protection of wages, are more abundant in the U.A.R. than in Sudan. Wages should be personally payable to the worker in both bountries, though this is by express provision in Sudan, and by deduction in the U.A.R. Authorizing another to receive the wages is allowed in both countries, though it is expressly sanctioned in Sudan, but not in the U.A.R. Wages should be paid in legal tender, in both countries. The worker is not obliged in either country to buy anything from the employer, or from any particular shop, though this is by express provision in the U.A.R., and is only by reference to the English Common Law in Sudan. In the U.A.R. wages should be paid on a working day and at the place of work; but there is no such obligation in Sudan, though reference to the Indian Law, gives grounds for a submission to the effect that wages should be paid in the place of work. Payment of wages to the bank with the consent of the worker, is a valid payment in both countries. Periodicity of the payment of wages is more regulated by statute in the U.A.R. than in Sudan. The time within which the wages should be paid at the termination of the contract, differs in length in the U.A.R., according to whether the contract is terminated by the employer or the worker, but not in Sudan. In Sudan deductions from wages are left to authorization in the contract, and the parties' contracting freedom in this respect is not curtailed, except to a very limited extent. In the U.A.R. the parties' contracting freedom in this respect, is completely regulated by statute. The U.A.R. law expressly prohibits the charging of interest on loans, and precludes deductions of more than ten percent, for the satisfaction of loans. In the Sudan there is no percentage-limit on the said deductions, though they should be reasonable; but the charging of interest should be as the parties agree. Deductions authorized by any law, other than the labour law, are expressly sanctioned in Sudan, but in the U.A.R. their validity was presumed. Attachment and assignment of the wages is expressly limited in the U.A.R. Labour Code. In the Sudan Ordinance there is no such limitation; but the Civil Justice Ordinance expressly prohibits the attachment of the wages of the labourers and not of the employees. The worker's freedom to assign his wages is much wider in the Sudan than in the U.A.R. Priority of wages is provided for in the U.A.R. Labour Code, but not in the Sudan Ordinance.

CHAPTER V

LEAVES AND HOLIDAYS

SECTION I: ANNUAL LEAVE

Section 58 of the U.A.R. Labour Code provides:

"The employer shall grant to every worker who has spent one complete year[1] in his service an annual leave of fourteen days with full wages.

"The leave shall be increased to twenty one days when the worker shall have spent ten continuous years in the service of the employer."

"The worker shall not renounce his leave."[2]

Section 22(1) of the Sudan Ordinance provides that, "after the completion of two years of continuous service, an employed person shall be entitled to fifteen consecutive days' holiday at full wages in respect of each subsequent year of continuous service."[3]

The worker's right to annual leave in Sudan, does not start to accrue until the beginning of his third year of service. Thenceforward, the completion of one year of continuous service, is only relevant to the entitlement to fifteen consecutive days of leave, and does not preclude the taking of the due proportion of the leave, at any time during the year of accrual. This also means that, on the termination of the contract, the worker will be entitled to his said due proportion of the accrued leave.[4]

[1] Section 10 of the Code provides that "unless otherwise expressly provided a year shall for the purpose of this Code consist of 365 days and a month shall consist of 30 days." This is a new provision in the Labour Code. Section 3 of the Civil Code provides to the same effect.

[2] Cf. sections 13(1), 39, 47, 45(1,a), 39(1), 35(1) and 111 & 113 & 121, of the Iraqi, Kuwaiti, Qatari, Jordanian, Lebanese, Libyan and Tunisian Labour Codes, respectively, and section 47 of the Saudi Regulations; *vide* the *Labour Survey of North Africa*, pp. 235–6 and 238, for Algeria and Morocco, respectively; and *vide* the French Act. No. 56–332 of 1956 (reference thereto is in the I. & L., Vol. 15, 1956, pp. 524–6, in which it is stated that the said Act supplemented the Act of 20 June 1936).

[3] Cf. the provisions in section 6(e) of the Adenese Ordinance. Section 31(a) of the Bahraini Labour Code is more similar to section 85(1) of the U.A.R. Labour Code. In England the worker's entitlement to annual leave is contractiual, unless it is prescribed by a Wages Regulation Order, issued under the Wages Councils Act of 1959 (Cf. section 9 of the Sudanese Wages Tribunals Ordinance, which was modelled on the English Wages Councils Act of 1945); *vide* Samuels, pp. 37–8; Batt, p. 168; and I. & L., Vol. 22, 1959, p. 193.

[4] Section 31(b) of the Bahraini Labour Code expressly provides to this effect, much the same as section 61 of the U.A.R. Labour Code, to be presently quoted.

It is submitted that the rightful or wrongful termination of the contract is irrelevant to the said entitlement to leave.[5]

In the U.A.R. the wording of section 58(1) of the Labour Code, has occasioned a division of opinion, on the question whether the spending of the first complete year of service by the worker, is or is not a precondition to the worker's entitlement to take his first annual leave.[6] It is submitted that the answer to the question is in the affirmative,[7] because otherwise, the word ***annual*** in the section, would have been sufficient, without the need for the words "who has spent one complete year in his service."[8] This submission is further supported by section 61 of the Labour Code, which provides that "the worker shall be entitled to the wages for his due days of leave which he has not taken before he left the service."[9] This provision was enacted to guarantee for the worker, a payment in lieu of the leave, which has already become due under the said section 58. So it does not, as some writers allege,[10] entitle the worker to any leave which section 58(1) denies to him, if he has not already completed his first year of service.[11] Once the entitlement to leave is established, the worker's right in the payment in lieu

[5] The submission is based on the lack of any relevant provision in the Sudan Ordinance, whereas sections 10(2) and 25 of the Ordinance deprive the worker of his notice of termination and of his termination gratuity, respectively (*vide* Chapters VI and VII, for these two sections, respectively). *Vide* Batt, p. 168, for the prevailing view in England, that "where there is a right to a holiday once a year, if the servant is dismissed by notice or otherwise rightfully before the end of the year in which the holiday is earned, he is not entitled to any pay or damages in respect of the loss of the holiday, since his absolute right to the holiday only accrues or matures when that year is completed."

[6] Murad, p. 485; Habeeb, p. 349; Zaki, p. 285 (though not expressly); El-Fakahani, Book I, Vol. II, p. 193; and Faheem, p. 80, give a negative answer. Those who give an affirmative answer, are Badawi, K.M., p. 208 and p. 215, where he quotes as an authority, Cairo Labour Court in Case No. 2585 of 1952; Rashed and Hashem, p. 90; Badawi, Z., Vol. 1, pp. 80 and 82; and Naguib and Bakr, p. 97.

[7] *Vide* in support, Cairo Court of Cassation in case No. 1445 of 1955 (in El-Fakahani, Book I, Vol. II, p. 230); and the same Court in case No. 265 of 1956 (in El-Hawwari, p. 122); Cairo Labour Court in case No. 6252 of 1959 (*Ibid.*, p. 123); and the same Court in case No. 2585 of 1952 (in Badawi, K.M., p. 215); and Cairo Court of Arbitration in dispute No. 143 of 1954 (in Habeeb, p. 349).

[8] The Explanatory Note to Law 317 of 1952, whose section 20 is the predecessor of section 58 of the Labour Code, says that the section was based on the international convention for paid annual leaves. The convention in question is the *Holidays with Pay Convention*, No. 52 of 1936: *vide* Article 2(1) thereof, whose wording is almost identical with the U.A.R. provision, *vide* also para. 1(3) of the *Holidays with Pay Recommendation* No. 47 of 9136.

[9] Cf. the provisions in sections 18, 31, 45(2), 35(3) and 118 and 125, of the Iraqi, Qatari, Jordanian, Libyan and Tunisian Labour Codes, respectively. Section 31(b) of the Bahraini Labour Code contains a similar provision; so the influence of the U.A.R. is apparent. *Vide* also Article 5(c) of the *Holidays with Pay (Agriculture) Convention* No. 101 of 1952.

[10] These are the first four writers, mentioned in footnote 6, *supra*.

[11] On the other hand, there is no division of opinion, on the worker's entitlement to the fourteen days of leave for the first year of service, once it is completed.

thereof, by virtue of section 61, is not affected by the justifiability or otherwise, of the termination of the contract.[12] On the other hand, the entitlement to the said payment in lieu is independent of his entitlement to the payment in lieu of the notice of termination of the contract,[13] because they arise "from two different legal texts having different objects."[14]

The calculation of the leave-year in the U.A.R., commences on the date of service of every worker, and not at the beginning of the calendar year. However, there is nothing to preclude the employer from agreeing with the worker on the adoption of the latter, provided that the employer initially grants to the worker his leave entitlements, for the portion of the year, from his service-date to the beginning of the next calendar year.[15] It is submitted that the same applies in the Sudan. On

[12] *Vide* Cairo Court of Appeal in appeal No. 253 of 1956; and Cairo Court of Cassation in the two cases Nos. 2504 of 1953 and 103 of 1954 (all three in Habeeb, p. 350); *vide* also Murad, p. 485; Zaki, p. 28; Rashed and Hashem, p. 90; and Faheem, p. 81. Cf., however, Article 6 of the I.L.O. Convention No. 52 of 1936, and Article 9 of Convention No. 101 of 1952, both of which disentitle the worker to his final leave, if he is justifiably dismissed by the employer.

The Explanatory Note to Law 317 of 1952, whose section 23 is the predecessor of section 61 of the Labour Code, attributes the said view to "the accrual of the right therein to the worker earlier than the dismissal." It is submitted that the better and clearer justification of the view is that payment for the annual leave is a wage, of which the worker cannot be deprived (*vide* Section I of Chapter IV, *supra*). This also is the ground of entitlement of the heirs of a deceased worker to the payment in lieu of the leave, which was due but he did not take before his death. Those who support the said entitlement of the heirs are Badawi, K.M., p. 206; and Faheem, p. 81. For contrary decisions (on the ground that the death of the worker does not amount to his leaving the employment, as prescribed by section 61, because the leaving of employment presupposes that the worker is alive, so as to be able to leave the employment), *vide* the two last-mentioned cases, in footnote 49 to Chapter IV, *supra*. Those who support this view are El-Fakahani, 1959 Supplement, p. 168 (who seems to have reversed his previous stand on this issue: *vide* his Book I, Vol. II, p. 193); and Rashed and Hashem, p. 90. It is submitted that these writers, together with the said decisions, are wrong, because they adopt a very narrow and too literal an interpretation, which results in an unwarranted prejudice to the worker, and because the payment in lieu of the leave, is a wage, which cannot be denied to those who succeed the worker. On the other hand, the distribution of the payment in lieu among the heirs, should be according to the Moslem *Shari'a* law, because it is a wage (*vide* Section III, G, of Chapter IV, *supra*). So the advocacy by Butros and Rajab, p. 314, of the application of the *Shari'a* Law, only after the exhaustion of the dependants as prescribed by section 82 of the Labour Code (re distribution of the termination gratuity: *vide* Chapter VII, *infra*), is, it is submitted, not correct.

[13] *Vide* Section II, A, 2, of Chapter VI, *infra*.

[14] I. & L., Vol. 4, 1950, p. 296, re the similar position in France. So it is submitted that the contrary U.A.R. decision of the Alexandria Court of Appeal in appeal No. 52 of 1955 (in El-Fakahani, Book I, Vol. II, p. 232), is wrong.

The position should also be the same in the Sudan, because the worker's entitlements to the notice and the holidays, arise from the two independent legal provisions in sections 10 (*vide* Chapter VI, *infra*) and 22 of the Sudan Ordinance.

[15] *Vide* Cairo Court of Appeal in appeal No. 1142 of 1955 (in El-Fakahani, Book I, Vol II, p. 200); and Cairo Labour Court in case No. 5483 of 1959 (in El-Hawwari, p. 124); *vide* also Badawi, K.M., p. 208; El-Fakahani, 1959 Supplement, p. 162; Butros and Rajab, p. 313; Habeeb, p. 349; Naguib and Bakr, p. 94; and Rashed and Hashem, p. 85.

the other hand, the year should be a year of continuous service, as is expressly prescribed in the Sudan provision. In the U.A.R. it had been judicially decided that the year should also be a continuous year of service.[16]

The provisions in the U.A.R. and Sudan, prescribe that the annual leave should be with full wages.[17]

By virtue of section 22(3) of the Sudan Ordinance, the annual leave is inclusive of the public holidays which may fall within the leave-period, but not of the weekly rest-days also falling within the said period.[18] This means an additional number of days of absence on leave with pay. On the other hand, the annual leave should also be exclusive of the sick leave, because each of them is independently prescribed in the Ordinance, and the objects thereof are totally different.[19]

In the U.A.R. there is no express provision, similar to the provision in Sudan. However, it has been judicially held that "the annual leave is exclusive of the other leaves, so that the sick leave and the public holidays are not deducted therefrom."[20] If this is the verdict of the law, it is submitted that the same should also apply to the weekly rest-

[16] *Vide* Cairo Court of Cassation in case No. 1911 of 1953; and El-Geeza Court of Cassation in case No. 322 of 1956 (both in El-Fakahani, Book I, Vol. II, pp. 202 and 201, respectively); cf., however, para. (1)2 of the I.L.O. Recommendation No. 47 of 1936.

[17] *Vide* the definition of wages in Section I of Chapter IV, *supra*; and *vide* Article 3 of Convention No. 52 of 1936; and Article 7 of Convention 101 of 1952. So it is submitted that the High Court of Appeal decision in the U.A.R., in appeal No. 11 of 1959 (in El-Hawwari, p. 124), is wrong, in excluding the cost of living allowance, from the calculation of payment for the leave.

For piece-rate workers, section 9 of the U.A.R. Labour Code provides that "the average daily wages for workers other than those who are paid by the month the week or the day shall be calculated on the basis of the average sums received by the worker for the actual days of work during the preceding year" – cf. the provisions in sections 29, 34, 19(2), 57 and 35(3) of the Kuwaiti, Qatari, Jordanian, Lebanese and Libyan Labour Codes, respectively, and section 13(1) of the Saudi Regulations; and cf. para. 4 of the I.L.O. Recommendation No. 47 of 1936. In Sudan there is no equivalent provision. Reference to the English Common Law, reveals that" there are no legal principles," which can readily be applied, though the "average earnings in the past over a period of six or twelve months," are usually taken as the basis of calculation: *vide* O. Kahn-Freund, in p. 276 of the *British Legal Papers*.

[18] Section 22(3) of the Sudan Ordinance provides that, "if a public holiday or holidays (other than the weekly holiday) falls within the period of the employed person's holidays with pay under this section, the period of such public holiday or holidays shall not be excluded in calculating the period of holidays with pay to which the employed person is entitled under this section"; cf. section 31(f) of the Bahraini Labour Code. *Vide* section 14(2) of the Sudan Ordinance, as amended in 1963, for the weekly rest-day.

[19] The sick leave is prescribed by section 21 of the Ordinance – *vide* the section quoted in Section II of the present Chapter, *infra*.

[20] Cairo Court of Cassation in case No. 1869 of 1954 (in El-Fakahani, Book I, Vol. II, p. 232); this is in line with Article 2(3,a) of the I.L.O. Convention No. 52 of 1936; section 35(1) of the Libyan Labour Code expressly excludes public holidays from the calculation of the annual leave; section 45(1,a) of the Jordanian Labour Code expressly provides to the contrary.

days,[21] because they are independently prescribed by the Labour Code, for different objects.[22] The conclusions reached in the Sudan in this respect, are equally applicable to the U.A.R.

The employer in the U.A.R., can grant to the worker more favourable terms in respect of the annual leave, because this is expressly sanctioned by section 6 of the Labour Code.[23] In Sudan section 23 of the Sudan Ordinance contains a similar sanction.[24]

However, the above-quoted section 58(2) of the U.A.R. Labour Code prescribes a more favourable leave to the worker, after he spends "ten continuous years in the service of the employer."[25] In Sudan there is no such provision, and the matter is left almost entirely to the agreement of the parties.[26]

The renunciation by the worker of his leave, is prohibited in section 58(3) of the U.A.R. Labour Code.[27] Presumably, this means in the first

[21] Those who support the exclusiveness of the annual leave from the sick leave the public holidays and the weekly rest-days, are El-Fakahani, Book I, Vol. II, p. 191 (*vide* also his 1959 Supplement, p. 176); Murad, p. 484; Rashed and Hashem, pp. 87 and 90; and Faheem, pp. 79, 85 and 87. Badawi, Z., Vol. I, p. 80, is against the exclusion of the weekly rest-days; and Naguib and Bakr, p. 99, are against the exclusion of the public holidays. Vide section 116 of the Tunisian Labour Code, which impliedly excludes weekly rest-days; and Article 5(d) of Convention 101 of 1952, which expressly does so.

[22] *Vide* sections 118 and 119 of the Code, for weekly rest-days in the commercial and other establishments, respectively.

[23] *Vide* the section quoted in Section V of Chapter II, *supra*. This presumably also covers the cases of teachers, whose summer leave is usually much longer than the statutory leave, which as a result, they cannot request as additional leave: *vide* the Cairo Labour Court in case No. 4384 of 1959 (in El-Hawwari, p. 125).

[24] Section 23 provides:

"Nothing in sections 21 and 22 shall be construed as preventing an employer from operating a scheme under which persons employed by him receive more favourable conditions than those prescribed by the said sections in respect of absences on account of illness or holidays with pay.

"Provided that where, under the provisions of such a scheme employed persons engaged on the basis of a monthly wage are entitled to more favourable conditions in respect of absences due to illness or holidays with pay than employed persons in the same grade and class engaged on the basis of a daily, weekly or fortnightly wage such employed persons engaged on the basis of a daily, weekly or fortnightly wage shall, after the completion of five years of service, be entitled to conditions in respect of such absences or holidays not less favourable than those to which employed persons in the same grade and class engaged on the basis of a monthly wage are entitled."

The first paragraph of this section is redundant, because section 35 of the Ordinance (*vide* the section quoted in Section V of Chapter II, *supra*), generally sanctions benefits to the worker, more favourable than those prescribed by the Ordinance.

[25] Zaki, p. 283; and Naguib and Bakr, p. 95, both submit that periods of suspension do not interrupt the continuity of the ten years. It is submitted that they are correct, because the legislator's emphasis is on the worker's continuity with the same employer, and not on the effective service. *Vide* Article 2(5) of the I.L.O. Convention No. 52 of 1936; para. 3 of Recommendation 47 of 1936; and Article 5(b) of Convention No. 101 of 1952.

[26] *Vide*, however, the legislator's interference in such an agreement, in favour of the daily, weekly or fortnightly workers, in section 23 of the Sudan Ordinance, quoted in footnote 24, *supra*. *Vide* section 31(a) of the Bahraini Labour Code, which expressly provides for the increase of the leave, after five years of continuous service.

[27] This provision is not necessary, because section 6 of the Code (*vide* footnote 23

instance, the illegality of any express agreement to renounce the leave, without any return. Whether renunciation for a monetary return is legal or not, is not settled.[28] It is submitted that such renunciation is also not legal, because otherwise, the legislator's interference so as to prescribe the leave, by way of exception to the rule that remuneration is the return for work,[29] would ultimately amount to no more than the granting of extra wages to the worker, whereas "the leave is necessary for the recuperation of the worker and for the increase of production."[30] In other words, the leave is a right of a public character, though it does not always remain so, as shall be presently mentioned. Further support for the said submission may be drawn from section 60 of the Labour Code, which provides that "the employer may deprive the worker of his wages for his period of leave or recover any wages he paid therefor if it is proved that the worker has been working for another employer during the said leave-period."[31] If the employer is thus entitled to

supra) serves the purpose. The only other Arab Labour Codes, which contain such express prohibition, are the Lebanese (section 43) and the Tunisian (section 128).

[28] Cairo Labour Court in case No. 5597 of 1954 (in El-Fakahani, Book I, Vol. II, p. 216); Butros and Rajab, p. 312; and Badawi, Z., Vol. 1, p. 81, favour the legality of such renunciation for return, if the leave to be renunciated has already accrued, Murad, p. 484; Rashed and Hashem, p. 84; Habeeb, p. 352–3; and Faheem, p. 80, favour the opposite view, mainly because such renunciation precludes the achievement of the legislator's goal of securing rest for the worker, which is necessary for the public good. *Vide* the *Labour Survey of North Africa*, p. 233.

[29] *Vide* the discussion on remuneration, in Section I of Chapter I, *supra*.

[30] *Vide* the Explanatory Note to section 20 of Law 317 of 1952, which is the predecessor of section 58 of the Labour Code; *vide* also Cairo Court of Cassation in case No. 490 of 1954 (in El-Fakahani, Book I, Vol. II, p. 220). Rashed and Hashem, p. 75, even advocate the view that the worker should be entitled, if the employer refuses to grant him the leave, to absent himself for a period equal to his leave due, after he serves notice of the same upon the employer. In this they emphasize the necessity of taking the leave in kind. But this is not consistent with their view that the leave is also a private right, which can be renounced (*vide* footnote 34, *infra*). Butros and Rajab, p. 315, oppose this view, because "this may justify the employer in dismissing the worker without granting him the termination gratuity," presumably for the unjustifiable absence of the worker. It is submitted that they are legally correct. The resulting harshness to the worker would be a rare occasion, because the employer would, as a result of his said refusal, not only be obliged to pay the worker in lieu of the leave (*vide* footnote 38, *infra*), but would also be subject to the penalty prescribed in section 221 of the Labour Code (*vide*, however, footnote 38 to this Chapter, *infra*, where it is pointed out how Butros and Rajab wrongly adopt this reasoning for a different purpose). *Vide* also Article 4 of Convention 52 of 1936, which expressly provides that "any agreement to relinquish the right to an annual holiday with pay, or to forego such a holiday, shall be void." In Morocco, "a worker may not relinquish his leave, even if he receives compensatory payment, except in special cases, such as for the performance of national defence work or for the provisioning of the country in general, and then only with the permission of the Labour Department": *Labour Survey of North Africa*, p. 238.

[31] *Vide* Article 5 of the I.L.O. Convention No. 52 of 1936. It is submitted that the employer would easily be adjudged a similar power, in Sudan.

It is to be noted that the legislator uses in this section, the word *recover* and not the word *deduct*. So if the worker refuses to pay back the wages, the employer can only recover the wages by a suit in Court; vide Butros and Rajab, p. 311–312, who wrongly submit 'penalize' the worker, when the latter works for another during the leave-period, the employer should not be allowed to have the worker work for him during the said period, even when that is for a monetary return.

In Sudan there are no provisions similar to sections 58(3) of the U.A.R. Labour Code. However, the illegality of the renunciation of the leave without any return, can be deducted from the provisions of sections 23(1) and 35 of the Sudan Ordinance.[32] It is submitted that renunciation for a monetary return is also not legal, for the same reason forwarded for the U.A.R.[33]

It appears that the tacit renunciation of the leave results at the end of each year of entitlement, from the worker's abstention from requesting his leave, and the employer's acquiescence in the same, as the year or the years pass by. Some Court judgments have, however, decided and some writers maintain that the leave continues to retain its public character, even after the expiry of the year of entitlement. So they conclude that the tacit renunciation at the end of the entitlement period, should be as invalid as the express renunciation at the outset or during the currency of that period. They then conclude that the worker's leaves, which he does not request, accumulate from year to year, by the force of the law.[34] Other Courts decided and other writers maintain that the right to the leave becomes a private right, at the end of the year of entitlement, which right the worker is then free to expressly or tacitly renounce, whether for a return or otherwise. Accordingly, the leave does not automatically accumulate.[35] It is submitted that the second is

that the employer can deduct in instalments. On the other hand, as long as the legislator thus provides the employer with a remedy, the latter cannot in this respect, take in addition, any disciplinary measures against the worker.

It is interesting to note that none of the other Arab Labour Codes, contains any provision similar to the U.A.R. provision.

[32] *Vide* footnote 24 to this Chapter, *supra*.

[33] Section 31(c,ii) of the Bahraini Labour Code, however, expressly sanctions the legality of such renunciation.

[34] *Vide* Alexandria Court of Cassation in appeal cases Nos. 534 and 568 of 1953 (in Naguib and Bakr, p. 95); Cairo Labour Court in case No. 5767 of 1959 (in El-Hawwari, p. 131); *vide* Zaki, pp. 285–9; and Faheem, p. 82. Rashed and Hashem, pp. 72–3, believe in the public and private characteristics of the worker's right to the leave all through. So they maintain that the right is not renouncable, in as far as it is of a public character; but side by side with that, it is renouncable in as far as it is a private right. The difficulties of reconciling their position are apparent. El-Fakahani, 1959 Supplement, p. 161, supports the above-mentioned decisions, but not in a sure way. He refers to his Book I, Vol. II, pp. 236–7, where he advocates the necessity of ascertaining, whether the worker did or did not abstain from requesting the leave, for his own convenience. If he did not, "it would be possible to say that the worker has freely renounced his right to the leave, and it would thereafter be unreasonable to surprise the employer, with a request for accumulated leaves for past years." This opinion definitely runs against the said decision.

[35] *Vide* the High Court of Appeal in appeal No. 11 of 1959 (in El-Hawwari, p. 126); Cairo Court of Appeal in appeals Nos. 1103/1031 and 1244 of 1955, and No. 253 of 1956

the correct opinion, because section 59(2) of the U.A.R. Labour Code expressly provides for the carrying over of part of the leave from year to year, but subjects the same to the agreement of both parties.[36] This provision would be violated, if the worker were to be allowed to accumulate his leave through the successive years, merely by making no request for the leave. On the other hand, those who hold the first opinion, maintain that the worker's accumulated leaves can be satisfied by payment in lieu.[37] This is not consistent with their contention that the leave retains its public character all through. If it so retains its character, and if the express renunciation of the leave for a monetary return is not valid, the invalidity should also extend to the tacit renunciation of the leave. Those who hold the second opinion, logically maintain that the right to the payment in lieu can only arise and as a result accumulate, only if the worker requests the leave during the entitlement year, and the employer refuses to grant it to him.[38] An ex-

(all in Habeeb, p. 253), and No. 22 of 1958 (in El-Hawwari, p. 103); Alexandria Court of Appeal in appeal No. 296/101 of 1955 (in Habeeb, p. 354); Cairo Court of Cassation in cases Nos. 415 and 3415 of 1953 (in Badawi, K.M., p. 25, and in Habeeb, p. 353, respectively), in cases Nos. 490 and 2032 of 1954 (in El-Fakahani, Book I, Vol. II, p. 220), in cases Nos. 792 of 1955 (*Ibid.*, p. 219), and 991 of 1956 (*Ibid.*, p. 222); Alexandria Court of Cassation in case No. 2254 of 1954 (in Habeeb, p. 354); Cairo Labour Court in cases Nos. 1962 and 3447 of 1953 and No. 501 of 1954 (in Badawi, K.M., pp. 209–10); ***vide*** also Butros and Rajab, p. 313; Badawi, K.M., pp. 210–5; and Rashed and Hashem, p. 74 (***vide*** the preceding footnote). Habeeb, pp. 353–4, used to support the same view; but ***vide*** the change of his position in p. 601, on account of the new provision in section 58(3) of the Labour Code, without further justification.

[36] Section 59(2) provides that "the employer may on a written request from his worker postpone the granting to him of the part of his leave in excess of the six days to a coming year." ***Vide*** section 59(1), quoted in the latter part of the present Section of this Chapter.

Cf. the provisions in sections 13(2) and 49, of the Iraqi and Qatari Labour Codes, respectively. The former permits the carrying over from year to year, of half the balance of the leave entitlements. The latter permits the accumulations of all the leave entitlements of the expatriate worker only, until he is transported back to his country, as provided in section 23 of the Qatari Labour Code. Section 116 of the Tunisian Labour Code permits accumulation of the leave entitlements for two years only; the Moroccan Law permits such accumulation for three consecutive years (***vide*** the *Labour Survey of North Africa*, p. 239). All the above laws subject the carrying over of the leave to the consent of both parties.

[37] ***Vide*** also Cairo Court of Cassation in case No. 114 of 1954 (in El-Fakahani, Book I, Vol. II, p. 224).

[38] This is based on section 203 of the U.A.R. Civil Code, which provides that "the debtor after being served with notice in accordance with sections 219 and 220 shall carry out his obligation in kind whenever that is possible. However, if the carrying out of the obligation in kind is too heavy on him he may tender a monetary compensation therefor provided that no serious loss thereby results to the creditor"; ***vide*** Alexandria Court of Appeal in appeal No. 18 of 1955 (*Ibid.*, p. 207); Cairo Court of Cassation in cases Nos. 1697 and 3031 of 1953 (*Ibid.*, p. 226); and Nos. 415 and 3447 of the same year (in Badawi, K.M., pp. 215 and 209, respectively); Cairo Labour Court in cases Nos. 215, 328 and 1697 of 1953 (*Ibid.*, p. 215), and Nos. 1933, 3437 and 4052 (in El-Fakahani, Book I, Vol. II, pp. 207, 210 and 225, respectively); Alexandria Labour Court in cases Nos. 553 of 1952 and 354 of 1953 (in Rashed and Hashem, pp. 77 and 75, respectively); ***vide*** also Badawi,

ception to this, however, is clear from the provisions of the previously quoted section 61 of the Labour Code. This section which guarantees the payment in lieu of the leave, to the worker whose services are terminated, was enacted because such worker is not expected to have requested the leave before termination.[39] The proponents of the second opinion do not deny that the employer's refusal brings him within the mischief of the Labour Code.[40] But this does not contradict their opinion.

In Sudan there is no controversy similar to that in the U.A.R. However, if any such controversy should arise, the provisions of section 22(2) of the Sudan Ordinance[41] lead to a conclusion similar to that in the U.A.R., with the assistance there of section 59(2) of the Labour Code.

Neither in the U.A.R. nor in Sudan is there any provision, concerning the period of the year during which the leave should be taken.[42] However, opinion in the U.A.R. leans in favour of giving to the employer, the right to appoint the date of the leave within the year, as the interests of the work require.[43] It is submitted that the exercise by the employer

K. M., pp. 205–6; and El-Fakahani, Book I, Vol. II, pp. 191–2, for the similar position in France. The French Law, as pointed out therein, does not favour the accumulation of the leave in kind. This, it is submitted, is the logical conclusion from the accumulation of the 'private right' to the leave.

Contrary to the reasoning of both opinions, the Cairo District Court (Commercial), in two (unnumbered) cases decided on 19 February 1949 and 3 April 1950 (*vide* Rashed and Hashem, pp. 78 and 77, respectively), held that the worker's sole remedy, when the employer refuses to grant him the leave, consists in his right to terminate the contract, without being deprived of the termination gratuity; Alexandria Court of Cassation followed suit, in case No. 471 of 1949; but reversed its stand in case No. 1302 of 1950 (*Ibid.*, p. 78). The worker's need for work will invariably preclude him from using this remedy; and the result is his deprivation of a remedy. Butros and Rajab, p. 315, advocate the reporting of the employer to the Labour Office, so as to have him prosecuted, as a "practical solution," and thus bring pressure upon him, in order to preclude him from the refusal to give the leave. This of course is no legal reasoning.

[39] *Vide* Cairo Labour Court in case No. 5722 of 1959 (in El-Hawwari, p. 128).

[40] *Vide* the penal provisions, in section 221 of the Labour Code.

[41] Section 22(2) provides that "an employed person may, with the consent of his employer, defer his holidays in any particular year to the next succeeding year, in which case he shall be entitled to thirty consecutive days' holiday at full wages" Cf. section 31(c) of the Bahraini Labour Code, which permits both the accumulation in kind, and in the payments in lieu of the leave. This is the only provision of its kind, in all the Arab Labour Codes. O. Kahn Freund, in p. 273 of *The Britsh Legal Papers*, points out that, "accoring to the English Common Law, and in the absence of a trade usage to the contrary, holidays cannot be deemed to" accumulate. So the parties can without limitation, agree on the accumulation of the leave.

[42] Sections 114 and 115 of the Tunisian Labour Code provide for such a period; *vide Labour Survey of North Africa*, pp. 236 and 239, for similar provisions in Algeria and Morocco, respectively.

[43] *Vide* Murad, p. 484; Zaki, p. 284; Habeeb, p. 351; Badawi, K.M., pp. 206–7; El-Fakahani, Book I, Vol. II, pp. 191 and 235, and his 1959 Supplement, pp. 163–4; and Faheem, p. 82.

Sections 40, 48, 39(2), 45(i,b) and 35(4) of the Kuwaiti, Qatari, Lebanese, Jordanian and Libyan Labour Codes, respectively, expressly give the employer an absolute power of this right, should be reasonable and should as far as possible, take the interests of the worker into consideration. For Sudan reference to the English Law reveals that the managerial powers of the employer include the appointment of the leave date.[44] The reasonable exercise by the employer of this power, should likewise obtain in Sudan.

The worker in the U.A.R., cannot insist on the taking of the leave in one stretch. This is clear from section 59(1) of the Labour Code, which provides that, "if the exigencies of the work so require the leave in excess of any continuous six days may be taken in instalments."[45] So the employer has the right to decide on the taking of the leave by instalments, "for if the workers have this right they would surprise the employer by their absence at any time, and thus would prejudice the proper carrying out of the work."[46] However, only the reasonable exercise of such right by the employer, with no other motivation than the interests of the work, should be the measure of the validity of the exercise of the right. In Sudan there is no similar provision. Reference to the English Law reveals that "the annual leave is to be taken on consecutive days, ... but when ... (it) ... is more than one working week the holiday may be divided into separate periods, one of which is at least one working week."[47] It is not clear here, whose right it is to decide on the instalments. So the apparent and equitable view is that neither party has this right alone. But failing any agreement thereon between them, the employer should be able to reasonably exercise that right, while taking the circumstances of the worker into consideration.

to appoint the date of the leave, in accordance with the work requirements. Section 13(3) of the Iraqi Labour Code, expressly provides for the appointment of the leave-date, by the agreement of the parties; and in any case, obliges the employer to grant the leave to the worker within one month, and in certain exceptional circumstances, within two months after the request of the leave by the latter.

[44] *Vide* O. Kahn-Freund, in p. 276 of *The British Legal Papers.*

[45] *Vide* the somewhat similar provisions in sections 40 and 48, of the Kuwaiti and Qatari Labour Codes, respectively. Sections 116 and 122 of the Tunisian Labour Code provide similarly re instalments, but only with the consent of the worker; *vide* also the *Labour Survey of North Africa*, p. 239, for similar provisions in Morocco, and p. 236, for the position in Algeria, which permits the taking in instalments, of any leave in excess of twelve days, but only with the consent of the worker – In this there is an exact similarity to the position in France: *Vide* the Holidays with Pay Act of 1956. *Vide* also Article 2(4) of Convention 52 of 1936; Article 6 of Convention 101 of 1952; and para. 2 of Recommendation 47 of 1936.

[46] Cairo Court of Arbitration in dispute No. 133 of 1952 (in Habeeb, p. 351); *vide* also Cairo Court of Appeal in the appeal on dispute No. 53 of 1957 (in El-Fakahani, Book I, Vol. II, p. 206).

[47] O. Kahn-Freund, in p. 275 of *The British Legal Papers.*

SECTION II: SICK LEAVE

Section 63 of the U.A.R. Labour Code provides that "the worker whose sickness is duly proved shall in any one year[48] be entitled to seventy per cent of his wages for the first ninety days and eighty per cent for the next ninety days."[49]

The sickness mentioned in the section, is the ordinary sickness, as the sickness resulting from a professional disease or an industrial accident, is dealt with under the Social Insurance Act.[49] On the other hand, the sick leave is due to the worker, even though the sickness results from his negligence or misconduct.

The worker is not obliged to prove his sickness by a medical certificate, as he may either seek treatment by the employer's doctor,[50] or the employer may accept the worker's word. However, the employer "is not precluded from requesting his own doctor to examine the worker."[51] Any difference between the employer and the worker in this respect, can be settled by the Arbitration Board mentioned in section 81 of the Labour Code.[52]

The wages mentioned in the section, are calculated on the basis of the wages to which the worker would have been entitled, if he did not fall sick.[53]

[48] *Vide* the definition of the year in footnote 1, *supra*. *Vide* also footnote 15 and the related text, re calculation of the leave year, which is also applicable to the sick leave; *vide* in this respect, Murad, p. 481; Habeeb, p. 358; Rashed and Hashem, p. 98; and El-Fakahani, Book I, Vol. II, p. 194. Butros and Rajab, p. 420, wrongly submit that the sick leave year is the twelve months preceding the sickness.

[49] The wording of the section leaves the absence of the worker to implication. This is bad drafting.

The provisions of section 63 are a great improvement on the provisions of its predecessor section 25 of Law 317 of 1952, which granted to the worker a sick leave of one month with full wages for the first ten days, half wages for the next ten days, and quarter wages for the last ten days.

The Explanatory Note to the Labour Code, says that " in due course, the application of this provision will be referred to the Social Insurance Corporation soon as the legislation on medical Insurance is enacted." Subsequently, Law No. 92 of 1959, re Social Insurance, was enacted; and Chapter I of Book II thereof, established the said Corporation.

Cf. the provisions in sections 14(1), 38, 50 and 63, of the Iraqi, Kuwaiti, Qatari and Lebanese Labour Code, respectively, and sections 18 and 47 of the Saudi Regulations. Section 37(1) of the Libyan Labour Code contains sick leave provisions for the workers, whose establishments are not covered by the Social Insurance Law. The Jordanian and Tunisian Labour Codes do not contain any relevant provisions.

[50] *Vide* Section I, F, of Chapter III, *supra*.

[51] The Explanatory Note to section 25 of Law 317 of 1952, which is the predecessor of section 63 of the Labour Code; *vide* also Zaki, pp. 290–1; and Habeeb, p. 58.

[52] *Vide* section 81 in Chapter VI, *infra*; *vide* also El-Fakahani, Book I, Vol. II, p. 195; Rashed and Hashem, pp. 95–6; and Naguib and Bakr, p. 101.

[53] *Vide* footnote 17, *supra*, for the provisions of section 9 of the Labour Code, concerning the wages of piece-rate workers. *Vide* Section I of Chapter IV, *supra*, for the definition of wages.

The sick leave is independent of the annual leave.[54] On the other hand, "the sick leave is not exclusive of the non-working days, even though the worker does not usually get any wages for these days, whether by virtue of the contract or the law."[55] The reference here is mainly to the public holidays and to the weekly rest-days,[56] whether the workers are ordinarily remunerated for them or otherwise.[57] The exclusion of both would prejudice the worker, because all the days of absence, including the public holidays and the weekly rest-days, will enter in the calculation of the days, after the expiry of which the contract is dissolved by virtue of section 81 of the Labour Code.[52] The worker who is ordinarily paid for the weekly rest-days, should, however, be entitled to the full wages for these days, and not the lesser percentage of wages to which he would otherwise be entitled by virtue of section 63 of the Labour Code. The worker who is not ordinarily paid for his weekly rest-days, would by their inclusion in the sick leave, be entitled to the said lesser percentage of wages for these days, instead of being altogether deprived of the wages. The employer cannot object to this, because of the two parties, it is he who benefits more from the provisions of the said section 81 of the Code. The acceptance of his objection would permit him to have the better of the two worlds. All the above should also apply to the inclusion of the public holidays in the calculation of the sick leave.[58]

The sick leave for a certain year, cannot be carried over to the following year or years,[59] because it is a yearly entitlement which is contingent upon the sickness of the worker in the same year. If during the sickness, a new entitlement year commences, the worker is entitled to continue

[54] *Vide* Alexandria Court of Appeal in appeal No. 85 of 1955; and Cairo Court of Cassation in case No. 1492 of 1955 (both in El-Fakahani, pp. 233 and 234, respectively); *vide* also El-Fakahani, 1959 Supplement, p. 716; Faheem, p. 87; and Rashed and Hashem, p. 87, all of whom hold the same opinion; *vide* also footnote 20, *supra*. Section 41 of the Lebanese Labour Code empowers the employer to reduce the annual leave to eight days, if the sickness exceeds one month. This peculiar provision is the only provision of its kind, in the Labour Codes of the Arab countries. The writer has also not found any precedent therefor in any other Law.

[55] The Explanatory Note to section 25 of Law 317 of 1952, which is the predecessor of section 63 of the Labour Code.

[56] Murad, p. 482; Butros and Rajab, p. 307; Rashed and Hashem, p. 97; and Faheem, p. 87, are of the same opinion.

[57] Cf. with the exclusion of the weekly rest-days from the annual leave; *vide* also Butros and Rajab, p. 307.

[58] *Vide* in this respect, the Council of State's opinion No. 2/5/2/2, delivered on 29 January 1953 (mentioned in Badawi, Z., Vol. II, p. 92). El-Fakahani, 1959 Supplement, p. 176; and Rashed and Hashem, p. 97, maintain otherwise, without reasoning.

[59] *Vide* Murad, p. 482; Faheem, p. 86; Zaki, p. 358; and Sabbour, p. 524, who are of the same opinion. Cf. section 14(1) of the Iraqi Labour Code, which permits the carrying over of the sick leave.

in his absence, by taking the sick leave of the new year,[60] without prejudice to the above-mentioned provisions of section 81 of the Labour Code. If the worker consumes his sick leave entitlements, he can, it is submitted, join his annual leave with it, but again subject to the limitations prescribed by section 81, for the frustration of the contract.[61] On the other hand, the worker can request the substitution of his annual leave for an equal part of his sick leave, if he wants to get the full wages. If the worker falls sick during his annual leave, he should if he chooses, be entitled to have his sick leave calculated as from the expiry of his annual leave;[62] so the running of the time for the purposes of the said section 81, should thus be delayed by the length of the annual leave.

Finally, a worker on probation,[63] is entitled to the sick leave.[64] The reason is that, contrary to the annual leave, the sick leave is due without the pre-condition of the passing of one year's service, before the first entitlement, though both of them accrue as from the beginning of the service.

In Sudan section 21 of the Sudan Ordinance provides:

"(1) After the completion of two years of continuous service, an employed person who is unable to attend at his place of employment owing to an illness which is not due to his misconduct or negligence shall be entitled in respect of the days on which he is absent on account of such illness[65] to full wages for thirty days and half wages for a further thirty days during each twenty four months of subsequent continuous service.

"(2) The employer shall incur no liability under this section unless the illness has been certified to be an illness which renders the employed

[60] Murad, p. 482; Butros and Rajab, pp. 305–6; Faheem, p. 86; and Naguib and Bakr, p. 102, are of the same view.

[61] Cairo Court of Appeal in appeal No. 1021 of 1955 (in El-Fakahani, Book I, Vol. II, p. 234) is a contrary decision. Badawi, K.M., p. 221; El-Fakahani, Book I, Vol. II, p. 195; and Butros and Rajab, pp. 306–7, advocate the said joining of the two leaves, without reference to the limitation in section 45 of Law 317 of 1952, which is the predecessor of section 81 of the Labour Code.

[62] Habeeb, p. 359, is of the same opinion. On the other hand, Badawi, K.M., p. 222; Sabbour, p. 524; and Rashed and Hashem, p. 300, maintain that the worker can during his sickness, request the annual leave. They add that the annual leave so taken, should be excluded from the number of days, after which the contract is dissolved by virtue of section 81 of the Labour Code. It is, however, submitted that they are wrong, because the frustration of the contract is by the force of law, automatic (*vide* Section I of Chapter VI, *infra*).

[63] Section 44 of the Labour Code limits probation to three months.

[64] Badawi, K.M., p. 223; Butros and Rajab, p. 308; El-Fakahani, 1959 Supplement, p. 175; and Badawi, Z., Vol. II, p. 91, are of the same view.

[65] The absence on sickness includes the periods of approaching illness and convalescence: *vide Davies v. Ebbow Vale Urban District Council* (1911), 27. T.L.R. 543 (*vide* Diamond, p. 94). The same should apply in the U.A.R.

person incapable of attending at this place of employment by a medical practitioner nominated by the employer and licensed in accordance with the provisions of section 14 of the Public Health Ordinance, or, where no such medical practitioner is available, by a person nominated for the purpose by the employer and agreed to by the employed person."[66]

The sickness mentioned in the section is the ordinary sickness, as is the case in the U.A.R., because the 'industrial' sickness is dealt with by the 1949 Workmen's Compensation Ordinance.[67] On the other hand, and contrary to the provisions in the U.A.R. ,the worker is expressly deprived of his right to the sick leave, if the sickness results from his "misconduct or negligence."[68]

Contrary to the U.A.R., the proof by the worker of his sickness is expressly provided for in Sudan. However, in respect of the settlement of any difference between the two parties, these parties are not on grounds as equal as they are in the U.A.R.

The wages due to the worker for his days of sick leave, are calculated on the basis of the wages which he would have earned, if he was working,[69] as is the case in the U.A.R.

The sick leave is independent of the annual leave.[70] On the other hand, there is no provision in Sudan equivalent to section 81 of the U.A.R. Labour Code, which frustrates the contract after the worker's absence on sickness reaches a certain number of days. So the inclusion of the weekly rest-days in the calculation of the sick leave, cannot be justified, especially where they are expressly excluded from the annual leave, by virtue of section 22(3) of the Sudan Ordinance.[18] However, public holidays enter in the calculation of the sick leave, because they do so in the calculation of the annual leave.[18] The submission made in

[66] Cf. section 32 of the Bahraini Labour Code; for the position under the English Common Law, cf. *Inglis v. East India Co.* (1851) 18 L.T.O.S., with *Cuckson v. Stones* (1858) L.J.Q.B. 25. Diamond, pp. 92–3, states the said position, as follows: "Unless the contract of service or apprenticeship contains an express or implied provision to the contrary, a master is bound, while the contract subsists, to pay the remuneration during the absence through illness of the servant or apprentice"; *vide* also the nice summary of the law in Barwell and Kar, pp. 252–3; and *vide* Batt, p. 199; Smith, p. 91; Samuels, p. 12; and Macdonell, p. 217.

[67] *The Laws of the Sudan*, Vol. 8, Title XXII, Sub-Title 4; *vide* also the English case of *Elliott v. Liggens* (1902), 2 K.B. 84, where a workman, after sustaining an injury and was compensated by virtue of the Workmen's Compensation Act of 1897, was held to be disentitled to wages.

[68] *Vide* a similar express deprivation in section 32(b, i) of the Bahraini Labour Code. The Sudanese and Bahraini provisions seem to follow the English Common Law, in this respect: *vide* Halsbury, Vol. 25, pp. 477–8.

[69] *Vide* the definition of wages in Section I of Chapter IV, *supra*; and *vide* footnote 17, *supra*, for the wages of piece-rate workers.

[70] *Vide* footnote 19, *supra*, and the related text.

the U.A.R., to the effect that sick workers should be entitled to the full wages for the public holidays falling within the sick leave, should also be applicable in Sudan, if the worker then is getting only half of the wages, by virtue of section 21 of the Ordinance.

The two years' entitlement of sick leave cannot be carried to any futuer years, for the same reason forwarded for the U.A.R.[71] But the joining of the sick leave for any two years, with the sick leave for the next two years, should be allowed without any limitation as prescribed in section 81 of the U.A.R. On the other hand, there is no objection to the taking by the worker of his annual leave after his sick leave, and there is no limitation thereon similar to that in section 81 of the U.A.R. Moreover, the converse case of joining these two leaves should be allowed in Sudan, as it is in the U.A.R. The substitution of a part of the sick leave by the annual leave, may arise in Sudan, because the latter half of the sick leave is paid for at half of the rate of the wages only, and the worker may prefer to get the full wages. It is submitted that there is nothing to preclude the worker from doing so, as is the case in the U.A.R. The taking of the annual leave by the worker during the sick leave, should be permitted without any limitation as is imposed thereon in the U.A.R.

Finally, there is no legislative provision in Sudan, to limit the period of probation, contrary to what we saw in the U.A.R. So the entitlement of a probationary worker to the sick leave will not present the query, which had to be answered in the U.A.R. The right of the worker, whether probationary or otherwise, only starts to accrue from the beginning of the third year of service, and not from the date of service, as it is in the U.A.R.

SECTION III: PUBLIC HOLIDAYS

Section 62 of the U.A.R. Labour Code provides:

"Every worker shall be entitled to leave with full wages[72] on such days as are prescribed in an order from the Minister of Labour provided that these days shall not exceed ten in any one year.[73]

[71] Cf. section 32(a) of the Bahraini Labour Code, which permits the carrying over of the sick leave. This section also preserves the sick leave entitlements, for the worker who is discharged on medical grounds. Section 50(4) of the Qatari Labour Code provides to the same effect. These are the only Labour Codes of the Arab countries, which contain such a provision.

[72] *Vide* the definition of wages, in Section I of Chapter IV, *supra*; and footnote 17, *supra*, for piece-rate workers.

[73] When the Labour Code was first issued, the number of days was seven; but it was made nine by Law No. 106 of 1960; and was later on made ten by Law No. 159 of 1961. *Vide* footnote 1, *supra*, for the definition of the year.

"The employer may put the worker to work on the said days if the exigencies of the work so require provided that he shall pay him twice the wages. Workers employed in the public establishments which shall be specified in an order from the Minister of Labour may be put to work on any of the said days provided that every such worker shall be allowed a day off in return."[74]

The section gives the authority to specify the public holidays, to the Minister of Labour. So any public holiday declared by a mere resolution of the Council of Ministers, will not be binding on the employers.[75]

On the other hand, it had been held that the employer could always grant his workers additional public holidays, to suit his religious or political convictions, and deduct them from the annual leave of the workers.[76] It is submitted that this is not justifiable in law, because this in effect, will give the employer a power to give the annual leave in instalments, for reasons other than the requirements of the work, as is prescribed in section 59(1) of the Labour Code.[77] However, there is nothing to preclude the employer from agreeing with his worker, to give him a holiday on the latter's religious feasts, either in lieu of the prescribed public holidays, or in addition thereto, for deduction later on from the worker's annual leave.

The employer alone has the authority to decide whether the work

[74] Cf. the somwehat similar provisions, in sections 15 and 16 of the Iraqi Labour Code, and 37 of the Kuwaiti Labour Code. Sections 46 and 49 of the Qatari Labour Code and the Saudi Regulations, respectively, provide for public holidays, without providing for work on these holidays. The Lebanese, the Jordanian and the Libyan Labour Codes do not contain provisions prescribing public holidays, though the latter two mention public holidays, for the purposes of calculating the annual leave only, in sections 45 and 35, respectively. *Vide* the *Labour Survey of North Africa*, pp. 229 and 231, for the provisions in Algeria (to which the provisions of Title 1 of Chapter IV of Book II of the French Labour Code, were extended), p. 229, for the provisions in Tunisia, and pp. 232–3, for the provisions in Morocco – in these two countries, the public holidays are not prescribed in the labour legislation. The holidays which are grantable in Tunisia by practice only, do not, when the worker is requested to work on them, entitle the worker to double pay, except when a collective agreement so provides.

[75] *Vide* Cairo Court of Arbitration in dispute No. 176 of 1954 (in El-Fakahani, Book I, Vol. II, p. 245).

[76] *Vide* Cairo Court of Arbitration in dispute No. 34 of 1955 (in Habeeb, p. 357, who approves of the decision); writers who agree, are Faheem, pp. 80 and 84; Rashed and Hashem, p. 93; and Badawi, Z., Vol. I, p. 83, and Vol. II, pp. 84–5. El-Fakahani, 1959 Supplement, pp. 172–3, also agrees, but advocates that the exercise by the employer of this power, should be reasonable; *vide* Cairo Court of Arbitration in dispute No. 13 of 1955 (in his Book I, Vol. II, p. 239), as an authroity for his proposition. *Vide* also Cairo Court of Appeal (*Ibid.*, p. 246), as an authority for the proposition, that the deduction from the annual leave of the additional public holidays, will not be valid, unless the employer had told his workers of his intention to so deduct, at the time of granting these additional holidays.

[77] *Vide* the section quoted in Section I of the present Chapter, *supra*.

requires that the worker should be put to work on a public holiday[78]; but the exigencies of the work should be the only consideration. If the worker refuses to work, he will be deprived of his wages, and will in addition, be subjected to a disciplinary action, for refusal to carry out the employer's orders.[79] On the other hand, if the worker volunteers to work on a public holiday, he will not be entitled to the double wages.[80]

Contrary to what we saw in the case of the annual leave,[81] it was held that the employer could not deprive the worker of, or recover from him the wages for any public holiday, on which the worker works for another employer.[82]

Finally, the public holidays are, as we saw above, excluded from the calculation of the annual leave;[83] but should not be excluded from the calculation of the sick leave. If a public holiday falls on a weekly rest-day, the worker who is ordinarily remunerated for that day, should be entitled to a compensatory day, because each of these is prescribed by a separate statutory provision, and because the denial of a compensatory day will deprive the worker of his wages for one day.[84]

Neither in the Sudan Ordinance nor in any other law, is there any provision to prescribe public holidays,[85] though these holidays are expressly included in the calculation of the annual leave, by section 22(3) of the Ordinance.[86] Due to the absence of a legislative provision, it is submitted that the matter becomes contractual at least on the grounds of custom, and that the employer has no right to oblige the worker to work on a public holiday.[87] If, however, the worker agrees or even volunteers

[78] Habeeb, p. 355, is of the same opinion.

[79] Of this opinion are Murad, p. 486; El-Fakahani, Book I, Vol. II, p. 197; Rashed and Hashem, p. 94; Habeeb, p. 355; Faheem, p. 85; and Naguib and Bakr, p. 99.

[80] *Vide* Cairo Labour Court in case No. 5597 of 1954 (in El-Fakahani, Book I, Vol. II, p. 241); *vide* also Badawi, K.M., pp. 216–7; Butros and Rajab, p. 316; and Habeeb, p. 356.

[81] *Vide* section 60 of the Labour Code, quoted in Section I of the present Chapter, *supra*.

[82] *Vide* the case quoted in footnote 80, *supra*.

[83] *Vide* footnote 20, *supra*; *vide* also Rashed and Hashem, p. 87; and Faheem, p. 85; *vide* the Council of State's contrary opinion, delivered on 10 September 1955 (in Habeeb, p. 356); and *vide* Naguib and Bakr, p. 99; and El-Fakahani, Book I, Vol. II, p. 196.

[84] Faheem, p. 85, is of the same opinion; El-Fakahani, Book I, Vol. II, p. 196, is impliedly of the contrary opinion.

[85] However, the writer knows from personal experience in Sudan, that public holidays are prescribed and amended from time to time, by executive resolutions of the Council of Ministers.

Vide the provisions in section 31(d & e) of the Bahraini Labour Code, which are similar to the U.A.R. provisions.

In England public holidays are usually provided for in the collective agreements. They average six days per year; and the entitlement thereto, is usually made conditional upon the passing of one year in service (*vide* I. & L., Vol. 22, 1959, p. 193).

[86] *Vide* the section quoted, in Section I of the present Chapter, *supra*.

[87] *Vide* the Indian case of *Amar v. Karam Singh*, A.I.R. 1914 Lah. 82, in Barwell and Kar, p. 381.

to so work, the amount of the wages due to the worker for such work, should be subject to the agreement of the parties. Moreover, the employer cannot object, if the worker agrees to work for another employer on a public holiday, nor can he deprive him of, or recover from him the wages for such holiday, unless the contract otherwise provides.

Finally, the public holidays are expressly included in the calculation of the annual leave, by virtue of section 22(3) of the Sudan Ordinance,[86] and their inclusion in the calculation of the sick leave has been advocated.[88] The same view advocated in the U.A.R., in respect of the weekly rest-days, is also advocated in the Sudan, mainly because of the issue of wages.

SECTION IV: OTHER LEAVES

Neither in the U.A.R. Labour Code nor in the Sudan Ordinance, nor in the labour legislation of either country, is there any provision, concerning the other kinds of leave which the worker may need, though both of them have laws or regulations, as the case may be, for such leaves for Government workers.

So the worker in both countries has no bereavement or compassionate leaves. If he needs to absent himself on the death or the sickness of a spouse, a parent, a child or a close relative, he has to request permission from his employer. If the latter refuses, the worker's absence if justified,[89] will be absence without pay.[90] Moreover, the worker has no right to absent himself for education,[91] or for the birth of his children,[92] or for making the pilgrimage to Mecca.[93]

[88] *Vide* Section II of the present Chapter, *supra*.

[89] *Vide* footnote 53 to Chapter III, *supra*; and *vide* Section II, A, 4, of Chapter VI *infra*.

[90] *Vide* El-Areef, p. 387; and Badawi, Z., Vol. II, p. 86–7. *Vide* sections 38 and 31(9) of the Lebanese and Bahraini Labour Codes, respectively, for provisions prescribing the bereavement leave.

Section 59 of Law 210 of 1951 in the U.A.R., prescribes an emergency leave for the Government officials and workers. The Administrative Regulations of 1934 in Sudan, grant the Government officials and workers, some local leave which can be used for an emergency.

[91] *Vide* section 17 of the Iraqi Labour Code, for provisions on educational leave without pay, for workers. *Vide* also the *Labour Survey of North Africa*, p. 237, for similar provisions in Algeria; and cf. these with the French provisions (*vide* I. & L., Vol. 22, 1959, p. 299).

Law 210 of 1951 in the U.A.R., grants leave for such a purpose, for Government officials.

[92] *Vide* provisions for leave on such an occasion, in pp. 235 and 239 of the *Labour Survey of North Africa*, in Tunisia and Morocco, respectively.

[93] *Vide* sections 51 and 35(5) of the Qatari and Libyan Labour Codes, respectively, for the worker's pilgrimage leave. In Saudi Arabia, section 48 of the Saudi Regulations empowers the Government to issue orders, to prescribe the granting of part-paid leaves and leaves without pay. The Saudi Government has not so far used this power.

In the U.A.R. the Financial Circular, No. 2 of 1943, grants such leave to the Government officials and workers.

Legislative provisions for the said leaves are necessary, not only for the benefit of the worker, but also for the solving of some problems related to the legality of the dismissal of the workers by the employer.

SUMMARY

The worker's right to the annual leave in the U.A.R., starts to accrue from the date of his service, though he can take his first leave only after he completes one year in service. In the Sudan the accrual date is the beginning of the worker's third year in service, but thenceforward, there is no limitation on the taking of his leave. On the termination of the contract, irrespective of who terminates it, and of its legal justifiability in the U.A.R., or its rightfulness in the Sudan, the worker is entitled to a payment in lieu of the leave already accrued but not taken. In the U.A.R. the employer is expressly empowered to deny to the worker or recover from him the wages for the leave holidays, on which he works for another employer, and the same should be applicable in Sudan. In both countries, the leave-year ordinarily starts as from the service-date of the worker, and should be a year of continuous service. The annual leave in the Sudan, is exclusive of the weekly rest-days and of the sick leave, but not of the public holidays. In the U.A.R. the exclusiveness extends to all these three. Longer leave for longer service, is prescribed in the U.A.R., but not in the Sudan, where any increase in the leave is purely contractual. In both countries, the renunciation by the worker of his leave, without any return or for a monetary return, is not legal. On the other hand, the leave should tacitly and completely be renounced by the worker in both countries, at the end of each leave-year, if he does not request the taking of the leave during the said year. If he makes the request, and the employer refuses to grant him the leave, the worker will have the right to a payment in lieu of the leave. This right is a cumulative right. The employer in both countries, has the right to appoint the date of taking the leave; but his exercise of this right should be reasonable. In both countries, the worker cannot insist on taking the leave in one stretch. This is deduced from an express provision in the U.A.R. Labour Code, but is only by reference to the English Common Law in Sudan. The employer in the U.A.R., is expressly empowered to divide the leave, in excess of any six continuous days. In Sudan the power to divide the leave should be subject to the agreement of both parties.

Sick leave in the U.A.R. and Sudan, is due for the worker's non-industrial sickness. The worker in the latter, is deprived of his leave, if the sickness results from his misconduct or negligence; but the case is otherwise in the former. Proof of the sickness is equally mandatory on the worker in both countries, but in settling any difference in this respect, the parties in the U.A.R., are on more equal grounds than they are in Sudan. In both countries, the sick leave is independent of the annual leave, but not of the public holidays. The weekly rest-days are included in the calculation of the sick leave in the U.A.R., but not in the Sudan. In neither country can the sick leave entitlement be carried over to future years; but if the sickness continues, successive entitlements can be joined, without limitation in Sudan, but with some limitation in the U.A.R. The taking of the sick leave after the annual leave, is permitted in both countries; but the converse case is permitted with some limitation in the U.A.R., and without limitation in the Sudan. The substitution of a part of the sick leave by the annual leave, is permitted in Sudan, but in the U.A.R., such substitution is permitted conditionally. Finally, the worker's right to the sick leave accrues as from the date of service, and there is no other limitation on the first entitlement thereto, as is imposed on the entitlement to the annual leave. In Sudan the accrual of the sick leave starts, as from the beginning of the third year of service, as is the accrual of the annual leave.

The U.A.R. Labour Code prescribes public holidays, but the Sudan Ordinance does not. The worker in the U.A.R. cannot refuse a reasonable request by the employer, to have him work on a public holiday. If he answers the employer's call, he is entitled to double wages. In Sudan the worker is not obliged to answer the call; but if he does, the wages payable therefor are for agreement between him and the employer. In neither country can the employer object to work by the worker for any other employer. The public holidays are excluded from the calculation of the annual leave in the U.A.R., but not in the Sudan. However, they are included in the calculation of the sick leave. If the public holiday falls on a weekly rest-day, a compensatory day is due in both countries.

Neither in the U.A.R. nor in Sudan, are there any provisions on the absence of the worker for compassionate reasons or bereavement, or for the purpose of education, the birth of children or the making of the pilgrimage. So the worker's absence for any of these reasons or purposes, should be subject to the consent of the employer. The employer also decides, whether to pay wages for the absence, or not.

CHAPTER VI

SUSPENSION, FRUSTRATION AND TERMINATION OF THE CONTRACT OF EMPLOYMENT

The rules of the civil law governing the suspension, frustration and termination of the civil contracts, are both in the U.A.R. and Sudan, generally applicable to the contract of employment. However, the peculiar nature of this contract, especially as concerns the worker, occasioned the legislator's interference in both countries, so as to provide some rules better suited to the contract. But these rules cannot be fully appreciated, without reference to the relevant rules of the civil law.

SECTION I: SUSPENSION AND FRUSTRATION OF THE CONTRACT[1]

Section 159 of the U.A.R. Civil Code provides that, "if in bilateral contracts it becomes impossible to perform an obligation, the corresponding obligation shall be excused and the contract shall *ipso facto* be frustrated."[2] The frustrating impossibility results from *force majeure*, which covers the occurrences which man can never avoid, like earthquakes, and any circumstances which the parties could not foresee, at the time of making the contract.[3] On the other hand, the impossibility need not be permanent.[4]

If the said *force majeure* affects the performance of the contract, but not to the extent of frustration, the contract is temporarily suspended.[5] This means the temporary relief of both parties of their contractual obligations, without liability.

[1] These two topics are discussed together, because as we shall presently see, they are well connected, under the general law.

[2] *Vide* section 14(c) of the Tunisian Labour Code, section 443 of the *Majallah*, section 1148 of the French Civil Code, and section 1639 W of the Netherland Civil Code.

[3] *Vide* El-Areef, p. 315. *Vide* footnote 7, *infra*.

[4] Cairo Court of Appeal in appeal No. 474 of 1957 (in El-Hawwari, p. 193); cf. Murad, p. 389.

[5] *Vide* Cairo Labour Court in case No. 140 of 1960 (*Ibid*., p. 258); *vide* also Badawi, K.M., p. 277; Sabbour, pp. 361 and 519; Habeeb, p. 428; Rashed and Hashem, p. 177; and Faheem, p. 114. Zaki, pp. 333–4, adds, however, that the contract will be frustrated, if time is of the essence of the contract.

In Sudan the rules of the English Common Law are applicable. Under these rules, "if further fulfilment of the contract is brought to an abrupt stop by some irresistible and extraneous cause for which neither party is responsible, the contract shall terminate forthwith and the parties be discharged."[6] The impossibility of performance of the contract may arise, either from an act of God or from *vis major*. These together are the counterparts of the frustrating causes in the U.A.R.[7] On the other hand, the frustrating impossibility need not be permanent, exactly as is the case in the U.A.R.

If the act of God or the *vis major* does not go to the root of the contract so as to frustrate its object, the contract is suspended.[8] The two parties who, as a result, are relieved of their contractual obligations, are bound to carry out these obligations, when the suspending cause ceases.

These are the rules of the general law in the U.A.R. and Sudan, which govern the frustration and suspension of the contracts. We shall now proceed to discuss some causes of suspension or frustration, in which the labour legislators of both countries have chosen to interfere, and to assess the effects of this interference on the rules of the general law.

Particular causes

(a) Sickness

Temporary sickness of the worker in the U.A.R. suspends the contract, by virtue of the rules of the general law.[9] This suspension

[6] Cheshire and Fifoot, p. 462; *vide* also in pp. 462–9 thereof, the historical development of the doctrine of frustration of the contract, from the old theory of the 'implied term' to the now more favoured theory of the 'just solution'; and note therein the cases of *Paradine v. Jane* (1647), Aleyn, 26; *Taylor v. Caldwell* (1863), 38. & S. 826; and *Davis Contractors Ltd. v. Fareham U.D.C.* (1956) A.C. 696, which help to clarify the said development. *Vide* also Cooper, pp. 50–1; Diamond, p. 215; I.S.D.L., Vol. 4, 1929, pp. 5–6; and Barwell and Kar, pp. 117 and 442.

[7] The term 'act of God' was interpreted in *Nugent v. Smith* (1876) I C.P.D. 423, to mean the elementary forces of nature, which are not connected with the agency of man, like floods and earthquakes. These also fall under the French term *force majeure*. On the other hand, the unforeseen occurrances of a different order, like a declaration of war or a rebellion, which are connected with man, are classified under *vis major*. The French term *force majeure*, covers such occurrances: *vide Matsoukis v. Priestman & Co.* (1915) I K.B. 681, where it was held that the French term *force majeure*, was a purely continental notion, and was wider than each of the act of God and the *vis major*, in England.

[8] In *Nordman v. Rayner and Sturges* (1916), 33 T.L.R. 87, it was held that the contract of an Alsatian was not frustrated, by his internment for one month, on account of his French sympathies.

[9] *Vide* Cairo Court of Cassation in case No. 1326 of 1955 (in Habeeb, p. 432); *vide* also El-Areef, p. 319; Murad, p. 390; and Sabbour, p. 349. *Vide* I.L.R., Vol. 79, 1959, p. 635, for the similar position in France.

relieves the employer of the payment of wages to the worker.[10] This necessitated the legislator's interference, so as to prescribe the sick leave with pay for the worker, in section 63 of the Labour Code.[11] This interference does, it is submitted, preclude the suspension of the contract.[12]

If the sickness extends over a long period, the contract, under the general law, is not frustrated as a matter of course. But the employer is ultimately entitled to terminate the contract. In this the legislator also interfered,[13] by enacting section 81 of the Labour Code. Section 81(1) provides that, "without prejudice to the provisions governing compensation for industrial accidents the contract of employment shall end by the worker's death or his disability from work or by a sickness which causes his absence from work for a minimum consecutive period of one hundred and eighty days or for non-consecutive periods exceeding two hundred days in any one year."[14] Section 81(5) provides that "the employer shall not during the sickness periods mentioned in the first paragraph exercise the right to terminate the contract to which he is

[10] Section 161 of the U.A.R. Civil Code provides that, "if in bilateral contracts the corresponding obligations are due either party may refrain from carrying out his obligations if the other party does not carry out his own obligations" – *Exceptio non ad impleti contractus*.

[11] *Vide* the section quoted and discussed in Section II of Chapter V, *supra*. As the paid sick leave by virtue of this section, is limited to 180 days in any one year, the extra 20 days necessary to make up the two hundred days mentioned in section 81(1), would presumably be leave without pay. This means that the contract, during these twenty days, is suspended, both by implication from section 81(1), and by virtue of the rules of the general law.

[12] This is supported by section 81(4) of the Labour Code, which guarantees for the worker, whose contract is frustrated by the operation of section 81(1), the termination gratuity ordinarily payable by the employer, by virtue of section 73 (*vide* Section I of Chapter VII, *infra*). If the legislator thus guarantees the payment of wages to the worker during his sickness, and of the gratuity on the frustration of the contract, there is no room left for the contention that the contract is suspended, during the worker's sickness.

[13] Section 697(2) of the U.A.R. Civil Code gives to the special laws, presumably meaning the labour laws in the first instance, an overriding effect over the Civil Code provisions, re dissolution of the contract by *force majeure* (*vide* the section quoted in part F of this Section of the present Chapter, *infra*).

[14] It is clear that the 180 consecutive days do not have to fall within one year.

Sections 14 and 59 of the Saudi Regulations, and 59 of the Kuwaiti Labour Code, respectively, contain provisions somewhat similar to section 81(1) of the U.A.R.

Section 81(2 & 3) of the U.A.R., provides for the proof of the disability or the sickness of the worker, as follows:

"The disability or the sickness shall be proved by a medical certificate provided that the employer may have the worker examined by another doctor, and if the two differ either party may request the Labour Office to refer the matter to a medical arbitration board for whose establishment and the procedure of referring disputes thereto and the assessment of fees an order from the Minister of Labour in agreement with the Ministers of Justice and Health shall be issued.

"The Labour Office concerned shall on the receipt of the medical arbitration decision communicate it fortwith to the worker and the employer both of whom shall carry out any obligations resulting from the decision, which shall be final."

entitled by virtue of section 72."[15] Thus section 81 (1) deems the sickness for either of the periods mentioned therein, to be *force majeure* which frustrates the contract, without the need for any decision from either party, and consequently without any need for a notice of termination by either of them.[16] The acceptance of the worker by the employer, after the expiry of these specified periods, is no more than an indication that the employer intends to keep the contract effective, which after all is open to him.[17] But the employer can always insist at the time of the return of the worker, that the contract has already been frustrated, and that any further service should only be under a new contract.[18] On the other hand, the employer is, by virtue of these provisions, precluded from using his power to terminate the contract by notice, before the expiry of the said specified periods of absence, whereas under the general law, he might, according to the circumstances of the case, use this power after the expiry of shorter periods.[19] The said specified periods are irrelevant to the sickness which results from a professional disease or an industrial accident. The frustration of the contract is caused by the disability which may result from the said sickness, irrespective of its length.[20] Finally, these specified periods do not prolong the duration of a limited contract which expires in the meantime.

In Sudan temporary sickness of the worker under the rules of the English Common Law, does not suspend the contract, as this is considered to be a 'visitation of God,' for which the worker should not be responsible, unless the parties provide otherwise in the contract.[21] Thus contrary to the position in the U.A.R., the worker is entitled to his

[15] Only the Saudi Regulations (section 14) contain a similar provision.

[16] *Vide* Cairo Court of Cassation in case No. 1486 of 1959 (in El-Fakahani, Book I, Vol. III, p. 413): "The contract is frustrated by the force of law (*de plein droit*)... without the need for the employer to take any further step"; *vide* also the Cairo Court of Appeal in appeal No. 1021 of 1955 (*Ibid.*, p. 409); the Cairo Labour Court in case No. 3620 of 1959 (in El-Hawwari, p. 201); and *vide* Sabbour, pp. 350–1; Butros and Rajab, pp. 381 and 421; and El-Fakahani, 1959 Supplement, p. 315. Of the contrary view which, it is submitted, is wrong, are the High Court of Appeal in appeal No. 74 of 1958 (in Zaki, p. 342); and Cairo Court of Cassation in case no. 1162 of 1957 (in E.-Fakahani, Book I, Vol. III, p. 408); *vide* also Badawi, K.M., p. 426; Zaki pp. 342 and 344; and Faheem, p. 123. Rashed and Kashem, p. 300, advocate this view; but they advocate the contrary view without explanation in p. 303. Habeeb does the same, in pp. 433 and 482, respectively; and so does Murad, in pp. 390 and 392, respectively.

[17] *Vide* Cairo Court of Cassation in case No. 1205 of 1955 (in El-Fakahani, Book I, Vol. III, p. 410); *vide* also El-Areef, p. 303.

[18] *Vide* Sabbour, p. 351, who is of the same opinion.

[19] The employer is, however, not precluded from dismissing the worker for a justifiable cause, during the latter's sickness, as he is entitled to do by virtue of section 76 of the Labour Code (*vide* Section II of the present Chapter, *infra*); *vide* Murad, p. 391.

[20] *Vide* Murad, p. 392, who is of the same opinion.

[21] *Vide Cuckson v. Stones*, 1 Ell & Ell. 248; *vide* also Macdonell, pp. 215–6; Halsbury, Vol. 25, p. 487; and Barwell and Kar, pp. 252–3.

wages during such sickness. The prescription of the sick leave with pay, in section 21 of the Sudan Ordinance,[22] does not change the Common Law principles in any material respect; but the section provides for a sure measure of the length of the temporary sickness.

If, however, the sickness extends beyond the statutory periods of the sick leave, it is submitted that the contract will then be suspended, unless the employer agrees to pay the worker's wages for such further period. The English Common Law cannot be invoked, so as to oblige the employer to pay those wages, because the Sudan legislator has in section 21, put a limit on the employer's obligation. On the other hand, a long sickness is, under the English Common Law, one of the three important considerations which justify the frustration of the contract; the other two being the terms of the contract and any prevailing custom.[23] This should also be the case in Sudan. However, such frustration does not have the same consequences, which frustration has both in the U.A.R. and England. Frustration in these two countries, relieves the employer of the obligation to serve a notice of termination on the worker, or to pay in lieu. In Sudan section 12 of the Sudan Ordinance,[24] which deems the contract dissolved by the employer's death, guarantees for the worker the said notice or payment in lieu. So the Sudan legislator should be taken to intend the same guarantee for the worker, in the more deserving case of the frustration of the contract by long sickness. If, however, the employer accepts the worker into his service, this should be a good indication that he intends to keep the contract effective, exactly as the position is in the U.A.R. On the other hand, the English Common Law permits the employer to terminate the contract, at any time during the worker's sickness, by giving due notice, unless the parties agree otherwise.[25] In Sudan section 10(1) of the Sudan Ordinance[26] permits such termination during sickness, by providing that the notice may be given "at any time," contrary to what we saw in the U.A.R. Finally, the termination of a limited contract by the effluxion of time, is not affected by the sickness.

Comparison of the law in the U.A.R. and Sudan, reveals that the effect of the worker's sickness on the contract, is basically the same in

[22] *Vide* the section quoted and discussed, in Section II of Chapter V, *supra*.

[23] *Vide Storey v. Fulham Steel Works Co.* (1907), 24 T.L.R. 89; and *Robinson v. Davidson* (1871), L.R. 6 Exch. 269 – cf. with *Bettini v. Gye* (1876), I Q.B.D. 183; *vide* also Batt, p. 71; Cooper, pp. 48–9; Cheshire and Fifoot, p. 470; Samuels, p. 13; and Halsbury, Vol. 25, pp. 477 and 487.

[24] *Vide* the section quoted in part F of this Section of the present Chapter, *infra*.

[25] *Vide Orman v. Saville Sportswear Ltd.* (1960), 3 A.E.R., p. 105.

[26] *Vide* the section quoted in Section II of the present Chapter, *infra*.

both countries. However, the frustration of the contract by a specified long sickness, results by the force of law in the U.A.R., but not in Sudan. On the other hand, the employer in the former, cannot terminate the contract by notice during the worker's sickness; but in the latter he can.

The sickness of the employer has no effect on the contract in the U.A.R., unless "his personal qualities are material to the performance of the work, in which case the contract is suspended, as it is in the case of the worker's sickness."[27] If the contract is so suspended, frustration of the contract may eventually result from the employer's long sickness. In Sudan it is submitted that, by analogy with the English Common Law rules, concerning the effect of the worker's temporary sickness on the contract, the contract will not be suspended by the employer's illness. By the same analogy, however, the contract may eventually be frustrated by the employer's long sickness.[28]

(b) Disability

The worker's disability from work may result either from a professional disease or an industrial accident or from his old age. But irrespective of the cause of the disability, it is considered by section 81(1) of the U.A.R. Labour Code,[29] to be *force majeure* which frustrates the contract. This is in line with the rules of the general law.[30] Contrary to the frustration by long sickness, there is here no limitation of time, for the ascertainment of the disability is the only material consideration.[31] On the other hand, it is sufficient that the disability precludes the worker from performing his contractual work,[32] for it need not be a total disability.[33] Furthermore, the disability need not always be

[27] El-Areef, p. 319. This can also be deduced by analogy, from section 697(1) of the Civil Code, which precludes the frustration of the contract by the employer's death, unless his personal qualities were taken into consideration, at the time of making the contract (*vide* the section quoted in part F of this Section of the present Chapter, *infra*).

[28] This can also be deduced by analogy, from section 12 of the Sudan Ordinance, which deems the contract terminated by the employer's death.

[29] *Vide* the section quoted in part A of this Section of the present Chapter, *supra*.

[30] *Vide* section 159 of the Civil Code, in this Section of the present Chapter, *supra*.

[31] El-Fakahani, 1959 Supplement, p. 316; Rashed and Hashem, p. 306; Badawi, Z., Vol. I, p. 90; and Naguib and Bakr, p. 183, are of the same opinion.

It is difficult to appreciate the reference in section 81(1), to industrial compensation. This compensation is prescribed in section 28 of the Social Insurance Law No. 92 of 1959. There is nothing in this Law, which concerns the subsistence of the contract, before the industrial disability is ascertained: *vide* Zaki, p. 346; and Butros and Rajab, p. 422.

[32] *Vide* Cairo Court of Cassation in case No. 3097 of 1953 (in Badawi, K.M., p. 428) *vide* also El-Areef, pp. 401 and 410; Murad, p. 390; El-Fakahani, 1959 Supplement, p. 317; Badawi, K.M., p. 423; Rashed and Hashem, p. 298; Badawi, Z., Vol. I, p. 90; Butros and Rajab, p. 419; and Naguib and Bakr, p. 193.

[33] *Vide* Murad, p. 390. Sabbour, p. 521, maintains otherwise, though with some

permanent, for a temporary disability may sometimes frustrate the object of the contract, as when time is essential to the contract.[34]

In Sudan similar rules are applicable, by reference to the English Common Law. "It is a condition implied in contracts of service or apprenticeship," says *A. S. Diamond*, "that they shall come to an end in the event of supervening physical or mental incapacity of the servant or apprentice such as to frustrate the object of the contract."[35]

On the other hand, both in the U.A.R. and Sudan, a limited contract, whose duration expires before the disability is ascertained, comes to an end without reference to the disability.

Finally, the effect of the employer's disability on the contract, should both in the U.A.R. and Sudan, be similar to the effect of his sickness on the contract.

(c) Criminal offences and imprisonment

Section 67 of the U.A.R. Labour Code provides:

"If the worker is accused of the commission of a crime or of the misdemeanour of participating in or the incitement of an unlawful strike or of any misdemeanour within the scope of the work the employer may suspend the worker from the date of reporting the same to the competent authority and until a decision is thereby given.

"If the competent authority decides not to prosecute the worker or if he is acquitted he shall be returned to his work and any failure so to do shall constitute an unjustifiable dismissal.

"If it is established that the accusation of the worker was contrived by the employer or his authorised agent his wages for the period of suspension shall be paid and if the competent authority or the Court discovers such contrivance it shall state the same in its decision or judgment."[36]

So the employer has the choice of suspending the contract, in the eventualities mentioned in the section.[37] If the worker is committed

hesitation, as he adds that the worker's smaller output due to old age, should justify the termination of his contract by notice (*vide* Section II, B of the present Chapter, *infra*, for the justification of the termination of the contract).

[34] Murad, p. 390, maintains otherwise, without any justification.

[35] P. 190; *vide* also *Harmer v. Cornelius*, 5 C.B.N.S. 236; and *Warburton v. Co-operative Wholesale Society* (1917), 1 K. B. 663 quoted by him as authorities.

[36] The only other Arab Labour Code which contains a similar provision, is the Iraqi Labour Code (section 46).

[37] *Vide* Alexandria Court of Cassation in case No. 999 of 1950 (in Badawi, K.M., p. 262); *vide* also El-Areef, p. 392; El-Fakahani, 1959 Supplement, p. 188; Badawi, K.M., p. 253; Rashed and Hashem, pp. 129–30 and 137; and Naguib and Bakr, p. 115.

Strikes will be discussed later. Misdemeanours "within the scope of work" mean those committed either during working hours or at the place of work: *vide* Badawi, K.M., p. 253; El-Fakahani, 1959 Supplement, pp. 187–8; and Rashed and Hashem p. 128.

to prison by the competent authority, pending the taking of a decision, whether the reporting to the authority be made by the employer or any other person,[38] the employer can consider the contract suspended, without the need for him to expressly do so.[39] This is in line with the general law, which considers the contract suspended by an unauthorized absence, as long as the contract is not terminated.[39] If the contract is suspended by virtue of section 67, there is no time-limit to the suspension,[40] as it has to wait for the decision of the competent authority or the judgment of the Court. Suspension of the contract means that the worker is not entitled to his wages during suspension. The exception to this rule, when the worker's accusation is by the contrivance of the employer or his authorized agent,[41] as provided in the last paragraph of section 67, is in accordance with the general law. On the other hand, the worker's return to work in accordance with section 67, presupposes that the employer has suspended the contract or considered it to have been suspended. If it had been suspended, it is submitted that the employer cannot justifiably terminate the contract, before the decision or the judgement, as the case may be, is given. He has to choose between suspension or termination, when the worker is accused. But if, for lack of sufficient evidence, the competent authority decides not to prosecute or the Court acquits the worker, the employer may still be entitled to terminate the contract, if the proven facts justify him in doing so.[42] On the other hand, neither the conviction of the worker of any of the offences mentioned in section 67 or of any other offence, nor the worker's absence on account of a detention pending the giving of the decision or the judgement, or on account of a sentence of imprisonment, *ipso facto* frustrates the contract. If the employer decides to have

[38] El-Fakahani, 1959 Supplement, p. 188; and Rashed and Hashem, p. 129, are of the same opinion. Naguib and Bakr, pp. 117–8, say the same thing, but they contradict themselves in p. 116.

[39] *Vide* Alexandria Court of Cassation in case No. 331 of 1950 (in Faheem, p. 108); *vide* also Butros and Rajab, p. 362; and Rashed and Hashem, pp. 130 and 132. *Vide* section 161 of the Civil Code; *vide* also El-Areef, p. 152.

[40] Rashed and Hashem, p. 132; and Naguib and Bakr, p. 115, are of the same opinion.

[41] *Vide* El-Areef, p. 394; Rashed and Hashem, p. 134; Habeeb, pp. 516 and 633; and Naguib and Bakr, p. 120. The contrivance of the employer or his authorized agent presupposes his *mala fides*: *vide* Abdeen District Court in case No. 2288 of 1949 (in Rashed and Hashem, p. 133); Cairo Labour Court in case No. 1687 of 1959 (in El-Hawwari, p. 173); and Cairo Court of Cassation in case No. 1462 of 1957 (*Ibid.*, p. 171); *vide* also Rashed and Hashem, pp. 135–6; and Naguib and Bakr, p. 120. El-Areef, p, 394; and Badawi, K.M., p. 254, add that the contrivance cannot be ascertained, unless the Court judgement is final.

[42] *Vide* Cairo Court of Cassation in case No. 17 of 1959 (in El-Hawwari, p. 170); and *vide* Section II, B, of the present Chapter, *infra*, for the justification of termination of the contract.

no more of the worker, he should expressly terminate the contract.[43] The same conclusions should be reached under the rules of the general law, because the said conviction or absence would, it is submitted, be ultimately attributed to the fault of the worker, so as to justify the termination of the contract by the employer, and would not be considered as *force majeure* which frustrates the contract.[44]

In Sudan there is no provision similar to section 67 of the U.A.R. Labour Code. However, Government workers who benefit from the Sudan Ordinance,[45] are subject to the Officials Discipline Ordinance of 1927. Section 35(1) of this Ordinance empowers the Government, "if the interest of the public service requires," to suspend the worker from "performing his duties," pending the result of criminal proceedings, "initiated in respect of an act which would constitute an offence under this ordinance."[46] The order or suspension "may direct that the official's pay be provisionally suspended either in whole or in part, until the decision of the (disciplinary) Board, which shall in the event of an acquittal, cancel the order for suspension, and in the event of a conviction make such order as appears to be just." It is submitted that the committing of the worker to prison, pending the result of the criminal proceedings, as is provided in the said section, will automatically suspend the contract, without the need for any order of suspension as above-mentioned. This suspension should also result to the contracts of other workers, not covered by the Officials Discipline Ordinance, because the worker's absence would be an unauthorized absence,[47] as

[43] Section 76 of the Labour Code (in Section II of the present Chapter, *infra*), entitles the employer to justifiably terminate the contract, for the commission of any crime or of a misdemeanour involving dishonour, or for unauthorized absences. So it can be concluded that the contract is not thereby automatically frustrated. *Vide* also Alexandria Court of Cassation in case No. 331 of 1950 (in Faheem, p. 108); Alexandria Court of Appeal in appeal No. 143 of 1954 (in El-Fakahani, Book I, Vol. III, p. 557); and Cairo Court of Cassation in case No. 140 of 1957 (*Ibid.*, p. 556); and *vide* El-Areef, p. 392; Sabbour, p. 525; El-Fakahani, 1959 Supplement, pp. 192–3; Faheem, pp. 107–8; Butros and Rajab, pp. 362–3; Rashed and Hashem, p. 130; and Naguib and Bakr, p. 117. Cairo Court of Cassation in case No. 991 of 1956 (in Sabbour, p. 521); and Cairo Labour Court in case No. 1912 of 1958 (in El-Hawwari, p. 195), decided that the contracts were frustrated, by the worker's detention for political reasons, and by the worker's imprisonment for over three months, respectively. It is submitted that these two decisions are wrong.

[44] *Vide* Cairo Court of Appeal in appeal No. 110 of 1959 (in El-Hawwari, p. 195). The last mentioned case in the preceding footnote, considered imprisonment to be *force majeure* under the general law, and wrongly identified it with the frustrating *force majeure*, mentioned in section 81(1) of the Labour Code (*vide* Section I, A, of the present Chapter, *supra*).

[45] *Vide* Section I of Chapter I, *supra*.

[46] *Vide* section 6 of the Officials Discipline Ordinance, which mentions these offences.

[47] *Vide* the English case of *Nordman v. Rayner and Sturges* (1916), 33 T.L.R. 87, where the internment of the plaintiff for one month, was held not to end the contract; but presumably the contract was suspended during that month.

it is under the general law of the U.A.R. If the worker's accusation amounts to a malicious prosecution by the employer or his authorized agent, the worker should be entitled to his wages for the period of suspension, as he is entitled in the U.A.R. On the other hand, if the Government worker's contract is suspended as above, section 34(1) of the Officials Discipline Ordinance[48] impliedly precludes the Government from terminating his contract, before the criminal proceedings are ended. In this there is similarity with the position of the U.A.R. However, it is submitted that the position is otherwise, in the case of other workers, for the employer in Sudan does not have to choose between suspension and termination of the contract, as the employer in the U.A.R. has to do. The acquittal of the Government worker does not, by virtue of section 34(3) of the Officials Discipline Ordinance, preclude the Government from proceeding against him and eventually dismissing him under this Ordinance, provided that "the charge under this ordinance does not raise substantially the same issue or issues on which he has been acquitted." In the case of other workers, it is submitted that the employer has the same power to rightfully terminate the contract,[49] as the employer in the U.A.R. has to justifiably do so. Finally, as in the U.A.R., the conviction of the Government or any other worker does not *ipso facto* frustrate the contract. However, contrary to the position in the U.A.R., the worker's long absence from work, on account of his detention or a sentence of imprisonment, may frustrate the contract.[50]

(d) Military service

Section 79 of the U.A.R. Labour Code provides:

"The worker who is called up for compulsory military service (the service of the flag) shall have the option either of requesting the cancellation of the contract and the taking of the termination gratuity as mentioned in section 73 or of availing himself of the provisions governing the military and national service (the service of the flag).

"The administrative authority concerned[51] shall notify the em-

[48] Section (34(1) provides that, "if proceedings are instituted against an official he shall not, unless the Council of Ministers so directs, be brought before a Board of Discipline on any grounds involved in the criminal charge while the criminal proceedings are still pending."

[49] *Vide* Section II, B, of the present Chapter, *infra*, for the rightful termination of the contract.

[50] *Vide Unger v. Preston Corporation* (1942) I A.E.R. 200, where nine months' internment was held to frustrate the contract. Comparison of this case with *Nordman's* case mentioned in footnote 47, *supra*, shows how every case is decided according to its own circumstances.

[51] The authority concerned is the Labour Office, within whose jurisdiction the place of work is situated (*vide* Order 134 of 1959).

ployer of the worker's option within three months of his recruitment."[52]

The provisions governing the military and national service, are contained in Law No. 505 of 1955 (as amended by Law No. 9 of 1958 and Law No. 149 of 1960), concerning compulsory military service,[53] and Law No. 314 of 1956, concerning service in the National Guard and the Liberation Army.[54]

Section 60 of the former Law prescribes that establishments employing at least fifty workers, should keep the same or equivalent work for their workers, who are called up for military or national service, until they are discharged therefrom. Section 61(2) thereof prescribes that the worker should after his discharge from the military service, request his re-instatement in his work, within thirty days after the discharge, that the employer should, if the worker is medically fit, take him back within sixty days of the worker's request, and that the worker should return to the work, within ten days after the employer requests him so to do. Section 61(1) thereof provides that, "if the worker becomes unfit (for his previous work) because of a disability which he suffers during his compulsory service, but he can perform any other work, he shall be returned to that other work without prejudice to his old service and wages." As these provisions and those of section 79(1) of the Labour Code are general provisions, they are equally applicable to contracts of limited as well as contracts of unlimited duration.[55] If the call to military service is made during the probationary period of the worker, the worker is deemed to have passed his probation successfully.[56] On the other hand, if the notification in accordance with section 79(2) of the Labour Code, does not reach the employer within the prescribed three months, the worker should be taken to have opted for keeping his contract,[57] because the contract is suspended during the three months, and this should presumably continue if a contrary choice is not exercised.

Section 13 of Law 314 of 1956, prescribes the keeping of their work, for the workers who either volunteer for the Liberation Army, or are called up for the National Guard; and prescribes the payment of their

[52] Cf. section 8 of the Tunisian Labour Code, which is the only other Arab Labour Code containing such a provision; cf. also section 25 of Book I of the French Labour Code.

[53] This Law repealed Law No. 226 of 1951.

[54] This Law repealed Law No. 510 of 1953.

[55] El-Areef, p. 180; and Faheem, pp. 115–6, are of the same opinion. Rashed and Hashem, p. 290; and Habeeb, p. 438; wrongly consider that the limited contract is frustrated by a *force majeure*, in these circumstances.

[56] This is the effect of the amendment of Law 505 of 1955, by Law 149 of 1960.

[57] Murad, p. 393, is of the same opinion; but Habeeb, p. 613, is of the contrary opinion, without reasoning.

wages by their employers, upto thirty days per year, provided that these workers do not exceed ten per cent of any one establishment. If the thirty days or the ten per cent are exceeded, section 14 thereof makes the Government liable for the wages until the workers are returned to their work, however long that may be. This, it is submitted, violates the provisions of section 79(1) of the Labour Code, in so far as the volunteers for the Liberation Army are concerned, because section 79(1) gives the choice to the worker to keep his contract, only in the case of compulsory military service. As the Labour Code was enacted after Law 314 of 1956, its provisions should prevail.

If the worker opts to keep his contract as is provided in section 79(1), his contract is suspended. This is contrary to the rules of the general law, which would in the circumstances, deem the contract frustrated by *force majeure* caused by an act of state, viz., the calling of the worker or employer to compulsory military service. However, an exception should be made in the case of the employer, whose personal performance of his obligations or personal qualities are not material to the contract.[58]

In Sudan there is no compulsory military service. This accounts for the lack of provisions, similar to those in section 79 of the U.A.R. Labour Code.[59]

(e) Strikes, lock-outs and other work stoppage

There is no provision in the U.A.R. Labour Code, to show the effect of a strike on the contract of employment, apart from what can be deduced from section 67 thereof.[60] This section entitles the employer to suspend the contract of the worker, who is "accused of the misdemeanour of participating in or the incitement of an unlawful strike," if the employer does not choose to justifiably terminate the contract,[61] as he is entitled to do under the general law. In other words, an unlawful strike[62] does not *ipso facto* frustrate the contract. On the other hand, under the rules of the general law, a lawful strike[62] suspends

[58] *Vide* Rashed and Hashem, pp. 289–90.

[59] Under the English Common Law, the call to military service, frustrates the contract: *vide Marshall v. Glanville* (1917) 2 K.B. 97. The statutory right of the worker to reinstatement, by virtue of the Reinstatement in Civil Employment Act of 1944 (as later on embodied in the National Service Act of 1948), "is independent of a contract of service," and is not permanent (*vide* Cooper, pp. 311 and 312). Cf. section 1639 H(3) of the Netherlands Civil Code, as amended in 1953.

[60] *Vide* the section quoted in part C of this Section of the present Chapter, *supra*.

[61] *Vide* Butros and Rajab, p. 340; Habeeb, pp. 472–3; and Sabbour, p. 373.

[62] In order to ascertain whether a strike is lawful or not, reference should be made to Book V of the Labour Code, concerning conciliation and arbitration in labour disputes,

the contract;[63] and this rule was not touched by the Labour Code.

In Sudan there are no legal provisions equivalent to section 67 of the U.A.R. Labour Code. However, the effects of a lawful and an unlawful strike[64] are similar to their effects in the U.A.R.[65]

The effect of a lock-out or any other work stoppage by the employer on the contract of employment, is not provided for in the U.A.R. Labour Code. Under the general law, it is submitted that, subject to the provisions of section 692 of the Civil Code,[66] the effect of a temporary work stoppage is that of suspension, if it is due to *force majeure*, and that of a breach if it is due to a lesser cause. As a lock-out does not result from *force majeure*, its effect is that of a breach of contract. However, section 209(2) of the Labour Code[67] obliges the employer to secure the Labour Minister's consent, before he stops the work for compelling reasons. This applies not only to lock-outs, but also to any work stoppage, whether temporary or permanent, partial or total. As the compelling reasons do not always arise from *force majeure*, the employer is, as it were, provided by section 209(2) with a partial relief from the liability for the breach of his workers' contracts. However, the employ-

to the wartime order No. 75 of 1940 (kept effective by Decree Law No. 102 of 1945), and to section 374 of the Penal Code, concerning the leaving or stoppage of work, which fulfils a public need.

[63] *Vide* Cairo Court of Arbitration in dispute No. 128 of 1954 (in Butros and Rajab, p. 340); and *vide* El-Areef, p. 298; Butros and Rajab, p. 343; Habeeb, p. 471; Sabbour, p. 373; Badawi, K.M., p. 387; and Rashed and Hashem, p. 262.

On the other hand, Badawi, K.M., pp. 387–8; and Rashed and Hashem, pp. 262–3, maintain that a lawful strike should entitle the employer to terminate the contract of a limited duration, as he is entitled to do with this and the unlimited contract, when the worker goes on an unlawful strike. The reasoning behind their contention, is that the worker bound by a limited contract, "should be taken to have renounced striking during the contracted period; so if he joins the strikers, he violates his contractual obligations" (Badawi). Sabbour, p. 373; Butros and Rajab, p. 340; and Habeeb, p. 472, are of the contrary opinion, because striking lawfully is a legal right for the worker, which he cannot renounce. It is submitted that there is nothing to preclude the worker from agreeing not to strike. But the mere entry by the worker into a limited contract, does not amount to his renunciation of the right to strike. The limitation of the contract is only relevant to the manner of termination of the contract.

[64] *Vide* the Trade Disputes Act of 16 February 1960 (in the *Laws of the Sudan*, Title XXII, Sub-Title 7), and particularly section 16 thereof, for the determination of the legality of a strike. *Vide* the Canadian Supreme Court decision on 25 June 1962 (in I.L.R., Vol. 87, 1963, p. 229).

[65] *Vide* the Indian case of *East Indian Railway Co. & anr. v. Shewbex Roy Ghanshyamdas* (1925) 32 C.W.N. 805.

[66] *Vide* the section quoted in footnote 10 to Chapter I, *supra*.

[67] Section 209(2) provides that "the employer shall not stop the work either wholly or in part unless he is compelled to do so by serious reasons and after he secures the consent of the Minister of Labour to whom he should apply by registered letter, and the Minister shall decide thereon within thirty days after the receipt thereof, provided that if the said period of time expires (without the Minister's decision), the employer may stop the work." *Vide* also section 374 of the Penal Code, which prohibits any stoppage in certain employment essential to the public. *Vide* section 21 of the Tunisian Labour Code.

er's obligation to obtain the Minister's consent limits his power under the general law, to stop the work when there is *force majeure*. If the employer does not secure the Minister's consent, the lock-out or work stoppage is illegal, and results in the breach of the worker's contracts.

In Sudan there are also no provisions to show the effect of a lock-out or other work stoppage, on the contract of employment. Reference to the English Common Law reveals that, if a work stoppage is occasioned by an act of God or *vis major*, as when a mine becomes unsafe,[68] the contract is suspended. But if there is neither, a breach of the contract results, unless the employer is expressly or impliedly authorized to suspend the contract.[69] When there is a dispute, as defined in section 2 of the 1960 Trade Disputes Act,[70] the employer in Sudan is permitted to declare a total or partial lock-out, if thereby he does not violate the provisions of section 16 thereof.[71] This statutory permission is free from the authorization provisions, prescribed in the U.A.R.

(f) Death

Section 697 of the U.A.R. Civil Code provides:

"The contract of employment shall not be frustrated by the death of the employer unless his personal qualities were taken into consideration in the making of the contract; but the contract shall be frustrated by the death of the worker.[72]

"The frustration of the contract by the worker's death or his long sickness or any other *force majeure* which precludes the worker from continuing with his work shall be governed by the provisions of the special laws."

These special laws are mainly the labour laws. Apart from what we have seen in section 81(1) of the Labour Code,[73] whose provisions deem the contract frustrated by the worker's death, there is no other relevant provision. Even this section adds nothing to section 697(1) of the Civil Code. So one of these two sections is redundant. On the other hand,

[68] *Vide Browning & ors. v. Crumlin Valley Collieries Ltd.* (1926) I K.B. 522.

[69] *Vide* Barwell and Kar, p. 339; Batt, p. 193; and Smith, p. 70.

[70] A trade dispute "means a dispute between employers and workers, or between employers and employers or between workers and workers which is connected with the employment or non-employment or with the terms of employment or with the conditions of labour of the same employers and workers."

[71] Section 16 prohibits a lock-out before negotation, or while conciliation or arbitration procedures are taking place, in accordance with the Act.

[72] Section 923 of the Iraqi Civil Code contains similar provisions.

[73] *Vide* the section quoted in part A of this Section of the present Chapter, *supra*. *Vide* also footnote 14, *supra*, section 14(c) of the Tunisian Labour Code, and section 1639 L of the Netherlands Civil Code.

there is no provision in the Labour Code concerning the employer's death. So section 697(1) remains to be the only relevant provision. That an employer's personal qualities and personal performance are material to the contract, is clear in such cases as the contract of a doctor and his nurse, or of the advocate and his clerk.[74] The frustration of the contract by the worker's death is in line with the general law. But the general saving of the contract from frustration by the employer's death, is contrary to the general law, which considers the death of either party to be a frustrating *force majeure.*

In Sudan section 12 of the Sudan Ordinance provides that, "unless otherwise expressly provided in the contract every contract of service shall terminate on the death of the employer... provided that the employed person shall be entitled to all the benefits of the contract up to such termination as provided in this ordinance, including due notice in accordance with section 10."[75] The English Common Law holds the contract frustrated by the employer's death.[76] This means that the worker is not entitled to a notice of termination or a payment in lieu. So the Sudan provision is not in line with the English Common Law. On the other hand, the Sudan Ordinance does not provide for the effect of the worker's death on the contract. This seems to have been left for reference to the English Common Law. This Law deems the contract frustrated by the worker's death, as it is frustrated by the employer's death, because both of them should carry out their obligations personally: *actio personalis moritur cum persona.*[77]

So the contract is fully frustrated by the worker's death, both in the U.A.R. and Sudan. The employer's death can in certain circumstances fully frustrate the contract in the U.A.R.; whereas in Sudan such frustration always occurs, but the worker is entitled to the payment in lieu of the notice.

(g) Bankruptcy, winding up and closing down of the establishment

Section 85 of the U.A.R. Labour Code deems the contract terminated, by the "winding up, bankruptcy and the authorized final closing down"[78]

[74] *Vide* Cairo Court of Cassation in case No. 780 of 1953; and the Alexandria Court of Appeal in appeal No. 305 of 1955 (both in Habeeb, p. 444).

[75] Section 17(a) of the Bahraini Labour Code contains similar provisions; cf. section 13(1, b) of the Adenese Ordinance.

[76] *Vide Farron v. Wilson*, L.R. 4C.P. 744; and *Davidson v. Reeves* (1892), 8 T.L.R. 391; *vide* also Diamond, p. 217; Macdonell, p. 235; and Smith, pp. 140–1.

[77] *Vide Hall v. Wright* (1859) E.B. & E. 746; *vide* also Cheshire and Fifoot, p. 470; Diamond, pp. 216–7; Cooper, p. 47; and Barwell and Kar, pp. 61–2.

[78] Authorisation of the closing down should be secured, as provided in section 209(2) of the Labour Code (*vide* footnote 67, *supra*).

of the establishment, in which the worker concerned is employed. But this "shall not constitute a bar to the fulfilment of all obligations."[79] Thus the employer is obliged to give a notice of termination or to pay in lieu, as prescribed in section 72 of the Labour Code. This is in line with the general law.

Under the general law, bankruptcy of the employer does not frustrate the contract, but deems the termination of the contract to be a termination by the bankrupt.[80] If *force majeure* causes the bankruptcy, it is the former and not the latter which frustrates the contract.[81] The winding up of the establishment has a similar effect on the contract, whether it is a compulsory or a voluntary winding up.[82] The effect of *force majeure* which causes the compulsory winding up, is similar to that which causes the bankruptcy.[83] The same rules apply to the dissolution of a partnership, in which the worker is employed,[84] unless it is agreed otherwise.[85] The authorized final closing down of the establishment has also the same effect on the contract; and the *force majeure* which causes it, has the same effect which it has, in causing a bankruptcy or a winding up.

In Sudan section 12 of the Sudan Ordinance provides that, "unless otherwise expressly provided in the contract every contract of service shall terminate..., if the employer is a firm or a company, on the dissolution or winding up thereof..., provided that the employed person shall be entitled to all the benefits of the contract up to such termination as provided in this ordinance, including due notice in accordance with section 10."[86] Thus, as in the U.A.R., the employer is obliged to give

[79] *Vide* section 85 quoted in footnote 69 to Chapter II, *supra*.

[80] El-Areef, pp. 318–9; Rashed and Hashem, p. 323; Faheem, p. 119; El-Fakahani, 1959 Supplement, p. 327; Murad, pp. 395–6; and Sabbour, p. 421, are of the same opinion.

[81] *Vide* the French decision of Trib. Civ. de Rouen of 10 June 1929, Gaz. du Palais, 1929, 2,445 (in I.S.D.L., Vol. 5, 1930, pp. 81–2), in which it was held that the employer's bankruptcy does not constitute a frustrating *force majeure*, because it is "due to his own fault and negligence"; *vide* also El-Areef, p. 319. El-Fakahani, 1959 Supplement, p. 327, maintains without reasoning, that the contract is not frustrated by the employer's bankruptcy even if it be caused by a *force majeure*. It is submitted that he is wrong.

[82] *Vide* El-Areef, p. 401; Faheem, p. 119; and *vide* Sabbour, pp. 428–9.

[83] *Vide* the French decision in *Comptoir d'excompte et autres v. Duboisset* (1937), D.H. 1937, p. 330 (in I.S.D.L., Vol. 13, 1939, p. 99), in which it was held that the winding up of an employer's business cannot be assimilated to a case of *force majeure*. *Vide* footnote 80, *supra*, for the wrong view of El-Fakahani, which he also maintains, in the case of winding up.

[84] Section 528 of the Civil Code provides that "the partnership shall be dissolved by the death of one of the partners or by a judicial attachment on him or by his bankruptcy." Section 529 thereof provides for the dissolution of the partnership, by the withdrawal of one of the partners, or by the agreement of the partners.

[85] *Vide* section 528 of the Civil Code.

[86] Section 17(a) of the Bahraini Labour Code contains similar provisions.

the notice of termination or to pay in lieu. This is in line with the English Common Law.

Under this Law, a compulsory winding up "operates as a termination of the contracts of service of the company's employees, such order being itself a notice of dismissal."[87] A voluntary winding up also "operates as a notice of dismissal if it involves a termination of the servant's employment by the company."[88] The dissolution of a partnership has the same effect on the contract.[89]

Neither the bankruptcy of the employer nor the closing down of the establishment are mentioned in section 12 of the Sudan Ordinance. Reference to the English Common Law, for their effects on the contract, reveals that neither frustrates the contract.[90]

SECTION II: TERMINATION OF THE CONTRACT

(a) Legal termination

Under the rules of the general law in the U.A.R. and Sudan, a limited contract[91] terminates by the expiry of the stipulated period or season, or by the performance of the work agreed upon.[92] On the other hand, a limited and an unlimited contract[91] are terminable by the Court at the instance of either party, for the other party's failure to carry out his obligations,[93] or by the agreement of both parties.[94] However, the English Common Law implies a term in the unlimited contract, that it is terminable by reasonable notice, if the contract or custom does not provide for such notice;[95] and recognizes for both parties, an extra-

[87] Batt, p. 86; *vide* also Diamond, p. 204; Cooper, p. 48; and Samuels, p. 17.

[88] Halsbury, Vol. 25, p. 484; *vide* also Cooper, p. 48; deduce from Diamond, p. 203; Samuels, p. 17; Batt, p. 86; and Smith, p. 136.

[89] *Vide* Cooper, pp. 47; Diamond, p. 204–5; Batt, pp. 79–81; and Halsbury, Vol. 25, pp. 483–4.

[90] For the effect of the employer's bankruptcy, vide Batt, p. 83; Diamond, pp. 203 and 218–9; Cooper, p. 48; Smith, p. 136; Halsbury, Vol. 25, p. 484; and Clark, p. 32. For the effect of the closing down of the establishment, *vide* Diamond, p. 214.

[91] *Vide* Section III of Chapter II, *supra*, re duration of the contract.

[92] *Vide* section 148 of the U.A.R. Civil Code. For Sudan, *vide* Cheshire and Fifoot, p. 442 *et seq.*

[93] *Vide* section 157 of the U.A.R. Civil Code. For Sudan, *vide* Cheshire and Fifoot, p. 488 *et seq.*

[94] *Vide* section 147 of the U.A.R. Civil Code. For Sudan, *vide* Cheshire and Fifoot, p. 452 *et seq.*

[95] *Vide Ryan v. Jenkinson* (1835) 25 L. J.Q.B. II; and *Re African Association, Ltd., and Allen,* (1910) I K.B. 396; and *vide* the Indian cases of *Nagpur Electric Light & Power Co. Ltd. v. Anand,* I.L.R. 1944 Nag. 66; and *Sundaresan V.C.O. & Berar,* A.I.R., 1946 Nag. 273; *vide* also Diamond, pp. 179–80; Cooper, p. 53; Samuels, pp. 10–11; Smith, p. 44; and Halsbury, Vol. 25, p. 488. The implication of the said term by the English Common Law, has been necessitated by the same motive, which necessitated the departure in the U.A.R., from the rules of the general law; "... its primary object,"

judicial remedy to summarily determine the contract without notice in certain circumstances, including the failure of the other party to carry out his contractual obligations.[96] We shall now discuss the effect on these rules, of the labour legilsators' interference in the two countries.

(1) Termination of limited contracts

Section 679(1) of the U.A.R. Civil Code provides that, "if the contract of employment is made for a definite period it shall *ipso jure* terminate on the expiry of its period."[97] Section 680(1) of the Code provides that, "if the contract is made for the performance of specific work it shall terminate when the work is completed."[98] Section 694 of the Code provides that "the contract of employment shall terminate on the expiry of its period or the completion of the work contracted upon." The redundancy of this section in the Code is clear. On the other hand, the provisions in these three sections, preserve the rules of the general law.[99]

If a limited contract contains a term, that it is terminable by a notice of a certain length, it terminates on the expiry of the duration of the contract, even though the notice has not been given.[100]

Contracts for life and long-term contracts for more than five years,[91] are by virtue of section 678(2) of the Civil Code, terminable only by the worker, after the lapse of five years, by the service of six months notice upon the employer. In this the legislator has departed from the rules of the general law.

In Sudan there is no direct provision on the termination of the limited contracts. However, it can be deduced from sections 11 and 10(1) of the Sudan Ordinance,[101] that a contract for a specified period of time and a contract for specific work, terminate on the expiry of the period and the completion of the work, respectively. This deduction is possible only by reference to the English Common Law, whose rules are similar to the rules of the general law in the U.A.R.[102]

says Diamond (pp. 179–80), "is to enable the servant to obtain similar employment elsewhere, or the master to obtain a servant" (*vide* footnote 105, *infra*, and the related text).

[96] *Vide* Batt, p. 60 *et seq.*, and pp. 189–90 and 197–8; *vide* also *Spain v. Arnott* (1817), 2 Stark. 256.

[97] *Vide* similar provisions in section 915(1) of the Iraqi Civil Code, and section 14 of the Tunisian Labour Code; *vide* also section 1639 F of the Netherlands Civil Code, as amended in 1953.

[98] *Vide* similar provisions in section 916(1) of the Iraqi Civil Code, and section 14 of the Tunisian Labour Code.

[99] *Vide* Sabbour, p. 328

[100] *Vide* footnotes 24 and 39 to Chapter II, *supra*.

[101] *Vide* section 11 in footnote 71 to Chapter II, *supra*, and section 10(1) in this Chapter, *infra*.

[102] *Vide* Diamond, p. 214.

By the rules of the English Common Law, a limited contract terminates on the expiry of its period, even though any notice prescribed therefor in the contract is not served, exactly as is the position in the U.A.R.[103]

Contracts for life or long-term contracts are not terminable by notice, unless the contract or a binding custom provides otherwise, or the servility of the worker is involved. In this the legislator has not interfered.

(2) Termination of unlimited contracts by either party with notice

Section 694 of the U.A.R. Civil Code provides that, "if the contract duration is not limited by agreement or the type or purpose of the work either party may terminate his relationship with the other provided that the exercise of this right shall be preceded by a notice whose manner of service and duration shall be provided for in the special laws."[104]

Section 72 of the Labour Code provides that, "if the contract duration is unlimited either party may terminate the contract after he serves a notice in writing upon the other party thirty days before the termination in the case of the workers appointed on monthly wages and fifteen days in the case of other workers."[105]

This unilateral power of termination was first prescribed by the 1883 Civil Code. This prescription constituted then a departure from the rules of the general law. It was necessitated by the fear that the contract would otherwise become perpetual and would prejudice the freedom of work or of employment.[106]

[103] *Vide Langeton v. Carleton* (1873), 9 Ex. 57; and *vide* footnote 39 to Chapter II, *supra.*

[104] *Vide* similar provisions, in section 917 of the Iraqi Civil Code.

[105] Cf. the provisions, in sections 95(1), 54, 18, 16, 13 & 50, 15(1 & 2) and 14, of the Iraqi, Kuwaiti, Qatari, Jordanian, Lebanese, Libyan and Tunisian Labour Codes, respectively, and in section 12 of the Saudi Regulations; *vide* also sections 347 of the Swiss Code de Obligations, and 1639 G of the Netherlands Civil Code. Section 16 of the Jordanian Labour Code contains a peculiar pre-condition to the exercise of the right of termination by notice, viz. the passing in service of six and three months, by the monthly paid and other workers, respectively. Section 23 of Book I of the French Labour Code (as amended by an Act dated 19 February 1958 – *vide* I. & L., Vol. 20, 1958, pp. 272–3), contains such peculiar pre-condition. Section 15(1) of the Libyan Labour Code, makes the notice of termination equal in length, to the pay-periods of the wages; *vide* in this respect, sections 1639 I, J and K of the Netherlands Civil Code. *Vide* the *Labour Survey of North Africa*, p. 211, for the provisions in Algeria and Morocco.

[106] *Vide* Cairo Labour Court in case No. 5282 of 1959 (in El-Hawwari, p. 187); *vide* also Murad, p. 403; Rashed and Hashem, pp. 159 and 191; and Sabbour, p. 328 – So the notice provision is for the benefit of both parties: *vide* El-Areef, p. 335; Murad, p. 403; Rashed and Hashem, p. 167; Butros and Rajab, p. 381; Habeeb, p. 477; and El-Fakahani, Book I, Vol. I, p. 642. An agreement to partially or totally relieve the worker of the notice or of the payment in lieu, is valid by virtue of section 6 of the Labour Code (*vide* Section V of Chapter II, *supra*), because such agreement affords to him more favourable treatment than that of the Labour Code. But an agreement to so relieve the employer is invalid by

The requirement that the notice should be in writing, does not render an oral termination ineffective,[107] though the terminating party would be subject to the mischief of the Code, and may thereby prejudice his cause in a suit for unjustifiable termination.

Whether the notice can be given by the employer, so as to run concurrently with the worker's annual leave, does not seem to have been fully mooted.[108] It is submitted that the answer to the query is in the negative, because the annual leave and the notice are prescribed for two different objects, by two different legal provisions.[109] Service of the notice by the employer during the worker's sickness, is expressly prohibited by section 81 of the Labour Code.[110]

The contract *prima facie* subsists until the expiry of the notice; and in the meanwhile, both parties should carry out their contractual obligations.[111] However, section 695(1) of the Civil Code provides that

virtue of the same section. An agreement to provide for a notice longer than that prescribed in section 72, would presumably be invalid, for it is less favourable to the worker, when he wants to terminate the contract; *vide*, however, Cairo Court of Appeal in appeal No. 625 of 1955 (in El-Fakahani, Book I, Vol. I, p. 647), where it was presumed that the longer notice was favourable to the worker and was valid. It is submitted that this decision is wrong. *Vide* sections 917(2), 918(3) and 920 of the Iraqi Civil Code.

[107] *Vide* Cairo Labour Court in case No. 2966 of 1953 (in El-Fakahani, Book I, Vol. I, p. 641); and *vide* Butros and Rajab, p. 380; Badawi, Z., Vol. I, p. 86; and Naguib and Bakr, p. 133; *vide* also section 90 of the Civil Code. Murad, p. 404, merely states that an oral notice is not sufficient. El-Fakahani, 1959 Supplement, pp. 214–5, shows that he does not appreciate the problem involved, by dismissing it as non-existing, in view of the provisions of section 72, re writing.

[108] The only decision found by the writer on the question, is the old decision of the Mixed Courts, decided on 8 December 1948 (in El-Areef, p. 338 footnote 2). The decision answered the question in the affirmative; and El-Areef supports this answer, without reasoning.

[109] *Vide* the French decision in *Bonnières et Colombes v. Viguier* (1937), Gaz. du Palais, 1937, I, p. 387 (in I.S.D.L., Vol. 13, 1939, p. 123); and *vide* I. & L., Vol. 4m 1950, p. 296. Sections 52 and 52(3) of the Qatari and Lebanese Labour Codes, respectively, expressly provide as is submitted above.

[110] *Vide* the section quoted in Section I, A, of this Chapter, *supra*. Sections 14 of the Saudi Regulations, and 96 and 52(3) of the Iraqi and Lebanese Labour Codes, respectively, expressly provide to the same effect; and so does section 1639 H of the Netherlands Civil Code, provided that the duration of the sickness should be less than two years.

[111] *Vide* Cairo Labour Court in case No. 1103 of 1956 (in El-Fakahani, Book I, Volume I, p. 646); and Alexandria Court of Appeal in appeal No. 167 of 1957 (in Habeeb, p. 483); *vide* also Murad, p. 407; El-Areef, p. 335; Badawi, K.M., p. 286; Butros and Rajab, p. 132; and Rashed and Hashem, p. 161. *Vide* the two French decisions in *Dumont v. L'Ami du Peuple (1932)*, Dalloz Hebdom, 1933, p. 79; and *Manufacture Lyonnaise de Chaussures du Sud-Est v. Mrs. Brunet* (1927), Gaz. du Palais, 1927, 2, 395 (both in I.S. D.L., Vol 9, 1935, p. 81, and Vol. 3, 1928, p. 102, respectively).

If the employer agrees to grant some time-off to the worker, during the notice period, so as to enable him to look for another job, or if there is an effective custom which sanctions the granting of such time-off, the worker will not be paid wages therefor, unless the employer agrees to pay or the custom prescribes payment (*vide* El-Areef, p. 340; and Zaki, pp. 383–4). Section 959 of the Draft Civil Code of 1948, expressly provided for the said time-off, to the tone of nine hours per week. But the section was not adopted, though the Mixed Courts had already adopted the French *Usage des deux heures* "if the contract is made for an unlimited period, and either party, terminates it without giving notice or before the expiry of the notice he shall pay to the other party a compensation for the notice period or the unexpired portion thereof and without prejudice to the provisions of the special laws the said compensation shall include all ascertainable and regular payments in addition to the fixed wages."[112] Section 72 of the Labour Code further provides that, "if the contract is terminated without the said notice the terminating party shall pay to the other party a compensation equal to the worker's wages for the period of the notice or the remainder thereof."[113] From these two sections, it can be deduced that the non-service of the prescribed notice or the total or partial non-observance of a served notice does not invalidate the termination of the contract.[114] In this case, however, the termination of the contract takes effect immediately on the exercise by the party concerned of his choice to pay in lieu, and not on the expiry of the prescribed notice or of the balance thereof.[115]

The statutory fixing of the compensation for the notice, without reference to any actual loss and without imposing a duty on the worker to minimize his loss by looking for other work, constitutes a departure from the rules of the general law.[116] The calculation of this compensa-

(*vide* Habeeb, p. 483; *vide* also El-Areef, p. 340; and Zaki, pp. 383–4). Section 143 of Law 279 of 1946 in Syria, which was supplemented by the U.A.R. Labour Code, also contained a similar express provision. The non-adoption of this provision in the Labour Code, is without justification. Sections 19(b) and 51, of the Qatari and Lebanese Labour Codes, respectively, provide for the said time-off; and *vide Labour Survey of North Africa*, p. 211, for similar provisions in Tunisia and Morocco. *Vide* I.L.R., Vol. 80, 1959, p. 270. for the provisions in Germany; *vide* also I.L.R., Vol. 32, 1936, p. 195. The I.L.O.'s Report No. V(1) of 1963, provides for the said time-off, in the *Proposed Recommendation Concerning Termination Of The Contract At The Initiative Of The Employer.*

112 *Vide* similar provisions in section 918(1) of the Iraqi Civil Code.

113 *Vide* similar provisions, in sections 54, 16, 13 and 53, and 15(3), of the Kuwaiti, Jordanian, Lebanese and Libyan Labour Codes, respectively, and in section 12 of the Saudi Regulations. Section 19 of the Qatari Labour Code gives the choice to pay in lieu of the notice, only to the employer. Section 95(2) of the Iraqi Labour Code provides to the same effect; but section 95(4) penalizes the worker, who does not serve the notice, by the loss of "half of all the sums due to the worker under the provisions of this law." This peculiar penalty has no counterpart in the other Arab Labour Codes. *Vide* I.L.R., Vol. 79, 1959, p. 631, for the law in France.

114 *Vide* Murad, p. 405; Badawi, K.M., p. 282; El-Areef, pp. 333 and 339; Rashed and Hashem, p. 171; and Habeeb, p. 479.

115 *Vide* the French case of *Romestant v. Pical* (1936), Gaz. du Palais, 1937, 1, 142 (in I.S.D.L., Vol. 12, 1938, p. 152), in which it was held that a worker dismissed without notice, can insist on the payment in lieu of the notice, and can refuse to go back to work, because the employer cannot alone re-establish the legal relationship, which he has broken.

116 *Vide* section 221 of the Civil Code. Before the enactment of the Civil Code (section 695), the Mixed Courts used to apply the rules of the general alw, to the payment in lieu of the notice: *vide* a relevant decision on 18 May 1938 (in Habeeb, p. 480). The departure from these rules, was justified by "the compensation also connoting a penalty"

tion is based on the worker's wages which he would have received, had he worked through the period of notice.[117]

Finally, it has been judicially held, though only once to the knowledge of the writer, that neither the notice nor the payment in lieu is due, when the unlimited contract is terminated by the agreement of the parties,[118] unless of course the parties agree otherwise. It is, however, submitted that section 6 of the Labour Code[119] invalidates such a decision, in so far as the worker is deprived of the notice which the employer is obliged to give by virtue of section 72 of the Code. The case would be otherwise, if, during the currency of an unlimited contract, the parties agree to transform it to a limited contract, subsequently terminable by the effluxion of time. The non-coincidence of the termination by effluxion with the date of the said agreement, precludes the operation of section 6 of the Code.[120]

In Sudan section 10(1) of the Sudan Ordinance provides:

"Subject as hereinafter provided, every contract of service wherein no agreement respecting notice of longer duration is expressed, not being a contract to perform some specific work without reference to time, shall be determinable by either party:

(a) where the employed person is engaged on the basis of a monthly wage, at the expiration of one month's notice which may be given at any time;

(b) where the employed person is engaged on the basis of a weekly wage:

(i) if he has completed less than two years of continuous service[121] at the expiration of one week's notice which may be given at any time;

(ii) if he has completed two, but less than five years of continuous service, at the expiration of two weeks' notice which may be given at any time;

(*vide* the Explanatory Note to section 961(1) of the Draft Civil Code, which was enacted as section 695(1) of the Civil Code); *vide* also I.L.R., Vol. 32, 1936, p. 204; and I.L.O. Report VII(1) of 1962, pp. 27–8.

[117] *Vide* Section I of Chapter IV, *supra*, for the definition and components of wages.

[118] *Vide* Cairo Court of Cassation in case No. 1770 of 1953 (in El-Fakahani, Book I, Vol. I, p. 644); the writers who advocate the same view, are Murad, p. 388; El-Areef, pp. 315, 334 and 400; El-Fakahani, 1959 Supplement, p. 214; Husseini and Hawwari, p. 335; and Sabbour, p. 324 (though only impliedly). Habeeb, p. 481, advocates the same view; but is against it in p. 420.

[119] *Vide* the section quoted in Section V of Chapter II, *supra*; *vide* also Article 12 of the I.L.O. Convention No. 64 of 1939.

[120] El-Areef, p. 411, says that an agreement to terminate an unlimited contract, "actually amounts to the transformation of the contract into a limited contract"; Rashed and Hashem, p. 184, support this view. It is submitted that this indirect justification by him, of the worker's non-entitlement to notice or payment in lieu, is not legally warranted.

[121] Section 2 of the Sudan Ordinance defines 'continuous service,' as "continuous service with the same employer..."

(bA) where the employed person is engaged on the basis of a fortnightly wage and has completed less than five years of continuous service, at the expiration of two weeks' notices which may be given at any time;
(c) where the employed person is engaged on the basis of a daily wage, whether paid daily or not:

(i) if he has not completed six months of continuous service, at the close of any day without notice;
(ii) if he has completed six months but less than two years of continuous service, at the expiration of one week's notice, which may be given at any time;
(iii) if he has completed two but less than five years of continuous service, at the expiration of two weeks' notice which may be given at any time;

(d) where the employed person in engaged on the basis of a daily, weekly or fortnightly wage and has completed not less than five years of continuous service, at the expiration of one month's notice which may be given at any time."[122]

With the exception of the provision in (c, i), the section is in line with the English Common Law.

Contrary to the position in the U.A.R., there is no requirement that the notice should be in writing. This is also in line with the English Common Law, which sanctions an oral notice even though the contract provides for written notice.[123]

Under the English Common Law, the notice can run concurrently with the annual leave[124] or the sick leave[125]. However, it is submitted that this should not be the case in Sudan, because the annual leave, the sick leave and the notice are prescribed for different objects, by different legal provisions with penal sanctions, much the same as was submitted concerning the concurrence of the annual leave with the notice in the U.A.R.

As in the U.A.R, the contract *prima facie* subsists during the notice period in Sudan.[126] There are no provisions equivalent to sections 695(1)

[122] *Vide* similar provisions, in section 12(a) of the Bahraini Labour Code. In Aden section 12(1) of the Adenese Ordinance makes the termination by notice, subject to the consent of the authorized officer. This is in line with Article 12(3) of the I.L.O. Convention No. 64 of 1939.

[123] *Vide Latchford Premier Cinema v. Ennion* (1931) 2 Ch. 409; *vide* also Samuels, p. 11; Batt, p. 59; and Barwell and Kar, p. 358.

[124] *Vide Yardley v. Laws* (1957), Current Law Yearbook No. 1260, quoted by O. Kahn-Freund, in p. 274 of the *British Legal Papers*.

[125] *Vide* Cooper, p. 49; and Samuels, p. 12.

[126] It is submitted that the law in Sudan, would treat any time-off which the worker takes during the notice period, in order to look for other work, as the law in the U.A.R. treats it (*vide* footnote 110, *supra*).

and 72(2) of the U.A.R.[127] However, under the English Common Law, the payment in lieu of the notice by the employer is valid, unless the employer is obliged by the contract, not only to pay remuneration, but also to provide work to the worker.[128] But the worker does not have a corresponding right of such payment in lieu, because "it is not wages but services to which the master is entitled."[129] On the other hand, the non-service of the notice constitutes a breach of the contract. The damages which may be awarded therefor, are not necessarily equal to the wages for the period of the prescribed notice, contrary to what we saw in the U.A.R. They may be less or more, depending on the actual loss suffered by the party aggrieved, who in addition has a duty to minimize the damage.[130]

Finally, the English Common Law holds that "the termination of a contract by consent is good whether the stipulated notice is given or not."[131] It is, however, submitted that section 35 of the Sudan Ordinance[132] precludes the application of the Common Law rule; and that the position in Sudan should be similar to that in the U.A.R., concerning the effect of an agreement to transform an unlimited contract to a limited contract.

Presumably, both in the U.A.R. and Sudan the entitlement to the payment in lieu of the notice, arises only when the contract is terminable by notice. We shall now discuss the cases in which either party may terminate an unlimited contract without notice, or a limited contract before its expiry, and the cases in which the employer may alone so terminate the contract.

(3) Termination by either party of unlimited contracts without notice or limited contracts before expiry

(i) Failure to carry out contractual obligations. Section 76(6) of the U.A.R. Labour Code provides that "the employer shall not terminate the contract without serving notice upon the worker and without paying the termination gratuity[133] or without compensation... (unless) the

[127] Section 12(b) of the Bahraini Labour Code is similar to section 72(2) of the U.A.R.
[128] *Vide Konski v. Peet* (1915) I Ch. 530.
[129] Batt, p. 198; and *vide* p. 191 thereof.
[130] *Vide* the Sudan case of *El-Sayed El-Hag El-Dosh v. President, Ahlia Intermediate School* (1958), AC-Revision-164-58 (in the S.L.J.R., 1958, p. 75); *vide* also the two English decisions in *Brace v. Calder* (1895) 2 Q.B. 253; and *Reid v. Explosives Co.*, 19 Q.B.D. 264; and *vide* Macdonell, p. 191; Smith, pp. 122–3; and Barwell and Kar, p. 410.
[131] Diamond, p. 173, footnote 45.
[132] *Vide* the section quoted in Section V of Chapter II, *supra*.
[133] *Vide* Chapter VII, *infra*.

worker fails to carry out his essential obligations under the contract of employment."[134]

Section 77(2) of the Code provides that "the worker may leave the work before the expiry of the contract or without notice... if the employer fails to carry out his obligations towards the worker in accordance with the provisions of this Code."[135]

The provisions in these two sections constitute a departure from the rules of the general law, under which the parties are supposed to apply to the Court, which after examining all the circumstances, decides whether the contract should be terminated or not.[136] The reasons behind this departure are the personal qualities of the contract of employment, which preclude its specific performance by a judicial order, and prejudice to a great extent the continuation of the contract, while the Court is examining the matter.[137] The departure does not, however, preclude the aggrieved party from resorting to the Court, in order to have the validity of the other party's termination of the contract determined.[138]

The legislator mentions the "essential obligations under the contract of employment," in section 76(6), and the "obligations... in accordance with this Code," in section 77(2). Some writers made a distinction

[134] Cf. some similar provisions, in sections 56(b), 20(4), 74(4) and 18(e), of the Kuwaiti, Qatari, Lebanese and Libyan Labour Codes, respectively; *vide* also section 1639 P (10, 11 and 12) of the Netherlands Civil Code; and *vide* I.L.R., Vol. 79, 1959. p. 633, for the position in France. Section 14(b) of the Tunisian Labour Code entitles either party to summarily determine the contract, for a "grave mistake," meaning, it is submitted, an important reason; vide I.L.R., Vol. 80, 1959, pp. 267–8, for the similarity with Germany, in this respect.

Section 963 of the U.A.R. Draft Civil Code expressly provided for such power of termination, for both the employer and the worker (when the employer fails to carry out his obligations); but the section was not adopted.

The employer's power of termination, by virtue of section 76, is exercisable, not only when the contract is unlimited, but also when it is limited. The rules of the general law (section 157 of the Civil Code), are equally applicable to both contracts; and the labour legislator should not be taken to have differentiated between them in section 76, whereas he does not so differentiate in section 77 (to be presently quoted); Sabbour, pp. 369–70; Zaki, p. 354; Badawi, Z., Vol. I, p. 95; El-Areef, p. 327 (though only impliedly); and Rashed and Hashem, p. 207, are of the same opinion.

[135] Cf. some similar provisions, in sections 98(c, d and e), 58(a), 21(1), 18(b and c), 75(2), 20(b) and 14(b), of the Iraqi, Kuwaiti, Qatari, Jordanian, Lebanese, Libyan and Tunisian (only by deduction) Labour Codes, respectively, and in section 17(b) of the Saudi Regulations; *vide* also section 1639 Q (3–8) of the Netherlands Civil Code; and *vide* for the position in France, the French case of *Vauvrecy v. Marsil* (1925), Gaz. du Palais, 1925, 2, 729 (in I.S.D.L., Vol. 1, 1926, pp. 97–8).

[136] *Vide* footnote 93, *supra*.

[137] *Vide* Cairo Court of Cassation in case No. 415 of 1955 (in Habeeb, p. 447); *vide* also El-Areef, p. 322; Murad, p. 396; Sabbour, pp. 392–3; El-Fakahani, 1959 Supplement p. 290; Badawi, K.M., p. 278; Zaki, p. 353; Butros and Rajab, p. 414; and Rashed and Hashem, p. 255.

[138] Rashed and Hashem, pp. 246 and 248, are of the same opinion.

between the two provisions, so as to deny to the worker his right of termination, when the obligations not carried out by the employer emanate from the contract or the Civil Code.[139] It is submitted that the distinction is too artificial to sustain,[140] though it is admitted that the legislator should have used the same terms. On the other hand, the obligations in section 76(6) are qualified by essentiality,[141] whereas they are not so qualified in section 77(2). This means that the legislator deems the employer's obligations under the Labour Code to be all essential.

In Sudan section 10(2) of the Sudan Ordinance provides that "an employer may dismiss without notice an employed person for wilful disobedience of a lawful order, or gross misconduct in or connected with his employment, or serious negligence or wilful misconduct calculated seriously to injure the employer's business."[142] This general provision warrants the dismissal of the worker by the employer, for the reason mentioned in section 76(6) of the U.A.R. Labour Code. However, it does not constitute any departure from the rules of the English Common Law. "A master or servant is entitled to determine a contract of service summarily," says *A. S. Diamind*, "in case of any breach by the other party of a condition precedent, expressed or implied, in the contract."[143] A breach is constituted by the wilful failure or neglect of either party to carry out his contractual obligations, for it is a fundamental principle of the law that a person cannot 'approbate and reprobate,'[144] at the same time. Reference to the English Common Law rules is further necessary in Sudan, because the Sudan Ordinance does not give a terminating power to the worker, similar to that of the employer under section 10(2). Under these rules, the worker has a similar power.[145]

[139] Badawi, K.M., p. 411; and Sabbour, p. 399. Rashed and Hashem, p. 285, maintain the contrary opinion, without any reasoning.

[140] *Vide* Cairo Labour Court in case No. 1541 of 1959 (in El-Hawwari, p. 216).

[141] *Vide* Cairo Court of Appeal in appeal No. 1206 of 1959 (in El-Hawwari, p. 237).

[142] *Vide* similar provisions in sections 13(a) of the Bahraini Labour Code, and 7 of the Adenese Ordinance.

[143] P. 185; *vide* also *Neyger v. London Passenger Transport Board* (1935) L.J.N.C.C.R.; 46; *Harvey v. Crampain Fishing Co. Ltd.*, (1934), L.J.N. C.C.R., 405; *Boston Fishing Co, v. Ansell* (1888), 39 C.D. 339; *The Marina* (1881), 50 L.J.P. 33; *Lomax v. Arding* (1855). 10 Ex. 734; *Spotswood v. Burrow* (1850), 5 Exch. 110; *Baillie v. Kell* (1838), 6 Scott, 739; *Spain v. Arnot* (1817), 2 Stark., 256; and the Indian case of *K.R.V. Alagappa Chettiar v. Sundaram Annuvi & ors.*, 49 M.L.J. 516 (quoted by Barwell and Kar, p. 381); and *vide* Cooper, pp. 62 and 63; Samuels, p. 13; Smith, p. 80; Macdonell, p. 209; and Halsbury, Vol. 25, p. 485.

[144] Batt, p. 60; *vide also Clouston & Co. Ltd. v. Corry* (1906) A.C. 122; and *vide* Halsbury, Vol. 25, p. 516.

[145] *Vide* Diamond, p. 193, and p. 185; *vide* also *The Castilia* (1822), I Hag. Adm. 59; and *vide* Batt, p. 186; Cooper, p. 79; and Halsbury, Vol. 25, p. 488.

The terminating cause by virtue of section 10(2), should be an "act of some gravity,"[146] so as to justify termination without notice. This by deduction, is also applicable to the termination by the worker.

(ii) Misrepresentation. Section 76(1) of the U.A.R. Labour Code entitles the employer to terminate the contract without notice, "if the worker assumes a false identity or produces false testimonials or recommendations."[147]

Section 77(1) of the Code entitles the worker to leave the work, without notice or before the expiry of the contract period, "if the employer or his representative had misrepresented to him the conditions of employment at the time of making the contract."[148]

The terminating powers in these two sections, are based on the rules of the voidability of the contract because of misrepresentation.[149]

[146] *Vide* the Sudanese case of *Vassili Bamboulis v. Osman Abdulla* (1960), KHC-Revision-167-1960 (in the S.L.J..R, 1960, p. 168); *vide* also the English decision in *Gould v. Webb*, 4 E. & B. 236.

[147] Cf. some similar provisions, in sections 20(1), 17(c), 18(a) and 14(b), of the Qatari, Jordanian, Libyan and Tunisian (only by deduction) Labour Codes, respectively, and section 16(a) of the Saudi Regulations; *vide* also section 1639 P (1 and 2) of the Netherlands Civil Code. Section 74(1) of the Lebanese Labour Code grants the power of summary determination to the employer, only when the worker tenders a false statement as to his nationality.

[148] Cf. some similar provisions, in sections 98(a), 21(3), 18(a), 75(1), 20(a) and 14(b), of the Iraqi, Qatari, Jordanian, Lebanese, Libyan and Tunisian (only by deduction) Labour Codes, respectively, and in section 17(a) of the Saudi Regulations (this section limits the worker's exercise of this power to one month, after the making of the contract; the provision seems to have been copied from section 31 of Law No. 41 of 1944 of the U.A.R.).

[149] Section 125 of the U.A.R. Civil Code provides:

"The contract may be avoided for misrepresentation if the devices employed by either of the contracting parties or his representative, are of such gravity that the other party would not have entered the contract without them.

"Such misrepresentation is constituted by the wilful silence in respect of any fact or circumstance which would have precluded the deceived party from entering the contract had he known of it."

Vide Rashed and Hashem, p. 283; and Habeeb, p. 468.

In the U.A.R. opinion leans in favour of considering the summary determination of the contract by the employer, on any of the grounds mentioned in section 76, as no more than an application of the ground mentioned in section 76(6), and by the worker on any of the grounds mentioned in section 77, as no more than an application of the ground mentioned in section 77(2): *vide* El-Areef, pp. 397, 398 and 414; Zaki, p. 360; Rashed and Hashem, pp. 244, 254 and 280; and El-Fakahani, 1959 Supplement, p. 298 – *Vide* I.L.O. Report VII(1), 1962, p. 63: "In view of the gravity of a dismissal for serious misconduct, regula- tions frequently provide for additional safeguards to the worker, including, for example, a detailed definition of instances to be considered as serious misconduct"; *vide* also I.L.R., Vol. 79, 1959, p. 633. However, it is submitted that the correctness of the abovementioned opinion in the U.A.R, does not extend to the dismissal by virtue of subsection 76(1), because the misrepresentation occurs before the contract is made, or to the dismissal by virtue of 76(2), re probation, because the dismissal thereunder, does not really amount to the non-carrying out by the worker, of his essential contractual duties.

However, these powers are extra-judicial powers for the parties,[150] and in this there is a departure from the rules of the general law. The misrepresentation should in accordance therewith, go to the root of the contract.[151] The production by the worker of a false certificate, with the sole purpose of earning higher wages, was held not to have gone to the root of the contract, because it was not a material consideration in the making of the contract.[152] This, however, should not be taken as a rule of general application, as the circumstances of the case may justify a different decision.

The testimonials mentioned in section 76(1), should presumably have been made by persons other than the worker. However, it was held that they also included testimonials made by the worker himself.[153]

In Sudan section 10(2) of the Sudan Ordinance entitles the employer to summarily dismiss his worker, for "gross misconduct in or connected with his employment... or wilful misconduct calculated seriously to injure the employer's business." Reference to the English Common Law reveals that material misrepresentation by the worker at the time of making the contract, falls under misconduct, justifying the summary dismissal of the worker. "The failure to afford the requisite skill which had been expressly or impliedly promissed," says *C. M. Smith*, "is a breach of legal duty, and therefore misconduct."[154] This legal duty is "an implied warranty that he is of skill reasonably competent to the tasks he undertakes – *spondes peritiam artis*."[155] This ground of summary dismissal had been equated with the wilful failure of the worker to carry out his contractual duties. "It appears to us that there is no material difference," said *Lord Ellenborough* in *Spain v. Arnott*,[156] "between a servant who will not, and a servant who cannot perform the duty for which he was hired."

[150] *Vide* El-Fakahani, 1959 Supplement, p. 273.

[151] *Vide* Murad, pp. 374 and 398; El-Fakahani, 1959 Supplement, p. 301; and Naguib and Bakr, pp. 164–5.

[152] *Vide* Cairo Court of Cassation in cases Nos. 287 of 1954 and 324 of 1956 (in El-Fakahani, Book I, Vol. I, pp. 162 and 161, respectively); *vide* also Butros and Rajab, p. 401; and Naguib and Bakr, p. 165.

[153] *Vide* Cairo Court of Appeal in appeal No. 801 of 1955 (in El-Fakahani, Book I, Vol. I, p. 160), in which it was held that a false testimonial by the worker, as to the number of his children, with the result that the employer had to pay a bigger family allowance, was a testimonial covered by section 76(1); *vide* also El-Fakahani, 1959 Supplement, pp. 274–5.

[154] P. 90.

[155] *Willes*, J., in *Harmer V. Cornelius* (1858), 5 C.B. (N.S.) 236; and *vide* Diamond, p. 190; Cooper, p. 77; Samuels, p. 11; Macdonell, p. 214; and Halsbury, Vol. 25, p. 486; *vide* also the Indian case of *Ramaswamy Aiyar v. Madras Times Printing & Publishing Co. Ltd.*, A.I.R., 1918, Mad., 1257 (quoted by Barwell and Kar, p. 76); and *vide* Clark, pp. 3 and 27.

[156] 2 Stark 256, N.P.

The worker who has been misled as to the conditions of work, at the time of making the contract, has similar powers of summary determination of the contract, under the rules of the English Common Law.[157] This substitutes the lack of legislative provisions, in this respect, in Sudan.

The above-mentioned Common Law rules are in line with the rules relating to the rescission of all the contracts, which are voidable because of misrepresentation.[158] The deceived party can "repudiate the transaction without resort to legal proceedings... (or) he can also bring an action for rescission."[159] This differs with the rules of the general law in the U.A.R.

As in the U.A.R., the misrepresentation should go to the root of the contract.[160]

(iii) Assault. Section 76(10) of the U.A.R. Labour Code entitles the employer to terminate the contract without notice, "if the worker assaults[161] the employer or the responsible manager or commits a grave assaults on any work supervisor[162] during the work or in connection therewith."[163]

Section 77(4) of the Code entitles the worker to leave the work without notice, or before the expiry of the contract, "if the employer or his representative assaults the worker."[164]

These statutory powers of termination constitute a departure from the rules of the general law, under which the Court should decide whether the contract should be determined or not.

[157] *Vide Woodley v. Metropolitan Railways* (1877), 2 Ex. D. 384.

[158] *Vide* Cheshire and Fifoot, p. 212 *et seq.*

[159] *Ibidem*, p. 230.

[160] *Vide* Halsbury, Vol. 25, p. 485.

[161] The Arabic word used in the section, is not limited to assault in the legal sense. It covers the legal as well as any other assault, which falls under the common sense of the word.

[162] The word supervisor was defined by the Court, as the person "who can supervise and guide a number of workers": Alexandria Court of Cassation in case No. 1504 of 1958 (in El-Hawwari, p. 262); and *vide* Cairo Court of Cassation (Commercial) in case No. 1582 of 1951 (in Murad, p. 378). The supervisor does not have to be the direct supervisor of the worker.

[163] Cf. similar provisions, in sections 56(f), 20(8), 17(a), 74(7), 18(i) and 14(b), of the Kuwaiti, Qatari, Jordanian, Lebanese, Libyan and Tunisian (only by deduction) Labour Codes, respectively, and section 16(i) of the Saudi Regulations; *vide* also section 1639 P (5) of the Netherlands Civil Code; and *vide* I.L.R., Vol. 79, 1959, p. 633, and Vol. 80, 1959, p. 268, for the position of the law in France and Germany, respectively.

[164] Cf. similar provisions, in sections 58(b), 21(2), 18(d), 75(4), 20(d) and 14(b) of the Kuwaiti, Qatari, Jordanian, Lebanese, Libyan, and Tunisian (only by deduction) Labour Codes, respectively; and *vide* section 1639 Q (1) of the Netherlands Civil Code. Similar grounds lie behind the summary determination powers, to be presently mentioned.

The employer was granted the power of summary determination, because "the relationship between the employer and the worker, should be based on obedience and respect; the failure thereof prejudices the carrying out of the work, for it affects the balance between the two parties, and as a result, the employer's power of control over the establishment vanishes."[165] This also explains the qualification of the assault by the condition of gravity, when it is committed on the supervisor,[166] because he is not the person invested with the power of control over the worker. On the other hand, the non-qualification of the assault on the worker, by any condition of gravity, is, however, understandable, because no such condition was imposed on the assault on the employer, who is the other party to the contract.

The assault mentioned in both sections does not have to be physical[167] nor criminal,[168] but it has to be real and not merely a hot argument,[169] provided that, for the purposes of section 76(10), the employer does not provoke the worker's assault.[170]

In Sudan section 10(2) of the Sudan Ordinance entitles the employer to summarily dismiss his worker, for "gross misconduct in or connected

[165] Cairo Court of Cassation in case No. 3447 of 1953 (in Habeeb, p. 463); *vide* also Alexandria Court of Appeal in appeal No. 74 of 1955 (in *Ibidem*, pp. 363–4); and Cairo Court of Cassation in case No. 1253 of 1959 (in El-Hawwari, p. 272).

[166] Badawi, Z., Vol. 1, pp. 102–3, maintains that the gravity of the assault depends on whether it constitutes a punishable criminal offence or not. It is submitted that he is wrong, because a grave assault may otherwise be committed: *vide* Alexandria Court of appeal in appeal No. 140 of 1954 (in Habeeb, p. 466), where it was held that the worker committed a grave assault, when he snatched the papers from the supervisor, during a disciplinary trial and tore them to pieces; *vide* also the Alexandria Court of Cassation in case No. 1504 of 1958 (in El-Hawwari, p. 262), and vide Sabbour, p. 388; Zaki, p. 361; and Naguib and Bakr, p. 175.

[167] *Vide* Cairo Court of Cassation in case No. 1657 of 1954; and the Alexandria Court of Appeal in appeal No. 148 of 1956 (both in Habeeb, pp. 466 and 465, respectively); *vide* also Rashed and Hashem, p. 276; and Naguib and Bakr, p. 174; and *vide* Cairo Court of Cassation in case No. 1709 of 1957; and Cairo Court of Appeal in appeal No. 41 of 1959, and cf. them with Cairo Court of Cassation in case No. 1165 of 1959 (all three in El-Hawwari, pp. 267, 268 and 269, respectively).

Section 41(4) of Law 317 of 1952, which is the predecessor of section 77(4) of the Labour Code, stipulated for the physical assault on the worker.

[168] *Vide* Cairo Court of Cassation in cases Nos. 271 af 1954 and 1716 of 1955 (both in Habeeb, pp. 466 and 463, respectively); and Alexandria Court of Cassation in case No. 1504 of 1958 (in El-Hawwari, p. 262); *vide* also Murad, p. 378; El-Areef, p. 399; Badawi, K.M., p. 405; Sabbour, pp. 388–9; and Rashed and Hashem, p. 276.

[169] *Vide* Alexandria Court of Cassation in case No. 1504 of 1958; and Cairo Labour Court in case No. 5131 of 1959 (both in El-Hawwari, pp. 265 and 266, respectively).

[170] *Vide* Cairo District Court (Commercial) in case No. 1017 of 1950 (in Rashed and Hashem, p. 277); and Cairo Court of Cassation in case No. 1151 of 1959 (in El-Hawwari, p. 265); *vide* also Murad, p. 378; Badawi, K.M., pp. 397 and 405; Zaki, p. 361; Sabbour, p. 389; Butros and Rajab, p. 349; Rashed and Hashem, p. 276; and Naguib and Bakr, p. 175. El-Fakahani, 1959 Supplement, p. 289; and Sabbour, p. 389, correctly add that the worker's assault should not exceed the right of self-defence.

with his employment."[171] Under the English Common Law, the misconduct which justifies the summary dismissal of the worker, includes "insolence, criminal conduct, and other conduct inconsistent with the relationship of master and servant,"[172] whether during the performance of the work or otherwise.[173] So assault by the worker on the employer, falls under misconduct. Presumably the assault on the employer's representative or on the work supervisor, also justifies the summary dismissal of the worker.

The grounding of the misconduct on its inconsistency with the employment relationship, explains the justification for granting the power of summary determination to the employer, similar to that in the U.A.R. This also should justify the granting of the power of summary determination of the contract to the worker, when he is assaulted by the employer.

The sufficiency of the justifying assault, not only on the employer or his representative or the work supervisor but also on the worker, should depend on the gravity of the assault and all the circumstances of the case.[174] The misconduct of the worker should, in any case, be gross, as is prescribed by section 10(2) of the Sudan Ordinance.

(iv) Breach of Safety Regulations. Section 76(4) of the U.A.R. Labour Code entitles the employer to terminate the contract without notice, "if the worker in spite of a written warning does not abide by the rules prescribed for the safety of the workers and the establishment provided that these rules shall be written and displayed in a prominent place."[175]

Section 77(5) of the Code entitles the worker to leave the work without notice, or before the expiry of the contract period, "if there is a serious danger to the worker's safety or health provided that the employer had knwon of the existence of this danger and did not carry out the

[171] *Vide* the more elaborate provisions in sections 13a and 7, of the Bahraini Labour Code and the Adenese Ordinance, respectively.

[172] Diamond, p. 188.

[173] *Idem.*

[174] *Vide Smith v. Allen* (1862), 3 F. & F. 157 N.P.; and *vide* Smith, p. 83; and Barwell and Kar, p. 383.

[175] Cf. some similar provisions, in sections 97(a, c and e), 56(b), 20(3), 17(e), 18(c) and 14(b), of the Iraqi, Kuwaiti (only by deduction), Qatari, Jordanian, Libyan and Tunisian (only by deduction) Labour Codes, respectively, and section 16(d) of the Saudi Regulations, which in addition, prescribes the service of a notice of the worker's breach of the safety regulations, on the Government authorities; *vide* also section 1639 P (8) of the Netherlands Civil Code; and *vide* I.L.R., Vol. 79, 1959, p. 633, for the similar position in France.

Vide section 109 of the Labour Code, which precludes the worker, under the pain of penalty, from wilfully or negligently violating the safety rules or damaging the safety equipment.

necessary measures or the measures prescribed by the authorities concerned within the prescribed time."[176]

These powers of summary determination constitute a departure from the rules of the general law.

The words "in spite of a written warning" in section 76(4), have given rise to the question whether the dismissal of the worker can only be effected after he commits a second breach of the safety rules, preceded by a written warning served upon him after his first breach, or it can be effected after his first breach, if he had already been warned in writing of the dangers of a breach. The wording of the section warrants the first alternative,[177] for otherwise the prominent display of the written rules would have sufficed. The grave consequences which may result from a first breach and which gave rise to the second alternative, warrant an amendment of the section, but do no warrant a limited interpretation.[178]

In Sudan section 10(2) of the Sudan Ordinance entitles the employer to summarily dismiss his worker, "for wilful disobedience of a lawful order... or serious negligence... calculated seriously to injure the employer's business." Safety rules are lawful orders; so the disobedience thereto or the infraction thereof, wilfully or by serious negligence, warrants the summary dismissal.[179] This is in line with the English Common Law, which sanctions the summary dismissal of the worker for any "conduct inconsistent with the relationship of master and servant."[180]

There is no provision in the Sudan Ordinance, to grant the worker the power of summary determination of the contract. Reference to the English Common Law, however, reveals that the worker has such a power. "A servant is justified in terminating his engagement and refusing

[176] Cf. similar provisions, in sections 98(d) and 20(1, e) of the Iraqi and Libyan Labour Codes, respectively, and section 17(e) of the Saudi Regulations. Sections 58(c), 21(1), 75(2) and 14(b) of the Kuwaiti, Qatari, Lebanese and Tunisian Labour Codes, respectively, give ground to the power of summary determination by deduction. *Vide* also section 1639 Q (9) of the Netherlands Civil Code.

Vide section 108 of the Labour Code, which obliges the employer to provide the worker with free protection from the risks at work.

[177] Cairo Labour Court in case No. 5574 of 1954 (in Butros and Rajab, p. 389); *vide* also El-Areef, p. 398; and Badawi, K.M., p. 386 ,who hold the same opinion, though without reasoning.

[178] *Vide* Cairo Court of Appeal in appeal No. 410 of 1956 (in El-Fakahani, Book I, Vol. I, p. 182); *vide* also Butros and Rajab, pp. 348 and 403; and Habeeb, p. 454.

[179] *Vide* section 26 of the Workshop and Factories Regulations of 1 August, 1952 (*The Laws of the Sudan*, Vol. 8, Title XXII, Sub-Title 5), which prohibits the worker to "wilfully and without reasonable cause do anything likely to endanger himself or others, or wilfully interfere with or misuse any means, appliance or other thing provided for the safety, health or welfare" of the workers; cf. the similar provisions in section 37(b) of the Bahraini Labour Code.

[180] Diamond, p. 188.

to go on further with his work if he has a reasonable apprehension of danger to life or of personal injury."[181] This follows from the employer's duty to protect the worker from the dangers at work.[182]

(v) Criminal offences, dishonesty and immorality. Section 76(8) of the U.A.R. Labour Code entitles the employer to terminate the contract without notice, "if the worker is finally convicted of the commission of a crime or of a misdemeanour involving dishonesty breach of trust or the violation of the public morals."[183]

Section 77(3) of the Code entitles the worker to leave the work without notice, or before the expiry of the contract, "if the employer or his representative commits an immoral act on the worker or a member of his family."[184]

The employer's power under the former section, constitutes a departure from the general law, "which deems the outside behaviour of the worker out of the jursidiction of the employer's power of control... unless that behaviour seriously affects the interests of the establishment."[185] The offence under this section does not have to be related to the work.[186] On the other hand, the final conviction of any crime is

[181] Halsbury, Vol. 25, p. 488; *vide* also Diamond, p. 125; and *vide Burton v. Pinkerton* (1867), L.R. 2 Ex. 340; and *O'Neil v. Armstrong, Mitchell & Co.* (1895) 2 Q.B. 418.

[182] *Vide Bartonshill Coal Co. v. Reid* (1858) 3 Macq. 266; and *vide* Section I, F, of Chapter III, *supra*.

[183] Cf., but distinguish the somewhat similar provisions, in sections 97(f), 56 (d and e), 20(6), 17(a), 74(6), 18(9) and 14(b) of the Iraqi, Kuwaiti, Qatari, Jordanian, Lebanese, Libyan and Tunisian (only by deduction) Labour Codes, respectively, and section 16(h) of the Saudi Regulations (*vide* also the Royal Decree No. 2629/13/2/18 of 22 June 1956, which gives to the employer the power to summarily dismiss the worker, who is convicted under the Decree, of the offence of striking, incitement of strikes or of demonstrating); *vide* also section 1639 P (4 and 6) of the Netherlands Civil Code; and *vide* I.L.R., Vol. 80, 1959, p. 268, for the position of the law in Germany.

The reason behind the granting of this power to the employer, is that the misconduct of the worker "violates the moral order in the establishment and deprecates its reputation" (Zaki, p. 359). The worker's power of summary determination is a counterpart for the employer's power. This counterpart is necessary, for otherwise the employment relationship will be devoid of one of its essential elements.

[184] Cf. some similar provisions, in sections 98(b), 21(2), 20(c) and 14(b) of the Iraqi, Qatari, Libyan and Tunisian (only by deduction) Labour Codes, respectively; *vide* also section 1639 Q (2) of the Netherlands Civil Code. Sections 18(d) and 75(3) of the Jordanian and Lebanese Labour Codes, respectively, add the requirement that the act should amount to a criminal offence.

The Labour Code does not define family: *vide* in this respect, footnote 233 to Chapter I, *supra*; and *vide* section 222 of the U.A.R. Civil Code.

[185] Zaki, p. 359.

[186] *Vide* Cairo Court of Cassation in case No. 1954 of 1955 (in Habeeb, p. 459); *vide* also El-Areef, p. 399; Badawi, K.M., pp. 389 and 390; Sabbour, p. 385; and El-Fakahani, 1959 Supplement, p. 287.

Section 40(9) of Law 317 of 1952, the predecessor of section 76(8) of the Labour Code, granted the power of summary determination to the employer, "if the worker commits sufficient, whereas the misdemeanour should constitute an offence against honesty, trust or the public morals.[187]

The immoral act of the employer or his representative, mentioned in sectin 77(3), which also constitutes a departure from the rules of the general law, does not have to constitute a criminal offence, nor should it be committed in the place of work.

In Sudan section 10(2) of the Sudan Ordinance entitles the employer to summarily dismiss the worker, "for gross misconduct in or connected with his employment... or wilful misconduct calculated seriously to injure the employer's business." This provision may, but does not necessarily justify the summary dismissal of the worker, as does section 76(8) of the Labour Code. The test in Sudan is always the effect of the worker's behaviour on the employer's interests. This is in line with the English Common Law. "If a servant is guilty of such a crime outside his service," said *Lord Esher*, M.R., in *Pearce v. Foster*,[188] "as to make it unsafe for a master to keep him in his employ, the servant may be dismissed by his master; and if the servant's conduct is so grossly immoral that all reasonable men would say that he cannot be trusted, the master may dismiss him."[189] So the conviction of a criminal offence is not a condition for the exercise of the power of termination, as it is in the U.A.R.; and the rightfulness of the dismissal is determined by the circumstances of every case.

There is no provision in the Sudan Ordinance equivalent to section 77(3) of the U.A.R. It is, however, submitted that, apart from public policy, the immoral behaviour of the employer towards his worker or any member of his family, would both in England and Sudan, be held to be inconsistent with the employment relationship, and would thus justify the summary determination of the contract by the worker.

(4) Termination by the employer of unlimited contracts without notice or limited contracts before expiry

(i) The worker's absence from work. Section 76(5) of the U.A.R. Labour Code entitles the employer to terminate the contract without notice,

an immoral act," in the place of work. The replacement of the commission of the act. by the final conviction thereof, is commendable.

[187] Zaki, pp. 359–60, criticizes the absolute effect of the commission of a crime, by implying that a crime does not always seriously affect the interests of the establishment, Murad, p. 377; Sabbour, pp. 385; Habeeb, p. 461; Rashed and Hashem, p. 274; and Faheem, p. 104, justify the absolute effect of the crime, by its serious public effect.

[188] (1886), 17 Q. B.D. 536.

[189] *Vide* also Diamond, pp. 188–190; Smith, p. 85; Cooper, p. 76; Samuels, pp. 14–5; and Halsbury, Vol. 25, pp. 485–6.

"if the worker without justifiable cause absents himself for more than twenty days in any one year or more than ten consecutive days provided that the dismissal shall be preceded by a written warning which shall be served by the employer upon the worker after ten days of absence in the former case and five days in the latter case."[190]

This power of dismissal constitutes a departure from the rules of the general law.

The justifiability of the cause of absence depends on the circumstances of every case.[191] The preclusion of the employer's power of dismissal, when there is a justifiable cause, is because the contract is thereby only suspended.[192]

The warning in accordance with the section is valid, even if it is served before the expiry of the ten or the five days, as the case may be,[193] because this is more favourable to the worker. But a warning served at a date later than that provided in the section, takes effect as from the date of service, so that the worker will be allowed the following ten or five days, as the case may be, in order to return to the work;[194] otherwise the legislator's goal will not be fulfilled.[195] On the other hand, the warning, in order to be valid, should be served upon the worker, and not his trade union or the Labour Office,[196] for the warning is without value, if it is not directly driven home to the worker.[197] Some Court

[190] Cf. some similar provisions, in sections 17(d) and 18(a) of the Jordanian and Libyan Labour Codes, respectively. Sections 97(h), 56(c) and 74(5) of the Iraqi, Kuwaiti and Lebanese Labour Codes, respectively, justify the dismissal of the worker after specified absences, without the prescription of a warning, as in the U.A.R. Dismissal for "a grave mistake," by virtue of section 14(b) of the Tunisian Labour Code, depends on the length and the circumstances of the absence, in every case. *Vide* I.L.R., Vol. 79, 1959, p. 633, for the position of the law in France.

[191] *Vide* Rashed and Hashem, p. 253; El-Fakahani, Book I, Vol. I, p. 99; and El-Areef, p. 398, who submits that the cause should arise from *force majeure*.

Detention in prison was held to be a justifying cause: Cairo Court of Appeal in appeal No. 1334 of 1956; and Cairo Labour Court in case No. 4655 of 1956 (both in El-Fakahani, Book I, Vol. III, pp. 211 and 212, respectively); *vide* also El-Areef, p. 398; Butros and Rajab, pp. 390 and 430; and El-Fakahani, 1959 Supplement, p. 280.

[192] *Vide* Alexandria Court of Appeal in appeal No. 227 of 1958 (in El-Fakahani, Book I, Vol. III, p. 207).

[193] Butros and Rajab, p. 405, hold the same view, but without reasoning. Murad, p. 375; and Naguib and Bakr, p. 169, insist on the service of the notice, in the prescribed date, also without reasoning; and as a result, they advocate the renewal of the warning in the prescribed date.

[194] Badawi, K.M., p. 386; Rashed and Hashem, p. 252; and Butros and Rajab, p. 405, hold the same opinion.

[195] *Vide* Cairo Labour Court in case No. 1541 of 1959 (in El-Hawwari, p. 228); *vide* also Alexandria Court of Appeal in appeal No. 116 of 1956 (in El-Fakahani, Book I, Vol. III, p. 212); and *vide* Rashed and Hashem, p. 252; Habeeb, p. 455; and Naguib and Bakr, p. 169.

[196] Zaki, p. 358; and Naguib and Bakr, p. 169, are of the same opinion.

[197] *Vide* Cairo Court of Appeal in appeal No. 597 of 1956; Alexandria Court of Cassation in case No. 870 of 1957 (both in El-Fakahani, Book I, Vol. I, pp. 199 and 206, respectively) and Cairo Labour Court in case No. 3280 of 1958 (in El-Hawwari, p. 229).

decisions have ruled[198] and some writers maintain[199] that the warning is not valid, unless it contains the direction of the worker's attention to the probability of a dismissal. Though the employers do usually make such express direction, it is submitted that in law, they are not obliged to do so.

The year mentioned in the section is calculated as from the commencement of the worker's service,[200] and not backwards from the date of the absence in question.[201] This is consistent with the calculation of the year, for the purposes of leaves and holidays.[202]

Finally, some of those who maintain that the dismissal by virtue of section 76 of the Labour Code, should be a disciplinary dismissal,[203] advocate the view that the employer cannot exercise his power by virtue of section 76(5), after the lapse of the twenty days of intermittent absence, if he had already disciplined the worker and fined him for the previous absences, which form parts of these twenty days. Others who also maintain that the dismissal should be disciplinary, maintain the contrary opinion, for fear that "the employers would otherwise refrain from calling the workers to account for their intermittent absences, in order not to loose the right of dismissal, a thing which will encourage the workers to absent themselves without justifiable cause within the time limits which preclude the dismissal."[204] But this overlooks the violation of section 2 of Order 147 of 1959, which prohibits the imposition of two penalties for one offence.[205]

In Sudan section 10(2) of the Sudan Ordinance entitles the employer to summarily dismiss the worker, "for serious negligence or wilful misconduct calculated seriously to injure the employer's business."[206] Absence from work without justification is, under the English Common

[198] *Vide* Cairo Court of Appeal in appeal No. 361 of 1956; and Alexandria Court of Appeal in appeal No. 116 of 1956 (both in Habeeb, p. 454).

[199] El-Fakahani, 1959 Supplement, pp. 280–1; Rashed and Hashem, p. 253; and Habeeb, p. 454.

[200] *Vide* Cairo Court of Appeal in appeal No. 509 of 1954 (in Naguib and Bakr, p. 168); and Alexandria Court of Cassation in case No. 871 of 1957 (in El-Fakahani, Book I, Vol. III, p. 201); *vide* also Badawi, K.M., p. 386; El-Fakahani, 1959 Supplement, p. 280; Sabbour, p. 381; and Faheem, p. 100.

[201] Butros and Rajab, p. 404; and Habeeb, pp. 456–7, hold such opinion.

[202] *Vide* Chapter V, *supra*.

[203] *Vide* Section I, E of Chapter III, *supra*, especially footnote 134 thereto, and the related text.

[204] Murad, p. 376; *vide* also Butros and Rajah, pp. 405–6, who hold the same view.

[205] This Order is the main ground, on which those who advocate the disciplinary dismissal, depend; *vide* the Order in Section I, F, of Chapter III, *supra*.

[206] Section 20 of the Sudan Ordinance (*vide* Section III, E, iv, of Chapter IV, *supra*), concerns deductions for absences, and not the termination of the contract.

Law, "only an instance of neglect,"[207] or misconduct,[208] which "affords a good ground of dismissal."[209] Whether an absence justifies the dismissal or not, depends on the circumstances of the case, for "even absence for a day or a single hour might, in certain circumstances, show such wanton disregard of his employer's interests as to excuse dismissal."[210]

(ii) Serious material damage to the employer's property. Section 76(3) of the U.A.R. Labour Code entitles the employer to terminate the contract without notice, "if the worker commits a wrongful act which results in a serious material loss to the employer provided that the employer shall notify the authorities of the same within twenty four hours of his knowing of its commission."[211]

This power of dismissal constitutes a departure from the rules of the general law.

The wrongful act mentioned in the section does not have to be committed with intent,[212]nor should it constitute a criminal offence.[213] On the other hand, if the employer fails to notify the authorities concerned,[214]

[207] Samuels, p. 14.

[208] *Vide* Halsbury, Vol. 25, p. 464.

[209] Barwell and Kar, p. 367.

[210] Macdonell, p. 209; *vide Fillieul v. Armstrong* (1837) 7 A. & E., 557; and the Indian case of *Chatra Serampore Cooperative Credit Society v. Becharam Sarkar & ors.*, A.I.R., 1938, Cal. 829.

[211] *Vide* similar provisions, in sections 20(2) and 18(b) of the Qatari and Libyan Labour Codes, respectively. Sections 16(c) of the Saudi Regulations prescribes in addition, that the wrongful act should be committed with intent. Section 74(3) of the Lebanese Labour Code prescribes that the act schould onstitute a criminal offence, and the worker should be convicted thereof. Section 97(b) of the Iraqi Labour Code prescribes the service of the warning upon the worker, before the dismissal power can be used. Sections 56(a) and 17(b) of the Kuwaiti and Jordanian Labour Codes, respectively, grant the power of summary dismissal, without the requirement of the warning. Dismissal for "a grave mistake," by virtue of section 14(b) of the Tunisian Labour Code, should be according to the circumstances of every case. Section 1639 P (7) of the Netherlands Civil Code, is similar to the Iraqi provision. *Vide* I.L.R., Vol. 80, 1959, p. 268, for the position of the law in Germany.

[212] *Vide* Cairo Court of Appeal in appeal No. 1254 of 1960 (in El-Hawwari, p. 221); *vide* also El-Areef, p. 397; Sabbour, p. 377; El-Fakahani, 1959 Supplement, p. 275; Butros and Rajab, p. 402; Rashed and Hashem, p. 248; and Habeeb, p. 452.

[213] *Vide* the High Court of Appeal in (an unnumbered) appeal decided on 9 April 1953 (in Sabbour, p. 378); and Cairo Court of Cassation in (an unnumbered) case decided on 10 October 1954 (in Badawi, K.M., p. 396); *vide* also Zaki, p. 356; Butros and Rajab, p. 402; Habeeb, p. 453; Rashed and Hashem, p. 249; Badawi, K.M., p. 385; and Sabbour, p. 378. Murad, p. 375; El-Areef, pp. 397–8; and El-Fakahani, 1959 Supplement, p. 276, maintain otherwise. The reason behind the dividion of opinion, is the prescription in section 76(3), of the notification to the authorties concerned. The last three mentioned writers interpret this to mean the Police authorities; but the other writers correctly maintain that not every act notified even to the Police, should constitute a criminal offence

[214] *Vide* The High Court of Appeal in the appeal, mentioned in the preceding footnote and *vide* Cairo Court of Appeal in appeal No. 1279 of 1959 (in El-Hawwari, p. 220); *vide* also Badawi, K.M., p. 395.

or notifies them later than the time prescribed,[215] he cannot use his power of dismissal, because the worker will in the former case, be deprived of the protection which the investigation of the authorities may afford to him, and the employer will in the latter case, be taken to have waived his right of summary dismissal. But notification is sufficient, if it is made by any person other than the employer, provided that it is made within the prescribed time.[216]

If the loss resulting to the employer is not serious, the employer's remedy is the deduction of the compensation therefor, by virtue of section 54 of the Labour Code, and not the summary dismissal.[217] Finally, the apprehension of the danger of a serious loss is not sufficient for the justifiable use by the employer of his power of summary dismissal.[218]

In Sudan section 10(2) of the Sudan Ordinance entitles the employer to dismiss the worker without notice, "for serious negligence... calculated seriously to injure the employer's business." Serious material loss to the employer, as mentioned in the U.A.R., falls under this section, if it results from serious negligence. This is a more strict requirment than that of the U.A.R. Under the English Common Law, the measure is the seriousness of the loss resulting to the employer, and not that the loss should result from a serious negligence.[219] In this there is some similarity between the English Law and the law in the U.A.R.[220]

If the negligence of the worker is not likely to seriously affect the business of the employer, it will not justify the employer in summarily dismissing the worker.[221] However, unlike the position in the U.A.R., the actual happening of the serious loss to the employer is not a precondition to the exercise of the power of summary dismissal.

(iii) Disclosure of professional secrets. Section 76(7) of the U.A.R. Labour Code entitles the employer to terminate the contract without

[215] El-Areef, p. 398; and Rashed and Hashem, p. 250, hold the same opinion.

[216] Badawi, K.M., p. 385; and Butros and Rajab, p. 402, hold the same opinion.

[217] *Vide* section 54 quoted and discussed, in Section I, C, iii, of Chapter III, *supra*; *vide* also Cairo Labour Court in case No. 42 of 1960 (in El-Hawwari, p. 222); and *vide* Sabbour, pp. 378–9.

[218] *Vide* Alexandria Court of Cassation in case No. 1753 of 1957 (in El-Hawwari, p. 223)

[219] *Vide Baster v. London and County Printing Works* (1899), 1 Q.B. 901. Every case is decided according to its own circumstances: vide *Horton v. McMurtry*, 5 H. & N. 667; *vide* also Batt, pp. 62 and 157; Smith, pp. 84 and 88; and Barwell and Kar, p. 374.

[220] However, the English Law justifies the dismissal, if the serious loss results to the colleagues of the worker: *vide Baster's* case in the preceding footnote. In view of the lack of the mention of such loss, in section 10(2) of the Sudan Ordinance, this part of the English Law should not be applicable in Sudan, and the same should be true in the U.A.R.

[221] This is in line with the position under the English Common Law: *vide Gould v. Webb*, 4 E. & B. 933.

notice "if the worker discloses the secrets of the establishment in which he works."[222]

This power of summary dismissal constitutes a departure from the rules of the general law.

We have already seen that the preservation of the employer's secrets is one of the essential duties of the worker.[223] As the breach of this duty, which is the backbone of the power of summary dismissal by virtue of section 76(7), can justify the dismissal by virtue of section 76(6),[224] and as the former does not add any qualification to the latter, contrary to the other grounds of dismissal in section 76, it is submitted that the enactment of section 76(7) is not necessary.

The reporting by the worker of a breach of the law by the employer, does not amount to a disclosure of the employer's secrets.[225]

In Sudan section 10(2) of the Sudan Ordinance entitles the employer to summarily dismiss the worker, "for gross misconduct in or connected with his employment... or wilful misconduct calculated seriously to injure the employer's business." Under the English Common Law, the disclosure by the worker of his employer's secrets is termed misconduct.[226] The rightfulness of the worker's dismissal by such misconduct, depends on all the circumstances of the case.[227] This applies in Sudan, subject to the gravity and the wilfulness of the misconduct, as provided in section 10(2).

As in the U.A.R., the disclosure by the worker of his employer's breaches of the law, will not justify his summary dismissal. "No liability could attach for revealing the frauds or malpractices of his master," says *F. R. Batt*, "indeed he may be under a public duty to disclose these."[227]

[222] *Vide* similar provisions, in sections 20(5) and 18(f) of the Qatari and Libyan Labour Code, respectively. Section 97(g) of the Iraqi Labour Code speaks of the employer's, instead of the establishment's secrets... cf. section 1639 P (9) of the Netherlands Civil Code. Sections 16(g) of the Saudi Regulations, and 17(f) of the Jordanian Labour Code, speak of the secrets of the work. Section 14(b) of the Tunisian Labour Code, which speaks of "a grave mistake," permits dismissal for the disclosure of the employer's or the establishment's secrets, according to the circumstances of the case. *Vide* I.L.R., Vol. 80, 1959, p. 268, for the position of the law in Germany.

[223] *Vide* Section I, C, iv, of Chapter III, *supra*.

[224] Zaki, p. 359, holds the same opinion: *vide* footnote 149, *supra*.

[225] *Vide* Cairo Court of Cassation in case No. 1713 of 1957 (in El-Hawwari, p. 257); cf. with a decision of the same Court in case No. 2548 of 1953 (in Habeeb, p. 459), in which it was held that the unauthorised taking by the worker of the employer's accounting books to the tax authorities, so as to substantiate his information of tax racketeering by the employer, constituted a disclosure of his employer's secrets, justifying his summary dismissal; *vide* also El-Fakahani, 1959 Supplement, pp. 285–6.

[226] *Vide* Batt, p. 63.

[227] *Ibid.*, p. 160.

(iv) Intoxication. Section 76(9) of the U.A.R. Labour Code entitles the employer to terminate the contract without notice, "if the worker is found during the hours of work in an apparent state of drunkenness or affected by any narcotics he has taken."[228]

This power of summary dismissal constitutes a departure from the rules of the general law.

The drunkenness or the inebriety of the worker by the influence of narcotics, should be voluntary; otherwise the employer will not be justified in his summary dismissal of the worker.[229]

In Sudan section 10(2) of the Sudan Ordinance entitles the employer to summarily dismiss the worker, "for gross misconduct in or connected with his employment... or wilful misconduct calculated seriously to injure the employer's interests." Drunkenness and inebriety resulting from narcotics, are classified as misconduct by the English Common Law.[230] Under this Law, the misconduct in question justifies the summary dismissal of the worker, only if it interferes with the proper discharge of his duties. "When the alleged misconduct consists of drunkenness," said *Lord James*, in *Clouston v. Corry*,[231] "there must be considerable difficulty in determining the extent or conditions of intoxication which will establish a justification for dismissal. The intoxication may be habitual and gross, and directly interfere with the business of the employer or with the ability of the servant to render due service. But it may be an isolated act committed under circumstances of festivity and in no way connected with or affecting the employer's business. In such a case the question whether the misconduct proved establishes the right to dismiss the servant must depend upon facts."[232] This measure of justification applies to Sudan.

Contrary to the U.A.R., there is no requirement that the worker be

[228] Cf. similar provisions, in sections 97(d), 20(7) and 18(h) of the Iraqi, Qatari and Libyan Labour Codes, respectively. The Kuwaiti and Jordanian Labour Codes and the Saudi Regulations do not contain relevant provisions; nor does the Lebanese Labour Code, though section 65 thereof prohibits the entry of narcotics and any person affected by narcotics, into the place of work. Drunkenness or intoxication by narcotics, may constitute the "grave mistake," which justifies dismissal by virtue of section 14(b) of the Tunisian Labour Code. Section 1639 P (3) of the Netherlands Civil Code justifies the worker's summary dismissal, "if he indulges, despite warning, in drunkenness or other dissolute conduct." *Vide* I.L.R., Vol. 79, 1959, p. 633, for the position of the law in France.

[229] *Vide* El-Fakahani, 1959 Supplement, p. 288; Sabbour, p. 387; Butros and Rajab, pp. 349 and 411; Zaki, p. 360; and Habeeb, p. 462, who are of the same opinion.

[230] *Vide* Smith, p. 84; and Batt, p. 65.

[231] (1906) A.C. 122.

[232] *Vide* also *Wise v. Wilson*, 1. C. & K. 662; *Speak v. Phillips* (1839) 5 M. & M., 279; and *Hands v. Simpson* (1928), 44 T.L.R. 295.

found drunk or inebrious, during working hours. But as in the U.A.R., the effect on the worker should result from a voluntary act.

(v) During probation. Section 76(2) of the U.A.R. Labour Code entitles the employer to terminate the contract without notice, "if the worker was appointed under probation."[233]

This power of summary dismissal constitutes a departure from the rules of the general law.

The power belongs only to the employer, in order that he may be satisfied with the worker, before he takes him into permanent employment. Though the employer and the worker may agree to deprive the former of this power or to bestow it upon the latter, the worker cannot exercise it without such agreement.[234] On the other hand, the judicial and juridical opinion leans in favour of holding the employer unjustified in his summary determination of the contract, if it was prompted by reasons extraneous to the purpose of probation.[235]

In Sudan there is no relevant provision. So the power of either party to determine the contract during the probation period, if any, depends

[233] Section 95(7) of the Iraqi Labour Code entitles the employer and the worker to terminate the contract without notice, during the fifteen days following the date of making the contract (*vide* the *Labour Survey of North Africa*, pp. 211–2, for some similarity with the law in Morocco). This is without reference to section 25(1) of the Code, which prescribes that the period of probation should not exceed three months. Section 17 of the Kuwaiti Labour Code, which limits the period of probation to one hundred days, entitles the employer alone to summarily determine the contract, before the expiry of these hundred days. Section 16(b) of the Saudi Regulations entitles only the employer to summarily determine the contract, during the three months following the making of the contract (which are impliedly the probation period), only if the employer is dissatisfied with the performance of the worker. Section 74(2) of the Lebanese Labour Code is similar to the Saudi Arabian provision. None of the other Arab Labour Codes contains a relevant provision. Section 1639 N of the Netherlands Civil Code grants the employer and the worker the power to summarily determine the contract; and section 502 of the *Majallah* does the same.

[234] *Vide* Cairo Court of Cassation in case No. 1713 of 1957 (in El-Hawwari, p. 219); *vide* also El-Areef, p. 417; Sabbour, p. 117; Butros and Rajab, p. 34; and Habeeb, pp. 265 and 266–7. Those who advocate the contrary view, with no more justification than that of equity, in spite of the express provision in section 76(2), are Badawi, K.M., p. 88; Rashed and Hashem, p. 14; and Faheem, p. 24; *vide* also Cairo Labour Court in case No. 5979 of 1955; Cairo Court of Cassation in case No. 1317 of 1956; and Cairo Court of Appeal in appeal No. 215 of 1957 (in El-Fakahani, Book I, Vol. I, pp. 296, 302 and 293, respectively). Section 939 of the Draft Civil Code granted the power of summary termination of the contract to the employer and the worker; but the section was not adopted.

[235] *Vide* Cairo Labour Court in case No. 6565 of 1955 (in El-Fakahani, Book I, Vol. I, p. 287); Cairo Court of Cassation in case No. 70 of 1955 (in Badawi, K.M., p. 394); Alexandria Court of Cassation in case No. 952 of 1955; and Cairo Court of Appeal in appeal No. 215 of 1957 (both in Habeeb, p. 268); and Cairo Court of Cassation in case No. 35 of 1958 (in El-Hawwari, p. 72); *vide* also Murad, p. 251; Badawi, K.M., p. 89; El-Fakahani, Book I, Vol. I, pp. 306–10; Butros and Rajab, p. 36; Habeeb, p. 268; and Naguib and Bakr, p. 75. *Vide* Section II, B, of this Chapter, *infra*, for the justification of the termination of the contract.

on the terms of the contract,[236] subject to the provisions of the Sudan Ordinance, in respect of the length of the prescribed notice. On the other hand, the employer should not use his contractual power to dismiss the worker maliciously.[236]

* * *

Such are the powers of either party, on the one hand, and of the employer, on the other hand, to terminate the contract without notice. These powers should be exercised within a reasonable time, after the occurrence or the discovery of the terminating cause; otherwise the terminating party will be taken to have waived his power of termination.[237]

The summary determination of the contract by virtue of any of the said powers, relieves the terminating party of the obligation to serve the notice of termination or of the payment in lieu; but it does not entitle him to the payment in lieu from the other party, though it is the other party's conduct which drove him to terminate the contract.[238]

In order that a terminating party may be relieved of the payment of any damages to the other party, his termination of the contract should be justifiable in the U.A.R. and rightful in Sudan.

(b) Unjustifiable and wrongful termination

The above-mentioned rules concerning the legal termination of the contract, are further restricted in the U.A.R. by the provisions of sections 695(2) of the Civil Code and 74 of the Labour Code.

[236] *Vide* the Indian case of *Wechsler v. Johnston & Hoffman* (1928), Calc. suit 455, mentioned by Barwell and Kar, p. 66.

[237] For the U.A.R., *vide* Alexandria Court of Cassation in cases Nos. 471 and 1802 of 1949 (both in Rashed and Hashem, p. 244 – It is interesting to note that these writers, in citing these cases, forget that they advocate the view that the worker's dismissal in accordance with section 76 of the Labour Code, should be a disciplinary dismissal. If it is, the time within which the dismissal should take place, is fifteen days after the discovery of the cause of dismissal – *vide* footnote 134 to Chapter III, *supra*); *vide* also the Alexandria Court of Appeal in appeal No. 428 of 1959 (in El-Hawwari, p. 239); and *vide* El-Fakahani, Book I, Vol. I, p. 95; and Rashed and Hashem, p. 283.

For Sudan, *vide Phillips v. Foxall* (1872), L.R., 7 Q.B. 666: *Horton v. McMurtry* (1960), 5 H. & N. 667; and *Federal Supply and Cold Storage of South Africa v. Angehrn*, 103 L.T., 150; *vide* also Diamond, p. 188; Cooper, p. 78; and Smith, p. 80; and *vide* I.L.O. Report VII(1), 1962, p. 39, and paragraphs 12(3 & 4) of the *Proposed Recommendation Concerning Termination At The Initiative Of The Employer*, in Report V(1), 1963, p. 36.

[238] *Vide* section 696(1) of the U.A.R. Civil Code (in footnote 258, *infra*), which entitles the worker to compensation for the unjustifiable termination of the contract, even though he be the terminating party, if it is the employer's conduct which obliged him to terminate the contract. This compensation does not include the payment in lieu of the notice of termination (*vide* Badawi, K.M., pp. 286–7; and Butros and Rajab, p. 412, who maintain otherwise). *Vide* Cairo District Court (Commercial) in case No. 21 of 1949 (in Rashed and Hashem, p. 281); the Cairo Court of Cassation in case No. 415 of 1953 (in *Ibid.*, p. 410); and the same Court in case No. 473 of 1954 (in El-Fakahani, Book I, Vol. I, p. 644); and El-Geeza Court of Cassation in case No. 229 of 1958 (in El-Hawwari, p. 347); *vide* also El-Areef, pp. 324 and 408–9; El-Fakahani, 1959 Supplement, p. 214; and Naguib and Bakr, p. 161.

Section 695(2) of the Civil Code provides that, if a contract made for an unlimited period "is terminated by either party unjustifiably the other party shall, in addition to the compensation due for the non-observance of the notice, be entitled to damages for the loss he suffers by reason of the unjustifiable termination of the contract."[239]

Section 74 of the Labour Code provides that, "if the contract is terminated without a proper cause, the party who thereby incurs a loss shall without prejudice to the provisions of sections 72 and 73[240] be entitled to damages which the Court after investigating the circumstances of the termination shall assess while taking into consideration the nature of the work the extent of the loss the length of the service and the prevailing custom."[241]

From these provisions, it is clear that the termination of the unlimited contract by notice does not put an end to the matter. The terminating party, in spite of serving the notice, may still be liable to pay damages for the lack of justification or proper cause[242] for his termination. To use the English Law phraseology, the terminating party may still be liable to pay damages (of a tortious character), though he commits no breach of the contract.

This doctrine of unjustifiability or lack of the proper cause in the U.A.R., was based on "the exercise of a right in a manner which is

[239] *Vide* identical provisions in section 918(2) of the Iraqi Civil Code. Cf. some similar provisions, in section 1639 S of the Netherlands Civil Code.

Before the enactment of section 695(2) of the U.A.R., and even before the enactment of section 22 of Law 41 of 1944 (*vide* the Introduction, *supra*), the Mixed Courts, following in the steps of the French Law, developed the doctrine of justification of termination on the grounds of equity (*vide* Murad, p. 428; Sabbour, p. 336; and Rashed and Hashem, pp. 179 and 191–2).

[240] Section 72 prescribes the notice necessary for the termination of the unlimited contract (*vide* the section quoted in Section I, 2, of this Chapter, *supra*). Section 73 prescribes the payment of the termination gratuity (*vide* Chapter VII, *infra*).

[241] This provision was drawn from section 23(5) of Book I of the French Labour Code (*vide* I.S.D.L., Vol. 4, 1929, p. 84); *vide* also the French decisions in *Cauzier v. Dame Malude* (1929), Gaz. du Palais, 1930, 1, 143; *Ballot v. Auzémery* (1931), Dalloz Hebdom., 1932, p. 90; *Bon Marché v. Rongeat* (1932), Gaz. du Palais, 1932, 2, 140; and *Société Au Bon Marché v. Staudenmeyer* (1936), Dalloz Hebdom., 12, 265 (all in I.S.D.L., Vol. 6, 1931, p. 77; Vol. 8, 1934, pp. 104 and 107; and Vol. 12, 1938, p. 149, respectively); and *vide* I.L.R., Vol. 32, 1936, p. 200; and I.L.O. Report VII(1), 1962, on the *Termination of Employment*. This was and still is applicable to Algeria. *Vide* some similar provisions in section 23 of the Tunisian Labour Code, which seems to be the only Arab Labour Code containing such an express provision. A similar provision can be deduced from section 16 of the Libyan Labour Code. *Vide* I.L.R., Vol. 80, 1959, pp. 274–6, for the more protective provisions in Germany.

[242] These two terms are synonymous: *vide* the High Court of Appeal in appeal No. 202 of 1958 (in Habeeb, p. 629). Section 67(2) of the Labour Code uses the former term (*vide* the section quoted in Section I, C, of this Chapter, *supra*), whereas the latter term is used in section 74.

considered wrong, and which as a result the ordinary man will avoid."[243] The wrong exercise of a right can only be defined, by the reference to sections 4 and 5 of the U.A.R. Civil Code. Section 4 provides that "whoever exercises his right lawfully shall not be responsible for the loss that may result therefrom." Section 5 provides that "the exercise of the right shall be unlawful in the following cases (a) if only the infliction of a loss upon others is thereby intended, (b) if the interests intended to be served be so trivial as to be totally out of proportion with the loss which is thereby inflicted upon others, (c) if the interests intended to be served are unlawful." These two sections are concerned with the tortious liability in the U.A.R.[244] Thus the tortious liability has, by the doctrine of justification of the termination of the contract of employment, been grafted upon the contractual liability. It can be maintained of course, that the prescription of the liability for damages, both in section 695(2) of the Civil Code and section 74 of the Labour Code, for what in reality is a wrong in tort, had become a part of the law of the contract of employment.[245] But the liability remains juridically a tortious liability.[246] This is supported by the Court judgments which decided that no damages are due, unless a loss has resulted from the unjustifiable exercise of the right of termination.[247] Under the rules of the general law, the damages which can be awarded for a breach of a contract,[248] are

[243] Cairo Court of Cassation (commercial) in case No. 1225 of 1952 (in Habeeb, p. 486).

[244] *Vide* also section 163 of the Civil Code, which provides that "every wrong which causes a loss to others binds the person who commits it to pay damages."

[245] *Vide* Cairo Court of Cassation in case No. 723 of 1952 (in Rashed and Hashem, p. 360); Cairo Court of Appeal in appeal No. 1388 of 1960 (in El-Hawwari, p. 434); and the Cairo Labour Court in decisions Nos. 193, 195, 196, 198, 1106 and 1378 of 1960 (in *Ibid.*, pp. 437 and 439); *vide* also Zaki, p. 309; and El-Fakahani, 1959 Supplement, p. 27, where he points out that section 148 of the Civil Code, re the *bona fide* carrying out of the contractual obligations, and the exercise of the contractual rights (*vide* footnote 98 to Chapter III, *supra*), provides a legal ground for the doctrine of justification of the termination of the contract. It is submitted that he is wrong, because the *mala fides* is not essential to the doctrine of justification (*vide* Zaki, p. 486; and Naguib and Bakr, p. 142).

[246] *Vide* Alexandria Labour Court in case No. 57 of 1953 (in Rashed and Hashem, p. 220); and Cairo Labour Court in case No. 1903 of 1954 (in Badawi, K.M., p. 308); *vide* also Murad, p. 429; Sabbour, pp. 414 and 338; El-Areef, p. 355; Badawi, K.M., p. 303; and Rashed and Hashem, pp. 194, 200 and 208.

[247] *Vide* the High Court of Appeal in the two appeals Nos .210 of 1958 and 228 of 1960 (both in El-Hawwari, p. 369); *vide* also Cairo Labour Court in case No. 2480 of 1953; Cairo Court of Cassation in case No. 55 of 1955; and Alexandria Court of Appeal in appeal No. 167 of 1957 (all three in Habeeb, p. 508); *vide* also section 224 of the Civil Code.

[248] Section 221 of the Civil Code provides:

"If the damages are not fixed in the contract or in a provision of law, the Judge shall assess them , and they shall include the loss which the creditor has inccurred and the gain he has missed provided that they (the loss and the gain) are the natural consequences of the failure to carry out the obligation or of the delay in carrying it out, and the loss shall be considered as a natural consequence if the creditor could not avoid it by the exertion of a reasonable effort.

more strict than the rules applicable to the damages awarded for the commission of a tort.[249] The latter rules have been applied in the assessment of damages for the unjustifiable termination of the contract.[250] In this there is further support that the liability for these damages is still a tortious liability. It is accordingly submitted that the specification in section 74 of the Labour Code, of what the Judge should take into consideration for the assessment of the damages, is not exclusive, as section 170 of the Civil Code prescribes the taking into consideration of all the circumstances.[251] On the other hand, the damages may include damages for a moral loss.[252] It has also been correctly held that the damages could be awarded for the psychological pains, which resulted to the worker from his unjustifiable dismissal.[253]

The legislator does not, and indeed cannot enumerate the cases in which the termination of the contract would be unjustifiable or not. So every case will depend on its merits.[254] However, the legislator expressly states some cases, in which the worker's dismissal will be deemed unjustifiable or otherwise. Section 695(2) of the Civil Code provides that "the dismissal shall be unjustifiable if it is the result of any attachments of (the worker's) entitlements still in the hands of the employer, or because of the worker's debts to others." Section 696(2) of the Code deems the transfer of a worker to a lower position, not to be unjustifiable, if it was required by the interests of the work and was not effected *mala fide*.[255] Section 67(2) of the Labour Code expressly deems the non-reinstatement of the worker in his position, after he is acquited

"However, if the obligation is a contractual obligation, the debtor shall not be obliged to pay damages for more than the loss which could have been ordinarily contemplated at the time of making the contract unless he has committed a fraud or a grave mistake."

[249] Section 170 of the Civil Code provides that "the Judge shall assess the damages for the loss incurred according to the provisions of sections 221 and 222 while taking the circumstances into consideration."

[250] *Vide* section 695(2) of the Civil Code; *vide* also El-Areef, p. 357 (where he says that "the damages should be... equal to the loss," and not to what could have been contemplated at the time of making the contract); Murad, p. 437; and Rashed and Hashem, p. 203. Zaki, p. 403, says the same thing, though he maintains that the liability is contractual (*vide* footnote 245, *supra*).

[251] El-Areef, p. 405, submits to the same effect; *vide* also Cairo Court of Appeal in appeal No. 1021 of 1959 (in El-Hawwari, p. 373), in which the Court's considerations were wider than the specification in section 74. Section 962 of the Draft Civil Code, which was copied from section 23 of Book I of the French Labour Code, and which formed the basis of section 695(2) of the Civil Code, expressly provided for the taking into consideration of all the circumstances of the case.

[252] Section 222 of the Civil Code expressly provides to this effect.

[253] *Vide* Cairo Labour Court in case No. 364 of 1959 (in El-Hawwari, p. 371).

[254] *Vide* the decisions in which the termination was held unjustifiable, and those in which it was held to be justifiable, in El-Hawwari, p. 281 *et seq.*, and El-Fakahani, Book I, Vol. III, p. 652 *et seq. Vide* section 19 of the Libyan Labour Code.

[255] *Vide* the section quoted in Section I, C, ii, of Chapter III, *supra*.

of a criminal charge, or when the competent authority decides not to prosecute him, to be an unjustifiable dismissal.[256] Section 78 of the Labour Code provides that, "if the worker leaves the work for any of the reasons mentioned in the preceding section[257] the employer shall pay to him the service gratuity as provided in section 73 without prejudice to any damages which the Court may award."[258] Section 76 of the Labour Code[259] expressly relieves the employer from the payment of damages for the termination of the contract, on any of the grounds mentioned in the section. On the other hand, section 75(7) impliedly deems the dismissal of the worker to be unjustifiable, if it is for no reason other than his trade union activity.[260] Section 79(1) of the Labour Code[261] impliedly deems the termination of the contract of the worker, who is called up for military service, to be unjustifiably dismissed, even though the employer pays him in lieu of the notice of termination. Section 81(5) of the Code,[262] which precludes the employer from terminating the contract with notice, during the periods of the worker's sickness mentioned in section 81(1), impliedly deems such termination to be unjustifiable.[263] It is, however, submitted that this will not preclude the employer from dismissing the worker without notice, if he is justified in doing so under section 76 of the Code, even before the expiry of these sickness periods.[264]

The aggrieved party finds his remedy in damages, as is prescribed in section 74 of the Labour Code. This is in line with the rules of the general law, which preclude the specific performance of the contract of employment because of the personal qualities of the contract.[265] How-

[256] *Vide* the section quoted in Section I, C, of this Chapter, *supra*.

[257] This is section 77, whose provisions were quoted in Section II, A, 3, of this Chapter, *supra*.

[258] Section 696(1) of the Civil Code provides that "damages may be awarded for the dismissal even though the employer has not ordered it, if he by his conduct and particularly by his unjust treatment or by the violation of the contract terms has driven the worker to be seemingly the terminating party."

[259] *Vide* the section quoted and discussed in Section II, A, 3 and 4, of this Chapter, *supra*.

[260] Section 75 contains extensive provisions intended to provide the worker, who believes that his dismissal is unjustifiable, with a speedy procedure of complaint against the dismissal, and with a temporary compensation payable to him by the employer, until the matter is finally settled in Court (the section was inspired by section 23 of Book I of the French Labour Code; cf. section 1639 T of the Netherlands Civil Code). The discussion of these procedures falls outside the scope of this study.

[261] The section is quoted and discussed in Section I, D, of this Chapter, *supra*.

[262] The section is quoted and discussed in Section I, A, of this Chapter, *supra*.

[263] *Vide* El-Geeza Court of Cassation in case No. 130 of 1956 (in El-Fakahani, Book I, Vol. III, p. 407).

[264] Butros and Rajab, p. 423; and Rashed and Hashem, p. 304, submit to the same effect.

[265] *Vide* Alexandria Court of Cassation in case No. 1978 of 1957 (in El-Fakahani, Book I, Vol. III, p. 702); *vide* also Murad, pp. 436 and 430; El-Areef, pp. 357–8 and 426; and Rashed and Hashem, pp. 221–2.

ever, section 75(6) of the Code provides that "the Court may decide on the reinstatement of the worker whose contract is terminated in his work if his termination constitutes the offence mentioned in section 231 of this Code."[266] This forms an exception to the rules of the general law.

Finally, section 74 of the Labour Code speaks of the contract, without specifying that it should be an unlimited contract. Section 78 of the Code refers back to section 77 thereof. The latter section speaks of the limited and the unlimited contracts. Section 695(2) of the Civil Code clearly refers to the unlimited contract only. The question which has arisen from these provisions, is whether section 74 applies to a limited contract or not. Both the judicial and the juridical opinion has been, and still is divided into negative[267] and affirmative[268] directions. It is submitted that the answer is in the negative, because the party terminating a limited contract before the expiry of its period, would be liable to questioning by the other party in Court, on the ground that he has *prima facie* committed a wrong. So there is no need for further justification, as is prescribed by section 74; the case remains to be a case of pure breach of contract. In line with this, the damages grantable for such breach, have to be assessed as is provided in section 221(2) of the Civil Code,[269] and cannot be based on grounds identical with the wider grounds of the damages for the unjustifiable termination of the unlimited contract.[270]

In Sudan there are no provisions equivalent to those of the U.A.R. Reference to the English Common Law reveals that the U.A.R. doctrine of justification of the termination of the contract is not recognized in England.[271] If a contract is terminable by notice, and the notice is served, that puts an end to the matter; and the other party cannot, for the lack

[266] The offence mentioned in section 231, is committed by "the employer or his representative who terminates the contract of the worker or penalises him in order to oblige him to join refrain from joining or withdraw from the trade union or on account of the worker's carrying out of the union's work or its lawful resolutions."

[267] *Vide* Alexandria Court fo Appeal in appeal No. 326 of 1957 (in El Fakahani, Book I, Vol. III, p. 698); *vide* also El-Areef, pp. 355, 404 and 417; Sabbour, pp. 328–9; Zaki, pp. 369, 415 and 427–8; Habeeb, p. 542; Badawi, Z., Vol I.., p. 112; and El-Fakahani, 1959 Supplement, pp. 291 and 226.

[268] *Vide* Alexandria Court of Cassation in case No. 2031 of 1955; and Cairo Court of Appeal in appeal No. 1159 of 1958 (both in El-Fakahani, Book I, Vol. III, pp. 689 and 700, respectively); *vide* also Butros and Rajab, p. 383; Naguib and Bakr, pp. 147–8; and Rashed and Hashem, p. 204 (these writers depend on the fact that section 22 of Law 41 of 1944 limited the doctrine of justification to the unlimited contracts expressly, whereas Law 317 of 1952 was silent, thus according to them, evidencing a contrary intention of the legislator).

[269] *Vide* the section quoted in footnote 248, *supra*.

[270] *Vide* section 170 of the Civil Code, in footnote 249, *supra*.

[271] The social and economic benefits which result to the aggrieved party (especially when he is the worker), from the U.A.R. doctrine of justification, are lacking in Sudan.

of a complaint against him by the terminating party, allege that the contract had been wrongfully terminated.[272] "An action lies for damages," says *A. S. Diamond*,[273] "for wrongful dismissal by the master or wrongful departure by the servant. Wrongful dismissal or departure consists of a repudiation of the contract of service. There is a repudiation of the contract of service, where the servant is dismissed without notice or leaves the service without due notice and without justification, or where the acts and conduct of a party evince an intention no longer to be bound by the contract." The justification which *Diamond* mentions, is the justification of the non-service of the notice, and is not of the dismissal itself, contrary to the position in the U.A.R.[274] The damages in England are only payable for a breach of the contract, which may result from the breach of an express or implied term in the contract. The term in question may relate to the notice, when the contract is unlimited, to the duration of the contract, when it is limited, or it may relate to any other matter. But the consequences are the same. This liability to pay damages is purely contractual, and is clean and clear of the tortious liability.

In order to decide whether a breach of the contract has been committed or not, the terms of the contract and all the circumstances of the case are examined, as is the case in the U.A.R. In *Hadley v. Baxendale*,[275] it was decided that "the damages which the other party ought to receive in respect of such breach of contract should be such as may fairly and reasonably be considered either arising naturally, i.e., according to the usual course of things, from such breach of contract itself, or such as may reasonably be supposed to have been in the contemplation of the parties, at the time they made the contract, as the probable result of the breach itself."[276] Damages include the damages representing the loss of reputation or publicity of an actor,[277] but not the injured feelings of the dismissed worker,[278] contrary to the position in the U.A.R.

As in the U.A.R., and for the same reason, the remedy for the breach of the contract in England and Sudan lies in damages and not in the

[272] *Vide Dennis & Sons v. Tunnard Bros. and Moore* (1911), 56 Sol. 162; *vide* also *Siddall v. Wallsey Corporation* (1932), reported in I.S.D.L., Vol. 8, 1934, p. 28.

[273] P. 203.

[274] *Vide* the Sudanese case of *El-Sayed El-Hag El-Dosh v. President Ahlia Shool* (1958), AC-Revision-164-58 (in the S.L.J.R., 1958, p. 75).

[275] (1854), 9 Exch. 341; *vide* also Cheshire and Fifoot, p. 498 *et seq.*

[276] Thus the two requirements in section 221 of the U.A.R. Civil Code, are in England in the alternative (*vide* footnote 248, *supra*).

[277] *Vide Clayton v. Oliver* (1930) A.C. 209.

[278] *Vide Addis v. Gramophone Co.* (1909) A.C. 488.

specific performance of the contract.[279] There is no exception to this rule, as is contained in section 75(6) of the U.A.R. Labour Code; indeed, the Courts in England have specifically refused to make such an exception.[280]

SUMMARY

The suspension and frustration of the contract of employment are in the U.A.R. and Sudan, mainly governed by the rules of the general law of each country. These rules are similar. However, the suspending or frustrating *force majeure* in the U.A.R., has a wider effect than the Act of God or the *vis major* in Sudan. The legislators in both countries interfered in these rules, in varying degrees.

The contract is suspended by the worker's sickness, both in the U.A.R. and Sudan. During the suspension, the employer in the former cannot terminate the contract by notice, whereas in the latter he can. On the other hand, the contract in the U.A.R. is frustrated by the worker's long sickness of a specified length of time. In Sudan the notice of termination or the payment in lieu thereof, should be due to the worker; so the frustration of the contract is not complete. The employer's short sickness in the U.A.R. results in the suspension of the contract, only when the personal qualities of the employer are of material consideration in the contract. The employer's long sickness frustrates the contract, but only in the same eventuality. In Sudan the employer's sickness does not suspend the contract, but his long sickness may result in the frustration of the contract, without the express condition in the U.A.R.

Both in the U.A.R. and Sudan, the contract is frustrated by the worker's disability which prevents him from performing the contractual work. The effect of the employer's disability on the contract is similar to the effect of the sickness.

The contract is not frustrated in the U.A.R., by the worker's detention in prison or his sentence to imprisonment. If the employer does not justifiably terminate the contract, the contract during the worker's absence is suspended. If the worker is waiting for trial, but not under detention, the contract is not suspended unless the employer expressly decides to suspend it. During the suspension of the contract, the employer should not be able to terminate the contract, however long the

[279] *Vide Johnson v. Shrewsbury & Birmingham Railway Co.* (1853), 3 De G.M. 914; *Rigby v. Connol* (1880), 14 Ch.D. 482; and *Ryan v. Mutual Tontine Westminister Chambers Association* (1893), 1 Ch. 116; *vide* also Cheshire and Fifoot, p. 515 *et seq.*; Diamond, pp. 79 and 210; Clark, pp. 12–3; and Barwell and Kar, p. 61.

[280] *Vide R. v. National Arbitration Tribunal, Ex, p. Crowther* (1948) 1 K.B., 424.

suspension may be. If the worker is acquitted or his case is filed, the employer is expected to reinstate him in his work; but he can still terminate the contract, if he has justifiable reasons to do so. In Sudan the contract is suspended by the worker's detention in prison, or by his sentence to imprisonment; and such long absence may result in the frustration of the contract. However, except in the case of Government workers, the employer can rightfully terminate the contract, whether before, during or after the trial.

When the worker is called to military service in the U.A.R., he has the choice between the termination of his contract and its suspension, until he returns from his military service. The lack of similar rules in Sudan is due to the non-prescription of compulsory military service; but under the English Common Law, the call to military service frustrates the contract.

In the U.A.R. an unlawful strike entitles the employer to justifiably terminate the contract; but the contract is not *ipso facto* frustrated. A lawful strike can only suspend the contract. The rules of the law in these two respects in Sudan, should be similar. A lock-out in the U.A.R. does not suspend the contract nor frustrate it. If, however, the lock-out is authorized by the Minister of Labour, the contract is suspended. In Sudan a lock-out has the same effect as in the U.A.R.; but the employer may suspend the contract, if he is authorized to do so in the contract itself, or if he exercises his statutory right of suspension in certain circumstances.

Both in the U.A.R. and Sudan, the death of the worker completely frustrates the contract. The death of the employer frustrates the contract in the U.A.R., only when his personal qualities are material to the contract. In Sudan the employer's death entitles the worker to the payment in lieu of the notice of termination.

Neither in the U.A.R. nor in Sudan does the bankruptcy of the employer or the winding up or the closing down of the establishment frustrate the contract.

Under the rules of the general law both in the U.A.R. and Sudan, the limited contract terminates by the expiry of its period, or by the performance of the work agreed upon. An unlimited contract is not terminable by notice in the U.A.R., but it is terminable by a reasonable notice in Sudan. The termination of the contract for the failure to carry out the contractual obligations, can only be effected in Court in the U.A.R.; whereas in Sudan such termination can be effected in and out of Court. The legislators in both countries interfered in varying degrees, in these rules of the general law. On the other hand, both the limited and the unlimited contracts are terminable by the agreement of the parties.

Contracts for life and long-term contracts are in the U.A.R., terminable by a prescribed notice, after a certain number of years of service, but only by the worker. In the Sudan neither party can so terminate these contracts.

Both in the U.A.R. and Sudan, the legislators granted both parties the right to terminate the unlimited contract by notice. In Sudan the contract of a daily-paid worker can, however, be terminated without notice, at any time before the first six months of the service are completed. In the U.A.R. the notice of termination should be in writing, though this does not render an oral termination of the contract invalid. In Sudan there is no such requirement. The notice cannot be served during the sickness of the worker in the U.A.R.; whereas in the Sudan it can. Service of the notice during the annual leave, is not precluded in either country. In both countries the notice should not have effect, before the end of the annual leave. This should also apply to the notice served during the worker's sickness in Sudan. In both countries the contract subsists during the notice period. In the U.A.R. payment in lieu of the notice or the unexpired portion thereof, is permitted. The compensation for the non-service or the non-observance of the whole notice period, is thus fixed by statute, without reference to whether any loss was incurred or to the extent of the loss. In Sudan the payment in lieu of the notice is permitted to the employer, except when he is obliged to provide work and not only to pay remuneration to the worker. The non-service of the notice by the worker, or by the employer in the said excepted case, or their non-observance of the whole notice period, constitutes a breach of the contract. The compensation for this breach may be equal to, less or more than the notice pay. Termination of the contract by agreement of the parties, may relieve the worker in both countries of the liability to serve the notice, but the employer should not be so relieved.

The termination of the contract by either party without notice, is in both countries permitted, for the other party's failure to carry out his essential contractual obligations. Instances of such failure are catalogued in the U.A.R., but not in Sudan. The worker is expressly given the power to summarily determine the contract in the U.A.R., in certain circumstances; whereas in the Sudan he is not given this power, though the law warrants it. The employer is entitled to summarily determine the contract, during the worker's period of probation. In

Sudan the position is mainly contracutal, but is subject to the statutory provisions governing the termination of the contract of employment.

In the U.A.R. the terminating party must justify his termination; otherwise the termination will be unjustifiable. In Sudan this doctrine of justification is not knwon. If the notice of termination is served, the termination is rightful.

CHAPTER VII

THE TERMINATION GRATUITY

The workers in the U.A.R. and Sudan, came to be entitled since 1944 in the former,[1] and 1948 in the latter,[2] to the payment by their employers, at the termination of their contracts, of a sum independent of the payment in lieu of the notice of termination, or of the damages due for the unjustifiable or wrongful termination of their contracts, as the case may be. This sum was originally prescribed by the law, in order that the workers may find therein, "a means of sustenance, after they have reached an old age, which generally precludes them from carrying out their work; for it is not just that workers should be thrown out, after they have devoted all or a part of their lives in the service of the employer, without any consideration for their service."[3] The proper description of this sum then is that of 'indemnity' to the worker for the loss of his service, rather than the description of 'gratuity' which has been bestowed upon it by the legislator, both in the U.A.R. and Sudan.[4]

SECTION I: CONDITIONS OF ENTITLEMENT AND CALCULATION OF THE GRATUITY

Section 73 of the U.A.R. Labour Code provides:

"If the duration of a limited contract expries or if the employer terminates an unlimited contract he shall pay to the worker a gratuity for his service at the rate of half a month's wages for every year[5] of the first five year of service and one month's wages for every year thereafter without prejudice to the rights acquired by the worker by virtue of the repealed laws.

[1] *Vide* section 23 of Law 41 of 1944 (*vide* Section II of the Introduction, *supra*).

[2] *Vide* section 25 of the Sudan Ordinance, quoted in Section I of the present Chapter, *infra*.

[3] Cairo Court of Appeal in appeal No. 1332 of 1956 (in Habeeb, p. 399). This is true both of the U.A.R. and Sudan. *Vide* Section II of the present Chapter, *infra*.

[4] *Vide* in this respect, Zaki, p. 302, for the U.A.R, and Barwell and Kar, p. 237, for Sudan.

[5] *Vide* the definition of the year in section 10 of the Labour Code, quoted in footnote 1 to Chapter V, *supra*.

"The worker shall be entitled to a gratuity for a part of the year proportional to that worked by him.

"The last wages shall be taken as the basis of the calculation of the gratuity."[6]

This section expressly applies its provisions to limited contracts.[7] A limited contract includes a contract for seasonal work. However, section 71(2) of the Labour Code redundantly provides that, "if the contract is for seasonal work or the like and it expries the worker shall be entitled to the gratuity due therefor which is prescribed in section 73."

The entitlement to the gratuity of a worker bound by an unlimited contract, arises when the employer terminates the contract. The termination should presumably be the termination by notice, in accordance with section 72 of the Labour Code.[8] However, the gratuity is expressly due by virtue of section 78 of the Labour Code,[9] when the worker summarily determines the contract, for any of the justifying reasons mentioned in section 77 of the Code.[9] Section 79(1) of the Code[10] expressly entitles the worker who is called up to military service, to the gratuity, if he decides to have his contract cancelled. Section 81 (4) of the Code[11] prescribes the payment of the gratuity, when the contract is frustrated by the death of the worker or his disability from work, or his sickness for specified periods of time. The gratuity is due, even though the disability or death results from a professional disease or an industrial accident. The gratuity should also be due, even though the

[6] Cf. the somewhat similar provisions in section 100(1 & 2, a & c) of the Iraqi Labour Code, and sections 54, 57 and 58 of the Lebanese Labour Code, provided that the worker has spent one year in service (section 56). Sections 55 and 24 of the Kuwaiti and Qatari Labour Codes, respectively, provide that the gratuity is payable at the termination of the contract, without stipulating that it should be an unlimited contract. An additional requirement in Qatar, is that the worker should have spent at least one year in service. Sections 13 of the Saudi Regulations, and 19, 19 and 22 of the Jordanian, Libyan and Tunisian Labour Codes, respectively, make the gratuity payable only when an unlimited contract is terminated. The worker should, in addition, have spent six months of service in Jordan, and one year in Tunisia. In France only the journalists and commercial representatives, travellers and agents, are entitled to gratuity, under conditions similar to those in the U.A.R. (*vide* section 29 B–J and K–R of Book I of the French Labour Code). Collective agreements in France do, however, sometimes provide for the payment of a gratuity (*vide* I.L.R., Vol. 79, 1959, pp. 631–2). *Vide* I.L.O. Report VII(1), 1962, pp. 31–2, for the relevant provisions in various countries.

[7] *Vide* the definitions of the limited and the unlimited contracts, in Section III of Chapter II, *supra*.

When the gratuity was first prescribed by section 23 of Law 41 of 1944, only the unlimited contract workers were entitled to it. Section 37 of Law 317 of 1952, made the gratuity payable to the limited contract workers.

[8] *Vide* the section quoted and discussed in Section II, A, 2, of Chapter VI, *supra*.

[9] *Vide* sections 77 and 78 in Section II, A, 3, and B, of Chapter VI, *supra*, respectively; and *vide* therein section 696(1) of the Civil Code.

[10] *Vide* section 79 quoted in Section I, D, of Chapter VI, *supra*.

[11] *Vide* section 81 quoted in Section I, A, of Chapter VI, *supra*.

worker or his beneficiaries receive industrial compensation, because the gratuity and the compensation are for two different objects, and are prescribed by independent legal provisions.[12] If and when the contract is frustrated by the employer's long sickness, disability or death, the gratuity should, on the same analogy, be due to the worker. Section 85 of the Code[13] impliedly preserves the worker's right to the gratuity, when the contract is either transferred to a succeeding employer, or is frustrated by the winding up, bankruptcy or the authorised final closing down of the establishment. On the other hand, section 76 of the Code[14] entitles the employer to deprive the worker of the gratuity, if he summarily determines the contract for any of the reasons mentioned in that section.

If the contract is frustrated by *force majeure*, the worker seems to be entitled to the gratuity, on the analogy of his entitlement thereto by virtue of the said section 81 of the Labour Code.[15]

On the other hand, section 80 of the Code provides that "the worker may resign from the work by serving upon the employer the notice prescribed by section 72 and in such a case he shall be entitled to one third of the gratuity prescribed by section 73 if his service exceeds two years but has not reached five years and two thirds thereof if his service has not reached ten years and he shall be entitled to the whole gratuity if he resigns after ten years."[16] This presumably should apply to the resignation of the worker, who is bound by a contract for life or for more than five years, by six months' notice, after the lapse of the first five years of service, by virtue of section 678(2) of the Civil Code.[17] If, how-

[12] Murad, pp. 413 and 427; Badawi, K.M., pp. 422–3; El-Areef, p. 410; Sabbour, p. 511; El-Fakahani, 1959 Supplement, p. 314; Rashed and Hashem, pp. 307–8; and Faheem, p. 126, are all of the same opinion.

[13] *Vide* section 85 quoted in Section IV of Chapter II, *supra*, and in Section I, G, of Chapter VI, *supra*.

[14] *Vide* section 76 quoted in Section II, A, 3 and 4, of Chapter VI, *supra*.

[15] *Vide* Cairo Court of Cassation in case No. 932 of 1955 (in El-Fakahani, Book I, Vol. I, p. 620); the Alexandria Court of Appeal in appeal No. 400 of 1956 (in Habeeb, p. 391); and the Cairo Court of Appeal in appeal 474 of 1957 (in El-Hawwari, p. 194); *vide* also Butros and Rajab, p. 429; Rashed and Hashem, p. 184; Zaki, pp. 306–7 (though hesitatingly); and Faheem, p. 125. The line of reasoning adopted by these Courts and writers, is that the gratuity is due, except in the cases where it is expressly excluded. They conclude that the gratuity is due, when the contract is frustrated by *force majeure*. Murad, p. 414, submits that the frustration of the contract, by the burning down of the employer's establishment, should not entitle the worker to the gratuity.

[16] Cf. some similar provisions in sections 57 and 95 of the Kuwaiti and Libyan Labour Codes, respectively. Sections 100(2, f) and 55 of the Iraqi and Lebanese Labour Codes, respectively, entitle the worker to the gratuity, if he resigns at the age of sixty years, or if he completes fifteen years of service in the former, and twenty five years in the latter. The other Arab Labour Codes do not contain any relevant provision.

[17] *Vide* section 678(2) quoted and discussed in Section III of Chapter II, *supra*; and

ever, he does not serve the notice as prescribed in section 72 of the Labour Code or section 678(2) of the Civil Code, as the case may be, or does not pay in lieu of the notice, the worker will not be entitled to any gratuity, as this will entitle the employer to summarily determine the contract for the worker's failure to carry out his contractual obligations.[18]

If the contract is terminated by the agreement of the parties, the worker seems to be entitled to the gratuity, whether the contract was a limited or an unlimited contract. If it was limited, its termination by agreement, amounts to no more than the shortening of its life and does not change its limited nature. If it was an unlimited contract, its termination by agreement should not deprive the worker of the payment in lieu of the notice of termination.[19] So in either case, the conditions of entitlement to the gratuity in accordance with section 73, are fulfilled.[20]

Section 73 of the Labour Code prescribes the payment of the gratuity for the worker's service, "without prejudice to the rights acquired by the worker by virtue of the repealed laws." Section 2 of the Presidential Order issuing the Labour Code, provides:

"Persons who work in establishments not operated by mechanical power and ordinarily employ less than five workers and whose proprietors are not according to the last estimation liable to pay more than twenty pounds per annum as commercial and industrial tax and the workers of the non-commercial employers whose professional tax does not exceed the said sum according to the last estimation shall not benefit from the provisions of this Code except from the date of the coming into force of the Code.

"The provisions of section 73 of the attached Code concerning the gratuity for the service preceding the coming into force of the Code,

vide Section II, A, 1, of Chapter VI, *supra*; *vide* also El-Areef, p. 415; Butros and Rajab, pp. 418–9; Badawi, K.M., p. 417; and Habeeb, pp. 401–2, who are of the same opinion.

[18] *Vide* section 76(6) of the Labour Code, in Section II, A, 3, of Chapter VI, *supra*. *Vide* in support of the same conclusion, Cairo Court of Cassation in case No. 923 of 1955 (in Habeeb, p. 401); and the same Court in case No. 1041 of 1957 (in El-Hawwari, p. 211); and Cairo Court of Appeal in appeal No. 1196 of 1957 (in El-Fakahani, Book I, Vol. III, p. 341); and *vide* Murad, p. 416 (though his support is not express). Those who oppose the conclusion, on the ground that the service of the notice is a mere formality, are Habeeb, p. 401; and Zaki, p. 305 (though not whole-heartedly).

[19] *Vide* Section II, A, 2, of Chapter VI, *supra*.

[20] Those who support the entitlement to the gratuity when an unlimited contract is terminated by agreement, are Butros and Rajab, p. 429; El-Areef, pp. 410–1; Rashed and Hashem, p. 184; and Faheem, p. 125; *vide* also in support, the Alexandria Court of Appeal in appeal No. 176 of 1957 (in El-Fakahani, Book I, Vol. III, p. 340). Murad, p. 388 and Sabbour, pp. 324 and 495, are of the contrary opinion, because the entitlement to the gratuity in these circumstances, is not prescribed by the Labour Gode.

shall not apply except within the limits set by the provisions of Law 317 of 1952 and Law 279 of 1946 and on the basis of the wages (payable) at the time the contract is terminated."[21]

So the gratuity for the part of the worker's service, preceding the coming into force of the Labour Code, should be calculated in accordance with Law 317 of 1952, which differentiated between the monthly-paid and other workers. On the other hand, the said subsection 2(2), which purports to prescribe the basis of calculation of the gratuity, does not answer the question whether the preceding service does or does not include the part of the worker's service, before the coming into force of Law 317 of 1952, or even that preceding the coming into force of Law 41 of 1944.[22] It is submitted that an affirmative answer is warranted by the lack of any negative provision, and by the rule of interpretation which gives the benefit of the doubt to the worker.[23] Before the enactment of the Labour Code, the weight of the judicial authority was in favour of entitling the worker to the gratuity, as calculated in accordance with the rules prescribed in section 37 of Law 317 of 1952, not only for his service since 15 August 1944 when Law 41 was enacted, but also for the service preceding that date.[24] This judicial trend has not been reversed, after the enactment of the Labour Code.[25]

On the other hand, section 73 of the Code prescribes the gratuity for the worker's service, without defining whether it should be actual service or just a continuous relationship of employment (or continuous service as it is sometimes called). This lack of definition does, it is submitted, give ground for an interpretation in favour of the worker,[23] so

[21] The second sub-section was added by Law 227 of 1959 (*Al-Jaridat-ul-Rasmiyyatu* No. 211 (*bis*) of 1 October 1959), which made the new provisions applicable as from 7 April 1959, the date on which the U.A.R. Labour Code came into force. The reason for this retrospective effect, was 'justified' by the Explanatory Note to Law 227, by saying that this Law was no more than an interpretation of section 73 of the Labour Code. Law 279 of 1946 is the Syrian Labour Code, which was repealed by the U.A.R. Labour Code.

[22] *Vide* Section II of the Introduction, *supra*.

[23] *Vide* Section V of Chapter II, *supra*.

[24] *Vide* the decisions in El-Fakahani, Book I, Vol. I, pp. 589, 591, 594, 595, 596 and 602 – For the decisions which excluded the service preceding 15 August 1944, *vide* pp. 590, 592, 598 and 599.

[25] *Vide* Alexandria Court of Appeal in appeal No. 524 of 1959 (in El-Hawwari, p. 357), which held the worker entitled to the gratuity, for the part of his service from 10 March 1938 to 7 April 1959, as calculated in accordance with section 37 of Law 317 of 1952, and for the balance of his service up to 20 June 1959, as calculated in accordance with section 73 of the Labour Code; *vide* also Cairo Court of Cassation in cases Nos. 1733 and 2271 of 1959 (in El-Hawwari, pp. 359 and 214, respectively); *vide* also El-Fakahani, 1959 Supplement, pp. 219–22; Zaki, pp. 311–3, however, submits that the worker should not be entitled to any gratuity, for the part of his service preceding the enactment of Law 41 of 1944.

as to interpret service as continuous service. This means that the worker should be entitled to the gratuity for all the period, from the commencement of his service up to the moment it is terminated, irrespective of whether the worker was paid or not for any part of this period. Thus there should not be excluded from the said period, the worker's service for the last twenty days of his intermittent sickness period of two hundred days, which frustrate the contract in accordance with section 81 of the Labour Code,[11] or his absence for the compulsory military service in accordance with section 79(1), or any suspension period by virtue of section 67, when he is accused of the commission of certain offences,[26] or any disciplinary suspension by virtue of section 66,[27] or the worker's absence without justifiable cause, up to the limits mentioned in section 76(5) of the Code.[28] In line with this reasoning, if the period of the notice of termination of the contract as prescribed in section 72 of the Code,[29] is served, it will enter in the calculation of the gratuity. If, however, the terminating party pays in lieu of the notice, as he is permitted to do by section 72, the contract should terminate immediately on such payment,[30] and the period of the prescribed notice should be excluded from the calculation of the gratuity.[31] The same conclusion should be reached where the notice is not served, for the non-service of the notice does not invalidate the termination of the contract, as from the date the terminating party withdraws from the contract.[32] That also is the reason for the exclusion of the period during which the worker's dismissal is temporarily suspended, by virtue of section 75 of the Code,[33] because the contract is not revived during this period of suspension.[34] However, an exception to this results when the worker, dismissed for his trade union activities, is returned to his work by the order of the Court, in accordance with section 75(6), for then the contract is deemed not to have been affected.[35] On the other hand, the periods during which the worker goes on a lawful strike, or during which the employer

[26] *Vide* section 67 quoted and discussed in Section I, C, of Chapter VI, *supra*.
[27] *Vide* section 66 quoted and discussed in Section I, E, of Chapter III, *supra*.
[28] *Vide* section 76(5) quoted in Section II, A, 4, of Chapter VI, *supra*.
[29] *Vide* section 72 quoted and discussed in Section II, A, 2, of Chapter VI, *supra*.
[30] *Vide* footnote 115 to Chapter VI, *supra*, and the related text.
[31] *Vide* the contrary decision of the Cairo Labour Court in case No. 1103 of 1956, quoted with approval by Habeeb, p. 396.
[32] *Vide* the contrary decision of the Alexandria Court of Cassation in case No. 159 of 1950, quoted with approval by Rashed and Hashem, p. 170.
[33] *Vide* the section mentioned in footnote 260 to Chapter VI, *supra*.
[34] *Vide* Cairo Labour Court in case No. 1790 of 1953 (in Butros and Rajab, p. 439); and Cairo Court of Cassation in case No. 931 of 1959 (in El-Hawwari, p. 356); *vide* also Sabbour, p. 507; and Naguib and Bakr, p. 140.
[35] *Vide* section 75(6) mentioned in Section II, B, of Chapter VI, *supra*.

declares an unlawful lock-out, should be included in the calculation of the gratuity.[36]

The gratuity should be calculated on the basis of the wages[37] payable to the worker, at the time of the termination of the contract. The wages of the piece-rate workers are, however, calculated in accordance with section 9 of the Labour Code, on the basis of the average wages received by them for the actual days of work, during the preceding year.[38]

Finally, there is no provision in the Code to limit the time, within which the gratuity should be paid after it becomes due, equivalent to the provisions in respect of wages, in section 48 of the Labour Code.[39] So the gratuity should be paid, either within the customary period, if any, or within a reasonable time.

In Sudan section 25 of the Sudan Ordinance provides:

"When a contract of service is terminated by the employer otherwise than by the dismissal of the employed person in accordance with section 10 subsection(2), the employer shall pay to the employed person a gratuity in respect of his period of service calculated as follows:

"For employed persons who have completed not less than five years of continuous service, one half of one month's basic pay plus cost of living allowance in respect of each completed year of service up to twelve years, and one month's basic pay plus cost of living allowance in respect of each additional completed year of service, calculated on the basis of the average basic pay plus cost of living allowance paid to the employed person during the three years preceding the termination of the contract. The maximum gratuity payable under this section shall not exceed nine month's basic play pus cost of living allowance, except in the case of an employed person who has served for a period of not less than twenty completed years of continuous service, when the gratuity shall be a sum equivalent to one year's basic pay plus cost of living allowance calculated in accordance with the provisions of this section."[40]

Section 24 of the Sudan Ordinance adds that "an employed person shall not be entitled to receive any gratuity payable on termination of his contract of service under the provisions of this Ordinance until he has

[36] Butros and Rajab, p. 436, are of the same opinion.

[37] *Vide* the definition of wages, in Section I of Chapter IV, *supra*.

[38] *Vide* section 9 quoted in footnote 17 to Chapter V, *supra*.

[39] *Vide* section 48 quoted in Section III, D, of Chapter IV, *supra*; *vide* also therein Section 676(2) of the Civil Code.

[40] Cf. some similar provisions in section 19 of the Bahraini Labour Code. The Adenese Ordinance contains no relevant provision. The payment of any gratuity in England, is contractual.

completed five years or more of continuous service and has reached the age of twenty three years."[41]

So contrary to the U.A.R., the worker will not be entitled to any gratuity, if his contract is rightfully terminared by notice by his employer, before a worker completes five years of continuous service and before he reaches twenty three years of age.[42] On the other hand, the expiry of a limited contract does not entitle the worker to any gratuity, contrary to the position in the U.A.R. But as in the U.A.R, the employer is entitled to deprive the worker of the gratuity, if he summarily terminates the contract by virtue of section 10(2) of the Ordinance.[43]

If the worker is obliged to terminate the contract without notice, because of the employer's conduct,[44] it is submitted that he would be entitled to the gratuity, for the real terminating party should be taken to have been the employer and not the worker. If this would not be the position, the employer would be provided with a weapon of two vicious sides, for he can at one and the same time drive the worker to leave the service and deprive him of the gratuity. On the other hand, the frustration of the contract by the death of the employer, or the dissolution or winding up of the establishment in which the worker is employed, by virtue of section 12 of the Sudan Ordinance, preserves for the worker "all the benefits of the contract up to such termination as provided in this Ordinance."[45] Section 33(1) of the Ordinance provides that, "in the event of the death of an employed person his dependants shall be entitled to receive a gratuity equal to any gratuity to which the deceased would have been entitled if his contract of service had been terminated by his employer otherwise than by dismissal on the day of his death."[46]

If the contract is frustrated by an Act of God or *vis major*, the worker should, on the analogy of the entitlement in accordance with

[41] The worker in Bahrain, is not entitled to any gratuity, "for less than one year of continuous service," by virtue of section 19(a, i) of the Labour Code; but there is no age restriction.

[42] Section 2 of the Sudan Ordinance empowers a person to enter into a contract of employment, at the age of fifteen years. If the five years mentioned in section 24 of the Ordinance, are added to the said fifteen years, the result is twenty years. So without commenting on the unreasonable length of the service itself, before whose expiry the worker will not be entitled to any gratuity, the extra age requirement of another three years, seems only to have the effect of lessening the employer's burdens.

[43] *Vide* the section quoted in Section II, A, 3, of Chapter VI, *supra*.

[44] *Vide* Section II. A, 3, of Chapter VI, *supra*.

[45] *Vide* section 12 quoted in Section, I F, of Chapter VI, *supra*.

[46] There is no similar provision in the Bahraini Labour Code. However, by analogy with the worker's entitlement to the gratuity, in accordance with section 17(a) of the Code (which is the equivalent of section 12 of the Sudan Ordinance), the worker's heirs should be entitled to the gratuity on the worker's death (*vide* section 36 of the Bahraini Labour Code).

sections 12 and 33(1) of the Sudan Ordinance, also be entitled to the gratuity.

In the eventuality of the worker's resignation, section 26 of the Sudan Ordinance provides:

"An employed person who, after the completion of not less than fifteen years of continuous service and subject to the notice prescribed in section 10, himself terminates the contract of service shall be entitled to a gratuity equal to one half of the amount which would otherwise be payable in accordance with the provisions of the preceding section.

"Provided that if he has completed not less than thirty years of continuous service he shall be entitled to a full gratuity in accordance with the preceding section."[47]

As in the U.A.R., and for the same reason, the worker will be deprived of the gratuity, if he does not serve the prescribed notice of termination.

If an unlimited contract is terminated by the agreement of the parties the worker as in the U.A.R, and for the same reason, should be entitled to the gratuity.[48]

Section 25 of the Sudan Ordinance mentions 'continuous service.' This is defined in section 2 of the Ordinance, as the "continuous service with the same employer from the date on which this Ordinance comes into force." So the worker will not be entitled to any gratuity for the part of his service which precedes 12 February 1949, the date on which the Ordinance came into force.[49] This continuous service should, as in the U.A.R., mean all the period from the commencement of the service to the time of the termination of the contract, irrespective of whether or not the worker was paid for any part of this period. In this respect, similar conclusions, where relevant, should also be reached in Sudan.

Contrary to the position in the U.A.R., the wages on the basis of which the gratuity is calculated, are the "average basic pay plus cost of living allowance, paid to the employed person during the three years immediately preceding the termination of the contract." Basic pay is defined in section 2 of the Sudan Ordinance, as the "basic rate of remuneration payable to an employed person by an employer but excludes all other remuneration." On the other hand, the average is made out of the basic pay and the cost of living allowance actually paid to the

[47] Section 20 of the Bahraini Labour Code entitles the worker to the full gratuity, if he resigns by notice after five years of service.

[48] *Vide* Section II, A, 2, of Chapter VI, *supra*.

[49] Section 19(b) of the Bahraini Labour Code, provides similarly though such previous service is taken into consideration, for the purposes of entitling the worker to a bigger gratuity for longer service.

worker, during the preceding three years, and not what was supposed to have been paid to him. This applies both to piece-rate and other workers.

If the worker's service is terminated, at any time after the completion of five years' service, he should, if the termination is effected during the year, be entitled, as in the U.A.R., to a proportional part of the gratuity for the year of termination.

There is a ceiling on the gratuity payable in Sudan, contrary to the position in the U.A.R.

Finally, no provision is made in Sudan for the period of time during which the gratuity should be paid, after it becomes due, equivalent to section 15 of the Sudan Ordinance,[50] in respect of wages. So the payment of the gratuity within the customary period, if any, or within a reasonable time, should also apply in Sudan.

SECTION II: SUBSTITUTION OF THE GRATUITY BY OTHER BENEFITS

Section 83 of the U.A.R. Labour Code provides:

"If the establishment has a workers' savings fund[51] and if the rules of the fund state that the employer's contribution to the account of the worker in the fund is in satisfaction of the employer's legal obligation to pay the termination gratuity the contribution shall be paid to the worker provided that it is equal to or exceeds the gratuity due to him in accordance with the provisions of this chapter;[52] otherwise the gratuity shall fall due.

"If, however, the rules of the fund do not state that the employer's contribution was meant to be in satisfaction of his legal liability for the termination gratuity the worker shall be entitled to receive what is due to him in accordance with the rules of the fund over and above his legal entitlement to the gratuity.[53]

"If the establishment makes a pension scheme the pensionable worker

[50] *Vide* section 15 quoted in Section II, D, of Chapter IV, *supra*.

[51] Section 84 of the Code provides:

"Any person who sets up a savings assistance or pension fund in an establishment shall before its registration secure the consent of the competent administrative authority to its rules.

"The non-objection of the said authority to these rules within sixty days of their submission shall be deemed to be an approval of the rules."

[52] This is Chapter II of Book II (sections 42–88) of the Labour Code, which regulates the individual contract of employment.

[53] This provision was necessitated by the protests of the workers who were employed in establishments, which provided savings funds benefits, much earlier than the prescription of the gratuity by Law 41 of 1944: *vide* Butros and Rajab, p. 443.

shall be entitled to choose between the pension and the prescribed gratuity provided that if his service be terminated before he becomes entitled to the (full) pension he shall be entitled to the prescribed gratuity or what falls due to him of the pension fund whichever is greater."[54]

Section 3 of the Presidential Order issuing the Labour Code, provides that, "when the old age pension scheme comes into force the members of the workers' Insurance and Savings Corporation[55] shall be entitled to convert their due entitlements of the termination gratuity prescribed by this Code and their due savings in the (Corporation's) fund into pensions in accordance with a schedule which shall be issued in an order from the Minister of Labour on the proposal of the board of management of the Corporation provided that the conversion value of the said sums shall not be less than two pounds per month in the Egyptian region or twenty Syrian pounds in the Syrian region."[56]

The old age pension scheme was established by the Social Insurance Law No. 92 of 1959,[57] which was later amended by Decree Law No. 143 of 1961. Section 4 of Law 143 made the subscription in the pension scheme established by Law 192, obligatory both on the worker and the employer. By virtue of section 63 of Law 92, the employer's liability for the termination gratuity under section 73 of the Labour Code, was substituted by his contribution to the Social Insurance Corporation established by Law 92.[58] If, at the termination of the worker's service, the employer's contribution be less than the amount of the gratuity which should otherwise be due to the worker, the employer is obliged to pay the difference to the Corporation. Section 61 of Law 92 deprives the worker of the employer's contribution to the pension fund, if he is summarily dismissed in accordance with section 76 of the Labour Code,[59]

[54] Section 100(5) of the Iraqi Labour Code, re savings funds, substitutes the benefit thereunder for the gratuity, if it is more than the gratuity; but there is no requirement of the express statement of the same in the fund's rules. As in the U.A.R., the choice is the worker's choice. Section 27 of the Qatari Labour Code, re provident funds and pension schemes, provides in terms similar to the Iraqi. The Iraqi and Qatari provisions bear some similarity to section 39 of Law 41 of 1944 of the U.A.R. Section 95 of the Libyan Labour Code expressly substitutes the gratuity, by the benefits under the Social Security Act No. 53 of 1957. The other Arab Labour Codes do not contain relevant provisions.

[55] This is the corporation established by Law 419 of 1955, which was repealed by Law 92 of 1959.

[56] *Vide* footnote 150 to Chapter IV, *supra*, for the value of the Egyptian and Syrian pounds.

[57] *Al-Jaridat-ul-Rasmiyyutu* No. 71 (bis) B, dated 7 April 1959, p. 28.

[58] Section 56 of Law 92 prescribes a contribution by the employer, amounting to fourteen per cent of the worker's wages. The worker contributes one half of this sum. In addition to both, the pension is made up of the income of the investment of these contributions, and of any gifts the corporation decides to accept.

[59] *Vide* the section quoted and discussed in Section II, A, 3, of Chapter VI, *supra*.

or if he resigns before he *completes* two years of service.[60] Then the section proceeds to provide for the worker's entitlement to one third of these contributions for the service up to five years, and two thirds for the service up to ten years, exactly as section 80 of the Labour Code provides in respect of the gratuity.[61]

In Sudan section 27 of the Sudan Ordinance provides:

"(1) Where a Provident Fund, Pension, Life Assurance or other similar scheme has been established by an employer to provide benefits to employed persons on termination of their contracts of service, and the scope and provisions of such scheme have been approved by the Commissioner of Labour, and where any employed person who is eligible to subscribe to such approved scheme neglects or refuses without good and sufficient cause to subscribe thereto, the employer may at his discretion withhold payment of all or part of the gratuity to which the employed person would otherwise be entitled under the provisions of this Ordinance.

"(2) Where an employed person is entitled as part of his conditions of service to benefits on termination of his contract of service under the provisions of a Provident Fund, Pension, Life Assurance or other similar scheme approved by the Commissioner of Labour, he shall be entitled to receive:

(a) the benefits to which he is entitled under the Provident Fund, Pension, Life Assurance or other similar scheme; or

(b) gratuity calculated in accordance with the provisions of this Ordinance plus any sums paid by him by way of contribution to such scheme together with any interest accrued thereon which may be prescribed under the provisions of the said scheme, whichever total is the greater.

"Provided that if a pension is payable under (a) it shall always be considered greater than any capital sum payable under (b) for the purpose of this section."[62]

From this provision it is clear that, contrary to the position in the U.A.R., the worker's subscription to the Provident, Pension, Life Assurance or other similar scheme, is not absolutely obligatory. If, however, the worker refuses to subscribe "without good and sufficient cause," he may be liable to be penalized by the employer, by depriving

[60] Section 80 of the Labour Code deprives the worker of the gratuity, unless "his service *exceeds* two years."

[61] For further enlightenment on the pension scheme established by Law 92, *vide* sections 55–64 of this Law.

[62] Cf. some similar provisions, in section 21 of the Bahraini Labour Code.

him of all or part of the gratuity which otherwise would be due to him. The Sudan does not yet have any social insurance legislation, and this somehow explains the said non-absolute obligation on the worker. On the other hand, as in the U.A.R., it is submitted that the employer's contribution to the said scheme will not be due to the worker, if he is summarily dismissed by vitrue of section 10(2) of the Sudan Ordinance,[63] or wherever the worker is deprived of the gratuity.

Finally, both in the U.A.R. and Sudan, the legislative provisions aiming at the substitution of the termination gratuity by other benefits, do hold that the gratuity or an equivalent sum should, in any case, be the minimum which is due to the worker. Section 27 of the Sudan Ordinance deems any pension which may fall due to the worker, to be always more favourable to the worker than the gratuity. There is no similar provision in the U.A.R.

SECTION III: DISTRIBUTION OF THE GRATUITY OR THE SUBSTITUTED BEBEFITS AMONG BENEFICIARIES

Section 82 of the U.A.R. Labour Code provides:

"The total gratuity shall on the termination of the contract by the worker's death be divided as follows:

1. If children and parents who were supported by him are left the child or children in equal shares shall be entitled to seventy-five per cent, (and) the other twenty-five per cent shall be given to the two parents in equal shares or to either (surviving) parent.
2. If children who were supported by him are left but no parent or parents brothers or sisters who were supported by him are left the gratuity shall be divided among them in equal shares and if only one (such) child is left he shall be given the whole gratuity.
3. If the two parents who were supported by him are left but no children are left the gratuity shall be divided between them in equal shares and if one parent is left he shall be given the whole gratuity.
4. If a spouse is left together with children and parents who were supported by him the spouse shall be entitled to forty per cent and the child or children forty per cent and the parent or parents twenty per cent but if no children are left the spouse shall be entitled to two thirds of the gratuity and the parents one third, and if no parents are left the spouse shall be entitled to one half of the gratuity and the child or children

[63] *Vide* section 10(2) quoted in Section II, A, 3, and 4 of Chapter VI, *supra*.

the other half, and if no children or parents are left the spouse shall be given the whole gratuity.

"The brothers and sisters who were supported by the worker shall take the place of the parents if neither parent is left, and if none of the aforementioned is left the gratuity shall be divided in equal shares among those who were supported by the male or female worker and if none of these is left the gratuity shall be divided among the heirs according to the law of succession.

"The child or children shall include the males and the females and the spouse shall include the wife and the husband who was disabled from earning his living and was supported by his wife."[64]

So the heirs will not be entitled to any share in the gratuity, unless the classes of the beneficiaries enumerated in the section are respectively and fully exhausted. This constitutes a departure from the Moslem *Shari'a* Law of succession, which is applicable in the country as a whole.[65] On the other hand, the support of the beneficiary by the deceased worker is the measure of entitlement to the gratuity. This support is the actual support, and is not limited to support by the order of the Court.[66]

Section 98 of Law 92 of 1959,[67] provides for the distribution of a deceased worker's pension, exactly in the same way as does section 82 of the Labour Code, in respect of the gratuity. However, section 61 of Law 92 provides for the accrual of the pension or the other entitlements of the worker to the Corporation established by this Law. So heirs would not be entitled to any share, contrary to case of the gratuity. This constitutes a far-reaching departure from the rules of the Moslem *Shari'a* Law.

In Sudan section 33(2) of the Sudan Ordinance provides that "the

[64] Cf. the provisions in sections 100(6) and 72(d) of the Iraqi Labour Code. Sections 84 and 26 of the Kuwaiti and Qatari Labour Codes, respectively, and section 37 of the Saudi Regulations provide for the distribution of the gratuity among the heirs, in accordance with the Moslem Law of succession. The gratuity should be paid in Court which will make the distribution, both in Kuwait and Qatar. The Government in Saudi Arabia, is the authority concerned. Section 57 of the Lebanese Labour Code entitles the heirs of the deceased worker to the gratuity, but does not provide for its distribution among them. So the personal law of the deceased should be applicable. The Jordanian, the Libyan and the Tunisian Labour Codes are silent all through.

[65] Another departure from the *Shari'a* Law, is the equation of the males and the females, for under this Law, the male inherits double the share of the female. The Christian community also applies the *Shari'a* Law voluntarily, as indeed is generally the case all over the Middle East.

[66] Sabbour, p. 498, is of the same opinion; and he correctly adds that residence with the deceased worker, is not necessary – *Vide* Section III of Chapter I, *supra*, for the definition of the dependent members of the employer's family.

[67] *Vide* Section II of this Chapter, *supra*.

employer shall pay such wages, gratuity or other payment to any District Judge of the 1st or 2nd grade who, where the deceased is a Moslem shall distribute the same to the dependants in the proportions laid down in the Schedule to this Ordinance, and where the deceased is a non-Moslem shall distribute the same to the dependants as he shall think fit having regard to the personal law of the deceased."[68] Dependants are defined in section 2 of the Sudan Ordinance, as "those members of the family of an employed person who are wholly or in part dependent upon his earnings."[69] Thus the dependant should be a member of the employer's family, whereas in the U.A.R. dependants other than such members can ultimately share in the gratuity.

The Schedule mentioned in section 33 of the Ordinance, for the distribution of the gratuity, provides as follows:

"Note: (1) Brother and sister includes half-brother and half-sister
(2) If deceased Moslem is a female the word 'widower' shall be substituted for the words 'widow or widows' in the schedule.

DEGREE OF RELATIONSHIP	DISTRIBUTION
1. When the deceased leaves a widow or widows, and a child or children under 17 years of age or physically incapable of earning their living.	(a) For the widow or widows and one child: 60% for the widow or widows (in equal shares); 40% for the child. (b) For the widow or widows and two children: 60% for the widow or widows (in equal shares). 20% for each child. (c) For the widow or widows and more than two children: 50% for the widow or widows (in equal shares). 50% for the children (in equal shares).

[68] Section 36 of the Bahraini Labour Code prescribes the payment to the Government, or to the British Political Agent in Bahrain (when the British Bahraini Orders 1953–56, extend to the deceased), for distribution to the heirs, in accordance with the *Shari'a* Law, if the deceased was a Moslem.

[69] *Vide* Section III of Chapter I, *supra*, for a discussion of the word *dependent*.

2. When the deceased leaves a widow or widows, but no children under 17 years of age or physically incapable of earning their living and a father or mother or both.	75% for the widow or widows (in equal shares). 25% for the father or mother or for both (in equal shares).
3. When the deceased leaves a widow or widows, but no children under 17 years of age or physically incapable of earning their living, and no father or mother.	100% for the widow or widows (in equal shares).
4. When the deceased leaves no widow but leaves a child or children under 17 years of age or physically incapable of earning their living.	100% for the child or for the children (in equal shares).
5. When the deceased leaves no widow nor any children under 17 years of age or physically incapable of earning their living, but leaves a father or mother or both, and brothers or sisters under 17 years of age or physically incapable of earning their living.	$66\frac{2}{3}\%$ for the father or the mother or for both (in equal shares). $33\frac{1}{3}\%$ for the brothers and sisters (in equal shares).
6. When the deceased leaves no widow, children, brothers or sisters under 17 years of age or physically incapable of earning their living, but leaves his father or mother or both.	For the father or mother or both (in equal shares).
7. When the deceased leaves no widow nor children under 17 years of age or physically incapable of earning their living, nor his father or mother, but leaves brothers and sisters who are under 17 years of age or physically incapable of earning their living.	In equal shares between the brothers and sisters.

8. When the deceased leaves no widows, child, father, mother, brother or sister, but leaves other members of the family as defined in section 2 of the Ordinance.	In equal shares among those members of the family."

This distribution constitutes a departure from the rules of the Moslem *Shari'a* Law of succession, as does the distribution in the U.A.R.[70] On the other hand, there is no provision as to what becomes of the gratuity, if none of those mentioned in the Schedule survives. It seems very likely that the gratuity in this case does not devolve to the heirs of the deceased, because section 33(1) of the Sudan Ordinance expressly leaves the gratuity to the depedants, and does not merely provide for the distribution of the gratuity.[71] So the employer will be relieved of the payment of any gratuity, if none of those mentioned in the Schedule is left after the deceased. This apparent drastic departure from the Moslem *Shari'a* Law, in contrast with the partial saving for heirs in the U.A.R., requires interference from the legislator, so as to preserve the rights of the heirs in the gratuity, after the dependants, if any,[72] or at least to clarify what becomes of the gratuity if no dependants are left.

SUMMARY

When a limited contract expires, the worker in the U.A.R. but not in Sudan, is entitled to a termination gratuity. When an unlimited contract is terminated by the employer by notice, the worker in the U.A.R. is entitled to the gratuity for all the years of his service, and a proportional part of the gratuity for an unfinished year of service. In Sudan he will not in such eventuality be entitled to any gratuity, unless he had finished five years of service and reached the age of twenty three. But if the gratuity is due, it is due for all the years of service, and a proportional part of the gratuity is due for an unfinished year of service, as is the case in the U.A.R. The gratuity is also due in the U.A.R., if

[70] The equation of the males and the females in this distribution, constitutes another departure from the *Shari'a* Law, as is the case in the U.A.R.

[71] *Vide* section 33(1) quoted in Section I of this Chapter, *supra*.

[72] *Vide* Section III, G, of Chapter IV, *supra*, where the more unjustifiable departure from the rules of the *Shari'a* Law, in respect of the wages of the deceased worker, was discussed.

the worker terminates his contract summarily for certain justifying reasons, or if his contract is frustrated by a long sickness or by a disability, death, winding up, bankruptcy or authorised final closing down of the establishment, or by *force majeure*. In Sudan the worker should likewise be entitled to the gratuity, subject to the aforementioned service and age requirements. If the worker in the U.A.R. resigns, he will not be entitled to any gratuity, if he has not completed more than two years of service. The equivalent period in Sudan is fifteen years. If in the former he resigns after ten years of service, he will be entitled to the full gratuity. The equivalent period in Sudan is thirty years. One third of the gratuity is due to the worker in the U.A.R., if he has completed five years of service, and two thirds if he has completed ten years of service. In Sudan he is entitled to one half of the gratuity, if he has completed fifteen years but less than thirty years of service. If the contract is terminated by the agreement of the parties, the worker in the U.A.R. whether his contract was limited or unlimited, and the worker in Sudan provided that his contract was unlimited, should be entitled to the gratuity as aforementioned. The worker in the U.A.R. is entitled to the gratuity for his service preceding the enactment of the Labour Code, whereas in Sudan no gratuity is due for any service preceding the enactment of the Sudan Ordinance. In both countries the gratuity is due for continuous service, and not actual service. The gratuity in the U.A.R. is calculated on the basis of the last wages due to the worker before the termination; but the gratuity of piece-rate workers is calculated on the average actual earnings, during the year preceding the termination. In Sudan the gratuity is calculated on the average of the basic rate of pay and the cost of living allowance only, paid to the worker during the three years preceding the termination, and not the full wages. In Sudan there is a ceiling on the maximum gratuity that can be paid; but in the U.A.R. there is none. Finally, there is no provision in either country, limiting the time within which the gratuity should be paid, after it becomes due. So payment should be effected according to custom, if any, or within a reasonable time.

In the U.A.R. the gratuity was substituted by the pension provided for by the social insurance legislation. So the gratuity provisions are only important to measure the minimum benefits which become due to the worker, on the termination of his contract. In Sudan the substitution of the gratuity by other benefits, is not absolutely obligatory, though the worker may suffer if he does not agree thereto. When there is substitution, the residual importance of the gratuity is similar to that in the U.A.R. There is a provision in Sudan deeming a substituted pension to be greater than the gratuity, whereas there is no such provision in the U.A.R.

Distribution of the gratuity is expressly provided for in both countries. The distribution violates the Moslem *Shari'a* Law of succession, though more in the Sudan than in the U.A.R. The dependency of the beneficiaries on the deceased worker is the measure of their entitlement to the gratuity in both countries. However, those dependent beneficiaries can only be the members of the deceased worker's family in Sudan, whereas they can be non-family members in the U.A.R. On the other hand, the gratuity devolves to the heirs in the U.A.R., if no dependants are left by the deceased worker. In Sudan the contrary will very likely be the case.

SELECTED BIBLIOGRAPHY

BOOKS

Badawi, K. M., Al-Marje' Fi Kanun 'Akd El-'Amal El-Fardi Wa Al-Mabadé El-Kanuniya Likanunai Isabat El-'Amal Wa Amrad El-Mihna (in Arabic), 1955, Cairo (*Reference Book For The Law Of The Individual Contract Of Employment And The Legal Principles Relating To Industrial Injuries And Professional Diseases*).

Badawi, Z., Sharh Tashree' El-'Amal Fi Misr (in Arabic), 1953, Cairo, (*Commentary On The Labour Legislation In Egypt*), 2 Volumes and a supplement.

Barwell, N., and Kar, S. S., The Law Relating To Service In India, Volume I: The Law Of Master And Servant, 1st edn., 1952, Orient Longmans, Ltd., Bombay.

Batt, F. R., The Law Of Master And Servant, 4th edn., 1950, Pitman & Sons, Ltd., London.

Beling, W. A., Pan -Arabism And Labour, 1960, Harvard.

Bentham, J., The Theory Of Legislation, 1950, London.

Brinton, J. Y., The Mixed Courts of Egypt, 1930, New Haven University Press.

British Legal Papers, presented to the fifth International Congress of Comparative Law, Palace of Justice, Brussels, August 1958, edited by Kiralfy, A. K. R., Stevens & Sons, Ltd., London.

Butros, R., and Rajab, A. E., Sharh El-Kawaneen Al-Munadhemma Li 'Akd El-'Amal (in Arabic), 1957, Cairo (*Commentary On The Legislation Regulating The Contract Of Employment*).

Cheshire, G. C., and Fifoot, C. H. S., The Law Of Contract, 5th edn., 1960, Butterworth & Co., (Publishers), Ltd., London.

Cooper, W. M., Outlines Of Insustrial Law, 7th edn., by Wood, J. C., 1962, Butterworths, London.

Diamond, A. S., The Law of Master And Servant, 2nd edn., 1946, Stevens & Sons, Ltd., London.

El-Areef, Sharh Tashree' El-'Amal Fi Misr, Al-Guz' Ul-Awwal, Al-Madkhal Wa 'Akd El-'Amal El-Fardi (in Arabic), 2nd edn., 1955, Cairo (*Commentary On The Labour Legislation In Egypt, Volume I: The Introduction And The Individual Contract Of Employment*).

El-Fakahani, H., Al-Mudawwanat-ul-Ummaliyyatu (in Arabic), 2nd edn., 1959, Cairo (*The Labour Handbook*), Book I (3 volumes and a supplement).

El-Hawwari, I., Al-Mawsu'ah Al-Kadha'iyyah Fi Munaz'at El-'Amal (in Arabic). 1960, Cairo (*The Judicial Encyclopaedia Of Labour Disputes*).

El-Sa'eed, S. M., Min Hukuk Wa Wagebat El-'Ummal Wa Ashab El-'Amal Fi Kanun El-'Amal El-'Iraqi (in Arabic), 1962, Baghdad (*Some Rights And Obligations Of The Workers And The Employers In The Iraqi Labour Code*).

Faheem, M., Kanun 'Akd El-'Amal El-Fardi Wa Ahkam El-Kada' (in Arabic), 1955, Cairo (*The Law Of The Individual Contract Of Employment And Court Judgments*).

Fawzi, S. E., The Labour Movement In The Sudan, 1957, Oxford University Press, London.

Habeeb, S. A., Sharh 'Akd El-'Amal Fi El-Kanun El-Muwahhad (in Arabic), 1959, Cairo (*Commentary On The Contract Of Employment In The Unified Labour Cide*).

Halsbury, H. S. G., Laws of England, 3rd edn., Butterworths, London.

Husseini, M. H., and El-Hawwari, I.. Dai'rat-ul-Ma'aref El-'Ummaliyyatu (in Arabic), 1961, Cairo (*The Labour Encyclopaedia*).

Industrial Relations, Ministry of Labour, 1961, London.
International Labour Code 1951, I.L.O., Geneva, Switzerland, 1952 (2 volumes).

Labour Survey of North Africa, 1960, I.L.O., Geneva, Switzerland.
Laws of The Sudan, prepared and arranged for the Laws Commission by Cummings, C., and edited by Bennett, C. H. A., Haycock Press Ltd., London: Volumes, 1, 4, 8, 10.

Macdonell, The Law Of Master And Servant, 1883, Stevens & Son, London.
Madkour, M. T., Sharh Wa Tahleel Kanun El-'Amal El-Kuwaiti Fi El-Kita' El-Ahli (in Arabic), 1960, Kuwait (*Commentary On And Analysis Of The Kuwaiti Labour Code In The Private Sector*).
Magmu'at Kawaneen El-'Amal (in Arabic), The Ministry Of Social Affairs, 1954, Cairo (*A Handbook Of The Labour Legislation*).
Majalla (in Arabic), edited by El-'Aseer, Y., 1904, Beirut (*The Moslem Law Codified*).
Murad, M. H., Kanun-ul-'Amal Wa Al-Ta'meenatu Al-Ijtima'iyyatu (in Arabic), 4th edn., 1961, Cairo (*The Labour And Social Insurance Laws*).

Naguib, F., and Bakr, A. E. R., Kanun El'-Amal El-Muwahhad 'Ilman Wa 'Amalan (in Arabic), 1959, Cairo (*The Unified Labour Code – Theory And Practice*).

Rashed, J. E., and Hashem, M. K., Al-Tashree' El-Asasi Li 'Akd El-'Amal, Kanun 'Akd El-'Amal El-Fardi, Dirasat Mukarana 'Ala Al-Nusus (in Arabic), 1954, Cairo (*The Basic Legislation On The Contract Of Employment, The Individiual Contract Of Employment Law, A Comparative Study Of The Successive Enactments*).

Sabbour, F. A., Al-Waseet Fi 'Akd El-'Amal El-Fardi (in Arabic), 1961, Cairo (*A Handbook On The Individual Contract Of Employment*).
Samuels, H., Industrial Law, 6th edn., 1961, Pitman & Sons, Ltd., London.
Smith, C. M., A Treatise On The Law Of Master And Servant, 7th edn., 1931, Sweet & Maxwell, London.
Stone, J., The Province And Function Of The Law, 1950, Sydney.

The Changing Law In Developing Countries, edited by Anderson, J. N. D., 1963, George Allen & Unwin, Ltd., London.
The System of Industrial Relations In Great Britain, Its History, Law And Institutions, edited by Flanders, A., and Clegg, H., 1954, Basil Blackwell, Oxford.

Zaki, M. J. E., Al-Wageez Fi Kanun El-'Amal (in Arabic), 1962, Cairo (*Resumé Of The Labour Legislation*).

PERIODICALS

Industry And Labour, published by the International Labour Office, Geneva, Switzerland (stopped in December 1961), Volumes 4, 6, 15, 20, 22, 23.
International Labour Review, published monthly since 1921 by the International Labour Office, Geneva, Switzerland, Volumes 7, 28, 30, 32, 34, 77, 78, 79, 80, 83, 84, 86.
International Survey Of Legal Decisions On Labour Law, published yearly from 1926 to 1939, by the International Labour Office, Geneva, Switzerland, Volumes 1–13.
The International And Comparative Law Quarterly, published by the British Institute Of International and Comparative Law, London, Vol. 6, 1957.

I.L.O. CONVENTIONS, RECOMMENDATIONS, REPORTS AND RESOLUTIONS

Conventions

Holidays With Pay Convention, No. 52, 1936.
Contracts of Employment (Indigenous Workers) Convention, No. 64, 1939.
Labour Standards (Non-Metropolitan Territories) Convention, No. 83, 1947.

Contracts Of Employment (Indigenous Workers) Convention No. 86, 1947.
Protection of Wages Convention, No. 95, 1949.
Protection of Wages (Agriculture) Convention, No. 101, 1952.

Recommendations

Utilisation Of Spare Time Recommendation, No. 21, 1924.
Holidays With Pay Recommendation, No. 47, 1936.
Apprenticeship Recommendation, No. 60, 1939.
Protection Of Wages Recommendation, No. 85, 1949.

Reports

The Termination Of Employment, No. VII(1), 1961.
Termination Of Employment At The Initiative Of The Employer, No. V(1), 1962.

Resolutions

Of The Advisory Committee On Professional Workers, Concerning The Protection Of Inventions by Workers (No. 62, G.B. 160, in December 1929).
Of the Advisory Committee On Salaried Employees, Concerning The Protection Of Inventions by Salaried Employees (No. 62, G.B. 197, in April 1931).

LEGISLATION

Aden

The Contracts Of Employment (Indigenous Workers) Ordinance, 1945.
The Minimum Wage And Wages Regulation, 1945.

Bahrain

The Labour Code of 28 December, 1957.

England

The Crown Proceedings Act, 1947 (10 & 11 Geo. VI, C. 44).
The Employers And Workmen Act, 1875 (38 & 39 Vict. C. 90).
The Partnership Act, 1890 (53 & 54, Vict., C. 39).
The Patents And Designs Act, 1907 (7 Edw. VII, C. 29).
The Patents Act, 1949 (12, 13 & 14 Geo. 6, C. 87).
The Payment Of Wages Act, 1960 (8 & 9 Eliz. II Ch. 37).
The Servants' Character Act, 1792 (32 Geo. III, Ch. 56).
The Statute Of Frauds, 1677 (29 Car. II, C. 3) – and the repealing Law Reform (Enforcement of Contracts) Act, 1954 (2 & 3 Eliz. 2, C. 34).
The Truck Act, 1831 (1 & 2 Will. 4, C. 37).
The Truck Act, 1887 (50 & 51 Vict., C. 46).
The Truck Act, 1896 (59 & 60 Vict. ,C. 44).
The Wages Attachment Abolition Act, 1870 (34 & 35 Vict. 30).
The Wages Councils Act, 1945 (8 & 9 Geo. 6, C. 17).
The Wages Councils Act, 1948 (12, 13 & 14, Geo. 6, C. 7).

France

Code de Travaille (Book I).
The Holidays With Pay Act, No. 56-332, 1956 (Journal Officiel de la République français, 88th year, No. 78, 31 March 1956, pp. 3120–3122).

India

The Indian Contract Act, No. IX, 1872.
The Industrial Employment (Standing Orders) Act, 1946.
The Payment Of Wages Act, No. IV, 1936.

Iraq

The Civil Code, Law No. 40, 1951.
The Labour Code, Law No. 1, 1948 (The Official Gazette No. 4115, 16 March 1958).

Italy

The Patents Law, 1949.

Jordan

The Labour Code, Law No. 21, 14 May 1960 (The Official Gazette No. 1491, 21 May 1960).

Kuwait

The Labour Code In The Private Sector, 15 March 1959 (The Official Gazette, No. 216, 15 March 1959).

Lebanon

Code de Obligations, 1934.
The Labour Code, 23 Spetember 1946.

Libya

The Labour Code, 22 November 1962 (The Official Gazette No. 17, 24 November 1962).

Netherlands

The Civil Code, 1907 (as amended by an Act dated 17 December 1953, Staatsblad van het Koninkrijk der Nederlanden, No. 619 (1953), pp. 1135–1139).
The Patents Act, 1910.

Qatar

The Labour Code, Law No. 3, 1962 (The Official Gazette No. 2, 2 April 1962).

Saudi Arabia

The Labour And Workman's Regulations, 10 October 1947.
Royal Decree No. 2629/13/2/18, 22 June 1956, re prohibition of strikes.

Sudan

The Administrative Regulations, 1934.
The Advocates Ordinance, September 1935 (Laws Of The Sudan, Vol. 10, Title XXVI, Sub-Title 2).
The Apprentices Ordinance, 1908 (Laws of the Sudan, Vol. 8, Title XXII, Sub-Title 2).
The Civil Justice Ordinance, 1900 (repealed).
The Civil Justice Ordinance, 1 May 1929 (Laws Of The Sudan, Vol. 10, Title XXVI, Sub-Title 1).
The Companies Ordinance, 1925 (Laws Of The Sudan, Vol. 4, Title XII, Sub-Title 5).
The Domestic Servants Ordinance, 1921 (repealed).
The Domestic Servants Ordinance, 15 May 1955 (The Laws Of The Sudan, Vol. 8, Title XXII, Sub-Title 3).
The Employers And Employed Persons Ordinance, 12 February 1949 (Laws Of The Sudan, Vol. 8, Title XXII, Sub-Title 8).
The Employers And Employed Persons Rules, 15 March 1949 (Laws Of The Sudan, Vol. 8, p. 136).
The Expatriate Officials Compensation Ordinance, 15 August 1954 (Laws Of The Sudan, Vol. 1, Title II, Sub-Title 2).
The Government Provident Fund Ordinance, 1 July 1930 (Laws Of The Sudan, Vol. 1, Title II, Sub-Title 2).
The Officials Discipline Ordinance, 15 July 1927 (Laws Of The Sudan, Vol. 1, Title II, Sub-Title 3).
The Partnership Registration Ordinance, 15 November 1933 (Laws Of The Sudan, Vol. 4, Title XIII, Sub-Title 6).
The Prescription And Limitation Ordinance, 1928 (Laws Of The Sudan, Vol. 10, Title XXVI, Sub-Title 4).
The Trade Disputes Act, 1960 (Laws Of The Sudan, Vol. 8, Title XXII, Sub-Title 7).
The Wages Tribunals Ordinance, 15 February 1952 (Laws Of The Sudan, Vol. 8, Title XXII, Sub-Title 7) – And the two orders issued thereunder, both dated 15 August 1958, re shop-assistants and the Arabic clerical workers.

The Workmen's Compensation Ordinance, 1949 (Laws Of The Sudan, Vol. 8, Title XXII, Sub-Title 4).
The Workshops And Factories Ordinance, 31 December 1949 (Laws Of The Sudan, Title XXII, Sub-Title 5).
The Workshops And Factories Regulations, 1 August 1952 (Laws Of The Sudan, Tite XXII, Sub-Title 5).

Switzerland

Code de Obligations.

Syria

The Civil Code, Legislative Decree No. 84, 18 May 1949 (The Official Gazette, No. 27, 21 May 1949).
The Labour Code, Law No. 279, 1946 (repealed).

Tunisia

The Labour Code, No. 60–18, 1960 (The Official Gazette No. 36, 29 July 1960).

United Arab Republic (arranged chronologically)

The Merchant Shipping Act, 13 November 1882 (repealed).
The Civil Code, Law No. 131, 28 October 1883 (repealed).
Decree Law dated 9 January 1890, re abolishing of the guild system.
The Domestic Servants Regulations, 8 November 1916.
Law No. 14, 1939, re income tax.
Order No. 75, 1940 (as kept effective by Law No. 1202, 1945), re illegal strikes.
Law No. 62, 1942, re use of the Arabic language in certain documents.
Order No. 358, 1942 (The Official Gazette No. 221, 9 December 1942), re the cost of living allowance for commercial and industrial workers.
Law No. 41, 15 August 1944 (The Official Gazette No. 69, 8 June 1944), re the individual contract of employment (repealed).
The Advocates Law, No. 98, 1944.
Law No. 123, 1944 (superseded by Law 81, 1955), re the Worker's identity card.
Order No. 468, 1944 (The Official Gazette No. 23, 28 February 1944), as amended by Law No. 241, 1953 (The official Gazette, No. 40(bis), 14 May 1953), re cost of living and minimum wages for agricultural workers.
Order No. 469, 1944, as extended by Order No. 522, 1944, re lunch meals for workers in certain areas.
The Draft Civil Code, 1948.
The Civil Code, Law No. 131, 1948.
The Patents Law, No. 132, 1949.
Order No. 99, 1950 (The Official Gazette, No. 32(bis), 21 February 1950), re cost of living and minimum wages for workers.
Law No. 210, 1951, re the conditions of service in the Government.
Decree Law No. 119, 1952, re the worker's contracting capacity.
Decree Law No. 317, 1952 (The Official Gazette No. 157(bis), 8 December 1952), as amended by Law No. 165, 1953 (The Official Gazette No. 30(bis), Extraordinary, 9 April 1953), re the individual contract of employment (repealed).
Decree Law No. 318, 1952, re trade unions (repealed).
Decree Law No. 319, 1952, re conciliation and arbitration (repealed).
Law No. 505, 1955 (as amended by Law No. 9, 1958, and Law No. 149, 1960) re compulsory military service.
Law No. 314, 1956, re service in the National Guard and the Liberation Army.
Law. No. 32, 1957, re the Presidential power to declare establishments to be separate legal entities.
The Labour Code, Law No. 91, 1959 (The Official Gazette, No. 71(bis), B, 17 April 1959) – And the Presidential Decree issuing the Code.
Order No. 134, 1959 (The Official Gazette No. 72, 14 September, 1959), re specification of the authorities mentioned in the Labour Code.
Order No. 145, 1959, re limitation of places far from inhabited areas (section 64 of the Labour Code).

Order No. 146, 1959, re kinds and quantities of food to be provided for every worker (section 64 of the Labour Code).
Order No. 147, 1959, re disciplinary regulations, procedures and penalties (section 66 of the Labour Code).
Order No. 148, 1959, re model disciplinary rules (section 68 of the Labour Code).
Order No. 149, 1959, re disposition of fines (section 70 of the Labour Code).
Order No. 197, 1959, re limitation of the duration of the contract of apprenticeship (section 39 of the Labour Code).
The Social Insurance Law, No. 92, 1959 (The Official Gazette No. 71(bis, B, 7 April 1959), as amended by Law No. 143, 1961.
Law No. 158, 1959 (The Official Gazette, No. 158(bis), 20 June 1959), re contracts of maritime workers.
Law No. 227, 1959 (The Official Gazette, No. 211(bis), 1 October 1959), re amendment of the Presidential Decree which issued the Labour Code.
Law No. 106, 1960, re number of public holidays (amended section 62 of the Labour Code).
Law No. 265, 1960, re nationalised enterprises.
Law No. 267, 1960, re nationalised enterprises.
Order No. 58, 1960, re rules concerning the medical treatment of workers (section 65 of the Labour Code).
Order No. 195, 1960, re conditions and specifications of housing (section 64 of the Labour Code).
Law No. 159, 1961, re number of public holidays (amended section 62 of the Labour Code).

INDEX

ABSENCE, *vide* WORKER
ACCIDENT, 117, 119
- industrial, 203, 215, 216, 218, 266.
ACCOUNTING, duty of, 122.
ACTIONS,
- barring of, 170 (n).
- limitation of, 170 (n).
ACT OF GOD, 214, 272.
ACTOR, 62.
ADMINISTRATIVE,
- authority, 144, 274 (n).
- law, 74.
- regulations, *vide* REGULATIONS.
- unit, 73.
ADVOCATE, 45 (n), 52, 57-9.
AGENCY, 29 (n), 36, 41, 45-8, 50, 57, 59 (n), 62.
AGENT, *vide* AGENCY, COMMERCIAL and INSURANCE.
ALIMONY, 187, 188.
ALLOWANCE,
- cost of living, 160, 161, 166, 196 (n), 271, 273.
- family, 160, 166.
- travelling, 161.
APPRENTICE, 13, 14, 40, 76-8.
- definition of, 76, 78 (n).
ARAMCO, 18 (n), 173 (n).
ARTIST, 62.
ASSAULT, 241-3,
- criminal, 242.
- gravity of, 242, 243.
- physical, 242.
AUTHORITY,
- administrative, 144.
- competent, 129, 274 (n).

BAILMENT, 41 (n), 124, 151, 181.
BAR BOY, 72.
BASIC PAY, 271, 273.
- definition of, 161 (n).
BENEFICIARY, 277, 278.
BONA FIDES, *vide* EMPLOYER and WORKER.
BONUS, 160, 161, 164, 165, 183.
BREACH OF TRUST, 245.
BRITISH,
- judges, 4.
- Labour Party, 14.
- Ministry of Labour and National Service,
- an expert from, 14.
- occupation of Egypt, 8.
- protection,
- in Bahrain, 19 (n).
- in Kuwait, 17 (n).
- in Qatar, 17 (n).
BROTHER, 277, 279, 280, 281.
BUTLER, 72.

CAPACITY, contracting, 55, 78 (n), 83-4, 272.
CASE LAW, 35.
CERTIFICATE,
- false, 240.
- free of charge, 150.
- medical, 203.
- service, of, *vide* SERVICE.
CHARACTER, (*vide* SERVICE, certificate of), 147 (n), 150, 151 (n).
CHILD, 277, 278, 279, 280, 281.
CLASS, working,
- consciousness of, 8 (n).
- lack of organisation of, 10.
- political influence of, 8.
- power of, 8.
- weakness of, 8, 9, 10.
CLOTHING, 162, 163, 187.
CLUB, 71.
CODE NAPOLEON, 7, 41.
COERCION, 83.
COLLECTIVE AGREEMENT, 16, 17 (n), 38(n), 39, 83, 92 (n), 127, 174, 208 (n).
COMMERCIAL,
- agent, 61 (n).
- representative, 36 (n), 46 (n), 61, 114, 163, 182.
- traveller, 61, 114, 163, 182.
COMMISSION, 29 (n), 49 (n), 61, 62, 163, 182, 183.
- secret, 122.
CONDOMINIUM IN SUDAN, 13.
CONSENT, 37, 39, 40, 43, 47, 77, 83.
CONSTRUCTIVE KNOWLEDGE, 166.
CONTRACT OF ADHESION, 38, 39, 104.
CONTRACT FOR CASUAL WORK, 92.
CONTRACT OF EMPLOYMENT (OR SERVICE),

- acceptance in the, 37.
- actionability of, 85.
- assignment of, 36, 43, 44, 45, 99 (n).
- attested, 83, 87, 91 (n), 108, 174.
- breach of, 112, 115, 117 (n), 121 (n), 225, 236, 255, 256, 259.
- consensual nature of, 37-40, 83.
- collective, 26, 38, 39, 40, 102, 127, 141 (n), 160, 164 (n), 172 (n), 174 (n), 266 (n).
- definition of, 23-51.
- duration of, 35-88, 96.
- extension of, 95 (n), 98.
- form of, 49, 77, 84-8.
- formation of, 83-107.
- freedom of entering in, 37, 38 (n), 39, 40, 101, 173, 175, 183.
- frustration of, 204, 213-29.
  - death, by, *vide* DEATH.
    - of employer, 48, 50, 51, 113, 218, 226-7, 267, 272.
    - of worker, 113, 182, 226-7, 266.
  - disability, by, 218, 266, 267.
  - long sickness, by, 215, 217, 267.
- human element in, 10.
- implication of, 28, 60.
- language of, 87, 88 (n).
- life, for, 89, 93, 230, 231, 267.
- limited, 89, 90-95, 110, 216, 218, 219, 229, 230, 234, 236, 246-9, 265, 272.
- long-term, 89, 93, 98 (n), 230, 231, 267.
- novation of, 98-101, 113.
- nullity of, 83.
- offer in the, 37.
- performance of, 113, 114.
  - delegation of, 113, 114.
  - specific, 237, 258.
  - vicarious, 98-101, 113.
- piece-work, for, 93.
- privity of, 46.
- proof of, 86, 87.
- renewal of, 95 (n), 96-8, 151 (n), 153,
  - express, 96, 97.
  - tacit, 96.
- rescission of, 241.
- seasonal work, for, 92, 97, 266.
- specific work, for, 93, 96.
- subject-matter of, 83.
- suspension of, 213-29.
  - discipline, by, 131, 133, 270.
  - imprisonment, by, 219, 220, 221.
  - lock-out, by, 225-6.
  - military service, by, 222-4, 270.
  - sickness, by, 215, 217, 270.
  - strike, by, 224-5.
- termination of, 43, 47, 113, 114, 229-61.
  - agreement, by, 234, 236, 268, 273.
  - gratuity, *vide* GRATUITY.
  - justifiability of (*vide* WORKER, dismissal), 3 (n), 10, 11, 110, 145, 182, 195, 222, 232, 237, 254-9, 266.
    - compensation for the unjustifiable termination, 172, 181, 236, 255.
  - legal, 229-54.
  - life, of contract for, 230, 231.
  - limited contract, of, 230, 246-9.
  - long-term contract, of, 230, 231.
  - notice, by, 118, 227, 228, 231-6, 266,
    - concurrence with annual leave, 232, 235.
    - form of, 235.
    - length of, 231-2, 234-5.
    - non-observance of, 233, 255.
    - non-service of, 233, 236, 270, 273.
    - payment in lieu of, 171, 195, 227, 228, 233-4, 236, 258, 268, 270.
      - assignment of, 187 (n).
      - attachment of, 187 (n).
      - deprivation of, 194 (n).
      - priority of, 189 (n).
    - reasonable, 45, 229.
    - relief from, 231 (n).
    - service of, 232.
    - time-off during, 232 (n), 235 (n).
  - rightfulness, 194, 222, 259-61, 272.
    - compensation for wrongful termination, 172.
  - sickness, during, 215, 216, 217, 232, 258.
  - summary, 230, 236-49, 266.
    - reasonable time, within, 254.
    - waiver of right, of, 254.
- terms of, 38, 39, 40, 101-6,
  - ambiguous, 104, 106.
  - amendment of, 104, 106, 117.
  - binding effect of, 126.
  - implied, 214 (n), 229 (n).
  - interpretation of, 104, 106, 269.
  - mixed, 102, 105.
  - validity of, 103.
  - violation of, 116.
- theatrical, 112.
- transfer of, 99, 267.
- unlimited, 89, 95-6, 230, 231, 267.
- validity of, 86.

CONTRACT FOR INDEPENDENT WORK, 8, 10, 13, 36, 40, 41-5, 53, 59, 62, 63, 64, 65.

CONTRACT OF LEASE, 7, 8, 10, 11, 13, 16, 18, 54 (n).

CONTRACT OF SERVICES *vide* CONTRACT FOR INDEPENDENT WORK.

CONTROL,
- administrative, 34, 53, 57, 59 (n), 62 (n).
- continuous, 35.
- definition of, 30.
- delegation of, 34 (n), 35 (n).
- direct, 35.

– economic, 32, 34.
– element in the contract of employment, as, 8, 10, 11, 13, 15, 30-37, 42, 44, 46, 49, 50, 53, 57, 58, 59, 62, 63, 64, 65, 67, 127, 161, 242.
– legal, 32-3, 36, 58 (n).
– origin of, 30, 31.
– professional, 34.
– statutory, 33-4.
– technical, 34, 52, 57, 58 (n), 59 (n).
CONVENTION, *vide* I.L.O.
COOK, 71, 72.
COSTUME, 124 (n).
COVENANT IN RESTRAINT OF TRADE, 40.
– breach of, 154.
– consideration for, 155, 156 (n).
– definition of, 154.
– reasonableness of, 153, 154.
– relief from, 154, 155.
– severability of, 155.
CRIMINAL OFFENCE, 219-22, 245, 270.
CUSTOM, 27, 70 (n), 71, 72, 76, 102, 114, 160, 174, 176 (n), 180 (n), 209, 217, 229, 231, 254, 271, 274.
– antiquity of, 165.
– certainty of, 165.
– comprehensiveness of, 164.
– continuity of, 164.
– establishment of, 164, 165, 168.
– locality, of, 26, 28, 109, 121, 172 (n).
– non-variability of, 164.
– reasonableness of, 165.
– trade, of, 26, 28, 39, 109, 119, 166, 172 (n), 182, 183.
– uniformity of, 165.

DAMAGES,
– contractual, 256, 259, 260.
– tortious, 255, 257, 258 (n).
DEATH,
– employer, of, 48, 50, 51, 113, 114.
– worker, of, 113, 182.
DEPENDANT, 272, 279, 281.
– definition of, 69 (n).
DOCTOR, 52, 59-60, 134.
DOCUMENTS,
– return of, 148, 151.
DOMESTIC SERVANT, 13, 14, 63, 64, 70-73,
– definition of, 70.
– exclusion of, 53 (n).
DIRECTOR, company, 60-61.
DISABILITY,
– employer, of, 219.
– worker, of, 218, 223, 266,
  – permanent, 219.
  – proof of, 215.
  – temporary, 219.
  – total, 218.
DISCIPLINE, 30, 31, 184, 221, 222.
– board, 129.
– measures, 127-34.
– penalty, 55 (n), 130-31, 132, 172.
– rules, 116, 127-34.
  – amendment of, 129, 130.
  – model, 130.
DISEASE, professional, 203, 216, 218, 266.
DISHONESTY, 245.
DISMISSAL, *vide* WORKER.
DRIVER, 41 (n), 63, 71, 72.
DUTIES, *vide* OBLIGATIONS OF THE PARTIES.

EMPLOYEE, 54 (n), 55, 189 (n), 190.
EMPLOYED PERSON, *vide* WORKER.
EMPLOYER,
– bankruptcy of, 99 (n), 227, 267.
– *bona fides* of, 115, 123, 147 (n), 256(n).
– death of, *vide* DEATH.
– definition of, 51-3.
– *mala fides* of, 115, 220 (n), 222, 256(n), 257.
– orders of,
  – form of, 116, 125 (n).
  – legality of, 116.
– property of, 249.
ENACTMENT,
– Arabic, in, 6.
– comprehensive, 12.
– English, in, 6.
– lateness of, in Sudan, 14 (n).
– piece-meal, 9 (n).
EQUITY, 16, 26, 28, 141, 143, 172 (n), 255 (n).
ESTABLISHMENT,
– amalgamation of, 99.
– bankruptcy of, 99 (n), 267.
– closing down of, 99, 227, 267.
– dissolution of, 99 (n), 272.
– leasing of, 100.
– public, 73.
– taking by Government of, 100.
– transfer of, 99, 100.
– winding up of, 99 (n), 227, 228, 229, 267, 272.
EX-GRATIA PAYMENTS, 160, 161, 164 (n), 168.
EXPERT,
– British, 14.
– I.L.O., 9, 18.
– U.A.R., 17, 18.

FAMILY,
– definition, 68 (n), 69.
– member of, 68-9, 279.
FATHER, 280, 281.
FINE, *vide* DISCIPLINE, 128, 129, 130.
– deduction for, 184.
– distribution of, 134.
– register of, 133.
FOOD, 110, 139-40, 160, 161, 162, 163, 177, 187.

FOOTMAN, 72.
FORCE MAJEURE, 117, 213, 214 (n), 216, 218, 221, 224, 225, 226, 227, 228, 267.
FRAUD, 83.
FRENCH,
- mandate in Lebanon and Syria, 18(n).
- protection in Morocco and Tunisia, 19 (n).
- Revolution, 7.
FUEL, 161, 177.
FUND,
- provident, 75, 161, 186 (n), 276.
- savings, 274.

GARDENER, 71, 73.
GRATUITY, termination, 75 (n), 265-83.
- assignment of, 187 (n).
- attachment of, 187 (n).
- calculation of, 266, 271, 273.
- deprivation of, 128-9, 131, 169 (n), 170 (n), 194 (n), 267, 272, 273, 277.
- distribution of, 170 (n), 190 (n), 277-81.
- entitlement to, 67 (n), 69 (n), 118 (n), 222, 258, 265-71, 272.
- forfeiture of, 128.
- nature of, 169.
- payment of, time of, 271, 274.
- priority of, 189 (n).
- resignation, on, 267, 273.
- substitution by other benefits of, 274-7.
GUARDSMAN, 71.
GUILD, 7, 8, 38 (n).

HEIR, 170 (n), 195 (n), 278.
HELPER, 113, 114.
HOLIDAY, *vide* PUBLIC.
HOUSING, 110, 137-9, 140, 161, 162, 163, 177.
- cost of, 137, 138.
- married workers, for, 137.
- substitution of, by transportation, 139.
HUSBAND, 70 (n), 278.

I.L.O.,
- Convention, 15, 79 (n), 85 (n), 92 (n), 105 (n), 146 (n), 163 (n), 179 (n), 185 (n), 190 (n), 194 (n), 195 (n), 197 (n), 198 (n), 202 (n).
- Recommendation, 115 (n), 150 (n), 180 (n), 194 (n), 196 (n), 197 (n), 202 (n).
- Report, 148 (n), 239 (n), 255 (n).
- Resolution, 140 (n).
INDUSTRIAL,
- compensation, 267
- Revolution in Europe, 7 (n).
IMMORALITY, 245.
IMPRISONMENT, 220, 221, 222, 247 (n).
INSPIRATION,
- English Common Law, 4, 19, 23 (n), 24.
- French Law, 3, 16, 18, 19.
- Kuwait, 17.
- U.A.R., 17, 18.
INSURANCE
- agent, 36 (n), 46 (n), 61, 114.
- social, 203 (n), 218 (n), 275, 277, 278.
INTOXICATION, 252.
INVENTION, worker's, 140-43.
- assignment of, 143 (n).
- fair compensation for, 141.
- patent in, 142.
- payment for, nature of, 172.
- pre-emption right in the, 142.
- remuneration for, 141.
- trustee of, 143 (n).

JOURNALIST, 59.
JUSTICE, EQUITY AND GOOD CONSCIENCE, 4, 5, 6, 16, 116 (n), 128, 178, 180 (n), 181.

KEROSINE DISTRIBUTOR, 63.

LABOUR AGITATION, 14, 15.
LABOURER, 188, 190.
LAND DISTRIBUTION, 12.
LAND OWNERS, 10, 12.
LAW ARABISATION COMMITTEE, in Sudan, 6 (n).
LEASE,
- contract, *vide* CONTRACT
- persons, of, 7.
- things, of, 7.
LEAVES, 193-212,
- annual, 193-202.
  - accumulation of, 200.
  - calculation of, 196, 197 (n).
  - carrying over to another year of, 201 (n).
  - character, public, of, 198, 199, 200.
  - date of, 201-2, 206.
  - entitlement to, conditions of, 193-5.
  - length of, 193.
  - instalments, taking of, in, 200, 202, 208.
  - nature, private, of, 198 (n), 199, 201 (n).
  - payment in lieu of, 200.
  - payment for, nature of, 195 (n).
  - renunciation of, 193.
    - express, 198-9.
    - tacit, 199-201.
  - year of, 195.
- bereavement, 210.
- birth of child, for, 210.
- compassionate, 210.
- death of a relative, for, 210.

- pilgrimage, for, 210.
- sick, 203-7.
  - annual leave, during, taking of, 205, 207.
  - annual leave, substitution by, 205, 207.
  - calculation of, 204, 206.
  - carrying over to another year, of, 204, 207.
  - entitlement to, conditions of, 203, 205-6.
  - joining of, 204, 205, 207.
  - length of, 203, 205.

LIABILITY,
- contractual, 120, 124, 256, 260.
- tortious, 120, 121, 124, 136, 151 (n), 168, 185 (n), 255, 256, 257, 260.
- vicarious, 43 (n), 60.

LIBERATION ARMY, 223.
LIFE ASSURANCE SCHEME, 161, 276.
LOAN, *vide* WAGES, deduction from,
- interest on, 185.

LOCAL SALESMAN, 61, 114, 163 (n).
LOCK-OUT, 225-6, 270.
LORD CROMER, in SUDAN, 13.
LOSSES, 49, 50.
- moral, 257.

MAHDIA, 13.
MAJALLAH, 13 (n), 25 (n), 28 (n), 37 (n), 42 (n), 77 (n), 85 (n), 116 (n), 162 (n), 173 (n), 179 (n).
MALA FIDES, *vide* EMPLOYER.
MASTER, *vide* EMPLOYER.
MEALS, *vide* FOOD, 27 (n).
MEDICAL TREATMENT, 134-5, 136.
- place of, 135.
- preventive, 135.

MINIMUM STANDARD, 10 (n).
MINOR, 40, 84.
MISCONDUCT, 121, 128, 203, 205, 206, 238, 240, 242, 246, 248, 249, 251, 252.
MISREPRESENTATION, 83, 121 (n), 239-41.
MIXED COURTS, 7 (n), 8, 59 (n), 232 (n), 255 (n).
MOSLEM (*Shari'a*) LAW, 7, 8, 13, 16, 18 (n), 41 (n), 42 (n), 77 (n), 170 (n), 185 (n), 189, 190, 195 (n), 278, 279, 281.
MOTHER, 280, 281.

NATIONAL GUARD, 223.
NEGLIGENCE, 137 (n), 203, 205, 206, 238, 244, 248, 249, 250.
NURSE, 72, 73, 134, 136.

OBLIGATIONS OF THE PARTIES, 108-59.
- employment,
  - commencement, at the, of, 109-11.
  - during, 109-43.
  - termination, after the, of, 151-7.
  - termination, on the, of, 144-51.
- failure to carry out the, 229, 236-9, 268.
- specification of, 83, 108.

OFFICIAL, Government, 73-6.
OIL INDUSTRY,
- Bahrain, in, 19.
- Kuwait, in, 17.
- Qatar, in, 17.
- Saudi Arabia, in, 18.

ORDERS, *vide* EMPLOYER.
OVERTIME PAYMENT, 161, 168, 173, 175.

PAINTER, 62.
PARENT, 277, 278.
PARTNER, *vide* PARTNERSHIP.
PARTNERSHIP, 36, 41, 48-51, 63, 64, 65, 228, 229.
PENSION,
- fund, 161, 187 (n), 278.
- scheme, 274, 276.

PERCENTAGES, sales, 163.
PERSON,
- legal, 48, 51, 52.
- national, 48, 51, 52, 55.

PHAROES, 7.
PLACE,
- far from inhabited areas, 138.
- medical treatment, of, *vide*, MEDICAL TREATMENT.
- work, of, *vide* WORK.

PORTER, 71.
PRINCIPAL, *vide* AGENCY.
PROBATION, 205, 207.
- conditions of, 91.
- dismissal during, 131, 239 (n), 253.
- period of, 10, 55 (n), 86, 91 (n), 108.

PROFITS, 29 (n), 48, 49 (n), 64.
- sharing of, 163, 173, 176 (n).

PUBLIC,
- holiday, 30, 196, 197 (n), 204, 206, 207-10,
  - additional, 208.
  - calculation of, 209-10.
  - deduction from annual leave, of, 208.
  - wages for, 207, 210.
  - work on, 208, 209, 210.
- interest, 38 (n), 100, 105, 153, 154, 155.
- morality, 116, 152.
- order, 152.
- policy, 178, 246.
- welfare, *vide* PUBLIC, interest.

PURCHASE, freedom of, 178.

QUANTUM MERUIT, 28, 161.

REASONABLE MAN, care of, 115, 120.
RECOMMENDATION, *vide* I.L.O.

REGULATIONS,
- administrative, 75, 210 (n).
- safety, 243.
REMUNERATION, *vide* WAGES.
REPORT, *vide* I.L.O.
RESOLUTION, *vide* I.L.O.
- Council of Ministers, of, 208, 209 (n).
REST-DAY,
- other, 133.
- weekly, 133, 171 (n), 179 (n), 196, 197 (n), 204, 206, 209, 210.
RESTRICTION, profession, 52-3, 66.
RETIREMENT, 90-91, 92 (n), 95.
REVOLUTION,
- French, 7.
- Iraqi, 17.
- U.A.R., 11.
REWARD, 164, 183.
RIGHTS OF THE PARTIES, 108-59.
- compromise of, 102.
- disclaimer of, 102, 103.
- employment,
- commencement, at the, of, 109-11.
- during, 109-43.
- termination, after the, of, 151-7.
- termination, on the, of, 144-51.
ROMAN LAW, 7, 8, 16, 41 (n), 47 (n).

SANCTIONS,
- civil, 16.
- penal, 9, 14, 16.
SCULPTOR, 62.
SECRETS, professional or trade,
- definition of, 121.
- preservation of, 121-2, 151, 152 (n), 156, 250.
SERVANT, *vide* WORKER.
SERVICE,
- actual, 269.
- certificate of, 147-51.
- conditions of granting of, 148.
- contents of, 147, 149.
- damages for non-giving of, 148.
- delivery of, 149.
- language of, 147 (n).
- lien on, 150.
- public character of, 150 (n).
- continuous, 196, 269-70, 271, 272, 273,
- suspension of, 197 (n).
- exclusive, 27, 33, 35, 114-5.
- faithful, 115.
- military, 30, 222-4, 258, 266, 270.
- compulsory, 222, 223.
- national, 222, 223.
- personal, 113, 114.
- Sudan Civil, 75.
SHARI'A, *vide* MOSLEM (*Shari'a*) LAW.
SHEPHERD, 81 (n).
SHOE-MAKER, 65.
SICKNESS,
- employer, of the, 218.
- worker, of the,
- industrial, 206.
- intermittent, 215, 270.
- long, 214-8.
- proof of, 203, 206, 215 (n).
- temporary, 216.
SISTER, 277, 279, 280.
SPARE TIME, *vide* WORKER.
SPOUSE, 277, 278.
STANDARD, minimum, 103.
STRIKE, 224-5, 270.
SUB-CONTRACTING, 100 (n), 101, 173.
SUB-CONTRACTOR, *vide* SUB-CONTRACTING.
SUI GENERIS CONTRACT, 77, 78.
SUPERVISOR, *vide* WORK.
SUPPORT,
- actual, 68, 278.
- compulsory, 69, 278.
- main, 69.
- partial, 69.
SUSPENSION, *vide* DISCIPLINE, 128, 129, 130, 131 (n), 133.

TEACHER, 57, 96 (n), 197 (n).
TENANCY, 41 (n).
TERMINATION, contract, of, *vide* CONTRACT OF EMPLOYMENT.
TESTIMONIAL, 239, 240.
TIPS, *vide* WAGES, 23 (n), 27 (n), 160, 166.
- deduction from, 168.
- wages in lieu of, 168.
TOOLS, return of, 148, 151.
TRADE DISPUTE, 226 (n).
TRADER, 63, 64.
TRADESMAN, *vide* TRADER.
TRADE UNION, 187 (n), 258, 270.
TRANSPORTATION,
- costs of, 110.
- employment
- commencement, at the, of, 109-11.
- during, 109-11.
- termination of, at the, 144-7.
- place of medical treatment, to, 135.
- substitution by costs, of, 146.
- worker's body, of, 146.

UNDUE INFLUENCE, 83.
UNJUST ENRICHMENT, 28 (n), 161.
UNIVERSITY OF KHARTOUM, legal education in, 6 (n).
USAGE, *vide* CUSTOM.

VALET, 72.
VIS MAJOR, 214, 226, 272.

WAGES, 160-92,
- actual, 185.
- adequacy of, 29, 174 (n).
- agreement on, 172-5.

- alteration of, 172.
- amount of,
  - fixing of, 27, 28, 29, 172.
  - immateriality of, 27, 35.
  - variability of, 27, 29.
- assignment of, 187-9.
- attachment of, 171, 187-9.
- advances on, 179 (n), 186.
  - interest on, 186.
- cadre for, 169 (n), 172.
- deductions from,
  - compensatory, 132 (n), 133, 184, 250.
  - disciplinary, 184.
  - loans, in satisfaction of, 185-6.
- definition of, 160-62.
- element in the contract of employment, as, 27-30, 47.
- distribution of, 170 (n).
- entitlement to, 43, 44, 48.
- human and social aspects of, 29 (n).
- increase of, 169, 175.
- kind, in, 27, 29, 76, 162, 163, 176, 177.
- kinds of, 35, 163-72.
- minimum, 29 (n), 173, 175.
- money, in, 27, 29, 162.
- nominal, 185.
- overtime, for, *vide* OVERTIME PAYMENT.
- payment of,
  - bank, to, 180, 181.
  - cheque, by, 176, 177.
  - legal tender, in, 176-7.
  - periodicity of, 179-81.
  - personal, to worker, 175-6, 183.
  - place of, 180-81.
  - termination of contract, on, 181-3.
  - time of, 179-81.
- piece-rate, 133, 161 (n), 196 (n), 206 (n).
- priority of, 189.
- protection of, 162, 175-90.
- receipt for, 176.
- reduction of, 118, 128, 129, 172, 173 (n).
- Regulation Order, 39, 175 (n), 193 (n).
- time, 161 (n).
- undertaking to pay, 23, 29.

WAITER, 72.

WARNING, *vide*, DISCIPLINE, 130, 133, 243.
- form of, 243, 244, 247.
- renewal of, 247 (n).
- service of, 247.
- validity of, 247, 248.

WASHERMAN, 72.

WIDOW, 279, 280, 281.

WIDOWER, 279.

WIFE, 70 (n), 278.

WORK,
- abstension from, 26 (n).
- availability for, 25, 29, 42, 111, 171.
- casual, 26, 66, 92.
- commission, 112.
- compulsory, 81 (n).
- dangers at, 124.
  - protection from 135-6, 245.
- details of, 26.
- duration of, 66.
- element in the contract of employment, as, 25-7.
- equipment for, 65, 120-21.
- expenses incidental to, 169.
- form of, 25, 35, 54 (n), 55, 72, 73.
- freedom of, 152.
- gratuitous, 27, 172, 174.
- human and social aspects of, 27 (n).
- legal, 46 (n).
- limitations on, 153.
- manual, 55 (n).
- material, 46 (n).
- materials of, 65.
- negative, 26.
- performance of,
  - actual, 25, 29, 42.
  - personal, 42, 43, 113.
  - possibility of, 25, 26.
- piece, 93, 112, 182, 271, 274.
- place of, 109.
- positive, 26.
- provision of, 111-3.
- religious, 56.
- seasonal, 92, 97, 266.
- specific, 25, 44, 88, 89, 93, 96, 230.
- stoppage, 225-6.
- supervisor, 241, 243.
- temporary, 26, 66.
- undertaking to, 23, 25, 29.

WORKER,
- absence of, 220, 221, 246-9.
  - continuous, 247, 248.
  - deduction for, 248 (n).
  - intermittent, 247, 248.
  - justifiability of, 247, 248, 270.
- acceptance into service, of, 111.
- agricultural, 10, 12 (n), 14, 29 (n), 79-80, 173 (n).
- *bona fides* of, 115, 122-3, 143, 149 (n).
- care, duty of, 43.
- casual, 66-8.
- competence of, 120, 121, 131.
- competition of, with the employer, 121, 151-7.
- death of, *vide* DEATH.
- definition of, 53-81.
- dishonesty of, 123.
- dismissal of, 12,
  - disciplinary, 131, 248, 254 (n).
  - justifiability of, 38, 43, 91 (n), 117, 119, 132, 153, 216 (n), 219, 220, 224, 246, 249, 253, 254-9.

– probation, during, 131.
– rightfulness of, 147, 155, 246, 251, 260, 272.
– summary, of, 132 (n), 251, 252, 271, 272, 277.
– waiver of right of, 250, 254.
– suspension of, 270.
– Government, 73-6.
– home, 32, 33.
– maritime, 80-81.
– married, 110 (n).
– recruitment, place of, 110.
– safety of, 116, 119, 243, 256 (n).
– seasonal, 67.
– spare time of, 114, 115.
– transfer of, 99, 117, 118 (n), 119.
WORKMAN, 54 (n), 55, 188, 189 (n).
WORK RULES, 4 (n), 26, 28, 38, 39, 40, 83, 102, 116, 124-7, 160, 164 (n), 172, 174.
– definition of, 125.
– display of, 126.
– nature,
– administrative, of, 125-7.
– contractual, of, 125-7.
YEAR,
– definition of, 180 (n), 193 (n), 248, 265 (n).

French Terms

COMMISSION VOYAGEURS, 61 (n).
CONTRAT,
– à durée déterminée, 90 (n).
– d'adhésion, 38.
– d'entreprise, 41 (n).
– de louage d'ouvrage, 41 (n).
DÉPENDANCE,
– économique, 32 (n).
– juridique, 34 (n).
– professionelle, 34 (n).
– réglementaire, 34 (n).
– technique, 34 (n).
ENRICHISSEMENT SANS CAUSE, 161 (n).
GRATIFICATION, 164.
LIEN DE DÉPENDANCE OU SUBORDINATION, 3 (n), 30 (n).
POURBOIRE, 166.
RÈGLEMENT DE TRAVAIL, 4 (n).
REPRÉSENTANTS DE COMMERCE, 61 (n).
TRAVAILLEURS À DOMICILE, 32 (n).
USAGE DES DEUX HEURES, 232 (n).

GPSR Compliance

The European Union's (EU) General Product Safety Regulation (GPSR) is a set of rules that requires consumer products to be safe and our obligations to ensure this.

If you have any concerns about our products, you can contact us on ProductSafety@springernature.com

In case Publisher is established outside the EU, the EU authorized representative is:

Springer Nature Customer Service Center GmbH
Europaplatz 3
69115 Heidelberg, Germany

Batch number: 10830943

Printed by Printforce, the Netherlands